THE SPECTACULAR CITY,
MEXICO, AND COLONIAL
HISPANIC LITERARY CULTURE

Joe R. and Teresa Lozano Long Series in Latin American and Latino Art and Culture

The Spectacular City, Mexico, and Colonial Hispanic Literary Culture

Stephanie Merrim

UNIVERSITY OF TEXAS PRESS
Austin

Copyright © 2010 by Stephanie Merrim
All rights reserved
Printed in the United States of America
First edition, 2010

Requests for permission to reproduce material from this work should be sent to:
    Permissions
    University of Texas Press
    P.O. Box 7819
    Austin, TX 78713-7819
    www.utexas.edu/utpress/about/bpermission.html

♾ The paper used in this book meets the minimum requirements of ANSI/NISO Z39.48-1992 (R1997) (Permanence of Paper).

LIBRARY OF CONGRESS CATALOGING-IN-PUBLICATION DATA
Merrim, Stephanie.
  The spectacular city, Mexico, and colonial Hispanic literary culture / Stephanie Merrim. — 1st ed.
    p. cm. — (Joe R. and Teresa Lozano Long series in Latin American and Latino art and culture)
  Includes bibliographical references and index.
  ISBN 978-0-292-73746-4

  1. Mexico City (Mexico)—Social life and customs—16th century. 2. Mexico City (Mexico)—Social life and customs—17th century. 3. Festivals—Mexico—Mexico City—History—16th century. 4. Festivals—Mexico—Mexico City—History—17th century. 5. Mexico City (Mexico)—Intellectual life—16th century. 6. Mexico City (Mexico)—Intellectual life—17th century. 7. Mexico City (Mexico)—In literature. I. Title.
  F1386.2.M47 2010
  972'.5302—dc22

                                             2010019015

CONTENTS

Preface vii

INTRODUCTION *Road Map* 1

ONE *Agile Platforms of the Spectacular City: The New World and the Old* 13

TWO *Order and Concert* 49

THREE *Balbuena's "La grandeza mexicana" and the Advent of the Spectacular City* 91

FOUR *Balbuena's Spectacular City and the Creole Cause* 128

FIVE *Engaging Plurality: Baroque Plenitude and the Spectacular City in Mexico* 147

SIX *"To Know the All": The Spectacular Esoteric City in Mexico* 195

SEVEN *Babel: Wild Work of the Baroque* 247

APPENDIX *Chronology of Principal Works* 295

Notes 297

Works Cited 337

Index 355

PREFACE

Warm thanks go to my expert and attentive editor, Theresa May, and to everyone else who contributed to the book's production; to Yolanda Martínez-San Miguel and Nina M. Scott for invaluable suggestions on the manuscript; to Sara Snider for exquisitely proofing it; and especially to the friends, students, colleagues, and family who have sustained me and my work over the years. The memory of my sister, Andrea Goff Merrim, is a living inspiration. Another inspiration came from Anna Turner, who in a graduate seminar long ago asked a question that sparked the book's conceptual framework. More recently, the young students in my First-Year Seminar at Brown in the fall of 2008 gave me faith that the spectacular cities of this book and those of the Hispanic colonial period in general can have a vibrant life in the present.

To foster that life, I present all quotations in English, supplying only most poetry and theatrical dialogue in both Spanish and a fairly literal prose translation in English. Throughout, most translations are mine. However, where possible and appropriate I have cited published translations and provided page references to both the originals and the translations listed in the bibliography. *In all cases, the italicized page number refers to the published translations,* which occasionally have been slightly and silently modified to a more accurate or literal expression. All cited translations of Sor Juana's work derive from Alan S. Trueblood's *A Sor Juana Anthology*. To further facilitate comprehension of the book, a chronological list of the principal works that *The Spectacular City* discusses appears at the end of the text.

Previously published portions of this book include my "Spectacular Cityscapes of Baroque Spanish America," as cited in the bibliography, reprinted by permission of Oxford University Press, Inc.; "The Work of Marketplaces in Colonialist Texts on Mexico City," *Hispanic Review* 72, no. 2 (Spring 2004): 215–238, Copyright © 2004 Trustees of the University of Pennsylvania, reprinted by permission of the University of Pennsylvania Press; "Sor Juana Criolla and the Mexican Archive: Public Performances," *Creole Subjects in the Colonial Americas: Empire, Texts, Identities,* ed. Ralph Bauer and José Antonio Mazzotti, 193–218 (Chapel Hill: University of North Carolina Press for the Omohundro Institute of Early American History and Culture, 2009), reprinted by permission of the Omohundro Institute and the University of North Carolina Press; also, "*La grandeza mexicana* en el contexto criollo," *Nictimene sacrílega,* ed. Mabel Moraña and Yolanda Martínez-San Miguel, 81–97 (Mexico City: Universidad del Claustro de Sor Juana, 2003).

THE SPECTACULAR CITY,
MEXICO, AND COLONIAL
HISPANIC LITERARY CULTURE

INTRODUCTION
Road Map

At the beginning of William Faulkner's *Absalom, Absalom!* (1936), the demon-horse-man figure of Thomas Sutpen "abrupts" onto the scene (4). Bit by bit, piece by astonishing piece, he begins to take shape before the readers' eyes, first through the narrative of the haunted Rosa Coldfield. Speaking in a "grim haggard amazed voice" with an "air of impotent and static rage," Rosa sets in motion the "long unamaze" (3–4), the process of comprehending the amazing maze that Sutpen, with his near-colonialist design of forming a dynasty, foisted on her South. The narratives that ensue in *Absalom* fight their way through the labyrinth of personal, social, historical, and ideological circumstances that fueled Sutpen's design, ultimately reembodying them in their rich, interlocking complexity.

Rosa's amazement and urgent desire to "unamaze" speak to me of the issues that apprehending colonial Hispanic discourse presents. As a thick, long-gone universe of words and worldviews that continues to haunt, a maze of factors, colonial Spanish American discourse amazes, confounds, and resists narration. How to reembody and comprehend it? How to render a meaningful account of its myriad components, none of which exists in pristine isolation and each of which demands that its story be told? *The Spectacular City, Mexico, and Colonial Hispanic Literary Culture* takes the stand that for colonial Hispanic discourse to abrupt robustly and comprehensibly onto our scene as Faulkner's Sutpen did onto the stage of *Absalom*, we first need to embrace its complexity by considering the broad band of cultural formations that contribute to it. Then, and crucially, we may start to make sense of the colonial maze, even to "unamaze," by bringing the various cultural formations into active coherence.

My book casts this wide net into colonial Spanish America's literary culture, a term that connotes the field in which literary and other discourses are conceived, produced, and consumed (Valdés xviii). As its means of articulating colonial Hispanic literary culture or, if you will, its Ariadne's thread through the maze, the book tells the story of an interdisciplinary construct called the Spectacular City. A composite of elements that prove to drive colonial literary culture, the Spectacular City both shapes and facilitates the telling of stories that cut across the sixteenth and seventeenth centuries of colonial Spanish America, carrying Old World ideologies and epistemologies in tow. My book tells these diverse stories, yet in tracing the life and works of the Spectacular City it forms a narrative that has an almost novelistic shape.

Fittingly enough for a study that treats so many walking tours of colonial Spanish American cityscapes, the present introduction offers a road map to the book, a practical initial guide to the Spectacular City and to the interlocking stories whose telling it enables. The introduction sets up the stories that the study plays out, suggests the relationships between them and the directions in which the stories travel, and demarcates their boundaries, while paying particular attention to race and place. Practical as it may be, the road map, I hope, will impart a feel for the potential and drama of the approach to colonial Spanish American culture the book proposes and engage the reader for subsequent chapters, wherein walking tours and texture animate the Spectacular City that we now begin to traverse.

Motor of all the book's stories, the Spectacular City fundamentally derives from the actual, throbbing, propulsive, truly exorbitant cities of colonial Spanish America, locus of the Spanish "civilizing" campaign for the New World. The colonial city reached its fruition in the seventeenth century, when, reacting to the austerity of the Reformation, the Hispanic worlds fired back with spectacle and ostentation. The Spanish colonies in the New World produced the overblown wealth that brought those spectacular proclivities to a hyperbolic peak in statecraft, religion, architecture, consumerism, daily life, and so on. Accordingly, we will here experience a city grounded in the spectacular way of living and experiencing the world that Irving A. Leonard conveys in his classic *Baroque Times in Old Mexico: Seventeenth-Century Persons, Places, and Practices* (1959).

The Spectacular City that comes alive in the following pages, however, transcends its grounding in concrete places and practices. It becomes an abstract entity, an explanatory construct: an ensemble of broad elements that, as I wish to demonstrate, has dynamic generative and explanatory power for colonial Spanish American literary culture. This is the central life of the Spectacular City in the book at hand. And the three coordinates of the Spectacular City, each spectacular in its own right, are New World *cities,* their *festivals,* and various facets of that multiplex phenomenon, *wonder.*

Separately, each of the Spectacular City's three forces constitutes a powerhouse of colonial Spanish American culture across the board, a mainstay of it at once constant and protean. Over the arc of colonial discursive production, the city, festival, and wonder individually assume the host of distinctive, charged forms that my book sets out to disclose. Each of the three matrices functions as an extraordinarily capacious and malleable arena, equally available to the imperial colonizer and to the colonized. Quite purposefully in the hands of the colonized, or at times mercurially escaping the grasp of the colonizer, the components of the Spectacular City can become "structures of feeling" that from within the core of the dominant culture surreptitiously corrode it, heralding the emergence of new trends (Williams 133).

When the textualized city, festival, and wonder pull together to form the constellation or template that is the Spectacular City, they allow one to discern and to enunciate vital, wide-ranging stories. (We will see throughout that the Spectacular City both intersects with and exceeds Angel Rama's "ciudad letrada," or lettered city, which up to now has been one of the main tools for interpreting the real and literary colonial Hispanic city).[1] As it pushes through time and space, the composite Spectacular City proves to engender and to elucidate a spectrum of significant movements in colonial Hispanic literary history as well as their verbal monuments. In other words, the Spectacular City affords a platform from which to chart many large-scale trajectories of colonial culture, and it provides several fundamental bases for devising an intra-Hispanic, comparative literary history.[2]

The dynamic Spectacular City, as suggested above, organically calls other stories into telling as it evolves. One such story line is the education and modus operandi of the creole colonial intelligentsia, treated more contextually here than in Rama's *La ciudad letrada.* The palpitating life of wondrous objects and collections of them is another. The Spectacular City also convenes several quite conceptually driven stories. Wending back and forth between the Old World and the New, the tale of the Spectacular City exposes the hegemonic aspects of seemingly autonomous, abstract European epistemes, their guilty pleasures.

Analogously and principally, since the Spectacular City coalesces in the seventeenth century it dovetails with the magnificent, slippery phenomenon known as the New World Baroque. The second major story my book tells, therefore, tracks the intimate relationship between the New World Baroque and the Spectacular City, both of which militate against order and containment. Construing the New World Baroque as a precarious embodiment of the uncontainable, *The Spectacular City* necessarily attends to the work, the diverse and deeply efficacious specific jobs, that the quicksilver Baroque performed for the New World and its writers. For instance, one key plotline of the book contends that with its potent conjunction of city, festival, and wonder the Spectacular City triggers the genesis of the Baroque on New World soil rather than as an imported mode and subsequently plays a determining role in advancing the spirited work of the New World Baroque *for* the New World.

Who does this work? Although all sectors of society partake of colonial festivals and contribute to the discourse of the colonial period, the simple answer to the question is: mostly *radicados* (foreigners who had put down roots in the New World) and creoles (American-born Spaniards). I trust my readers will agree that the current lively, well-justified interest in Indian texts of all sorts need not block awareness that the radicados and, preeminently, creoles who occupy these pages continue to warrant close attention.[3] As those who for better or for worse enjoyed the greatest educational opportunities and the highest social positions, it was they who published most widely in the New and Old Worlds and thus momentously impacted the ideology and literary cultures of their times. By the beginning of the seventeenth century, creoles had come to dominate Mexican and Peruvian literary cultures. By the end of the century, they had utilized their position advantageously to formulate and propagate structures of feeling, which gathered into the protonationalism that would at long last spur independence from Spain.

Yet there is nothing simple about radicados, creoles, or any other subjects implicated in a colonial situation. For instance, received categories such as radicado and creole belie the fluidity of the colonial context. Some radicados eventually embraced the local milieu to the point of blending with the creoles or defending the Indians. Others never shed the touristic or deeply imperialist, yet ultimately erratic, perspective that informs the texts studied in chapters 2 and 3 here. More important, scholars estimate that from 20 to 40 percent of the individuals who identified themselves as creoles in the early years of colonization may actually have been mestizos seeking to elude racial prejudice (Mazzotti 11).[4]

The indistinction of categories ineluctably gives rise to, among other things, the fact that creole texts by no means tell a single or a monolithic story. In truth, owing to a matter that has recently received much scrutiny, they deliver some of the most tangled, challenging, and telling stories to issue from the colonial period. I refer to the sometimes conflicting investments of the creoles in both home and empire, attitudes which a raft of excellent scholars have brought to the fore.[5] Their collective efforts furnish a consummate picture of the creoles' Janus-faced, unstable identity and loyalties. On the one hand, creoles internalize deeply felt local attachments, paradigms, and alliances. On the other, they lean favorably toward the metropolis, Spain's cultural paradigms, ideologies, and, especially when mistreated by the viceregal system, imperial power structures. Conservative and dissident, dominant (as over/against Indians and mestizos) and subordinate (to viceregal officials, civil and ecclesiastic), creoles shift back and forth between polarities. Concomitantly, they find themselves well situated to mediate between stances in person and in writing, in the colonies and, as creole texts make their way across the ocean, in Europe.

We meet, in sum, an identity in the making and a conflict-ridden creole discourse "forged in the nexus of various circuits of identity and power" (Martínez-San Miguel 208). The dual positionality of creole writers catches both sides of the colonial divide. Creole writers meld the American and Spanish cultures that permeate every facet of their daily existence.[6] Their works hold official and nonofficial stories in tension. Such works subscribe to the official story wholeheartedly or in mimicry. Creole discursive production thus focuses an array of tensions inherent in the colonial situation.

Indians and self-proclaimed mestizos focus and face other significant tensions, tensions which generally distance their writings from the Spectacular City. Oppression and the obliteration of their past urgently preoccupy Indian writers, with the result that they often train their sights on protest and on recuperating indigenous history. Mestizo writers "concerned with the problems of lineage, inheritance, and remuneration," similarly defend "their claim to the future through an examination of the past" (Ross, "Historians" 142). On a lesser note, the improbability that subjected Indians or mixed-race writers would desire to pay homage to viceregal cities or festivals further separates their works from the Spectacular City. The two groups of writers therefore do not directly enter the ranks of Spectacular City texts, although the actions, writings, and history of the Indians play a tremendous, inalienable role in several creole and other works that come under study here. For example, as the seventeenth century progressed and creole protonationalism took shape, the movement increasingly aligned itself with the Indians, if, as we will find, mostly with their past.

In order to do justice to the trajectory of creole discourse together with the life force of the Spectacular City, this book centers on colonial Mexico City, capital of the viceroyalty of New Spain. Beyond the specifics of its literary culture, Mexico City constitutes a fertile arena for tracing the evolution and currency of the Spectacular City because of the viceregal capital's many paradigmatic and leading-edge features. Constructed atop the Aztec city of Tenochtitlán, a place whose strong history never faded from cultural memory, Mexico City combines aspects of the Peruvian cities of Lima and Cuzco. Mexico City also quickly experienced the brunt of Spain's urbanizing project, which included the early installation of a printing house (1535 in Mexico versus 1583 in Lima) and of a university housed in its own buildings (1554 in Mexico versus 1576 in Lima).[7] Both projects promoted the rapid, steady progress of literary culture in New Spain. Given its centrality to Atlantic, Pacific, and intracontinental trade, Mexico City imbibed foreign cultural currents; literary issues that would resonate throughout the colonies often manifested themselves first, and keenly, in Mexico City. By the same token, Mexico City did not fail to absorb the tidal waves of capitalism that would transform all that it touched. As the first modern, unwalled city of Latin America, the capital of New Spain early on pressed inexorably toward Latin America's problematic modernity.

None of this means to accord the literature of Mexico City any superiority to that of other colonial cities. In fact, being more distant from the metropolis, less controlled or controllable, other cities evidence a more unbroken dissentient literary tradition, albeit one that still can operate within the bounds of the Spectacular City and do the work of the New World Baroque. Chapter 1, therefore, contextualizes the Spectacular City with regard to colonial Spanish America at large, and the final chapter of this book chiefly scrutinizes the work of the Baroque in and for the spectacularly scandal-ridden cities of the South American continent.

Yet the heart and bulk of *The Spectacular City* lie in Mexico. Chapters 2 through 6 follow Mexico City and the cultural artifacts it yielded from the start of the sixteenth century to the end of the seventeenth. A case study, the chapters on Mexico aim to substantiate my broad claims about the Spectacular City and the New World Baroque. A chronologically organized book within a book, the Mexican chapters enact a sample literary history that revolves around the city, festival, and wonder—without intending to *be* a literary history, exhaustive or otherwise. Rather, the third major story told here, that of colonial Mexico City and its literary culture, will immerse readers in the dense texture and elusive gyrations of colonial texts, be they canonical or works that have almost faded from sight. To meet the challenge of the often daunting texts with the nuanced readings they demand and with the fresh readings the Spectacular City opens up is a primary job of the book at hand.

Exhuming and probing colonial works on Mexico City (historiography, treatises, poetry, drama, protonovels, and journalism) through the lens of the Spectacular City brings to the fore a pivotal aspect of Hispanic Mexico's early literary history: a conscious, sustained, cross-fertilizing discursive tradition enacted by creoles that spans most of the colonial period. As creole writers engage in an apologetics for Mexico City, one which models an apologetics for the New World at large, they instantly begin to assemble a vibrant intertextual corpus. Creole writers avidly read and insistently quote and rewrite one another, often polemically. Resourceful and intent on consolidating a textual edifice favorable to Mexico, they also exploit any available material that might suit their cause. Hence, creoles selectively redeploy and cannily reterritorialize extant writings on Mexico by Spaniards, radicados, and, later, Indians. From wayward, scant beginnings, creoles cobble together a *Mexican Archive* that never ceases to ramify or to entail astonishing acrobatics with received knowledge.

To label the intertextual body an archive is, of course, to activate Michel Foucault's construction of the archive as "the general system of the formation and transformation of statements" (*Archeology* 130) or, better yet for our context, Roberto González Echevarría's refinement of it as "an archive of stories and a storehouse of the master-stories produced to narrate from Latin America" that can manifest the "power to negate previous narrative forms from which it takes texts" (*Myth* 3, 34). And to identify the colonial Mexican Archive with creole writers invokes Kathleen Ross's characterization of Baroque creole intertextuality: "Baroque literature in Spanish America was the vehicle through which the criollos, or American-born Spaniards, engaged in an intertextual dialogue with the sixteenth century and the writing of the age of the Spanish conquest" (*Baroque Narrative* 7).[8] No less does the "creole archive" bring to mind Anthony Higgins's *Constructing the* Criollo *Archive*. Predicating his contentions on eighteenth-century texts, Higgins distinguishes "a genealogy through which *criollos* seek to articulate a body of practical and theoretical knowledge of their environment and the history of its inhabitants, with a view to constructing for themselves a position and space of authority within colonial society" (xii).

The investigations undertaken here should broaden and thicken the understanding of the creole-constructed archive that the preceding formulations have so importantly and trenchantly seeded. Chapters 3 and 4 redraw the chronological boundaries of that archive, demonstrating that it began to take shape long before the Baroque period or the eighteenth century. Moreover, it will become apparent that when, as Ross stated, Mexican writers dialogue with Spanish texts of the conquest, they conduct those dialogues in full awareness that they are also communing with compatriots who had cited the same Spanish-authored and, as time goes by, Mexican-authored texts.

By laying bare and working through how creoles signify upon their forebears of various provenances, the suite of chapters on Mexico City helps reembody a literary history that up to now has largely derived its coherence from extrinsic criteria like dates and places or from disciplinary criteria such as literary period characteristics.[9] The broadly based Spectacular City grows that literary history and contributes to its coherence. First, because the festival chronicles that often constitute the Spectacular City attained publication and wide dissemination. They thus had considerable impact on local writers. Second, because the Mexico City text that first conjoined city, festival, wonder, and the Baroque to crystallize the Spectacular City, the radicado Bernardo de Balbuena's 1604 "La grandeza mexicana" [Mexican grandeur], reverberated explosively into creole discourse.[10] This lengthy, elitist, convoluted poem remained a constant touchstone of Mexican *criollismo,* or "creolism," well into the eighteenth century. A towering, complex protagonist of my study, Balbuena's prodigiously influential pro–Mexico City text fueled Mexican creole patriotism and channeled its discursive history—in directions Balbuena would often not have countenanced. That is, Balbuena's overweening scorn for the Indian, the exile of the Indian from the poem except in its final, degrading allusion to the "indio feo" [ugly Indian] (124), sets a pattern that Mexican creole discourse would either adopt, modify, or overtly contest. Thus although Indian authors may not figure prominently in these pages, we will bear extensive witness to creole constructions of the Indian that incrementally supplement Balbuena's elitist poem.

The seven chapters of *The Spectacular City, Mexico, and Colonial Hispanic Literary Culture* most vitally bear witness to the complex birthing process and manifold life-forms over time of the mobile Spectacular

Introduction

City. Chapter 1 frames its components and their transatlantic genealogies. In essence, the book then follows the Spectacular City from its antecedents (chapter 2) to its advent (chapters 3 and 4) to its multifaceted Baroque apogee (chapters 5–7).

More specifically, chapter 1, "Agile Platforms of the Spectacular City: The New World and the Old," grounds the city, festival, wonder, and creole concerns in their historical contexts. It next places the Spectacular City in motion between the New World and the Old to conceptualize the crosscurrents that underwrite it, as deriving from the efforts of Spain in the Renaissance and Baroque eras to contend with the crises that the New World presented. From here, in an ever-shifting *ars combinatoria,* the book conjugates the city and its representation, the festival and festival chronicles, and wonder-as-emotion or wonder-as-object. While each coordinate of the Spectacular City comes into play throughout (except for chapter 2, where loaded representations of the communal marketplace stand in for the communal festival), each chapter or period inflects the mix differently, highlighting certain aspects. To flesh out the backstories and compass of the Spectacular City, the book frequently contemplates texts other than official festival chronicles or festival-allied works.

Chapter 2, "Order and Concert," considers the insidious fit between the epistemologies and esthetics of the European Renaissance, on the one hand, and Spanish imperialism, New World city planning, and sixteenth-century representations of Mexico City, on the other. The Renaissance Ordered City they all contrive to produce reaches expression in propagandistic and/or touristic city texts written by Hernán Cortés, Francisco Cervantes de Salazar, and Juan de la Cueva and in the hegemonic pastoral city crafted by the little-studied radicado author Eugenio de Salazar y Alarcón. Chapter 3, "Balbuena's 'La grandeza mexicana' and the Advent of the Spectacular City," breaks out of the Ordered City and gravitates toward the creoles. It locates Balbuena's works in the transition from the Mendicants to the Jesuits that formed a creole intelligentsia and that pulled Mexico City away from its previous austerity. Then, interrogating Balbuena's seminal, liminal poem, the chapter begins to sketch the special profile of the New World Baroque. With its effusive celebration of an exotic Mexico City and the disruptive particularity that the poem's economic bent occasions, "La grandeza mexicana" overflows the Apollonian Ordered City to debut the Dionysian Baroque Spectacular City.

That city spins off its imperialist axis and into orbit as creoles take it up for their own purposes. Chapter 4, "Balbuena's Spectacular City and the Creole Cause," details how creole writers appropriate and complicate "La grandeza mexicana" shortly after its publication. A short-term reception history of Balbuena's poem, the chapter examines its imploding esthetic and ironic returns in texts by Baltasar Dorantes de Carranza, Mateo Rosas de Oquendo, and Arias de Villalobos, all of which put pressure on Balbuena's sublime, elite city. Chapter 5, "Engaging Plurality: Baroque Plenitude and the Spectacular City in Mexico," explores the pluralized, multicultural landscape of Mexico City and the attendant discourses of plurality that surge forth irrepressibly in the late seventeenth-century cultural nationalism of Agustín de Vetancurt, Carlos de Sigüenza y Góngora, and Sor Juana Inés de la Cruz. In treatises and in festival texts, the three authors lift official discourses to new, plural, creolized heights.

Chapter 5 examines popular festivals, the enormously popular Guadalupanism that took root in the mid-seventeenth century, and texts on communal festivals for Mexico City, Querétaro, and Madrid. Conversely, chapter 6, "'To Know the All': The Spectacular Esoteric City in Mexico," turns to the elite counterparts of those phenomena. It analyzes the esoteric festival practices of the creole intelligentsia; their spectacular philosophical proclivities that rally around the enticing possibilities for knowing the All held out by the renowned German Jesuit Athanasius Kircher and his museum; and metaphorical renditions of the festival encountered in Sor Juana's and Sigüenza's works. The spectacular esoteric city of which these various enterprises are integral parts carries the Baroque to its peak, as Sor Juana and Sigüenza mount a literary fin de siècle based on the creole archive, and also to its devastation on epistemological and social grounds.

Finally, the upheaval of absolutist viceregal society that Sigüenza's account of the 1692 Mexico City food riot depicts leads into chapter 7, "Babel: Wild Work of the Baroque." This last chapter projects the Spectacular City onto texts from Mexico, Bogotá, Potosí, and Lima that attack colonial misrule, often championing the Indian. Unfettered, sensationalizing exposés, the works enact what would strike the imperial eye as the backfiring of the Baroque. Hence, the New World Baroque and Spectacular City that began in the imperialist "La grandeza mexicana" demonstrate their potency for denouncing colonial societies that have descended into malignant hegemonies and Babelic pandemonium.

From the beginning of the seventeenth century to its end, the Spectacular City and the New World Baroque display an extraordinary ability to overflow bounds, defying containment. To capture those energies as vividly as possible, several of my chapters have a pictorial epigraph. More than as illustrations, the pictures that preface the chapters serve as keys to the issues of verbal representation that the chapters broach. The visual epigraph of chapter 1, Hieronymus Bosch's effervescent, fearsome *Garden of Earthly Delights* (c. 1500–1505), suggests a mode of representation and a prevailing mood. Subsequent visual epigraphs progress sequentially from archetype to explosion. At heart, this is *the* story of the Spectacular City, and the transit from Sandro Botticelli's geometrical, airbrushed Venus (c. 1484) to Cristóbal de Villalpando's busy, particularized *Central Square of Mexico City, 1695* subsumes and tells that story as effectively, perhaps, as any words the following pages can muster on its behalf.

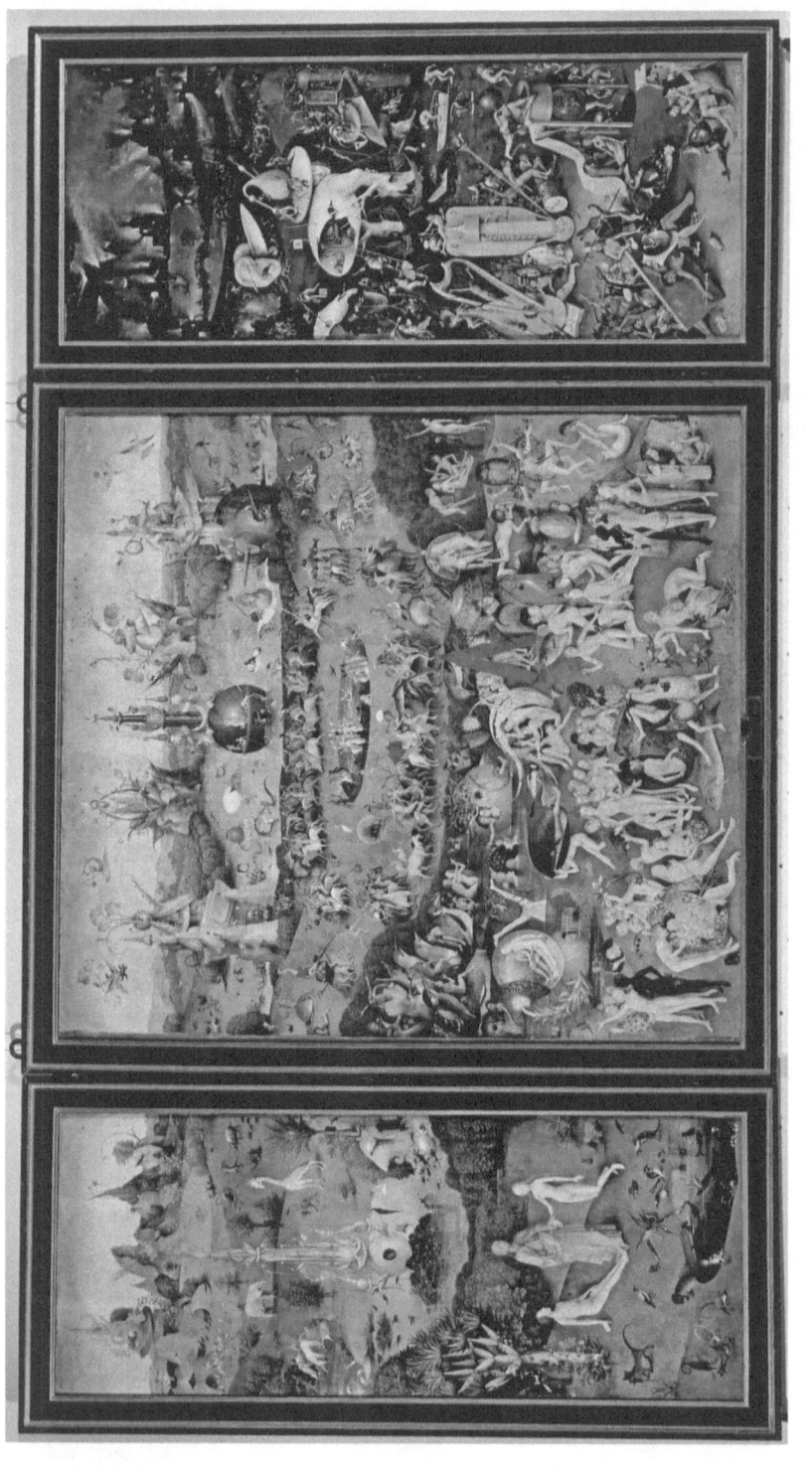

FIGURE 1. *Hieronymus Bosch (c. 1450–1516). Garden of Earthly Delights, c. 1500–1505. Left wing: Paradise (Garden of Eden); central panel: Garden of Earthly Delights; right wing: Hell (Inferno). Triptych with shutters. Wood. Central panel 220 × 195cm, wings 220 × 97cm. Museo del Prado, Madrid, Spain. Erich Lessing / Art Resource, N.Y.*

One   AGILE PLATFORMS OF
THE SPECTACULAR CITY
The New World and the Old

César Vallejo's breakout book of poetry, *Los heraldos negros* [The black heralds] (Lima, 1918), gives off shock waves that convulse a received, stable world picture into an "ultranervous axis" (68). *Los heraldos negros* leads off with a section entitled "Plafones agiles," which I loosely translate as "Agile Platforms."[1] Rather than grounding the cosmos, Vallejo's platforms inaugurate an offensive that swirls it into incoherence. The poet proceeds to execute a full-scale assault on the "virgin plenitude of the I," the sublime unity of a God-ruled universe "that is one / for all" (65). Claiming that the Inca race forges itself and smolders in his words (41), Vallejo hurls literary and philosophical thunderbolts at a once serene, intelligible world. *Los heraldos negros* decenters the universe, defaults from unity to multiplicity, lacerates lyricism with cacophony, wounds hope and pleasure with a serpent-ridden flow (65) of disillusionment and melancholy.

"But Lord," the poet implores in a piece entitled "Absolute," "can you do nothing . . . against what is ending?" (65). From his wartime, avant-garde moment, Vallejo mourns the loss of one world picture and heralds the advent of a new, more complicated one. His words echo the derangement of the received world that emanates from Hieronymus Bosch's *Garden of Earthly Delights,* painted as the "discovery" of a previously unknown New World was sending shock waves through Europe.[2] Then, as in Vallejo's transitional moment, previously stable platforms lost their bearings to become agile: supple, shifting, transitive, nervous, contingent, electric.

This chapter considers a broad array of the agile early modern platforms that bear on the Spectacular City, each of which constitutes a launching pad for our subsequent investigations. The first half of the chapter travels across colonial Spanish America to place the concrete elements of the Spectacular City—the New World creole, city, and festival—in their historical contexts. It sketches the force fields of the historical contexts and the strains on those force fields, the stuff of their kinetic agility. Entering the territory of the Spectacular City's other matrix, wonder, then draws us pointedly to Spain and into its fraught transactions with the New World. Via wonder we board the platforms by means of which Old World Spain labors to contend with the menacing tides of change. These tides had bombarded its stable, harmonious world pictures with very much the same kinds of thunderbolts that *Los heraldos negros* fires at the "virgin plenitude of the I" that had, in fact, long ago lost some of its innocence. Never ceasing to yearn for harmonious unity and singularity, the metropolis constantly seeks means of salvaging them, or at least of salving the crises. Ongoing efforts at damage control (with an emphasis on *control*) profoundly imprint the epistemes and esthetics of the early modern period. The several such palliative efforts that the chapter investigates lay the scaffolding for the quietistic machinery of the Renaissance Ordered City and for the breakout agility of the Baroque Spectacular City.

I. THE PERIOD OF STABILIZATION AND THE CREOLES

By the second half of the sixteenth century, Spanish America's so-called "period of stabilization" (Vidal 25) after the conquest had commenced. With all of the major colonial structures in place, all of the great colonial cities founded, and the Indians achieving a slow but sustained demographic recovery from the devastations of conquest, the colonies had reached a plateau that allowed for the vigorous, often tempestuous, creation and consolidation of a new society. The old tendency to view the era as inert or lethargic has fallen away, displaced by awareness that defining aspects of present-day Latin America took shape during the approximately 150-year period of stabilization. Rather than as a hiatus of calm, scholars now recognize the era as one of ferment, consistently jarred by tensions and uprisings.

Economic issues stood at the epicenter of storms on both sides of the Atlantic. Even as the Spanish empire's dependency on New World wealth grew, its capacity to monopolize New World resources diminished. By the end of the sixteenth century, Mexico had entered into independent trade with Manila and had evolved into the preeminent broker of intracolonial trade with Peru. Huge quantities of goods, especially luxury goods, moved through this circuit, bypassing Spain. The motherland soon realized that Mexico had begun to unseat Seville as the clearinghouse for commerce and that New Spain "had in essence become the metropolis of Peru" (Boyer 457, 473). Therefore, in the first decades of the seventeenth century Spain undertook, if ineffectually, to curtail trade between the colonies (see Israel, chaps. 1, 3). Diversification of colonial economies exacerbated the situation. Textile factories opened in the New World cities, and as the big silver strikes subsided, the colonies expanded their economic bases from mining into agriculture and cattle raising. Although Mexico diversified more notably and earlier on than Peru, over the course of the seventeenth century each of the New World colonies attained a considerable degree of economic autonomy.[3]

Against the backdrop of this "first emancipation of America" (Lynch 211) in economic terms, throughout the period of stabilization creoles struggled to attain prominent roles in viceregal society. They had at their disposal on the civil front a singular tool of the Spanish legal system, the *cabildo,* or municipal council. In a decree of 1523 Charles V extended the medieval Spanish tradition of strong, democratic city councils to the New World, stipulating that the white citizenry would elect them (Israel 95). New World creoles ran the municipal councils, which managed significant parts of the city budget and had the power to veto some of the viceroy's expenditures. The Spanish crown's tendency to reward service with offices rather than with money and its decision in 1558 to fill the royal coffers by selling offices and noble titles in the New World (Burkholder, "Bureaucrats" 82–84; Moraña, *Viaje* 34) facilitated the creoles' advancement into other civil positions. While the highest offices of the military and the government long stayed closed to them, by the end of the seventeenth century creoles had obtained some access to the elite high court and royal advisory board, the Audiencia.[4]

Creoles made the greatest headway in penetrating the ranks of the secular (noncloistered) clergy. They tended to occupy the leading positions in the ecclesiastic counterpart of the municipal council, the *cabildo eclesiástico,* or cathedral chapter. Their knowledge of Indian languages and, probably more so, their wealth commended creoles to the church officials. Consequently, toward the end of the sixteenth century, creole secular clergy were likely to have outnumbered peninsulars, except in the ranks of bishop and archbishop (Ganster 147). The involvement of creoles in the regular (cloistered) orders met with greater, but not insurmountable, obstacles. Requirements for ordination such as purity of blood (*limpieza de sangre*), ever-higher levels of education, and demonstrable means of lifelong support, though not always applied, generally kept a check on creoles' membership in the regular clergy. To further maintain their standing in the regular orders, European-born clergy secured decrees that ensured the *alternativa,* the regular rotation in the orders' offices between Spaniards and creoles.[5]

The ordination requirements and alternativa merely index the opposition creoles faced as they attempted to claim a place in the upper echelons of colonial society. Friction between creoles and the crown had in fact existed almost from the start of the colonial period, as the crown sought to strip the creoles of the *encomiendas* [grants of Indian labor] they had inherited from their conquistador forebears. Allegedly to reduce mistreatment of the Indians, yet in effect to prevent the formation of a powerful New World aristocracy, the Laws of Burgos promulgated in 1512 declared that encomiendas were counter to the interests of the native peoples and of the crown (Liss 34). In 1536 the crown limited the originally perpetual encomiendas to "two lives," that is, to two generations of the conquerors' heirs. When in the "New Laws" of 1542 Spain moved to abolish encomiendas and their attendant Indian slavery, tensions that had been percolating in the creoles came to a head, which led to unrest in Mexico and outright mutiny in Peru.

Ordinances escheating on the encomienda sparked the initial stage of creole activism, in thought and in word as well as in deed. Bernard Lavallé observes with regard to Peru that the word *criollo,* which formerly referred to Afro-Brazilian slaves, first assumed the meaning of "American-born Spaniard" in a letter of 1567 branding creoles as troublemakers (17–18). The same letter to the Council of the Indies also touches upon the penury of the creoles, now divested of encomienda and wealth. Poverty, relative or urgent, initiates the creoles' career as troublemakers. And acrimonious resentment of their disenfranchisement by the crown and by *gachupines,* recently arrived Spaniards who, according to the creoles, plunder the New World only to abandon it, pervades early creole writings. A representative line from the creole Baltasar Dorantes de Carranza's *Sumaria relación de las cosas de la Nueva España* [Summary account of the things of New Spain] (1604), the first consolidation of a creole Mexican Archive, already rings with a Baroque-sounding disillusionment:

> Oh Indies! Oh Conquerors full of troubles . . . , even in times of greater service and better circumstances you were stripped of your own haciendas and of the fruits of your

services and deeds, as those who governed in the first years awarded the results of your toils to upstarts who had earned nothing in the conquest. And now the time has arrived in which deception and lies, and idleness and injury to one's fellow man prevail, when anyone who sells wine or spices or ordinary cloth or old iron obtains a great estate to entail to his heirs. (112–113)[6]

The bitter complaint that characterizes early creole writings arose simultaneously in the major colonial centers, prompted by the same circumstances.

When the first-generation creoles, with their avowed direct stake in the spoils of conquest, died out, the platform and vindictive tone they had unleashed did not disappear. Rather, they coalesced into a generalized "spirit of *criollismo*" (Liss 114) and served as a lightning rod for many successive generations of creoles.[7] The end of the seventeenth century, for instance, still finds Carlos de Sigüenza y Góngora and Sor Juana Inés de la Cruz protesting Europeans' rape of Mexico in the exact terms their creole predecessors had employed.[8] Creole discourse, nevertheless, was neither monotone nor static. While the creole protonationalism that reclaimed the indigenous past (to be discussed in chapters 5, 7) surged in the seventeenth century, creole writings had branched out much before then. Around the beginning of the seventeenth century, at least in Mexico their writings had begun to adopt from the adulatory biography of Hernán Cortés by the Spaniard Francisco López de Gómara, *La conquista de México* (1552), the epic magnification of the conquest so advantageous to petitions for encomienda. The creole writers Arias de Villalobos, Dorantes de Carranza, Gabriel Lobo Lasso de la Vega, Antonio de Saavedra Guzmán, Francisco de Terrazas, and Gaspar Pérez de Villagrá all contributed to the so-called Cortés cycle of epic poems on the conquest.

The most educated creoles by then had also begun to lay hands on European scientific theories like those of the French Jean Bodin and the Basque Juan Huarte de San Juan,[9] which, following Aristotle, understood climate and geography to determine biology and thus the attributes of a given place's inhabitants. On the basis of these would-be scientific postures Europeans denigrated the New World, situated below the equator in a region that medieval cosmography had debunked as an uninhabitable torrid zone or antipodes. Juan López de Velasco, for instance, wrote alarmingly in his *Geografía y descripción universal de la Indias*

(1571–1574) of the "heat and vice of the land" (14), the phlegmatic, vile nature of the Indians (16), and the degeneration Spaniards would suffer with prolonged residence in the New World (20). The Dominican activist Bartolomé de Las Casas countered the pernicious trend with a scientific defense of the New World, his *Apologética historia* (composed 1527–1551), which went unpublished until 1909. Creoles, on the other hand, boldly framed and published their geographical-climatological-biological New World apologetics. In what is likely the inaugural text of the series, the *Primera parte de los problemas y secretos maravillosos de las Indias* (1591), the Jesuit-trained Mexican creole Juan de Cárdenas argues for the superiority of creoles thanks to the "great predominance of the Sun over all the peoples of the Indies," which tempers the choleric disposition their Spanish blood transmits to them and imbues them with a more lively intelligence than that of their peninsular counterparts (161). After Cárdenas, and proliferating for more than one hundred years into a vast corpus of works, vociferous creoles and others hammered away at a prejudicial European determinism.[10] Whence arose the profound involvement of creole writings with place, and especially with the New World city in all its redemptive magnificence.

II. CITY

Anyone who breathed the air of the great colonial urban centers would readily infer the surpassing value that the colonizers attached to the city. A primary feature of Spanish "conquest culture," the reduced version of Spanish culture purposefully exported to the colonies (Foster),[11] that value was deeply entrenched in the metropolitan worldview. Classical models that Spaniards and other Europeans took much to heart prized the city as the apex of civilization, the locus of culture, and the consecrated home of the elite. Religious models elevated the city into a divine space. Revelation 21:2 reads, "And I John saw the holy city, new Jerusalem, coming down from God out of heaven, prepared as a bride adorned for her husband." That St. Augustine's *City of God* (413–427 CE) depicted salvation as citizenship in an orderly, harmonious heavenly city promoted urban space as a site of evangelization; during the Reconquest, Spain trained its efforts on retooling Muslim cities into exemplary Christian polities (Kagan 26–27).

These strong, illustrious precedents paved the way for the emphatically urban cast of Spanish colonization of the New World, which

Hervé Théry deems "the greatest intentional and coherent urbanization project" in history (4). Spanish explorers rushed to stake their claims on the New World by founding cities—sometimes within days of entering an unknown territory, having but the vaguest notion of where they were. And if many of the cities thus unpropitiously inaugurated began as outposts, they soon burgeoned. European-born settlers, even those with rural landholdings, flocked to the cities. From 1580 to 1630 the urban population of Spanish America in general tripled. While Mexico City's population quadrupled (Hardoy and Aranovich 182), the Jesuit Bernabé Cobo records that by 1639 the colonial capital of Peru, Lima, had reached twice its originally projected size, with some six thousand white inhabitants, thirty thousand black slaves, and five thousand Indians (360).

The cities that concentrated the population and power structures of the viceregal world exercised an equal monopoly on its resources. Mexico City and Lima developed into the commercial and financial hubs of the colonies. As they brokered trade from outlying colonial regions, Europe, and the Orient, and as all manner of goods flowed through them, the cities "became important centers for the commercialization of Spanish American society and institutions" (Morse 97). Texts of the times unabashedly celebrate the emporium city. Bernardo de Balbuena's boundless delight in the mercantile capitalism of Mexico City, the focal point of my chapter 3, meets its match in coeval works on Lima. The radicado Cobo describes the Peruvian capital in 1629 as an "emporium," "a perpetual market day for the whole kingdom" (319). A year later in Lima, the creole Franciscan Buenaventura de Salinas y Córdova asserts that "the entire city is a market" (254). Intense trade teamed up with exorbitant wealth to shape the New World metropolis into the quintessential protocapitalist city. There resided the newly rich bourgeoisie, intent on styling themselves as aristocrats. The Spanish peasant "puts on noble airs" in the New World, and the commoner "schools himself in nobility," observed Bartolomé Arzáns de Orsúa y Vela of the silver boom city Potosí (2:333). Associating appearances (the notorious Spanish *quedar bien*) with reality and wealth with nobility, the would-be aristocrats engaged in conspicuous consumption with a vengeance.

All of these factors combine to produce the dramatic, ostentatious, excessive—in a word, spectacular—city life of the colonial elite that inspired a mixture of awe and umbrage in contemporary observers. The extravagance of Mexico City in 1625 scandalized yet tantalized the British Jesuit turned Dominican turned Puritan, Thomas Gage.

His renowned account remarks upon the silver-plated shoes and gold-encrusted waistbands of Spaniards' mistresses, the bejeweled hatbands of tradesmen, the church roofs "daubed with gold," and the astonishing liveries of the two thousand coaches that crowd the wide streets several abreast (66–73), which coaches "exceed in cost the best of the Court of Madrid and other parts of Christendom, for they spare no silver, nor gold, nor precious stones, nor cloth of gold, nor the best silks from China to enrich them" (67). Lima's wealth similarly impresses Cobo. He writes, for example, "The pomp and splendor of its citizens' manners and attire are so great and widespread that at festivals it is impossible to figure out from the way they look who is what; because everyone, nobles and commoners, dresses extravagantly and richly in silk and all manner of finery, without any moderation whatsoever" (320). We see that the ways in which spectacular wealth can shake dearly held class distinctions trouble even Cobo's considerable pride of place.

Cobo's dismay at the breakdown of boundaries exceeds mere religious pieties. It reflects the fact that the meticulously planned cities of the New World aimed to impose and police social hierarchies. City planning, to which we shall attend more deeply in later chapters, designed urban space as an incarnation of the dominant ideology. In other words, city planning amounted to social engineering. As Rama states, the New World's planned cities would be "ruled by an ordering form of reason that manifests itself in a hierarchical social order overlaid on a geometrical order" (4). Two axes, social stratification and ethnic segregation, structured them.[12] The center of the city contained the icons of wealth and power: a plaza, with its market and gallows; around the plaza, the cathedral or principal church, the city hall, and the viceregal palace. The city then radiated out from the center in tiers of decreasing social status. Closest to the center lay the homes of the wealthy, the buildings of the principal religious orders, the main schools and university. A second tier quartered merchants' and artisans' workplaces and dwellings. City engineering relegated to the outermost circle all edifices pertaining to the Indians, *castas* (individuals of mixed race), and impoverished whites, separated from the rest by a wall in Lima.

The crown's city-planning ordinances of 1573 desire that Indians who contemplate the center of the city from their designated place on the outer margins be struck with wonder at its grandiose edifices and "understand that the Spaniards are settling there permanently, not temporarily, so that they will fear them and not dare to offend them" (García Gallo 244). If such were the intended effects on an outsider's gaze, to walk the city from one end to another entailed an embodied experience of the social scale in its full compass—a rather perverse entertainment for the colonial *flâneur!* And yet, anyone who traversed the city in its entirety would quickly realize that the neat, Draconian divisions that city planning aspired to institute did not hold absolutely. The same servitude and commerce that divided society, ironically enough, increasingly rendered the city a contact zone. Streets, marketplaces, *obrajes* [sweatshop factories], taverns, government buildings, and private homes all served as venues for the confluence of groups that regulation strove to partition. Economic interests bonded the elite to other populations. Wealth or the lack thereof divided the city more along class than racial lines. Shared deprivation, for example, placed impoverished Spaniards in constant intercourse, including sexual, with other underprivileged groups. Along the same lines but conversely, as Cobo's words suggested, enhanced buying power wreaked havoc with sumptuary distinctions.

Layered and spectacular, generative motor of the viceregal world, the city was all but destined to constitute the prime colonial "scene of writing," in both the literal and figurative senses of the phrase. Power, patronage, prestige, and intellectual resources converged in the urban environment. So, naturally, did artists and writers, to the effect that the preponderance of cultural activity took place there. Writers ensconced in the city would not fail to make it the stuff of their works, the pith of their politics. Thus, a writing of urban place comes resoundingly to the fore in the works of Spaniards, radicados, and creoles alike. Their heterogeneous ideological positions along with the complexity of city life itself incite the remarkably diverse tropics of urban place that the sixteenth and seventeenth centuries produce and that coming pages here will probe. Cities from ideal to demonic, official to contestatory, sublime to satirical, bounded to open, monolithic to multiple, vanquished to living, central to marginal, sensual to intellectual, real to abstract or allegorical, and particularly from pastoral to unambiguously urban, spring forth from the writings of the times.

The age-old genre of city panegyric, or *laudatiae urbes,* acquires tremendous agency in this panorama. Derived from the classics, praise of cities enjoyed special currency in Spain, where regional loyalties often trumped national identifications. Urban panegyric spread like wildfire to and through the New World, for it behooved all and sundry to extol the virtues of the city, crowning jewel of Spain's new possessions. It should by now be abundantly clear, though, that creoles would have a special investment in the genre. Within the arena of city praise, creole writers could achieve a spectrum of attractive goals. They could communicate with Spain, where their empire-magnifying texts would reach publication, and broadcast their loyalty to the crown. Simultaneously, they could advance an "American" agenda by lauding the splendors, even the superiority, of their home ground, compatriots, virtues, and customs vis-à-vis Europe. Best yet, at least on a practical level, creoles complacently lodged in the city and rarely venturing beyond it could write of what they knew most closely and deeply. Praise of cities therefore emerges as a privileged, capacious, patently overdetermined "language" of criollismo in the seventeenth century, be it in literature or historiography. While creoles did continue their expansive vindications of the New World's climate and geography, the local city milieu, a main source of creole pride, ever more insistently commandeered their writings.[13]

As city panegyric eclipses other apologetics, as writers zoom in from the big picture onto their local milieu, certain modes of representation and certain urban spaces take center stage. A passage on the marketplace of Lima in the *Memorial de las historias del Nuevo Mundo, Pirú* [Brief on the histories of the New World, Peru] (1630) by Salinas y Córdova affords a quite savory taste of two such matters:

> Women—mulatto, and black, Indian, and mestizo—sell there, under tents to protect themselves from the sun: the Indian women place all their wares on the ground, on top of blankets, straw mats, or sleeping mats; the mulatto and black women put them on wooden tables. . . . They sell quinces, and pomegranates (so good that they defy comparison to those of Spain), pippins, and apples, melocotons, peaches, pears, apricots, two kinds of plums (from Spain and native), four kinds of grapes (white, black, mollar, muscatel), white and black figs, muskmelons, watermelons (white, red, and yellow); passion fruits, prickly pears, pineapples, green and dark-skinned *paltas* [Quechua for "avocado"]; many varieties of guavas, cucumbers (from Spain and native), plantains (native and from Guinea) [and so on, on and on]. (253)

So immersed is Salinas in the city, so given over to the siren call of its specificity, that he inundates his reader with minutiae. This exorbitant particularity (about which I will have much to say with regard to the Baroque) plays a starring role in city texts. And what better site can one imagine for it than the marketplace, abounding in peoples and things?

Salinas's is just one of the myriad marketplaces that, together with the great city plaza (and for reasons that in both cases overspill civic pride), will prove to dominate the topology of the textualized city.

III. FESTIVAL

Although the truism that everything in Latin America is outsized and larger than in Europe generally conjures up the New World's luxuriant natural phenomena, it could also put one in mind of the monumental colonial plaza. The grand central plaza first made its appearance in the New World and only afterward circled back to take root in Spain.[14] Article 113 of the 1573 ordinances suggests why, saying that the main plaza "shall be rectangular, its length being at least one and a half times its width because this shape is best for festivals with horses, or for any others that might be held" (García Gallo 242). New World cities designed for ideological consolidation and social stratification, in other words, made provision in their infrastructure for the display and spectacle crucial to imperial objectives. If power and wealth could parade arrogantly through the unusually broad city streets, the majestic plaza accommodated the public events on which absolutist Counter-Reformation society turned. The disproportionately large plaza, in Potosí and elsewhere called Regocijo [Rejoicing], became a kind of "performance machine" (Roach 14), an apt setting for festivals and entertainments as well as for punitive spectacles like autos-da-fé.

Along with the plaza, the celebrations on which imperial Spain clearly set such stock swelled in the New World. The exigencies of proselytizing and calculated assessments of preconquest Indian cultures spurred the escalation. Spanish missionaries rapidly surmised the ceremonial orientation of Indian cultures and hastened to exploit it. A letter from the cathedral chapter of Lima to the king baldly urges: "it is advisable to hold public events, and especially here because the native peoples are so moved by pomp and display" (qtd. in Ramos Sosa 204). Based on a similar appraisal of Indian culture, Franciscan missionaries in Mexico began to institute the liturgical calendar of Catholicism shortly after the fall of Tenochtitlán (Curcio-Nagy 3). To lure the Indians, whom the Franciscan historian Juan de Torquemada labeled "ceremoniáticos," or addicted to ceremonies (qtd. in Brading 287), the conquering Spaniards throughout colonial space and time were at pains to outstrip not just the frequency but also the magnitude of indigenous ceremonies. "Bishops and priests should endeavor that any acts of worship be performed with the greatest perfection and splendor possible," writes the Lima cabildo in 1583 (qtd. in Ricard 317). In conjunction with the delightful persuasions of fabulous festivals, Spanish edicts from 1539 to 1813 time and again sharply prohibited Indian ceremonies (Taylor 42–43).

Before entering more fully into the Hispanic celebratory universe so vital to colonial society and to our concerns, let us pause for a minute to collect a larger perspective on it through a work that the title of my book evokes, *The Society of the Spectacle* by the French theorist Guy Debord. Debord's trenchant aphorisms on the contemporary totalitarian society of the spectacle brilliantly elucidate the festival machinery of the colonial Spectacular City.[15] He acerbically examines the ways in which the symbolic manipulation of power enacted by the hegemonic state barrages its constituents with illusions rather than realities. These diversionary illusions or "spectacles" masquerade as entertainments yet in fact represent the "materialization of ideology" (150), "a Weltanschauung that has been actualized, translated into the material realm—a world view transformed into an objective force" (13). As it translates political and theological ideology into concrete, seductive forms (the spectacle's "very *manner of being concrete* is, precisely, abstraction" [22]), the spectacle despotically foists its singular worldview on the urban environment that it confiscates. "The spectacle appears at once as society itself, as part of society, and as a means of unification," writes Debord (12). It attempts to unify society, to combat instability, and to camouflage with its glorious entertainments a wretched underlying reality: the spectacle "is no more than an image of harmony set amidst desolation and dread, at the still center of misfortune" (41). Spectacles that veil actual historical conditions sing of the commodity, of "what society *can deliver*" (20), little as it might. A "parody of the gift" no less than a "travesty of dialogue" (113), mass festivals make play a hidden appendage of work (21-22) and community the incarnation of alienation (151).

Debord may offer a dark view of the spectacle-festival, yet it is probably none too dark for the festivals of absolutist Spain's so-called guided culture. We well know from history and from Antonio Maravall's *Culture of the Baroque* that to stanch the overwhelming religious and political turmoil of the seventeenth century, to block the tides of change, Spain imposed an absolute monarchy. What Maravall terms "Baroque guided culture" accompanied that absolute monarchy. A culture of crisis, it sought to "overcome the forces of deviance or opposition present in the society of the epoch" (125), among many ways, by utilizing extant organs of culture to interpellate the masses. The Baroque era, Maravall writes, witnessed the first concerted attempt to harness mass media for the cultural shaping of the populace (102). Baroque statecraft, an integral part of its guided culture for the masses and the elite, therefore hypertrophied. It theatricalized power in full recognition that power lives in representation and that representation generates more power. Expectably, the civil and religious festivals already ingrained in the culture of Spain comprised the principal dramatic artillery of what had become a veritable society of the spectacle.

With the stakes even higher, the society of the spectacle installed in the colonies hyperbolically ritualized events large and small, colonial and imperial, religious and secular, praiseworthy and shameful. Religious fiestas marked the holidays on the liturgical calendar, the dedications of new churches or additions to existing structures, the investiture or departure of ecclesiastic officials, the transfer of relics or sacred images, beatifications and canonizations, articles of doctrine, patron saints of the cities or its organizations, autos-da-fé, and more. State festivals commemorated events in the lives of royal or viceregal families, the punishment of criminals, the arrival or departure of new fleets and especially of government officials. As they had in Spain, Corpus Christi and the official entries of rulers continued to occasion the grandest celebrations.[16] The viceregal festival also absorbed popular, local, agricultural celebrations.

Analogously, the festival implicated all constituencies in the society of the spectacle. State and church bodies, trade guilds, and confraternities bore the expenses of and participated in the celebrations. The entertainments of the festival *octavario* [the customary week-long celebration] catered to every taste. Elite culture jostled with popular in diversions that ranged from chivalric tournaments, elegant masquerades, and complex emblems contrived to pique the educated mind to raucous *mojigangas* [masquerades of a carnivalesque ilk], mass banquets, and fireworks. The conventional route of festivals traversed the entire city. As the processions stopped at its principal monuments, the "nerve centers that articulate space" (Ramos Sosa 69), they effectively consecrated an ideal city, remaking the map. Yet the ceremonial parades did not bypass festively transformed indigenous zones, where they marched through the triumphal arches and partook of the entertainments the Indians had prepared.

Here one encounters the single greatest novelty, and trap, of the hegemonic New World festival: its extensive incorporation of the Indian. Linda Curcio-Nagy notes that celebrations "attempted to promote a shared history and values" and to "influence the creation of a colonial identity" in "potentially 'dangerous' groups" (5). Aspiring to resolve social tensions in symbolic yet palpable form, hegemonic festivals mimicked the topsy-turvy egalitarianism of carnivals by according the Indians and their songs and dances a prominent place in the events. To the untutored eye, festivals merged the populations of the world's most racially and ethnically mixed society into a harmonious collectivity.[17]

Festivals that transformed colonial subjects into witting or unwitting actors converted the whole city into a theater. Ephemeral festival architecture such as triumphal arches made of plaster or wood functioned as props that refocused and ideologized urban space. Temporary façades, tapestries, banners, and special illumination obliterated quotidian realities, estheticizing the city. To produce the sublime sensory experiences that would bind the populace to its goals, the festival tapped all available cultural resources. Art, architecture, music, dance, and literature collaborated on the spectacle's vast stage. Elaborate contraptions and special effects brought science and technology into the mix. The festival, writes Octavio Paz, "is the exaltation of culture in its supreme form" (*Sor Juana* 147; unless otherwise indicated, subsequent references to Paz in *The Spectacular City* derive from his *Sor Juana*). Celebration organizers therefore commissioned works from leading writers and showcased their creations. Engaging the intelligentsia, fiestas featured rounds of sermons, religious and secular theatrical performances, and poetry recitals. Cultural and material capital blended indissolubly in the poetry contests sponsored by various groups as writers vied for luxury goods normally beyond their means.

The viceregal world, we see, spared no pains or expense in mounting its festivals. Conjoined with New World wealth and ostentation, official efforts resulted in spectacles so lavish and costly as almost to defy credibility. The journal of Josephe de Mugaburu, a Spanish soldier residing in seventeenth-century Lima, invites us into the extravaganzas common to the Spanish American colonies. Mugaburu served as sergeant of the guard at the viceroy's palace in Lima's central square, and from 1640 to 1686 he registered the plaza's events. The physical vantage point of this staunch imperialist translates into a literary one as he faithfully transcribes, to the exclusion of nearly everything else, the excessive, incessant ceremonial life of the city. Mugaburu's journal dazzles the reader with its reports of merchants paving streets in silver; a masquerade that attracted fifteen hundred participants, five hundred of them in outlandish costumes; floats awash in gold and jewels; trains of mules swathed in silk and carrying food for the masses; fireworks issuing from allegorical religious floats; lackeys and midgets dressed in crimson finery, and so on. His accounts equally demonstrate the ways in which fiestas attempted to implement a shared history and values. Mugaburu's lines on a festival in 1659, for instance, catch the state in the act of worshiping itself in effigy: "There was a parade of floats . . . [with] figures of all the viceroys who had governed this kingdom; then eight costumed Incas; followed by a very large figure carrying the world on his shoulders and with veins of silver and gold, offering it all to the prince" (51). With a single sweep of the pen, Mugaburu encapsulates the Weltanschauung, ideology, esthetics, and economics integral to the colonial society of the spectacle.

However potent their devices, however totalizing their pretensions, the festivals around which the colonial society of the spectacle revolved by no means lacked fissures and unstable, exploitable spaces. The festivals' sheer spectacular volume and cost courted disaster by draining the economy of the state and of the private citizens increasingly forced to shoulder the burden.[18] Juan Rodríguez Freile, a Colombian creole, laments in *El Carnero* [The ram]: "The president was given a solemn reception [in 1569] with great festivals that lasted for fifteen days and incurred excessive expenses, which the country could more easily bear then because it was new. Nowadays [1638], I do not know how it can afford them" (143). Festivals themselves could go awry and erupt into disorder. The identitary civic pride they encouraged could and did, as coming pages of *The Spectacular City* will detail, take on a rebellious life of its own that set in motion a rift between the (officially constituted) state and the (independently emerging) nation.

Moreover, thanks to the calculated escape valves for social tensions that the celebrations furnished, agile platforms were built into the very body of the festivals. The otherwise monological festival contained two salient spaces for social critique and dialogue. One ensued from the festival's usurping of carnivalesque activities: every celebration, even the solemn Corpus Christi, included comical components. Debonair masquerades coexisted with biting burlesques, poetry praising the city and its administration with satires lampooning them. Irving A. Leonard views the burlesque masquerade as "a useful medium of criticism" in that "it provided opportunities to pillory prominent officials and unpopular dignitaries" (121). The seventeenth-century Mexican protojournalist Antonio de Robles describes an "utterly indecent" masquerade in Puebla, unchecked by its bishop, "in which statues of the viceroy and his wife the countess were paraded through the streets and brought to justice, with people shouting many terrible insults at them" (1:29). The festival's other aperture, the *speculum principis,* or Mirror for Princes, dates to the Middle Ages. Traditionally, citizens greeted an incoming ruler with a roster (declaimed and/or inscribed on triumphal arches) of the qualities their ideal Christian ruler should possess, qualities they preemptively lauded in the new leader. Renaissance festivals of entry often supplemented the Mirror for Princes with a list of issues that their cities faced and that they wished the incoming ruler to address (Strong 8).[19] Prescribing qualities of the ruler and his agenda gave the intellectual some voice in the viceroy's subsequent regime.

Chronicles of festivals, or *relaciones de fiestas,* the cornerstones of the Spectacular City, augment that voice. A genre imbedded with absolutism, the festival chronicle blossomed in Europe around the mid-sixteenth century. As Roy Strong observes of Europe, by 1660 "no major festival went unrecorded in print" (22). The absolutist society of the spectacle virtually demanded these developments, for without written and pictorial record the magnificent, ideologically loaded, short-lived festivals would evanesce. To preserve them for posterity, festival patrons commissioned chronicles from renowned writers who had experienced the celebrations firsthand, often the same individuals who had contributed to the festival program. Festivals received their due, as it were, in what tended to be large-format, well-disseminated publications. The chronicles could be long or short, in poetry or in verse, on civil or religious occasions, but their commemorative nature warranted specific verbal protocols. Literally adhering to protocol, the accounts adulated the patron and inflatedly praised the festival. Narration alternated with description. Both verbal tasks maintained a witty, urbane tone and exercised an optic of extreme particularity that replicated the fetishizing of detail inherent in the events themselves.

Given the usual time lag between the metropolis and the colonies, it is striking that the first festival chronicles of Mexico and Peru were published in the 1560s, concurrent with the European vogue.[20] Striking but not startling, for festival chronicles held as many benefits for the colonial writer as they did for the colonial state. Authors profited from the financially lucrative commissions and from the rare opportunity to publish in a prestigious venue or at all, to compound their fame, to ascend the social ladder on the wings of that fame, and to communicate with the metropolis. Under such pressures, writers generally complied with the dictates of the genre and told the official story in its requisite official mode. Having such a prestigious, public venue at their disposal, on the other hand, they would not refrain from transmuting the festival chronicle into a platform for their personal and political interests. The same opportunistic, productive bargaining occurs in uncommissioned texts that position themselves as (or satirize) official festival chronicles. From the almost ineluctable, rich template of hegemonic celebrations, the agile festival-involved texts of various sorts that we shall follow extract a means and a mode for their own agendas.

IV. WONDER

Through the festival the society of the spectacle works its transformative magic on the cityscape, with the aim of producing wonders that incite an entranced wonder in all concerned. For their part, texts that invoke wonder summon the phenomenon's representational power to "spectacularize" or monumentalize whatever it envelops, to imbue the quotidian or micro-event with a spark of the festival's spectacular potency. Infusing its subject with a heady jolt of excitement lies at the heart of the many jobs that the multitasking wonder performs in the early modern worlds and beyond.

The axial, explosive, sprawling role of wonder in Renaissance and Baroque writing has been brought home by the current vogue of early modern wonder studies.[21] Two poles of the lively debate have a special hold on the account of early modern wonder in the Old and New worlds that I wish to purvey. First, predictably enough, Stephen Greenblatt's *Marvelous Possessions: The Wonder of the New World*, with its strong sense of wonder's centrality to European "first encounters" with the New World ("Wonder is, I shall argue, the central figure in the initial European response to the New World, the decisive emotional and intellectual experience in the presence of radical difference" [14]) and no less acute sense of how wonder was arrogated to the discourses of colonialism. Second, Mary Baine Campbell's *Wonder and Science: Imagining Worlds in Early Modern Europe*, which has oriented my thinking on many matters. Campbell shadowboxes with approaches to wonder such as Greenblatt's in order "to discover functions besides colonialist complicity for poetic estrangement and the cognitive emotion" (21), in the desire of recuperating the pleasure of wonder, "the value of a pleasurable emotion, or relation to knowing" (3). Conjugating Greenblatt's and Campbell's positions, I offer a synoptic history of the wounding of early modern wonder, that is, the co-opting of its pleasures. The tarnished history yields its share of pleasures on a different level, for we will see that the more wonder is wounded in or with regard to the New World, the more fitting and agile it becomes for the decolonizing projects of New World writers.

Historically and philosophically, the cognitive emotion of wonder begins in innocence. Plato's dialogue *Theaetetus* posits wonder as the intellectual energy that motivates all philosophical inquiry (21, 155 c-d). When Socrates' young pupil Theaetetus has reached a point of total confusion and describes himself as "dizzy" with wonder, his mentor replies: "that experience, the feeling of wonder, is very characteristic of a philosopher: philosophy has no other starting-point" (21, 155 c-d). Similarly, centuries later René Descartes writes in *The Passions of the Soul,* "Wonder is a sudden surprise of the soul which causes it to apply itself to consider with attention the objects which seem to it rare and extraordinary" (362). Descartes views wonder as a first reaction to an object or experience, and, importantly, as prior to moral judgment (358–359; Greenblatt 24). Aristotle shares Plato's view of wonder as the impetus for philosophical inquiry and arguably conditions Descartes's discomfort with the onrush of "surprise" generated by ignorance. In the *Metaphysics* Aristotle writes, "For it is owing to their wonder that men both now begin and at first began to philosophize; they wondered originally at the obvious difficulties, then . . . they philosophized in order to escape from ignorance" (1554; 1.2 982b 10–18). Aristotelian wonder, in other words, exists only as an initial passion born of ignorance, which intellectual inquiry aspires to dispel (see Daston and Park, chap. 3). Aristotle's posing and then disposing of wonder led his followers in the Middle Ages, including Roger Bacon, Albertus Magnus, and Thomas Aquinas, to vilify wonder as a mere raw, fearsome steppingstone on the road to knowledge.

Aristotle's construction of wonder in the *Poetics,* on the other hand, inaugurates the phenomenon's long, full life as the generative locus of literary production and criticism. The *Poetics* invests literature with the basic function of producing a salutary, cathartic wonder. Broaching the thorny question of verisimilitude, Aristotle argues that to inspire wonder, or *admiratio,* the poet may present things as they are said or thought or ought to be rather than as they were (133, 1460 a-b). Over the course of the Renaissance and thereafter, Aristotle's loophole in mimesis for *admiratio* came to be identified with the full play of the imagination, *inventio,* in its all-embracing manifestations as textual subject, stylistics, and effect on the reader (see Hathaway, chap. 2). And wonder itself contracted the stream of variegated meanings that Baxter Hathaway lists: "As we pursue the history of this particular emphasis of Aristotle's through the Renaissance, it is necessary to link together a group of words that are partially interchangeable, 'wonder' or 'miracle' (*thauma*), 'admiration' (*admiratio*), 'astonishment,' 'marvel' (*meraviglia*), 'awe,' 'stupor,' the unusual, the perfect, the sublime" (57–58). If, continues Hathaway, at "its lowest level, the marvelous is merely that which holds our attention or interest," at "its highest level it is practically an access to the Godhead or a direct intimation of divinity" (58).

Wonder's ability to bridge the prosaic and the divine primes it for protagonism in Spain, whose Renaissance remained tethered to religion. Slowly and incompletely, Spain wrestled with the transition from all-consuming medieval piety to Renaissance humanism and with the transvaluation of the religious into the secular that the transition entailed. Wonder serves as a connective tissue between the seemingly inimical realms. It permeates Spain's first major foray into secular literature, the extremely popular late fifteenth-century novels of chivalry. Construing the marvelous as the supernatural, the novel of chivalry gambols from one marvelous event to another, each of which provokes an exaggerated reaction of wonder in the characters. The marvel as supernatural event and the thematized *admiratio* that supplies the emotional dimension of the chivalric romance both carry in their wake the pious literature of the Middle Ages. For wonder figures in the New Testament as the effect of the words and works of Christ; St. Augustine writes a mini-encyclopedia of wonder in his *City of God* that attributes all marvels to God (books 20–21); medieval hagiographies and other devotional works often revolve around the awe-inspiring properties of miracles. In the novel of chivalry, wonder can thus be seen as an errant form of or allusion to the divine, a secularized miracle making still resounding with religious echoes.

Nonetheless, while the public adored novels of chivalry, moralists abhorred them. Theologians and Erasmians raged against the romances' abdication of verisimilitude, their lack of moral purpose or utility. A Christianized form of Neoplatonism achieved a far more acceptable fit between humanism and religion. I refer to the efficacious, abiding notion of the world as a book in which one reads and wonders at God's awesome handiwork. The archi-trope of the world as a book written by God, medieval in provenance, effortlessly fuses with Neoplatonism's model of the cosmos as a chain of mysterious yet seamless similitudes to pose an especially appealing task for the inquiring Renaissance mind.

The Renaissance "Natural Magician"—poet, theologian, protoscientist, or anyone who reads the book of the world—will endeavor to ferret out the connections, to decipher the cryptic signs of God's handiwork, and thus to attain a heightened appreciation of the deity's miracles along with a heightened understanding of the natural world. As the sixteenth-century Spanish writer Luis de Granada so perfectly puts it, "What is this whole visible world but a great and *marvelous* book that you, Lord, have written and offered to the eyes of all nations of the world . . . so that everyone may study it and know You? And then what are all the creatures of the world, so beautiful and perfect, if not refracted, illuminated writing that declares the excellence and wisdom of its author?" (186; emphasis added). The act of reading the book of the world in order to fathom its marvels converts outwardly secular, empirical, scientific explorations into a completely proper, divinely mandated hermeneutics and heuristics.

Up to this point, we have visited landmarks in the remarkably expansive territory of early modern wonder that represent the cognitive passion in its purity, and as brimming with pleasures. The pleasures will remain, but the innocence and purity suffer extreme ravages in the next landmark, the *Diario* [Diary] (1493) of Columbus's first voyage to the New World. Something of a Natural Magician but actually an impresario of wonder, Columbus evokes *maravilla* [the marvel or marvelous] with numbing frequency.[22] Las Casas's transcription-cum-summary of the *Diario* confirms and amplifies Columbus's wonder-mongering: Las Casas appears to be on a hunt for the marvelous. Moreover, in the copious direct quotes from the *Diario* that the transcription includes, Columbus himself brandishes the marvelous in a dizzying, confounding array of contexts. How, for example, can one understand the application of the marvelous equally to the beguiled reception of the natives to the trinkets with which the interlopers bribed them ("and they were so won over to us that it was a marvel" [11 October]) and to Columbus's seemingly enraptured response to the diversity of New World nature ("large and small birds of so many kinds and so different from ours that it is a marvel" [21 October])? Or his denial of the "maravillas" of Bohío, the alleged home of exotic monsters, recounted to him by the natives (5 December)? Beyond the discrepancy of contexts, the first example (trinkets) smacks of hypocrisy; the second (nature) appears to reflect genuine esthetic pleasure; the third (no monsters) oddly sabotages the verification of Oriental models in which we know that Columbus was engaged; all of the examples implicitly sully esthetics with commercialism. At every step, Columbus registers what Alejo Carpentier famously calls "the marvel of the real" *and* creates catachreses that wound the already plethoric marvelous.[23]

Columbus works wonder to a frenzy, but not without a plan. Careful scrutiny reveals that each instance of maravilla in his diary serves to mark one or another of the deeply disjunctive aspects of Columbus's design. That design, we know, conjoined self-vindication with the religious goal of obtaining funds to reconquer Jerusalem (26 December) and with urgent mercantile interests. When the *Diario* pronounces some entity or statement marvelous, it signals the positive indications vis-à-vis Columbus's design of whatever it marks. When denied, maravilla signals the contraindications of the subject for his purposes. Wedding wonder to his objectives, Columbus overloads and impoverishes it. His catachrestic wonder loses denotative muscle, moral shading, esthetic import. Las Casas's transcription of the *Diario,* conversely, strives to reinstate the purity of wonder. The last direct words of Columbus he cites refer to the miracles God allegedly bestowed on the Admiral (15 March). For Las Casas, the marvelous-cum-miraculous tinges with the Divine each aspect of Columbus's design thus marked. The Dominican friar validates Columbus's enterprise by aligning it with the old Transcendental Signifier even as it races headlong into the new, wounding language and morality to the core.

Clearly we are witnessing in Columbus the inception of a colonialist discourse, which Peter Hulme defines in a manner germane to the present context as "an ensemble of linguistically-based practices unified by their common deployment in the management of colonial relationships" (xiv). Beginning with Columbus, colonialist discourse immediately discerns the efficacy of wonder for its purposes—and hijacks it, colonizes the marvelous (Greenblatt 25).[24] Henceforth, Spanish writings from and about the New World interpellate wonder not merely, as it were, for epistemology, poetics, or theology, but also for hegemonic history. The serviceability of the multifaceted yet always sweet wonder for problematic situations of all sorts, furthermore, recommends it to other hegemonic scenarios. I now want to zero in on two subsequent moments in the wounding of wonder, one Renaissance and one Baroque, which maneuver it into executing some monumental, paradigmatic tasks.

The first enterprise has disarmingly circumscribed, personal beginnings. To sell his writing projects to the crown in his debut work on the New World, the *Sumario de la natural historia de las Indias* of 1526, the early Spanish voyager Gonzalo Fernández de Oviedo devises the shrewd strategy of billing and building it as a wonderland. While Oviedo sojourns in Spain, he composes the *Sumario,* the first Hispanic natural history of the New World and his least bulky work on the colonies, as a sneak preview of the massive general and natural history of the Indies he was already writing. Eschewing for the occasion the actual history of the colonial project, Oviedo concentrates exclusively on the spellbinding natural and ethnographic aspects of the New World. He entreats the young Spanish king, Charles V, to overlook any deficiencies in his *Sumario* and instead to heed only "the new things in it, for they have been my chief purpose" (49, 5). The author reiterates at various points that his report centers on wonderful, incomparable, and very strange things. With this and in the "Dedication" (47, 3), Oviedo blatantly inscribes his work in the framework of Pliny's *Natural History,* a book of wonders, the precursor of medieval paradoxography. Oviedo goes on to produce the marvel with all the fanfare of a magician pulling a rabbit out of a hat. A "Natural Magician," Oviedo reads and reveals the "secrets" of the New World. He typically begins his vignettes on its nature and peoples by connecting them to European phenomena but then trots out the utterly new properties or "marvels of the world" (94, 46) that only the author, by virtue of his firsthand knowledge of the colonies, can supply. A former Erasmian, Oviedo replaces the objectionable otherworldly marvels of the novel of chivalry with the earthbound wonders of the New World.[25] The sensorial, practical delights of New World nature dominate Oviedo's *Sumario.* His verbal representations allow the king (a notorious gourmand with a weak stomach) to share the taste, smell, feel, look, and medicinal assets of the new foodstuffs, oddities easily convertible into commodities. Oviedo parses New World nature into something of a scientific taxonomy, into parcels as easy to consume and enjoy as Disneyland attractions. When, however, Oviedo applies his sensationalizing sensibility to the peoples of the New World, he erects not a Disneyland but a nightmarish, sinful wonderland akin to that of Bosch, a world upside down where anything can happen. Especially in chapter 10 of the *Sumario,* Oviedo rails at what he considers to be the savage, transgressive, immoral practices of the non-Christian Indians. He fixates on such damning curiosities as the alleged devil worship, rape, cannibalism, sodomy, polygamy, nudity, abortions, brutality, and so on of the Indians in Tierra Firme. Oviedo contorts ethnographic novelty into a credulous scandal sheet that packs a prurient punch designed, of course, to justify colonial subordination of the Indians. To promote the Christianization of his demonized Indians, to mitigate the fear they might inspire, the humanist Oviedo adduces a Pliny-inflected, humanist caveat that legitimates *variety:* no matter how diverse and marvelous New World peoples might appear to be, they are human beings (94, 46), and their practices have antecedents in other pagan societies (82, 35).[26]

Oviedo has wonderized the New World to complex, most enticing, and ultimately tenacious effect. By restricting the New World to a topography of wonder, he has prophylactically shelved that vibrant entity away into a taxonomic, verbal curio cabinet. To temper the radical novelty of the New World, Oviedo "museumizes" it: he prematurely freezes the vibrant colonial world into a museum of delights, a collection of phenomena ripe for the taking, and relegates it to the safe status of exotica. J. H. Elliott notes that the "sixteenth century collected facts as it collected exotic objects" and "lumped them together into an undifferentiated category of the marvellous or exotic," which "inevitably reduced their effectiveness as vehicles for change" (*Old World* 30, 32). Columbus and Cortés regaled the Spanish court with trumped-up processions of exotic Indians and parrots. Oviedo does the same in writing, opening the New World to the discursive tactics of exoticizing. What better way to moderate the new and still let it glisten tantalizingly than by presenting it as simply, statically, exotic? With its adept sleights of hand, exoticizing discourse neatly manages to differentiate *and* to domesticate the foreign by estheticizing, mystifying, and spectacularizing it.[27] The foundational *Sumario* illustrates the easy slippage between the original meaning of "exotic" as "foreign, from outside," and its present resting place as "the charm or fascination of the unfamiliar" (*Webster's*). Thus, just as the New World was entering the European horizon, Oviedo ensnares the incipient colonial entity in a verbal technology so laden with benefits that it would continue to mold the representation of Latin America throughout the colonial period and to this day, in the form of a charming yet occlusive magical realism.[28]

Less than a century after Oviedo hawked the New World as a wonderland congenial to imperialism and evangelization, Counter-Reformation Spain recruited wonder for its domestic guided culture. In a post-Tridentine Spain faced with Protestant disparagement of the Catholic penchant for miracles, the stock of wonder had risen belligerently. The Catholic Church pugnaciously, if with somewhat greater circumspection, sanctioned more and more miracles. Further, the extreme times of crises had given rise to the celebrated Baroque taste for the wondrously shocking or bizarre, a taste that pervaded elite and popular culture alike.

The absolutist machine cannily took possession of the widespread partiality to wonders. "Subjects are produced when . . . they succumb to dazzlement or charm of any origin" (Marin xii): as the case of the festival has already corroborated, Spanish guided culture called upon wonder to shape the absolutist subject. Since that subject might well fall prey to the seductions of novelty and change seeping into Spain from the New World and the rest of Europe, the conservative guided culture contrived a new job for wonder. To mask the lack of change on more substantive fronts, the hegemony would funnel novelty into the controlled arena of culture, that is, into cultural artifacts that it gorged with wonders. "The irruption of outlandish elements in poetry, literature, and art," writes Maravall, "compensated for the deprivation of novelty elsewhere" (138; see his chap. 9). Novelty, cordoned off and shunted onto wonder-provoking cultural artifacts, from special effects in popular theater to audacious metaphors in abstruse poetry, would pacify the public. Wonder thus became a holding pen for disruptive energies, and one of absolutism's principal weapons for the managing of modernity.

The Baroque esthetic of amazement contained the seeds of its own implosion. It stands to reason that a wonder-filled art sequestering the real change and novelty proscribed to society would transgress its intended bounds. In a rare admission of the guided culture's breaking points, Maravall acknowledges this volatility, saying: "it was unavoidable that the passion for the unknown, for the new and the extraordinary, and finally for its corruption in the outlandish would go to . . . extremes, already beyond its permitted limits" (230).[29] The Spanish historian cites as an example of wonder's irrepressible instability Francisco de Quevedo's satirical works, which translated the Baroque license for amazing licentiousness into a channel for criticism of the government.

The fact that Quevedo's works gave birth to reams of colonial political satires intimates the even greater likelihood that wonder could and did short circuit in the New World. While, as Greenblatt observes, the pluralized "experience of wonder" inherently resists "recuperation, containment, ideological incorporation" (17), the wounded, agile wonder whose vicissitudes we have followed was even more likely to do so in a New World characterized precisely by the dynamism, outlandishness, and radical novelty that Spanish wonder ardently wished to redirect. Importantly, the wonder deployed on the New World and exported to it from Spain would be seized by New World authors. Availing themselves of its privileged status, multifunctionality, and lability, they put wonder to new work.

Antonio de León Pinelo, a converted Jew and a radicado devoted to his adopted homeland of Peru, for example, rescues wonder for the New World at the exact site of its wounding, Columbus's writings. León Pinelo's *El Paraíso en el Nuevo Mundo* [Paradise in the New World] (1650) revisits Columbus's theorizing of the New World in the *Diario* and the *Relación del tercer viaje* [Account of the third voyage] (1498). León Pinelo concludes that because, according to Columbus and subsequent thinkers, Paradise lies in the East, and the East equals the New World, then his adopted homeland is "the origin of the best, most precious and strangest things that the land can produce" and "of infinite strange and singular things, for which reason the Indies should be accorded a supreme place in the globe" (3). As Bosch's *Garden of Earthly Delights* graphically attests, from Paradise there logically issue the "strange and singular things" that León Pinelo charts in the second part of his text, a natural history of the New World. A professed disciple of Oviedo in the exorbitant Baroque era, León Pinelo reproduces and magnifies his predecessor's wonderland, with attention to the New World's infinite natural wealth, teratological creatures, sensational practices (though, echoing Oviedo's caveat on the diversity of the world, he intones that human sacrifice "is nothing new to the world" [21]). León Pinelo's fervent patriotism decolonizes wonder and reclaims the exotic.

The exoticizing of the New World that León Pinelo passionately embraces epitomizes the new work of wonder in the New World that we will experience in coming pages. Colonial authors write back to the empire using its own tropes in a *self*-exoticizing or "self-ascription of otherness" (Rabasa 11) that gains no little sustenance from the New World's multiple connections with the actual Orient, its quite real "Orientalism." Colonial writers find pleasure and impetus as well in the received vision of the New World as a wonder cabinet (*Wunderkammern*). Spanish museumizing of the New World devolves into a homegrown anatomizing and celebration of Spanish America's marvels consistent with the inclination toward particularity noted earlier. The ready association of New World oddities with capitalist commodities induces the siting of all kinds of work, from ideological to epistemological, in wonderful objects. In the hands of New World authors an exotic fruit, a curiously wrought globe, or a resplendent rose will discharge the Herculean labors with which wonder's history had freighted it.

V. MANAGING THE NEW WORLD

Wonder takes its place among the battery of discursive moves the Old World cultivated to manage the shock of the New, a shock Bosch captures in the fantastic, decentered, forbidding pandemonium of his *Garden of Earthly Delights*. More soberly, Elliott observes, "The very fact of America's existence, and of its gradual revelation as an entity in its own right, rather than as an extension of Asia, constituted a challenge to a whole body of traditional assumptions, beliefs and attitudes," including cosmography and the classics (*Old World* 8).[30] Elliott then states that the "sheer immensity of this challenge goes a long way towards explaining one of the most striking features of sixteenth-century intellectual history—the apparent slowness of Europe in making the mental adjustments required to incorporate America within its field of vision" (*Old World* 8). With these words, written in 1970, Elliott introduces the conundrum of the New World's seemingly minimal impact on Europe in the century following the first encounters, a conundrum that sparked much healthy debate. Some ten years later, Michael Ryan's nuanced formulation of European responses to the crises that the New World activated significantly redirected the debate:

> The assimilation of the new worlds . . . involved their domestication. If the new worlds attracted comparatively little attention, if they provoked no intellectual crisis, if they remained on the periphery of European vision, it may have been in part because the process of assimilation tended to *rob them of their difference and blunt the force of their impact*. (523; emphasis added)[31]

In keeping with this line of thought, I maintain that to assuage anxiety Europe developed a host of verbal panaceas—Oviedo's museumizing and exoticizing among them—that blunt the new by regulating it, delimiting it, obliterating it, and so on.

Discursive tactics, of course, join with visual media such as cartography and with all sorts of legal measures to defuse the intensity of the new. Each medium in its own way employs one of the Old World's most forceful and enduring management technologies for the New World. I refer to similitude, the equating of the New World to the Old. Simply put, similitude manages most everything that the New World places in crisis. It radiates into the Renaissance and Baroque epistemes; we will ponder it often, as wielded offensively by early Spanish writers to subdue the New World into the Ordered City, and, as it circulates throughout the New World, defensively by later citizens of the colonies. For a meaningful, suggestive first contact with the historically productive "colonialogic" (Campbell 63 *et passim*) of similitude, we turn to historiography itself.

In 1528 the Spanish humanist Hernán Pérez de Oliva wrote that Columbus had embarked on his second voyage to unite the world "and to give those foreign lands the same shape as our own" (53–54). Such, too, was the weighty mission of much historiography on the New World during the first 150 years of its existence for the Old World. An early form of comparative ethnography that some have called syncretic history or, more precisely if more awkwardly, historiographic syncretism, evolved to do the hegemonic job of parlaying heterogeneity into similarity.[32] Historiographic syncretism relates to its more benign and resistant sociological counterpart, the religious syncretism enacted by indigenous peoples, in that it undertakes to coordinate the history and religions of the New World with those of the Old. Bolstered by the humanism we heard in Oviedo's words, and often by Oviedo's words themselves, colonial historiographic syncretism delves into the Old World's past to unearth the pagan precursors to New World cultures; their existence allowed the early modern Western mind once again to envision the planet as a single, somehow united world rather than as a universe riven into two.[33] Luis Harss states that the "key factor" was a "sense of an expanding world that required a new unifying scheme capable of accounting for cultural diversity" (16). In systematizing and partially effacing diversity, historiographic syncretism (which henceforth I will abbreviate to "syncretism") takes over the conceptual management of a problematically multiple universe for which wonder or exoticizing supplied only a tenuous, inadequate heuristics. In subsuming the new and the unknown within the old and the familiar, syncretism holds supremely healing explanatory power for the Old World.

Not surprisingly, then, syncretism begins to take shape early on, in Las Casas's Aristotelian *Apologética historia* and his *Historia de las Indias* (completed in 1559). From the Dominican Las Casas, it spreads to the writings of all major religious orders. It transcends religious denominations, exercises itself on Mexican and Peruvian precontact history, and exhibits both a substantial consistency and a marked intertextuality as it develops (chapter 5 herein examines the major issue that divided it). Of the numerous works in this vein, I will mention only a few, which play a part in upcoming chapters. The effervescent years around our axial "La grandeza mexicana" (1604) boast the publication of two milestone syncretic works focusing on Mexico that project the colony onto a global framework, the Jesuit José de Acosta's *Historia natural y moral de las Indias* (1589 in Latin, 1590 in Spanish) and the Franciscan Juan de Torquemada's highly influential *Monarquía indiana* [Indian monarchy] (1615), as well as a milestone attempt at synthesis, the Dominican Gregorio García's *Origen de los indios del nuevo mundo, e Indias occidentales* [Origin of the Indians of the New World, and West Indies] (1607).

Each of the above writers labors to integrate the diverse, globalized world. Syncretism is the distraught dream child of similitude, a sometimes hallucinated effort to unify the Old and New worlds under the aegis of Christianity. First and foremost, syncretism tries to settle the most burning problem posed by the previously unknown New World: does its existence repudiate the origins of humankind as narrated in the Old Testament? Syncretism salves the crisis by subjecting the Indians to the universal scheme of biblical history (Brading 195–196). This means, in essence, that syncretism derives the Indians from Adam and then from the survivors of the Flood. As Acosta writes, "The reason why we are forced to admit that the men of the Indies traveled there from Europe or Asia is so as not to contradict Holy Writ, which clearly teaches that all men descend from Adam" and that all perished in the Flood, "except those that were preserved in Noah's ark" (75, 61). Before the eighteenth century, no account of the origins of the New World's populations would dare transgress the biblical scheme (Huddleston 11). Most every account would execute convoluted gymnastics in order to confirm it.

The other motor of syncretism furnishes Christian teleology and its thrust toward oneness with an enabling methodology. To inscribe the New World in a known framework, syncretism applies a predisciplinary form of comparative ethnography, which turns on the principle that cultural similarities betoken a common ancestry. A syncretic history therefore generally lays out perceived similarities between the Amerindians and one (or more) Old World peoples or cultures and then submits the similarities as proof that Latin Americans originated there. The same methodology authorizes syncretic histories to fulfill the perilous task of composing substantive, comparative accounts of Indian culture and history. As the histories branch out from origin theories to adumbrate at length the parallels between ancient Indian civilizations and those of the Old World, they range from assertions of direct influence of one society upon another to mere comparisons, affinities that do not presuppose actual contact. Ryan notes "an almost childlike joy running through these lists of conformities, as if the *real* discovery were not the exoticism of the other but his ultimate similarities with peoples already assimilated into European consciousness" (59). Its guilty pleasures notwithstanding, when enacted by sympathetic writers syncretism could favor New World cultures. According to Las Casas and Torquemada, for instance, New World societies boasted civilizations no less complex and excellent, if not more so, than those of ancient Greece or Rome. Further, in syncretic scenarios both the achievements and the alleged sins of the Indians inevitably had some precedent, were not egregiously unique. Syncretism's comparative methodology exculpates Indian religions at least from the stigma of singularity.[34]

If syncretism tenders some saving graces for indigenous history and culture, it by no means fully redeems them.[35] The word "syncretism" derives from a Greek word meaning "to make two parties join against a third" (*Webster's*). New World syncretic histories materialize the violence bound up in the word's definition. In projecting indigenous societies onto a global canvas, syncretism perforce relativizes their cultural achievements. Even as it recuperates the indigenous worlds, syncretism substantially evaporates their uniqueness or difference into similitude, disregarding and dissolving incommensurability (see Pagden, *European Encounters,* chap. 1; Catalá, chap. 1). It reaches for a spurious "concert" that, as Severo Sarduy observes, fabricates "images of a mobile and decentered but still harmonious universe" (102).

Syncretism can attain a decentered harmony and accommodate difference only by summoning that perpetual source of dissonance, the devil. Binding similitude to catachresis, practically all syncretic histories assign the disruptive devil some foundational role.[36] Acosta proffers an especially full-bodied and influential assessment of the devil's reputed interventions in the New World. His work registers innumerable aspects of Aztec civilization worthy of "praise and remembrance" (506, *372*), yet he writes the history of Aztec religion as a story of the devil's works. To the diabolical cleverness of the devil, Acosta repeatedly avows, New World religions owe the similarities they share with such Christian institutions as baptism, monastic life, communion, and so on, including ritual sacrifices that eerily mirror Christian sacraments. Acosta states, "The devil's pride is so great and so obstinate that he always longs and strives to be accepted and honored as God and to steal and appropriate to himself in every way he can what is owed only to the Most High

God. He never ceases to do this in the blind nations of the world, those that the light and splendor of the Holy Gospel has not yet illuminated" (347, 253). In short, the devil jealous of God has ingeniously fashioned in the New World religious practices that mimic or caricature those of Christianity.

Syncretism's elaborate, unsavory pact with the devil underscores the lengths to which post-Columbian European writers would go to defuse the impact of the New World. Lengths *and* breadths: if historiographic syncretism confronts the shock of the New World head-on, in overt collusion with similitude, other discourses manage the New World obliquely and surreptitiously and pleasurably, as befits an explosive subject.[37] Important recent studies by Mary Gaylord, Roland Greene, and Diana de Armas Wilson (among others, including Campbell) have effected what amounts to a sea change in the quest for the New World's influence on the Old by attuning readers to the muted, oblique imprints of the New World on early modern peninsular texts. They have compelled us to quarry those texts not just for momentous paradigm shifts but also for the diffuse, symptomatic residue of the New World buried within them. Gaylord, for example, exhorts, "it is urgent for us to reread the entirety of what we are used to thinking of as the [Spanish] Golden Age literary canon, scanning it for the traces of the literal and figurative crossings made inevitable by the double nature of the Hispanic World" because the texts' "mirrors of reality cannot *not* have reflected the expanded, newly doubled horizons of their authors' worlds" ("True History" 224–225). It arises from this perspective that what Walter Mignolo calls the "darker side of the Renaissance," the complicity of its reborn classicism with the management of the New World, manifests itself in both the Renaissance and the Baroque.[38]

Practically any discourse of the times, humanist or not, could busily if obliquely occupy itself with micromanaging the idea of the New World in ways that may include but far exceed the tropes of "Orientalism." Campbell reminds us that era begets the modern novel, "whose very name recalls origins in the management of novelty and its associated wonder" (11). Wonder-laden novels of chivalry and their reincarnation, *Don Quixote,* as has often been noted, insouciantly fall into line with the would-be knights-errant of the New World.[39] Analogously, not by coincidence do monsters, newly resurrected from medieval lore and tentatively supplemented with their alleged American avatars, populate everything from the popular journalism to the medical tracts of the period.[40] Jeffrey Cohen comments, "Through the body of the monster fantasies of aggression, domination, and inversion are allowed safe expression in a clearly delimited and permanently liminal space" (17). Less obvious genres—perhaps the less obvious the better—transact the New World. Observing that "the Americas were conquered and settled by discourses as much as by conquistadores" (6), Greene exquisitely interrogates Petrarchan love poetry, which "often turns itself inside out, registering the complex outcomes of European imperialism and disclosing its own complicity in that project" (2). Gaylord brilliantly exposes the ways in which erudite treatises on poetics of the Spanish Renaissance and Baroque, fulfilling Antonio de Nebrija's pronouncement that "language always accompanies empire," craft a "literary ideology" ("El lenguaje de la Conquista" 469, 472). Elsewhere, Gaylord envisions Baroque Gongorism, whose difficulty and love for novel imagery ignited the most heated debates, at least in part as a "New World poetics" ("Jerónimo de Aguilar" 86).

The poetic treatise *Agudeza y arte de ingenio* [Wit and the art of inventiveness] (1642, augmented in 1648), by the Spanish Jesuit Baltasar Gracián, puts face and form to this work of the Baroque, which is central to my book's arguments. Gracián heroically attempts to systematize the intractable poetics of the Baroque on the basis of the *agudeza,* or difficult poetic conceit, and *ingenio,* the exertions of the mind to create or to puzzle through these attenuated, cryptic poetic images.[41] Two of Gracián's propositions, though as cryptic as their subjects, get at the core of the treatise for our purposes. First, an elucidation (or what passes for one in Gracián) of the correspondences that, however opaquely, underlie all poetic tropes worthy of the name:

> This correspondence is common to all conceits [*conceptos*], and it encompasses all the art of inventiveness, for even if inventiveness utilizes contraposition and dissonance, these too establish an artful connection between the objects [the terms that the image puzzlingly conjugates] (1:56)

Second, Gracián's definition of the *concepto,* which brings both agudeza and ingenio into play: "It is an act of the mind [*entendimiento*] that clearly expresses the correspondence between the objects" (1:55).

These two dense propositions yield just enough clarity for us to gather that *Agudeza* dives right into the breach, into the dissonance that rules the crisis-ridden Baroque age. Throughout the text, Gracián frames a grammar of crisis based on difference, disharmony, disproportion, plurality, variety, novelty, and "monstrously" (e.g., 1:61) mixed tropes. *Agudeza* throngs with martial terminology like "strife," "violence," "pacification," "valor," "stratagems." While the crises of the Counter-Reformation that Gracián himself experienced in Cataluña[42] certainly fuel the text, the New World infiltrates *Agudeza* directly and by implication. Gracián's ecumenical treatise absorbs New World writers like León Pinelo and Juan de Palafox, bishop of Puebla. Its formulations, such as the following, consort allusively with Spanish imperialism. The subject one ponders, writes Gracián, comprises a "center" that radiates into the "entities that surround it" or "adjuncts that crown it," and the reader goes about joining the adjuncts "to the subject and to one another" in order to discover "some conformity or concert" between them (1:64). *Agudeza* obviously operates at a high level of abstraction that insinuates and accepts meanings rhetorical, political, and epistemological. Still, whether or not one construes Gracián's words on the center and its peripheries as referring to Spain's relationship to the colonies, it is undeniable that above all else *Agudeza* grapples with difference (together with plurality, variety, novelty). The expanded original title of the work reads, *Arte de Ingenio, tratado de la Agudeza. En que se explican todos los modos y diferencias de Conceptos* [Art of inventiveness, treatise on wit. Which explains all the modes of and differences between conceits] (16). Gracián relocates difference into the miniature, manageable world of poetics. There, he destigmatizes, valorizes, and estheticizes it, making difference a thing of beauty, a wellspring of pleasure.

Agudeza, in which one scholar has discerned a "sociopoetic notion of the subject" (Francisco Sánchez 217), transposes into the pleasurable game-world of poetry the various kinds of work one does in the hard world of the seventeenth century.[43] As the two propositions cited above reveal, *Agudeza* then serves up the palliative and gestural interpretive moves that melt alterity and dissonance into similarity and harmony. T. E. May considers *Agudeza* ultimately to concern itself not with "tension or discord," but with "unity, beauty, and truth" (299). A reader who heeds the protocols of Gracián's primer, as much a manual for life as his treatises on the hero or the politician, will exit the labyrinth of difference and enter the promised land of correspondence and similitude, the same revered terrain that historiographic syncretism was then still toiling to preserve. At the apogee of the Baroque, in a broken world yearning for harmony, Neoplatonic correspondence has not lost its currency as a model or desideratum. One simply needs to look deeper and further for it. Whosoever "speaks of mystery," writes Gracián, "speaks of something pregnant, of a hidden and recondite truth, and any knowledge that requires effort is more esteemed and pleasurable" (1:88): how to massage catachresis back to a nostalgically held similitude constitutes the greatest mystery and pleasure of all, something of a Baroque miracle.[44]

The concerted attempts of Gracián's *Agudeza* to defuse crises, together with those of the novel of chivalry, Petrarchan lyric, and monsterfests discussed above, intensify the fact that in Golden Age Spain Horace's dictum *deleitar enseñando,* or instruct while entertaining, overpowers the more scientific poetics of Aristotle, which prevailed elsewhere in Europe (see García Berrio, vol. 1). Moreover, one could no doubt add to the list of discourses obliquely involved in managing the New World such genres as the pastoral (the subject of much discussion as we proceed), the Byzantine novel, the captivity narrative, and more. Perhaps of greater interest at this point than further mapping the discursive landscape are the rather pungent conclusions to which the preceding recalibrations of it give rise. The practically incontrovertible likelihood that venerable early modern Old World genres have indirect commerce with the New World, that they perspicaciously trade anxiety for pleasure, complicates some of the ages' most lambent, outwardly uncompromised literary artifacts. It wrenches them from any purported innocence or univocality, challenging the purity of their provenance. What appears autochthonous to Spain, in some cases harking back to classicism, emerges as quite literally exotic ("foreign, from outside"), shot through with alien energies. Putting pressure on early modern Spanish discourses, as we have seen, aligns them with similitude's epic, epistemic efforts at containment. The now visible agility of both *langue* and *parole* in the Old World, I believe, has critical implications for understanding colonial Hispanic literary culture.

VI. CONCLUSION: THE WORK OF THE NEW WORLD BAROQUE

The foregoing considerations afford fresh prospects on such pressing issues as the theorizing of the New World Baroque, an endeavor which tends to divide into two entrenched camps. One camp of scholars regards the New World Baroque as an unmitigated negative, as an imported, monolithic mode and an organ of absolutism that the guided culture of the Spanish hegemony imposed on its colonies.[45] Given what we know of both the Spanish guided culture and the creoles' dual investment in viceregal society, the Baroque could hardly fail to function hegemonically in the New World. Untold scores of often undistinguished creole writers did indeed buy into the Baroque as an absolutist mode, utilizing it to ascend the social ladder. Yet, what happens when one acknowledges the permeability of the Baroque on its native Spanish soil to exogamous influences, when one grants that shock waves from the New World in some measure impact the Old World Baroque? Understood thus, it becomes highly unlikely—almost a logical impossibility—that the Baroque would operate as a monolithic, immobile entity in the New World. The widely accepted image of the European Baroque as wrought of tensions or as a welter of throbbing antagonisms that strain to resolve into a harmonious discord (*discordia concors*), which Gracián's *Agudeza* consummately exemplifies, renders it even more improbable that the New World Baroque would settle into a static, monological apparatus of the state.[46]

The inherently tensile nature of the Baroque, instead, would appear to poise it for a dynamic life in the New World. An opposing approach therefore considers the ever-kinetic Baroque to have taken flight in the New World, where it succeeds in acting transgressively to subvert colonial power structures and transitively to advance matters like New World identity politics. Many partisans of this approach rally to the Cuban José Lezama Lima's battle cry for the Latin American Baroque in *La expresión americana,* a Baroque he associates with the triumph of the New World city and deems an art of the "counter conquest" (31) because it teaches the following lesson: "thanks to the heroism and aptness of the Baroque's symbols, we ascertain that we can approach the forms of any given style without complexes and without going astray, as long as we infuse it with the symbols of our destiny" (54). Scholars have accordingly combed the New World Baroque for manifestations of its differences or divergences from that of the Old World, particularly for its traces of indigenous cultures, which Lezama Lima exalts as emblems of the Baroque's transculturated, syncretic activism on American soil.

Spirited divergences between the Old and New World Baroques, if sometimes equivocal ones (as chapter 5 below details) are certainly to be found.[47] The most powerful hub of the New World Baroque's activity, however, may not lie in differences real or putative. Rather, it arguably resides in the inalienable agility of the Baroque. Iris Zavala observes that it "is difficult to imagine a style of representation better suited to capturing the paradoxes of seventeenth-century colonial life than the Baroque" (174). Zavala then christens the polyphonic, syncretic logic of the

Baroque as "that which was always already there" (175), in the racially complex colonies.⁴⁸ Her words overflow their bounds, to speak to the propitiousness of the metropolitan Baroque, partially forged in face of the New World, for New World writers. As later pages of *The Spectacular City* will bear out quite specifically, by layering contradiction on contradiction, paradox on paradox, New World writers avail themselves of the eminently available, capacious Baroque and make it work for them, for their worlds, without necessarily abrogating its logic or forms.

By virtue, at least in part, of the incestuous redundancy built into the New World Baroque, the serpent has circled back to bite its own tail, implicitly warning Spain to beware what it peddles to the colonies. This inverted version of caveat emptor, now a *seller* beware, robustly obtains for the overall picture of the New World Baroque that our contemplation of Mexican creole and other writings will produce. A line from Luis de Góngora y Argote's *Soledad segunda* [Second solitude] (1613), a poem laced with references to the colonies, elegantly catches the picture my book will convey of the New World Baroque—as a terrain "en que la arquitectura / a la geometría se rebela" [in which architecture rebels against geometry] (ll. 669–670). Or as Lezama Lima writes, articulating the ultranervous axis of the New World Baroque, the movement bodies forth a "plutonic energy that deranges forms as it does a sturdy wall" (34). In other words, and in the words that *The Spectacular City* will bring to life, the New World Baroque as a breakout mode, one which abides by the etiquettes of the Baroque willed to it by Spain yet still defies containment, troubles ontologies, ruptures boundaries, incurs pluralism.

The New World Baroque can carry out its apparently paradoxical activity thanks quite precisely to the kinetic, volatile innersprings of the Spectacular City that the foregoing pages have undertaken to expose. Converging in the Spectacular City, the disillusioned creole, the hyperbolic New World urban environment, the exorbitant festival, and a disturbed wonder all intrinsically resonate and make common cause with fundamental aspects of the Baroque that Spain bequeathed to them. In ways that we have begun to glimpse and in others that will unfold as we move through time and texts, the agile platforms of the Spectacular City vitally enable the work of the New World Baroque.

"¡Ah, mano que limita, que amenaza / tras de todas las puertas, y que alienta / en todos los relojes, cede y pasa!" (Vallejo, "Unidad")

[Oh, the hand that limits, that threatens behind all the doors, and that breathes in all the clocks, it surrenders and passes!]

FIGURE 2. *Sandro Botticelli (1444–1510). The Birth of Venus, c. 1484. Tempera on canvas. 68 × 109⅝. (172.4 × 278.5 cm). Uffizi, Florence, Italy. Alinari / Art Resource, N.Y.*

Two   ORDER AND CONCERT

> *So as not to tire Your Highness with the description of the things of this city . . . I will say only that these people live almost like those in Spain and in as much concert and order as there.*
> HERNÁN CORTÉS, *SEGUNDA CARTA-RELACIÓN* [SECOND LETTER-ACCOUNT] (1520)

I. ENTERING THE ORDERED CITY

Before the Spectacular City, as its precondition and antagonist, there was the Ordered City. Decimating the concert and order that Hernán Cortés perceived in Tenochtitlán, the Hispanic Ordered City sought to subjugate the Indian world, razing and then rebirthing it in accord with the aims of the empire and in consonance with European paradigms. "Almost like those in Spain," says Cortés: faced with the practical dilemma of conveying the New World to those who had no direct knowledge of it, basically every sixteenth-century Spanish writer took frequent recourse to comparisons with Spain and Europe in his writings. On a larger, far more devastating scale, the colonizers would batter away in deed and in word at the forbidding yet promising "almost" until it yielded the greater resemblance to home for which the conquerors, no less than their century, yearned. Hispanic New World city planners and city wordsmiths alike contributed to erasing the New World's particularity in the name of empire, to erecting the Ordered City.

A term familiar from Angel Rama's *La ciudad letrada,* the Ordered City is both a real being, the planned city, and the bundle of powerful abstractions that underwrites it. Rama views the Ordered City as a colonialist entity that sprung fully formed, like Minerva from Jupiter's forehead, from Renaissance classicizing and Neoplatonic thought into the New World, to the utter disregard and obliteration of extant realities. As he states of the planned city, "Before materializing in reality, cities had to be constructed as symbolic representations whose existence inevitably depended on signs," such as words and charts (8). I will corroborate and work through his seminal assertion over the course of the chapter, examining its dramatic implications for city texts dependent on archetypes.

At this entry point, though, it is crucial to observe that Rama folds the planned or Ordered City, which arose in the Renaissance, into the absolutist Baroque city of the seventeenth century. The first two chapters of his book mate and conflate the sixteenth century and the seventeenth. They synchronize the planned city, a closed entity overweeningly dependent on signs, with the community of intellectuals and bureaucrats immured in a self-contained world of papers and words that constitutes the seventeenth-century Baroque *ciudad letrada,* or lettered community.[1] Certainly, the planned city and the absolutist agenda and Renaissance ideals that formed it greatly outlive their inception points. However, as this chapter and this book hope to bear out, I maintain quite forcefully that the Baroque city (and my construct, the Baroque Spectacular City) stands apart from the Ordered City, which has a special pertinence to the sixteenth century. One does well to bear in mind Mariano Picón-Salas's observation that "Renaissance vitality, unlike the baroque, always sought a rule or archetype. . . . Renaissance pride, and consciousness of power, operated under an ordering intelligence. Everything had a rule, a special type" (89).

In "Order and Concert," we will experience the exigencies of the sixteenth century and of the Ordered City itself largely via the theory, praxis, and verbal representation of sixteenth-century Mexico City, the first full realization of the planned city in the New World. Paving the way for the Spectacular City, the chapter delves into the constellation of Western paradigms, city planning, and city writing that creates the early Ordered City of Mexico, rebuilt over the ruins of Tenochtitlán. We join walking and riding tours of Mexico City in a spectrum of genres at the beginning, midpoint, and last quarter of the sixteenth century that lay the foundations both for the New World city and for Mexican colonial literature. The authors of the tours are not creoles but Spaniards with varying degrees of rootedness in the New World, all of whose primary investment, generally pronounced enough to produce blatant propaganda, lies with empire. Accompanying the tours at a remove of five centuries, we explore the writing of place rather than of action under the assumption that colonialist discourse can take shape as forcefully in description as in the narration of heroic deeds. Proceeding on foot, on horseback, and on board a charging whale, the tours traverse cityscapes that brim with exultant similarities to Spain and Europe, with the guilty pleasures of order and concert. Such elation, almost needlessly to say, comes at the cost of the vast real and epistemic violence (Spivak 280–281) that the sightseeing concertedly suppresses.

II. EPISTEMIC VIOLENCE

The conquerors' incessant recourse to the resemblances between the New World and the Old, on the face of things a reasonable enough solution to cognitive and communicative problems, ends up being no mere rhetorical or a natural move. We know from chapter 1 that it ultimately flows into and merges indistinguishably with the arsenal of tactics the Old World contrived to manage the shock of the new, similitude primary among them. The jubilant sightseeing excursions through Mexico City to which we will be party therefore enclose an insidious colonialogic that penetrates the harmonious, happy episteme of the sixteenth century, setting it up as a vehicle for untold violence. Two pictures, one a portrait of Venus and the other the portrait of a theoretical design, capture the life force of that episteme, its innocence and potential to do veiled violence. Both of them by now high-level clichés, the two pictures model the order and concert that Cortés foregrounds. Seemingly worlds away from Tenochtitlán or from referentiality itself, they will prove to drive the burgeoning reality and representation of colonial Mexico City as it assumes the contours of the Ordered City.

Order: A quintessential visual image of the Renaissance, Sandro Botticelli's *The Birth of Venus* (c. 1484) proffers pleasures that are also worlds away from those of the *Garden of Earthly Delights* that Bosch painted just a couple of decades later but in a more disturbed world. Where the phantasmagoric, nimble figures of Bosch's masterpiece cavort in lusty pleasure, Botticelli's inhuman Venus delicately fingers a breast sculpted into a glacial form and covers her private parts with a cascade of tresses. The dead-eyed *Venus pudica* intimates but forecloses on eroticism. Her airbrushed body, the embodiment of Neoplatonic Forms and of the Greek ideals of love and beauty, has been reduced to pure form and sheer surface. Venus rises majestically from the sea, posed on a neatly fluted shell that triumphs over the murky, moving depths of the water. Mannequin-like, purified into an avatar of the Virgin Mary, Venus herself has no depth or weight, no confounding complexity. All in her, except what should not be, is patent visibility, Apollonian clarity.[2]

Venus's chiseled figure towers forth from the calm, luminous background, encompassing land and sea, of a *locus amoenus*. While receding fingertips of land reach into the sea and evoke perspective, the painting resolves into a flat, thoroughly geometric composition divided into three symmetrical panels. Reminiscent of a medieval religious triptych, the three scenarios unite like the Trinity. The three are as if one, inextricably united by the lyrical, sinuous forms of mythological deities. On one side, Zephyr and Chloris's airborne curves absorb the waves of the foamy sea, with the wind god's arrow of breath animating the central frozen column that is Venus. On the other, a nymph of springtime (one of the four Hours) reaches out to wrap the goddess in a cloak whose embroidered flowers come to life on the other side of the canvas. *The Birth of Venus* coheres in an enlightened, sea-defying still life of order, symmetry, reason, form, and number.

Concert: As it ties all loose ends into a concert of conjugated forms, *The Birth of Venus* aims at transparency, total knowability. Yet it leaves one wondering: why has Botticelli's deadpan, almost dead Venus accrued such life and enduring fame? Why the stark contrast between Botticelli's and Bosch's delights? One logically turns to Michel Foucault's celebrated big picture of the sixteenth-century episteme for some elucidation. In chapter 2 of *The Order of Things*, "The Prose of the World," Foucault maps out the all-encompassing symphony of similitudes that underwrites the paradigmatic rhyming construction of Botticelli's *Venus*. He begins his now-classic discussion of the sixteenth-century episteme with the following broad, bold statement: "Up to the end of the sixteenth century, resemblance played a constructive role in the knowledge of Western culture. It was resemblance that largely guided exegesis and the interpretation of texts; it was resemblance that organized the play of symbols, made possible the knowledge of things visible and invisible, and controlled the art of representing them" (17). In Foucault's rendition, resemblance is omnivorous. It implicates the spatially proximate, creating relationships through adjacency. This *convenentia* quickly escalates into the boundless energies of "sympathy," a "principle of mobility" unfettered by time and space that "plays through the depths of the universe in a free state" and can draw even the most distant things together (23). Resemblance can thus potentially, if invisibly, gather all phenomena into its web, weaving them into concert and harmony. Word and world, heaven and earth, nature and human beings all participate in the seamless fabric, with each piece ultimately aligned and signed by God. It only remains for the "Natural Magician," whom we met in the preceding chapter, to unearth that signature, bringing into full view the wholly interlocking "prose of the world."

The interpretive challenges and idealized worldview of resemblance, Foucault maintains, engrossed the semiotic, hermeneutic, and representational practices of the West in the sixteenth century. Similitude's harmonious Neoplatonic cosmology infiltrated not only natural histories like that of Oviedo but also the landmark literature of the sixteenth century and beyond. In Spain, for example (though not Foucault's example), a huge repertoire of works coinciding in part with the cast of characters involved in micromanaging the New World that I surveyed in chapter 1, bore its unmistakable traces. They include the novel of chivalry, the pastoral novel and poetry, humanist dialogues, treatises on language, Italianate Neoplatonism, mystical poetry, and so on.[3] From Garcilaso de la Vega's eclogues to Jorge de Montemayor's *Diana* to Luis de León's *El cantar de los cantares de Salomón* (Solomon's Song of Songs), works spanning the entire sixteenth century at first persistently and then anachronistically harked to similitude's delightful concert. Suspended in ideal, imaginary spaces, these texts replicate the disembodied disposition of Foucault's episteme. The worldview of the sixteenth century appears to arise ex nihilo and to exercise its "sympathies" in a force field populated only by abstract entities. An Olympian construct, it lives in a nameless void, with no apparent tethers to history, society, ideology, and so on.[4] Botticelli's Venus occupies a parallel space, an idealized, abstract locus amoenus replete with sensuous properties but anchored only to philosophy and myth.

Foucault does not in any case avoid placing the episteme in a certain critical perspective by assessing the kind of knowledge it engendered. According to the French theorist, the similitude that so seduced harbored obvious epistemological perils. "Sympathy," he observes, "has the dangerous power of assimilating, of rendering things identical to one another, of mingling them, of causing their individuality to disappear—and thus of rendering them foreign to what they were before" (23–24). Moreover, the sixteenth-century episteme "condemned itself to never knowing anything but the same thing" (30). The logic of resemblance, in short, can entail a "plethoric yet absolutely poverty-stricken" knowledge (30).

Foucault's pointed assessment discloses the monological and monotopical, conceivably anxious bent of the sixteenth-century episteme. His critique dovetails with the multiform definitions of "order" and "concert" in Sebastián de Covarrubias's dictionary of Spanish (1611). The dictionary defines *orden* as,

> The placement of things, when each is put in its place, from the Latin, *ordo. Dar orden para que se haga una casa,* to give the order and form for a house. *Estar en orden,* to be ready. *Guardar la orden,* to not exceed mandates. *Ir en orden,* for each person to be in his place. (838)

Of the verb *concertar* (the noun, *concierto,* does not have its own entry) the dictionary says,

> The same as to compose, to fit, to accord; from the Latin, *componere.* Concert, accord, composition, conformity, consonance. *Hombre concertado, medido, ajustado,* he who lives according to order and concert. *Desconcierto,* the opposite. *Ir concertados o de concierto,* to be prepared and informed about what one has to do. (345–346)

Integrally related, equally rife with moralistic, authoritarian implications, order and concert team up to discipline an unruly world.

Taken in tandem, Foucault's words and the words "order" and "concert" themselves display the remarkably easy fit between epistemic and colonialogic that underlies the disembodied, esoteric, ahistorical sixteenth-century episteme. Despite the patently idealized, abstract disposition of both the episteme and the artifacts that echo it, they traffic in the agendas deployed on the New World to justify eradicating its incommensurability with the Old. Of course New World nature, which Columbus purveyed as a symphony in greens and blues, concretized and fueled Old World utopian dreams of a locus amoenus. Yet we cannot forget that order and concert exercised their tenacious, superannuated purchase on representation during a century in which the irruption of the New World onto the European scene occasioned the disruption or crisis of received norms.[5]

As the present chapter will demonstrate, over the course of the sixteenth century, the Spanish empire wielded order and concert in a vital, self-saving conjunction with its colonies. Perhaps abstract or ideal in its inception, the prose of the world was fitted to the New World, not simply in conjunction but in *collusion* with the project of the Spanish empire. We will see that the bucolic, pagan paradigm came to act in concert, in a tacit pact or accord, with designs to subordinate the real pagan world. In this context of epistemic control, Botticelli would figuratively trump Bosch and endure precisely because his painting's airbrushed Venus, bucolic tokens of rebirth, closed classical Forms, and elegant concert of similitudes effectively kills off the pandemonium of the *Garden of Earthly Delights*. Flowers rout monsters.

That a similitude paired with a bucolic setting accorded with colonialist objectives was not lost on writers who defended the New World. By 1552 Bartolomé de las Casas had already taken aim at the loaded representational force of resemblance, its epistemic violence. His *Brevísima relación de la destrucción de las Indias* [Most brief account of the destruction of the Indies] parodies the perniciousness of that representational force by dramatizing how in every space of the New World, every originally bucolic space, the Spaniards wrought the same vicious chaos. The early seventeenth century finds a mestizo, the Inca Garcilaso de la Vega, temporizing with similitude but still primarily striving in his *Comentarios reales* [Royal commentaries] (1609) to homologize the Spanish and Indian worlds (chapter 5 of my study tackles the complexities of similitude with regard to histories of Indian civilizations). As Antonio Cornejo-Polar puts it, the Inca Garcilaso utilizes "homogenizing sutures" to draw the two worlds into "an impossible harmony" (91).

Under such circumstances, resemblance performs the same work as can its apparent opposite, wonder. Resemblance effaces the new, denying it. Wonder, as discussed in chapter 1, can throw the new into prominence but contain it in the exotic. Both resemblance and wonder undertake to manage the new, to bring epistemological coherence to a reality that strained similitude to the breaking point. Yet city-inspired wonder proved to be particularly formidable. The wonder aroused by Aztec Tenochtitlán, the first New World city the Spaniards encountered, a splendidly refined polity larger than any European metropolis of the time, would not be so easily discharged by exoticizing as was nature. Over the course of the Mexico City tours that we now join, along with the containment of the new in familiar paradigms and delimited spaces, one therefore finds a concerted effort to banish entirely both the new and the troubled wonder it incites. In the last instance, the ordered Apollonian city of the sixteenth century prefers literally to have commerce, or to have no commerce at all, with the Dionysian wild zone.

III. HERNÁN CORTÉS AND BERNAL DÍAZ DEL CASTILLO

Of the many places that the conquerors visited on their first tour of Tenochtitlán in 1519, the bustling marketplace of Tlatelolco in the northern reaches of the city held unusual appeal.[6] A space where nature and culture as well as countryside and city converged, a microcosm of the New World, and a plenum bristling with the enticements of "adventure capitalism" (Campbell 95 *et passim*), the marketplace with good reason enthralled the early Hispanic New World travelers. Hernán Cortés and Bernal Díaz del Castillo as well as many later writers leave detailed descriptions of marketplaces, which often stand in for the city at large. As the marketplace becomes one of the earliest topics or *loci* of New World city representation, its pleasure-laden wares become textualized objects that constitute the first colonial city collection texts, an echo of Oviedo's museumizing and a prototype of Baroque wonder cabinets. With a carefully calibrated mix of pain and pleasure, the textualized objects of the marketplace are called into service to transact all sorts of ideological colonial business. A festival of commodities and a spectacle of Indians solely devoted to the merchandise that the New World can deliver to Spain, the marketplaces of sixteenth-century texts provide a site in which the new could be enjoyed, contained, transformed, taxonomized, commodified, utilized—in short, possessed.

As they register the fact that they have chanced upon a fully embodied city totally new to Western eyes, Hernán Cortés and Bernal Díaz seek out its laws. The smooth-running Tlatelolco marketplace offers "an Aztec discourse, the means by which this society defined and talked about itself" (Walsh and Sugiura 38), and a felicitous, soothing blueprint. Hence, Cortés in the *Segunda carta-relación* and Bernal Díaz in the *Historia verdadera de la conquista de la Nueva España* [True history of the conquest of New Spain] (written 1551–1584) focus the marketplace through an optic of order. From beneath its profusion of merchandise and activities, the extreme order of the Aztec marketplace arrests and thrills Cortés. With his ever-operative imperial eye, Cortés takes particular pleasure in the justice system that maintains discipline in the plaza as well as in the orderly array of the merchandise. In the detailed inventory of the marketplace, which Cortés effects in a chaotic enumeration tamed by the anaphoric repetition of "Hay" [there are] and "Venden" [they sell] at the head his sentences, the myopically Machiavellian Cortés comes as close as he can to writing ethnography. Then again, nearly fifty years after the fact, the marketplace has engraved itself in Bernal's memory under the aegis of order: "When we arrived at the great market place, called Tlatelolco, we were astounded at the number of people and the quantity of merchandise that it contained, and at the good order and control that was maintained, for we had never seen such a thing before" (171, 215). For both writers, order and the familiar activity of shopping bring resemblance into play, resulting in continual comparisons to Spain's products and the venues that sell them.

At least in the legally astute, always canny Cortés the description of an orderly city metonymized in the marketplace signifies on two levels, to strategic purpose. By underscoring in a single paragraph (the same paragraph in which our chapter's epigraph appears) the "orden," "concierto," and "policía" [propriety] of Tenochtitlán (137), Cortés positions the Aztec empire as a polis. According to Aristotle, those inside a polis, a community of citizens joined by law, are civilized human beings. Those outside it are beasts or gods.[7] Peggy Liss remarks that "when the Spaniards discovered Indian communities living in 'all manner of good order and polity' they extrapolated, from what they observed to be the state of civilization of a community, the degree of rationality possessed by its members" (22). The Indians possess some measure of reason and polis; to be full citizens of the European Renaissance city, implies Cortés, they basically lack only Christianity. So, as he marched through Mexico, Cortés zealously toppled Aztec temples. Here his references to order and concert form the cornerstones of what Michel de Certeau calls a "scriptural economy," a record *for* rather than *of* (*Practice*, chap. 10). They suggest the ready perfectibility of the Indians and offer them up as merchandise to be seized.

The comforting order and concert of the marketplace in any case give the conquerors some respite from the disquieting ardors of wonder that inform their writings. Virtually every anthology of colonial Latin American writing extracts from Bernal Díaz's baggy monster of a text the passages surrounding his proclamation of transported wonder: "It is not to be wondered at that I here write it down in this manner, for there is so much to think over that I do not know how to describe it, seeing things as we did that had never been heard of or seen before, not even dreamed about" (159, *191*). Bernal's storied rapture matches, perhaps even imitates, Cortés's entranced professions of "maravilla": "The palace inside the city in which he [Moctezuma] lived was so marvelous that it seems to me impossible to describe its excellence and grandeur.

Therefore, I shall not attempt to describe it at all, save to say that in Spain there is nothing to compare to it" (138, *109*). In a uniquely candid admission, Cortés writes that he can convey to the crown only a fraction of the things he saw in his initial encounter with Tenochtitlán, though he well knows that they "will be so astonishing as not to be believed, for we who saw them with our own eyes could not grasp them with our understanding" (131, *102*). Neither Cortés nor Bernal Díaz, addressing petitions to the crown for reward, can afford not to purvey a heightened sense of wonder that aggrandizes his enterprise and the booty for the crown that it supplies. Impresarios of wonder, they exploit it to maximum effect. At the same time, we note a shared rhetorical tic in their statements, one that suggests a more vexed relationship to the marvelous: the two writers link wonder and aporia.[8] No doubt the context and the task of verbalizing it fully warrant aporia. Nevertheless, for reasons that Cortés's *Segunda carta-relación* brings to the fore, their aporia symptomatizes a wonder that entails something other than pleasure or reward.

Cortés faces a thick predicament that pits rhetoric against epistemology. To wit, the more he lauds Tenochtitlán's order, civility, and civilization, the less his received categories of civility as an exclusively Christian property obtain. His insinuations that the Indians' polity suits them for Christianizing may palliate the category crisis, but Cortés articulates and dwells on it: "considering that they are barbarous and so far from the knowledge of God and cut off from all civilized nations, it is truly remarkable to see what they have achieved in all things" (137, *108*). The next paragraph repeats the conundrum: "can there be any greater grandeur [*grandeza*] than that this barbarian lord should have all the things to be found under the heavens in his domain, fashioned [*contrahechas;* literally, "counterfeited"] in gold and silver and jewels and feathers . . . ? (137, *108*). If "grandeza" here assumes an equivocal sense on which W. H. Prescott would not fail to capitalize as an indication of Moctezuma's alleged fatal flaw of effeminacy, "contrahechas" carries even greater impact for its dual meaning of "imitation" and "deformity."[9] Cortés repeatedly qualifies as "marvelous" Moctezuma's monstrous objects (certainly ceremonial artifacts, little as Cortés realizes it) that reproduce the world in gold "with such perfection that they seem almost real" (130, *108*). The "counterfeits" of the world in a denaturalized gold at once evoke Columbus's unfulfilled dream, Midas's lethal reality, and Plato's mimetic nightmare. In the *Segunda carta-relación* wonder has acquired the negative connotations of aporia and crisis that remove it from the sphere of pleasure. Cortés activates a medieval-feeling and -sounding wonder that involves fear, ignorance, and physical paralysis. As Albertus Magnus described this pathologized wonder, "the heart flees the unfamiliar as it flees the bad and the harmful" (qtd. in Daston and Park 113).[10]

Fear and disorder of every conceivable kind would continue to dominate Cortés's life and writing, and would have to be dispelled. His *Cuarta carta-relación* [Fourth letter-account] of 1524 centers on the adversaries, Spanish and Indian, who threaten Cortés's leadership and Tenochtitlán, laboriously reconquered after the Spaniards' expulsion from the city in the so-called Night of Sorrows. The rhetorically denuded *Cuarta carta-relación* monotonously hammers in its picture of the incendiary chaos—the "desconcierto" and "desorden" and "alboroto" [uproar]—that swarms all around Cortés. Frequently construing "concierto" to mean "plot," the fourth report takes on the bathetic cast of a laundry list of complaints akin to Columbus's unusually forthright "Carta al ama" [Letter to the nurse] (c. 1500)[11] and Oviedo's *Historia general y natural de las Indias* (1535). All three texts vituperatively deplore the lawlessness of their respective settings. Order was unquestionably no mere philosophical desideratum in the sixteenth-century New World; the colonial enterprise had dire need of it. Alternating with the narration of the ceaseless rebellions, Cortés details his fruitless search for a channel connecting the Atlantic and Pacific oceans, for what Oviedo had rightfully called, and what would continue to be until the building of the Panama Canal, the doubtful strait.

Surrounded by doubt and disorder, Cortés styles himself as he who brings the "good order" (333) that will allow the New World to be populated and the Catholic faith to take root in it. The conqueror portrays the rebuilding of Aztec Tenochtitlán into a logically organized Hispanic city as his stellar accomplishment in the role of messiah of order. Creating a chiaroscuro contrast with the verbal and real pandemonium of the rest of the text, the conqueror sketches out the well-reasoned steps he took to restore the city and to endow it with order: bringing back the inhabitants who had fled, rebuilding the market, erecting a fort, distributing city homestead lots (*solares*) to his men, cordoning off the Indians in peripheral zones. He notes that thanks to his efforts the city now contains "some thirty thousand residents" and that "its markets and commerce have the same order as before" (321). As Cortés attempts to persuade the crown of his implausible successes in instituting order, reason coasts into magical, providential, colonialogical thinking and writing.

The author of the Fourth Letter performs equally magical and baleful sleights with resemblance, especially when he depicts the marketplace. Cortés arrogantly negates the trauma of rupture. According to him, the rebuilt Tenochtitlán retains the same positive features it had earlier boasted. To ensure order, Cortés has permitted the local Indian chieftains to exercise the same power as before the conquest of the city (320). Demonstrating the full restoration of the marketplace, recreating it in word as he allegedly did in deed, Cortés replays in miniature the inventory of its goods and varied tradespeople from the *Segunda carta-relación*. He emphasizes that the same produce as in Spain ("toda la hortaliza de España" [321]) is at present grown and sold in Mexico. The marketplace, once a microcosm of Mexico, now replicates Spain. Tenochtitlán springs resiliently back to life as the hub of diverse resemblances.

Nevertheless, in verbally purveying the city Cortés elides the most crucial resemblance of all. At no point in the Fourth Letter or elsewhere does he expound on the fact that he had forged the Spanish administrative center of the city (the Zócalo) on the physical bases of the Aztec temples of the sacred precinct. This most graphic of similes, which Cortés astonishingly omits, ecologically preserves and symbolically refunctions the already orderly Mexico City. With regard to maintaining the former Tenochtitlán, Cortés states only that he decided to rebuild the city in the same place "due to its grandeur and marvelous position" (320).

Surprisingly or predictably, in view of the powerful presence of "maravilla" in the Second Letter, the preceding statement contains the single instance of the word in the Fourth Letter. "Maravilla" here is mated with "grandeza," which, as we saw, had also lost its virtue. The stigmatized maravilla makes a ghostly, tacit reappearance in the shards of gold still for sale at the market. Cortés observes that the new native markets lack nothing they sold "at the time of their prosperity" (322). Yet then, in the text's sole, veiled owning of difference, trauma, and mourning, Cortés goes on to acknowledge, "It is true that now there are not any gold or silver ornaments, nor featherwork, nor rich things, as there used to be; a few small pieces of gold and silver may sometimes be found, but not as before" (322). Cortés leaves the tantalizing assertion hanging. He provides no sense of why the magnificent, monstrous objects that had so commanded his attention in the Second Letter have vanished or where they have gone. Suspended as they are, the mysterious textualized objects hover between the real and the symbolic. They figure the fate of maravilla and of the world to which it pertained. Like the rebellious Indians, now confined in their own districts, maravilla has been consigned to objects and "disappeared." Moreover, the lost artifacts, the last vestiges of a disconcerting epistemological emotion, stand in for the lost Indian city, dismantled and textually repressed. Cortés allows both perilous presences to survive only as sublated, phantasmal absences.

IV. URBAN PLANNING

Although Cortés's inflamed will to order, which produced the above "disappearances," in all likelihood owes more to circumstantial necessity than to philosophical impulses, the Ordered City of the New World that the conqueror began to institute owes much of its existence to the philosophical and theological scaffolding of the times.[12] In *The Vermillion Bird,* Edward Schafer gives an idea of the meaning making that such deep structures could facilitate: "Faced with the abnormal world of Nam-viet, the northerner lacked the help of any generally accepted world view, to which he could optimistically assimilate the unpalatable facts of the South. The Hua man of the T'ang period could not call with complacency on such metaphysical principles as 'order,' 'harmony,' 'unity in diversity' or even 'beauty'—all conceptions agreeable to our own tradition—to lubricate his difficult adjustment" (115). Despite the differences in context, the planned New World city depends on the entrenched principles Schafer invokes. Long a mental and physical construct before it took root in Spanish America, the planned city has a rich, meaningful genealogy. A bird's-eye view of that genealogy, from its principles to its praxis in Mexico City, renders the Ordered City legible. And writeable: it exposes the intimate relationship between transcendent principles and the concerns of the state, the epistemic violence that lies at the core of post-Cortés Mexico City texts awash in order and concert.

The early modern planned city gained impetus from the highest reaches of Renaissance philosophy, from the Neoplatonism that Plato's translator, Marsilio Ficino, set in motion. Given that architectural design replicates the very reason, logic, and symmetry that characterize the Platonic form, Ficino regarded architecture as emanating in an unbroken line from the Ideal (Wheelock 185). He emphasized that architecture should be judged "for a certain incorporeal order rather than for its matter" (qtd. in Panofsky 137). The Florentine Renaissance architect and theorist Leon Battista Alberti, who will reappear as a prime mover of a Mexican text, translated Neoplatonic impulses into detailed prescriptions for a planned city. In book 9 of *On the Art of Building in Ten Books* (1450), for example, Alberti identifies building with Platonic reminiscence: "within the form and figure of a building there resides some natural excellence and perfection that excites the mind and is immediately recognized by it" (302). Alberti, reinvigorating Vetruvius's classical treatise on architecture, easily conjugates the ideal properties of Platonic Forms with the geometric forms of classical buildings.

Thomas More's equally ideal *Utopia* moves the prescriptions closer to the New World, bringing to light the opportunities for crafting a new society bound up in it. Written in 1516, before the Spanish discovery of Tenochtitlán but in full view of the advent of the New World for Europe, the text famously masquerades as an account of a New World society.[13] The *Utopia* chronicles not just a city planned down to the slightest detail but a whole society designed to materialize the principles of order, uniformity, harmony, community, hierarchy, asceticism, and reverence for learning, nature, and God. With its minute social prescriptions, the *Utopia* underscores the paradox that to be faithful to the foregoing principles of what More calls "the law of nature" (45) requires the utmost premeditation and regulation. When the Ideal meets the *Utopia*, in other words, it enters the important terrain of early modern social engineering.

More's *Utopia* captures a hallmark of sixteenth-century political thought, a "belief in the steady perfectibility of the social order" (Hoberman 206). The social order could not be expected spontaneously to perfect itself. Rather, it required planning and control by the increasingly centralized state of the times. European Renaissance theorists and urban planners reached back to venerable, consecrated sources for usable models. In the classical world they encountered the geometric gridiron pattern that had structured ancient Greek and Roman metropolises: streets uniformly laid out at right angles around a central square holding the temporal and spiritual bodies of the state. A rudimentary, almost inevitable form of city planning, the gridiron pattern nonetheless corresponded specifically to the designs and thought of the Greek state. Dan Stanislawski notes that "its methodical regularity and orderly quality well suited the Greek philosophical view of worldly order created out of variety. The idea of the corporate whole is typical of Greek thought of the period" ("Origin" 115). Greeks and Romans imposed the gridiron pattern on vanquished cities as a mark of the civilizing mission that conquest claimed to accomplish. Each new instance of the premeditated gridiron pattern over the course of history indicated "some form of centralized control, political, religious, or military" ("Origin" 108). While the pattern fell away during the Middle Ages owing to the absence of centralized power, it resurfaced at the dawn of the Renaissance in England and France ("Origin" 117–119).

Unlike its European counterparts and sole among them, Renaissance Spain did not institute the gridiron in its own immediate climes. Even the expansion of Madrid after it became the royal residence in 1561 proceeded haphazardly, in the organic way of the medieval town rather than along the lines of the Renaissance planned city (Kubler 99). For early modern Spain, the Ordered City was an exclusively New World phenomenon, one advanced and necessitated by the unique challenges the colonies presented. In the eyes of the crown, Rama tells us, the New World was a tabula rasa on which, unencumbered by its own traditions or, worse yet, by indigenous realities, Spain could begin to dream the new dream of a colonialist, capitalist empire (2–3). Very early on, the crown began to demonstrate its desire to effect a planned society in the New World. The directive of 1513 from King Ferdinand to Pedrarias Dávila on the conquest of Tierra Firme included instructions for the distribution of city lots and the configuration of the plaza in which the word "order" sounds insistently (Rama 5–6). Ferdinand's directive indicates that the crown had turned to Vetruvius, the only classical source on architecture and Alberti's model (Stanislawski, "Earliest" 101), to chart its virgin course.

By 1573 the influence of Vetruvius and the no-longer-virgin course itself, tried and progressively perfected from Santo Domingo to Mexico and Lima, reached full fruition in the 149 articles of the Spanish city-planning ordinances that laid out the "Order" to be followed when founding new settlements in the Indies. Stanislawski observes that the "codification in the reign of Philip II shows the almost complete dependence of the Spaniards on Roman and Greek experience ("Earliest" 104). The micromanaging ordinances definitively codify the *traza*, or layout, that had already stamped a tight pattern onto New World cities. In brief, they dictate that plazas, streets, and homestead lots be laid out to exact measurements ("a cordel y regla" [García Gallo 242]), beginning with the central oblong plaza and radiating out to its environs; that the plaza, of specified proportions, contain the church, the royal palace, municipal council, customs house, hospital, and shops; that the most distinguished conquerors receive the choice lots nearest the plaza; that separate districts be created for the Indians; that streets be made wide enough for the easy passage of horses (of military troops); that open space and smaller plazas be incorporated into the design as the cities expand such that even if they grow in population, they will not become "ugly" or lack amenities (García Gallo 243).

The preceding summary suggests that the ordinances prescribe considerably more than the traza. Elizabeth Weismann reads the traza as "a great example of what the Spanish empire was like: the determination of the crown to control every detail of colonial life, its real effort to deal rationally with the new problems" (84). Similarly, Liss notes that for the Spanish crown "peace, order, and law were interdependent concepts, all reflecting the divinely regulated and harmonious universal scheme" (149). We see that the complex genealogy of Renaissance urban planning—with its interlocking theoretical, practical, and political strands—comes to bear on the Ordered City of the Hispanicized New World, a dream of pure reason devised in the compass of the imperial project. The very "order and concert" that characterize the gridiron pattern in fact constitute a euphemism with providential dimensions. According to Richard Kagan, the gridiron plan gave "physical expression to the fundamental principles that *policía* entailed," the principles of civic order, justice, and Christianity. It follows that a town laid out to exact measurements and with order and concert, "a euphemism for straight streets and a regular symmetrical design" (33), purports to actualize in each of its overdetermined inches or right angles the rectitude that Spanish polity meant to bestow on the New World.

The planned city first fully realized in the rebuilt Mexico City of the first half of the sixteenth century carries yet another model in tow, one that raises the stakes of the city's order and concert exponentially. Jaime Lara's *City, Temple, Stage: Eschatological Architecture and Liturgical Theatrics in New Spain* reveals the impact on the physical foundations of Mexico City of a theology that derived in no small way from the first religious order to arrive in New Spain, the Franciscans. Lara explains that the Franciscans, who from 1524 to the end of the century directed many building projects in Mexico City, wished them to incarnate eschatological prototypes of the New Jerusalem such as those of Revelation, Ezekiel, and St. Augustine's *City of God*. For concrete guidance in the city planning of their millennial kingdom, intended to reintroduce the purity of the primitive church, the missionaries relied on the *Lo Crestià* (Christendom) that their fellow Franciscan, Friar Francesc Eiximenis, had published in 1499. Eiximenis's encyclopedic guide, which would shape the Spanish Escorial (Lara 192), outlines an ideal political society and city of an eminently orderly, geometric nature.[14] The square city of

Eiximenis's design, with its checkerboard pattern of parallel and perpendicular streets, plaza lodging the central church, and mountainous background, dovetailed perfectly with the classical gridiron (see Lara, chaps. 2, 3). A theological counterpart of More's Erasmian *Utopia,* Eiximenis's plan infused secular or pagan models with Christian purpose and invested the planned city with divine authority.

Eiximenis's Christian city dovetailed just as beautifully with the mountain-ringed setting of Mexico City. As the Franciscans enact it there by means of forced Indian labor, they build a city of significance "to the history of urban forms in general" (Kubler 102).[15] Hispanic Mexico City's original traza, of about fourteen streets and four avenues around a central square, distinguishes itself, first, for its compliance with form, the utter regularity of its plan. Municipal legislation soon imposed uniformity of appearance on the porticos and façades of individual homes. Those that did not conform were torn down (Kubler 75–76). The geometrical rectilinearity of the traza finds its complement in the austere, monumental lines of the huge Franciscan buildings that defined the landscape of early colonial Mexico City. The crenellated ramparts, thick doors and walls, and sentry boxes of sixteenth-century church complexes, as well as of public buildings and houses, speak to the fortification that the city needed but belie one of the most important architectural developments that colonial Mexico City presents: it is the first great modern city not to be enclosed in walls.[16] Together with the other great architectural development of Mexico City, its monumental plaza, the unwalled capital bespeaks the ambitious expansionism of the colonial Ordered City. In a balancing act of growth and containment, it strives to mold the future in the image of the regulated present.

V. ALONSO DE ZORITA AND FRANCISCO CERVANTES DE SALAZAR

The Spaniard Alonso de Zorita, ally of the Franciscans in New Spain, remarks on the admirable precision of mid-sixteenth-century Mexico City: "The very great and much celebrated city of Mexico is very well planned and very well built, with very long and very straight streets" (in Valle-Arispe 263). A humanist who received his doctorate in Salamanca, and an activist who brought the ideals of Las Casas to bear on his work from 1554 to 1564 as magistrate of the Audiencia in Mexico City and elsewhere, Zorita also exercised his jurisprudential mind in the *Relación de la Nueva España* [Account of New Spain]. He wrote the text in Spain upon his return from Mexico and completed it in 1585. Chapter 12 of the *Relación* leads the reader on a topographer's walking tour of the principal edifices of Mexico's Zócalo that reduces the fullness of place to the space, function, and number intrinsic to Renaissance city planning. Of the royal palace, Zorita says,

> it has three doors that open onto the main plaza; the first is for the Viceroy and Audiencia, the second for the jail, and the third for royal financial officials; it has another door, which goes to the mint; it has four large halls: the first, for the royal Audiencia, has three large rooms, in two of which magistrates hold hearings on civil matters, and in the third criminal judges hold their hearings; this hall houses the civil secretaries, who have their ledgers and seals and bailiffs there, and off this hall are two jail cells with bars, for transactions with prisoners [and so on]. (Valle-Arizpe 264)

Zorita's pen implacably verbalizes and quantifies the world under its purview. The institutions of order and justice readily lend themselves to Zorita's X-ray view, which illuminates their symmetry, geometry, positionality, organization, and relationship.

One hesitates to make too much of Zorita's taxonomized Zócalo, which certainly owes much to a pragmatic, legal turn of mind. Nevertheless, Zorita's subdued, mechanized precision accords with the spirit of the Ordered City and actualizes the representational practices of the Renaissance encountered in *The Birth of Venus*. Zorita's mappable Ordered City locates the New World in the orbit of logic and reason. Rescued from the hazes of chivalric supernaturalism, the excesses of aporia, the fearsome underside of wonder, the city is newly available to language (and thus to control). The humanist Francisco Cervantes de Salazar, whose dialogues on Mexico City Zorita read (Vigil 163), proclaimed that any reader possessed of sanity would prefer works "whose brevity and lack of obscurity delight" and "whose order and lack of confusion give pleasure."[17] Both Zorita and Cervantes de Salazar, Zorita's partner in representational practices if decidedly not in ideology, write with a humanist's order and clarity of a recently verbalizable world. The Ordered City ordains and demands their accounts. Word and world now act *in concert* with each other, with Renaissance parameters, and in the case of Cervantes de Salazar with the aims of the state, to produce the signature discourse of the Ordered City.

If one needs to proceed with caution so as not to overread Zorita's unassuming account, Cervantes de Salazar's dialogues detailing Mexico City and its environs in 1554, written in Latin and much later translated into Spanish and English, require more interpretive zeal than they have received. Historians have mined the text with almost fetishistic fervor, annotating its every assertion, appealing to its wealth of detail on the city for documentary evidence where little exists.[18] Only a handful of literary scholars have undertaken to analyze rather than to annotate the colloquies, which turn out to be much more and less than a factual document, while deeply, even sinisterly, monological.[19] Cervantes de Salazar's deceptively documentary yet supremely analyzable dialogues set colonialist agendas and Renaissance models in unmistakable interaction, naturalizing the coexistence of the two entities by means of exemplary, as it were, colonialogical maneuvers. The dialogues on Mexico City will therefore emerge here as the quintessential textualization of the Ordered City: the architecturally and ideologically Ordered City made Word, the Ordered City laid bare, in sum, the essential Ordered City.

The first extensive treatise on the full-fledged colonial Mexico City and one that will loom large in the Mexican Archive, the dialogues form the core of the first textbook of the Latin language for students at the embryonic Mexican university. When Cervantes de Salazar crafted the foundational textbook, he obviously had more than teaching Latin in mind. His dialogues on Mexico City conduct the reader on a tour not only of the city but also of the new society's ideological and cultural bases. Piling task on ambitious task, the Mexico City conversations aspire to introduce students to the classical world and to the glorious culture of humanist Spain. Printed in 1554 in Mexico and intended by Cervantes for use in his own classes, the textbook also contains a variety of texts intended to serve its didactic humanist goals. They include a Dedication to the Mexican university; a synopsis by Cervantes of the life of the Spanish humanist Luis Vives; Vives's dialogue *Introductio ad Sapientam* [Introduction to knowledge] and Cervantes's commentary on it; a Dedication to Alonso de Montúfar, professor of theology and archbishop of Mexico; four dialogues written by Cervantes in Spain on the games of contemporary Spanish youth; and Cervantes's three dialogues on Mexico ("The University of Mexico," "The Interior of the City of Mexico," "The Environs of the City of Mexico").

Although only a few of this welter of texts will occupy our attention, the aggregate speaks to Cervantes's abilities and proclivities. Born in Toledo around 1513 and educated in Salamanca, Cervantes became the secretary of Cardinal García de Loaysa, archbishop of Seville and president of the Council of the Indies. He then taught rhetoric at the University of Osuna. In Spain, Cervantes published translations into Spanish and commentaries on humanist works written in Latin. He also met Cortés, whom he greatly admired, in Madrid. The first viceroy of Mexico, Antonio de Mendoza, anxious to import intellectuals for the university he wished to found, may have invited the famed humanist Cervantes to journey to New Spain.[20] Cervantes arrived in Mexico City between 1550 and 1551 and spent the rest of his life there. In 1553 he delivered the inaugural address in Latin for the university, and in the same year he obtained a position as its first professor of rhetoric. The ambitious Cervantes soon acquired three degrees from the university, including that of doctor of theology (theology being more prestigious than rhetoric), and took religious orders in 1555. In 1567, 1573, and 1574 he served terms as the university's rector. The publication of the *Dialogues*, together with his support of such creole concerns as the right to inheritance of encomiendas, won Cervantes an appointment from the creole cabildo as official chronicler of the city. In this role he produced his *Crónica de la Nueva España* (written c. 1557–1564), which to a significant degree plunders López de Gómara's worshipful biography of Cortés. Cervantes's rapid-fire ascent to the pinnacle of the colonial intelligentsia garnered him no small criticism. Recorded comments from clergy in Spain lament his thirst for praise, dubious religious vocation, and ambition (Benítez 12; Peña 126); at the end of the *Dialogues* one of his students attempts to rehabilitate Cervantes from the abundant defamation of which he had clearly been the target.

The preceding large and admittedly dry panorama allows us to envision a somewhat more dramatic scenario, one which has various ramifications for the *Dialogues*. Picturing Cervantes as he enters Mexico, we see a social climber avid to gain a foothold in a colonial society poised for cultural development. Hungry for the fame that his *Diálogo de la dignidad del hombre* [Dialogue on the dignity of man], written in Spain, had termed a product of virtue and study (Bono 68–69), Cervantes quickly surmises the efficacy of his humanistic knowledge for achieving his goals. He goes about peddling his knowledge in various venues, not the least of which is the *Dialogues*. There the scholar recycles a jumble of his previous works and adds new colloquies on Mexico, assembling a resplendent, sure-to-please package of humanist artifacts for a captive audience, the young elite of Mexico who will assure his future. In other words, both the *Dialogues'* nature as a textbook and Cervantes's desire to market his ticket to prominence contribute to the ostentatious, quintessentialized humanism of the work.

As if this were not self-advertisement enough, the *Dialogues* in fact do triple duty for their author. Leaving no doubt whatsoever that the text serves Cervantes's aspirations to social mobility, throughout it we also hear him loudly naming himself and praising his own abilities.[21] And much as Cervantes's shameless self-promotion shapes and skews the *Dialogues,* it pales in comparison with his blatant gambits to ingratiate himself with the power centers. From the start of the second opening of the *Dialogues,* the dedication to Montúfar, Cervantes impresses upon his reader that he fervently espouses a providential view of the conquest, the official story. Given Montúfar's dual role as professor of theology and archbishop of Mexico, writes Cervantes, "*Soon all will become of such spirit that they will cleanse from every stain this New World, formerly the abode of the devil and of infidels, and make it a domicile for the true, Almighty God*" (23; emphasis added). Each dialogue on Mexico contains a similar profession of allegiance to the evangelizing, draconian, teleological Spanish mission that set out to perfect the Indians, absolving them of the putative stain of paganism. In subtle and not in the least subtle ways, the entire text resounds with it. Working the dual angle of inculcating students with "right values" of diverse sorts and of appealing to the sympathies of those in power, the dialogues blazon their message. They make inflamed propaganda a bedfellow of quintessential humanism.

While the official story is by now relatively old, if enduring, news, Cervantes de Salazar's first dialogue on Mexico promotes a crucial new story just now breaking into the Mexican arena, the institutionalization of education. "The University of Mexico" ushers the reader and the Spanish tourist Gutiérrez through the incipient institution founded by the second viceroy, Luis de Velasco, primarily for the sons of Spaniards. Inaugurated a scant year before Cervantes penned his *Dialogues,* the university centered on a traditional scholastic curriculum intended to rein the as-yet-undisciplined minds of laypersons and burgeoning clergy alike into sanctioned forms. Concomitantly, the university sought to provide not just education but worthwhile activity for the sons of Spaniards. In Mexico, as in Spain, "authorities maintained a militant attitude toward all learning and looked upon schooling as a cure for temporal ills—including a lack of gainful employment" (Liss 16). The authorities' militant attitude toward education would pay off in unsuspected ways. Increasingly disenfranchised sons of conquerors and subsequent creoles soon began to seize on education as a springboard for social mobility. Cervantes de Salazar was but one of the flocks of parvenus who infiltrated the higher echelons of the colonial hierarchy on the vehicle of seemingly disinterested literary culture.

Celebrating the inauguration of higher learning's Mexican history, Cervantes de Salazar's "The University of Mexico" dexterously fits the desirability of education to the official story. Mesa, apparently a radicado, leads Gutiérrez, like the author a Spaniard recently arrived in Mexico, around the just-founded Mexican university. The dialogue depicts a society on the brink of culture, of the enlightenment that distinguishes the Renaissance city. At its axial point—also axial for the Mexican Archive—Mesa posits a new, postconquest identity for Mexico in which learning will temper the unmitigated materialism that up to now has constituted the image of the colony. Mesa introduces the university as "the molding place of the youth; those entering are students, lovers of Minerva and the Muses." Gutiérrez asks, "Has wisdom any place where avarice holds sway?" Mesa responds, "That conquers which is stronger and the more greatly desired" (26). Thomas More's Utopians seek the pleasures of the mind, equated to "the practice of virtues and the consciousness of a good life" (60); thanks to the university, the new utopians, Mexico's creole sons, will benefit from and advance the civilizing Spanish mission. Thus, at the end of the dialogue, duly impressed by the tour, Gutiérrez confirms: "your university, still in its infancy and situated in a region up to now barbarous and uncivilized, has been established with such beginnings that, in my belief, New Spain, hitherto known for its supply of silver, will be celebrated among other nations in the future for the multitude of its learned men" (36). The mother university, of which Cervantes declares himself a "foster child" (23), and the singularly gifted, dedicated professors who act as the students' fathers (29) will together give birth to an enlightened Mexico and complete the ameliorating mission begun by religion.

With its burden of foundational functions, the first dialogue proves as keen to model for the reader the humanist stance on learning that both the institution and Cervantes profess as it was to lavish praise on the university. It (like the second dialogue) opens with the two interlocutors indulging in some intellectual grandstanding as they exchange humanist commonplaces on learning. Gutiérrez, the tourist, declares his eagerness to imbibe new ideas from the New World, to be "carried away into the discovery of wisdom," which "delights us with its variety" (25). The walking tour briefly becomes an exercise in pedantry. Gutiérrez explicitly quotes Aristotle and without attribution references Pliny on the ways in which the diversity of nature always turns the mind "toward things new and never seen before" (25). New and Old World erudition mix in Gutiérrez's observation on variety, familiar to New World discourse from Oviedo's *Sumario*. Saying that the mind "grows weary with endless repetition everywhere" (25), Gutiérrez deplores the tedium of resemblance in words uncannily parallel to Foucault's assessment of similitude.

In an imperial context, in the context of the Ordered City, the denunciation of resemblance borders on the heretical. Hence, after initially inscribing itself in a liberal humanist framework, the first dialogue triumphantly reveals its embracing of difference to have been only gestural, a smoke screen. Gutiérrez expects novelty from the Mexican university and importunes Mesa with questions that might elicit disclosure of the new, but Mesa glories in revealing to him its sameness to Salamanca. The university's professors, quality, schedule, grading, examinations, and so on, compete with the University of Salamanca or even outstrip it. Gutiérrez then validates said resemblances, bestowing on them the Spanish seal of approval. What could better confirm excellence than sameness to Spain? Margarita Peña aptly considers the *Dialogues*' relentless comparisons to Spain "no mere rhetorical or stylistic technique, but a moral device, essential to the aims of the dialogue" (130). At worst, Gutiérrez learns how difference is in the process of being molded into sameness or what it lacks to achieve sameness (in the case of the university, better salaries for professors like Cervantes).

The coy reinforcement of similitude persists and expands in the second Mexican dialogue, "The Interior of the City of Mexico." New interlocutors, now two veteran residents of the city (Zamora and Zuazo) and one Spanish newcomer, or gachupín (Alfaro), ride through the city. As the hardy creoles mount horses and the Spaniard a gentle mule (38) suited to a woman, Alfaro converses with Zamora and Zuazo, A with Z, one end of the world with the other. The greater the apparent polarization, the greater the pleasures of dispelling it. Over the course of the dialogue, therefore, sham difference melts into sameness. Zuazo matches Alfaro point by point in intelligence and erudition. Mexico City compares favorably with the greatest European cities, with the exception of its modest cathedral, a shameful situation that Cervantes petitions the archbishop to remedy.

As Alfaro and Zamora join their twinned intelligences to celebrate the Zócalo, the exalted praise they heap on it begins to expose the dark side of resemblance for Mexico:

> Alfaro: Indeed, there is no reason why anyone who has seen this court should wish to see the ones at Granada or at Valladolid, which are by far the most important in Spain.
>
> Zamora: Adjacent to the palace and the shops below, immediately after crossing San Francisco Street, there are very wide, long porticos, more celebrated indeed than were the Corinthian, the Pompeian, Claudian, and Livian colonnades at Rome.
>
> Alfaro: "Where the Claudian colonnade spreads its wide shadows" [Martial, *Liber de Spectaculis* 2.9].
>
> Zamora: There is the Middle Janus, a place set apart for merchants and tradesmen, just as are the steps in Seville and the bourse in Antwerp; Mercury presides over these places. (45)

A and Z exuberantly deny the New World's difference from the Old and in so doing move toward denying the New World's identity. Speaking in one voice, outsider and insider dissolve Mexico City into a panoply of resemblances to the classical world, Europe, and Spain. The filigree of comparisons inserts New Spain in a diachronic and synchronic constellation, a transhistoric global network. Diffused and disarmed, the once problematically distinctive Mexico becomes a cog in the well-ordered machine of the civilized Renaissance world. Zamora says of the Portal de los Mercaderes on the ground floor of the royal palace, "One could justly affirm that there flows together here whatever is well known in the whole world" (43). What had stood apart from the "whole world" now takes its place as no less, nor more, than a microcosm of it.

Divesting Mexico City of its problematic and individual identity, Cervantes de Salazar resurrects it in ideal form, as Form itself. Zamora's pedantic roster of Roman columns, one of many instances in which the text brandishes technical terminology, intimates that Cervantes intends his already multitasking dialogue to serve also as a primer of architectural forms. As such, even as it conveys the specific detail on individual

Mexican buildings that has captivated historians, the text does so in calculated commerce with Platonically oriented architectural treatises and architecture. Conceivably keeping its erudition under wraps to make the text more digestible for students (as may have been the case with the references to Pliny), the colloquy dialogues with Alberti's architectural treatise.[22] George Kubler notes that "The Interior of Mexico" "reveals an intimate familiarity with the concepts of modular composition, canonical proportions, uniform street-façades, and monumental public squares" (100) typical of Italianate urban planning. Kubler also considers it highly likely that Cervantes interacted in the Mexican capital with the architect Claudio de Arciniega, who designed the proxy catafalque for Charles V that the writer chronicled in his *Túmulo imperial* of 1560. Arciniega's buildings, including contributions to the cathedrals of Mexico City and Puebla, introduced dramatic changes into Mexican architectural design. They "mediated the Renaissance language of form" for Mexico City, creating "the first work in Mexico to be composed according to the strict rule of formal order in Renaissance architecture" (Kubler 122–123). In other words, mid-sixteenth-century Mexico City owed appreciably to Arciniega the regularity of form and symmetrical design of the Ordered City's individual buildings. With Cervantes's dual investment through Arciniega and Alberti in the architecture of the Ordered City, theory and praxis as well as textbook and tour mesh to create the consummate embodiment of the Ordered City that the second dialogue constructs.

The majority of the dialogue memorializes the original, pristine Ordered City. Its walking tour lingers within the perimeters of the small early traza, still the heart of the city, and exudes the Franciscan spirit that first breathed religious and architectural life into the city. Seen from horseback and in its distilled essence, Cervantes's city assumes the ideal form of the millennial kingdom that the Franciscans endeavored to implant in the heathen New World, or even the abstracted purity of St. Augustine's City of God. The dialogue's first view of the city sweeps panoramically down Tacuba Street. Tacuba's levelness, length, breadth, and rectitude, says Alfaro, "exhilarates the mind and refreshes the eyes!" (38), a statement that exactly parallels Alberti's Platonic reminiscence. Unadulterated form leaps out from busy particularity in streets whose right angles form crosses, in the city's well-proportioned columns, even in the hospital tending to venereal diseases, praised for its "art" (49). Great height, size, and strength characterize the monumental, semi-fortified buildings of the capital. Cervantes's Mexico City, rendered with the same precision as Zorita's, boasts the chiseled Apollonian lines of a sculpture and of the traza itself.

Above all, Cervantes's description conveys how fully the *order* that the traza aimed to confer on barbarous chaos now rules the city.[23] The city, as does the university (35), runs like clockwork, regulated by the ringing of a bell "heard by the inhabitants of the city in every quarter" (41). In this panoptic world, regulation ensures the uniformity of houses "built so regularly and evenly that none varies a finger's breath from another" (39) and limits tradespeople to the streets specifically designated for their occupation. The Audiencia, source of regulation and itself a model of decorum and exclusion, commands "reverence" (44) from those who enter the courtroom and thus elevates order almost into a religion. For its part, the level, organized Zócalo, surpassing all the world's plazas in "size and grandeur" (41), affords an appropriate space for the text to articulate its central contention that order equals beauty: "What order! What beauty!" (41). Only the bustle of nameless individuals passing through the streets of the center—necessary proof of the vibrancy and success of the colonial Ordered City—vitiates its geometric form and chronometric organization.

Alfaro later fittingly concludes that there "is nothing in the City of Mexico undeserving of great praise" (53). While Cervantes takes pains to diffuse Mexico City into an international, archetypal framework, in order to promote the Spanish empire he cannot fail to praise the capital's special merits. The praise he accords the city lays the written bases for civic patriotism, bases which Bernardo de Balbuena's "La grandeza mexicana" will immoderately expand.[24] Hawking the city as the jewel of the Spanish empire and remaining within the Spanish value system, Cervantes advertises the city's aristocratic nobility. He has the walking tour wend deliberately through and finally outside the traza along the conduit of Tacuba Street, home to the elite, and other similar streets. One set of magnificent houses gives way to another, the traza physically ends but reassuringly continues in spirit. As Alfaro states, "The City of Mexico is everywhere; that is, it has no suburbs and is beautiful and distinguished on all sides" (51). The lion's share of the dialogue leaves the reader with the impression that Mexico City is composed of nothing but aristocratic zones.

Cervantes confers on the would-be homogeneous city governed by similitude a striking concert between building and owner. He contends that "the structure of all these houses matches the nobility of those that reside in them" (50). The author also notes that Martín Cortés's palace "bears witness to the invincible and peerless spirit of its builder" (47). Cervantes's oft-repeated assertions of the correspondence between house and inhabitant allow him to support the creole cause[25] by adulating the buildings' influential owners, especially Hernán and Martín Cortés, without exceeding his topographic Renaissance architectural agenda. At the same time, the near personification of the buildings dimensionalizes the map of the Ordered City into a communicentric view, a portrait of a city that transmits the *genius loci,* or signal spirit, of a community rather than merely conveying its surfaces as does a chorographic view (Kagan 108–109). Like Leonardo Bruni's Florence, Cervantes's Mexico City radiates virtue, a virtue allegedly epitomized in the two Corteses and fully consistent with the capital's noble neo-Spanish disposition.

Having ponderously ennobled, idealized, uniformized, eternalized, homologized, and internationalized Mexico City, the second dialogue is ready for its first carefully calibrated experience of difference. The text leads Alfaro, the visitor, directly from the elite residential district into a Dominican monastery whose school houses or "confines" mestizo boys and trains them in matters pertaining to the worship of God (55). With this image of purification and confinement still in the mind's eye, the dialogue fleetingly dips into the antithesis of the noble Ordered City, the huts of the Indians. Two sentences quickly dispatch the squat huts that ring the monastery and "spread along the ground . . . without orderly arrangement" (56). The dialogue then immediately bounces back to another religious institution of learning, the Colegio de Niñas founded by Conceptionist nuns to inculcate mestiza girls with Christian culture. A tall white church looms behind the school. Locked in between two emblems of redemption, for the moment the Indians have been textually contained.

Yet before moving on to its final pious stop at an Augustinian monastery, the second dialogue takes a walk full of textual trepidation through the city's Indian zone. In one of the most fraught and literarily influential moments of sixteenth-century Mexican *lettres,* the three sightseers enter the Indian zone through the native market of San Juan, lying southwest of the city. There, in the shadow of an elevated gallows, to the beat of a cymbal, the second dialogue at long last engages with and complexly transacts alterity.

As the three interlocutors wander through the market, commenting on its wares, they effectively decouple the Indians from their products. Safehoused in the marketplace, the Indians (according to the author, some twenty thousand of them! [62]) make their first and only appearance as actors in the dialogue as a function of the products they sell (57–58). "Ají [chili], beans, Persian pears, guavas, mameyes, zapotes, camotes, gícamas, cacomites, esquites, tunas, gilotes, xocotes" (58): the Indians offer for sale and consumption "what the earth [that is, not the Indian] brings forth," things that Alfaro has never found anywhere else, things with "outlandish names" (58–59). Oviedo had reveled in the sensuous, practical delights of New World nature while recoiling from signal aspects of its human landscape; Cortés had descried the New World's novelty in its human-made objects and then "disappeared" them from the Mexican marketplace. Here, autochthonous natural produce stands in for the Indians, for novel otherness, and is channeled into a glaring exoticism.

Taking his cue from Oviedo's exoticizing and medicinal bents (we recall that Cervantes also plundered López de Gómara), the author of the dialogues brokers the newness of Mexico by having Zamora point out at length the usefulness of a series of native plants, seeds, and roots with the exotic names he flaunts: "*Iztacpatli* purges phlegm; *tlalcacaguatl,* and *izticpatli* free one from fever; *culuzizicaztli* relieves head catarrh; *ololiuhqui* cures ulcers and hidden wounds" (59). The wonder cabinet resolves into a medicine chest holding a wealth of benefits that Alfaro and the reader who shares his profile can access by simply reaching out to consume the native produce.[26] With its peculiar colonialist form of multiculturalism, Cervantes's account cajoles Spanish and Spanish-leaning readers eagerly to ingest matters that culturally they cannot stomach.[27] What is truly for sale in Cervantes's textualized marketplace, what it effectively manages through merchandising, is alterity.

The transposition of marketplace into medicine chest also brings to blithe resolution the dramatic, paradigmatic tension between Spaniard and creole that animates the second dialogue. As Alfaro skeptically confronts the overwhelming exhibit of otherness unfurled before him, both Zamora and Alfaro himself attempt to palliate a foreigner's (including the European reader's) disquiet by reciting a litany of humanist aphorisms. Remarks such as Zamora's that the "nature, the productive quality, of the lands is as diverse as the characters and tongues of men" (58), return one to the Pliny-cum-Oviedo frame story of the outset of the first and second dialogues, now directly germane to the sights of the excursion. Zamora applies a humanist's sense of relativism to a moment that several scholars have deemed an exemplary expression of the transculturation or acculturation that Spaniards underwent in the New World.[28] Responding to Alfaro's comment that the Nahuatl terms for native products that his tour guide proffers with gusto are "Outlandish names!," Zamora states, *"As ours to them"* (59; emphasis added). Under the steady tutelage of Zamora and Zuazo, swayed by the medicinal properties of indigenous plants, Alfaro comes to embrace a more tolerant, transculturated position. At the end of the dialogue the erstwhile skeptical Spaniard can wholeheartedly proclaim with Oviedo and Pliny that "Nature is marvelous in the variety of its products" (63). The experience of the marketplace has massaged Alfaro from anxiety into pleasure. Presented with a contained, commodified, benignly utilitarian form of outlandishness, he has exchanged Cortés's pathologized, medievally inflected "maravilla" for the characteristic Renaissance delighted *admiratio*.

A happy resolution indeed, for Alfaro and for transculturation. However, one cannot forget that the *Dialogues* systematically corrode each seeming affirmation of difference. Alfaro's acceptance of otherness will be no less disingenuous; Cervantes just negotiates it more intricately than before. The Spaniard's "conversion" will stand but will not undo the striking, literally dirty denigration to which the text has subjected the Indians in the marketplace. Cervantes has sought to broker the Indians to his readers by morphing them into a beneficial, fecund Nature. He now slyly turns his own equation of Indians equal Nature against the native peoples by identifying them with the least palatable, both literally and figuratively, forms of earthiness: mud, clay, worms, insects. Alfaro inquires about the "dark liquid" with which the Indians' "limbs are smeared," the "filthy, clay-like stuff with which their heads are daubed and incrusted," and about the worms in such large supply (59). Each matter turns out to have a practical if highly unappetizing explanation, since the clay protects against lice and Indians reportedly eat the worms. When Alfaro associates worms with death, he adds the last element necessary fully to write the Indians into the realm of the demonized chthonian. With the grotesque portrait of the dark, clay-daubed and worm-eating, death-identified Indians, the text effects a didactic chiaroscuro that, I believe, irremediably sullies its *admiratio* and solidifies Cervantes's draconian (and now Manichean) propagandistic agenda more palpably than it corroborates any enlightened criollismo.

Fatal and flawed, nature cannot be left in its pure state. Therefore, wherever nature appears in the *Dialogues,* Cervantes has it succumb to the omnivorous civilizing, homogenizing energies of the Spanish mission. Particularly in the perambulations of the third dialogue ("The Environs of the City of Mexico") through the outskirts of the capital, that mission acts upon disparate natural phenomena, all of which it at once physically metamorphoses and tacitly transmutes into images of containment. Roman fascination with enclosing outdoor space finds a new home in the walled open-air churches, country estate gardens, and aqueducts of the environs of the New World city. The travelers ascend toward a monument to tamed nature, Chapultepec Park, formerly Moctezuma's pleasure grounds. Hillside vistas, nature arranged artfully, often warrant the travelers' consideration, as does the spring of Chapultepec, "so enhanced by nature and art" that it transcends classical fountains (72). Wild New World nature cedes to the enclosed garden, the *hortus conclusus* redolent of the Virgin Mary's purity.

Even when left untouched, nature acquiesces to civilization. Perennially green pastoral lands figure in the dialogue as pasturelands (70–71), delightful streams as potable water (72). Lands and streams feed the cattle the Spanish had introduced in the New World, which fact laces with colonialist nuance the genre of the pastoral that will occupy our attention shortly, and onward. When Cervantes de Salazar invokes Horace's pastoral "Beatus Ille" (78), in his view the countryside warrants the epithet by virtue of its harnessing of wayward nature. Nature must be saved from itself. So must the Indians. Cervantes informs readers that a wall has been built around Chapultepec's grove "to prevent the spring from being defiled by Indians crowding in" (71). In a final convolution of his earlier equation, Cervantes indicates that nature must be protected from the very Indians who metonymize it.

The travelers reach the culminating point of their third excursion and the *Dialogues* their well-orchestrated apogee atop the hill of Chapultepec. Alfaro, Zuazo, and Zamora pass through the gates that carry an inscription in Latin by none other than Cervantes de Salazar, and they then climb to the hill's summit, where the city comes into full overviewing view (74). Here, in a rapid concatenation whose climactic energy I would like my reader to share, the text lays bare its heretofore none-too-hidden designs. It excoriates the Aztec sacrifices that took place on the hill "as if in a butcher shop"; lauds the Spanish project that transformed the Indians "from their former great misery to their present happiness, and from their previous slavery to true liberty" together with the magnificent emperor under whose auspices the liberation took place; definitively deprives Mexico of its unique identity, saying that "both worlds have been joined and encompassed in this place," a "*microcosmus*" or "small universe"; and reads the symbolic arrangement of the extended city situated on a "level plain," in which the "proud and lofty buildings of the Spaniards . . . enclose and entirely surround the homes of the Indians in the suburbs" (74–75). Nothing escapes or fails to please the eye of the pilgrims witnessing the diaphanous, epiphanic "spectacle" of Mexico (74).

In this one orgasmic scene, the text and the city have together relinquished all their secrets. The Ordered City and Renaissance representational practices desire, and mutually conspire, to produce this scene in which the New World achieves a marvelous transparency, a thrilling knowability. Secrets that taunted Columbus, that spurred Oviedo's empirical investigations, that stunned Cortés, and that prompted Alfaro's questions have now ostensibly lost their intractability and have come into Apollonian clarity. They have, one might say, seen the light. A readable, writeable, conquered Mexico that has been stripped naked and surrenders itself to the pilgrim's gaze or reader's eye slides into line with Botticelli's knowably naked Venus and with Jan van der Straet's famous 1580 engraving of America as an unclothed woman rising from her hammock to welcome an erect, cross-bearing conqueror.[29] Anne McClintock notes that in such porno-tropical fantasies "the world is feminized and spatially spread for male exploration, then reassembled and deployed in the interests of massive imperial power" (23). It therefore comes as no surprise that Zamora tells Alfaro, "You have learned almost everything" (77).

Almost everything: Alfaro still wishes to learn about "the life and customs of the Indians" (77). In response to his request, the third dialogue closes with a bizarre, anomalous performance of disorder. Although two pages of Zamora's account of the Indians are, significantly enough, missing in the sole extant original edition of the *Dialogues,* the one remaining page shows Cervantes taking a final lesson from Oviedo. Its fevered, miscellaneous congeries of damning ethnographic information, which ranges from accusations of polygamy to drunkenness, reproduces chapter 10 of the *Sumario,* with just a few distinguishing Mexican touches. Textually and in reality the Indians contravene the Ordered City. Cervantes shrinks from walking on the wild side in any place other than the marketplace, from setting foot outside the Ordered City except as a reader of previous texts. Yet his dialogues and mission would have been well served had Cervantes foregone the reading tour of "the life and customs of the Indians." For in the margins of the text and the shadows of his enlightened Mexico, Cervantes unwittingly provides a forum in which the repressed Indian world asserts its still-potent ability to confound, disorder, and undo both the Ordered City and its prime literary exponent.

VI. JUAN DE LA CUEVA AND EUGENIO DE SALAZAR Y ALARCÓN

By the last quarter of the sixteenth century, the "estheticizing of domination" (Beverley 75) that the Latin textbook of 1554 achieves in all but its margins was exercising its agenda in the domain of the humanist poetry that epitomized the culture so coveted by the colony and so expedient to Cervantes de Salazar. To transmogrify the New World city into verse, the most sublime of discourses in the sixteenth century, is to temper a potentially fear-ridden subject with the promise of beauty. No matter what the poems' literary merit—a scarce presence in the three ideologically driven compositions to which we now turn—their estheticizing of Mexico City inevitably heightens its pleasure quotient. Replaying, in a kind of fin-de-siècle retrospective, the ideologized tropes of the authors whom we have already met, the Spaniard Juan de la Cueva offers a sensually exoticized Mexico City for the reader's delectation, and the radicado Eugenio de Salazar y Alarcón deflects the city onto a sensational mythological framework. Even, or especially, when the poems estheticize Mexico City to the point of unrecognizability, they enact the Ordered City's objective of defusing whatever might pose a threat.

The section of Juan de la Cueva's "Epístola al licenciado Sánchez de Obregón, primer corregidor de México" [Epistle to Licentiate Sánchez de Obregón, first magistrate of Mexico] (c. 1577)[30] on Mexico City, likely the first poetic depiction in Spanish of the viceregal capital, fulfills that objective in its own (m)eager way. An autobiographical vignette written in the first person, the Mexico City section of the "Epístola" shows the renowned Spanish poet and dramatist going native as happily as a Spaniard can. Though he is filled with longing for his native Spain, the three years that Cueva spent in Mexico (1574–1577) reportedly held their share of delights.[31] The author expresses his gratitude to the "lucky star" that brought him to Mexico City, where he finds himself at his pleasure (20). Rather than concealing his status as a newcomer, Cueva derives a lively, emotive poetic persona from it:

> De aquestas cosas que sin arte expreso,
> que admira el verlas y deleitan tanto,
> de que puedo hacer largo proceso,
> cuando las considero, bien me espanto,
> porque tienen consigo una extrañeza
> que a alcanzar lo que son no me levanto. (20)

> [Although the things of Mexico City that I express so artlessly astonish the eye and delight so greatly that I could discuss them at length, it truly frightens me to ponder them, because they are so alien that I am unequal to comprehending them.]

Cueva juggles wonder, fear, and delight as he sets forth what had been many immigrants' motley reaction to New Spain. The poem's rapid jaunt through Mexico City, consistent with Cueva's jaunty exposition of his interiority, takes on a merry, superficial touristic air. For the poem's poetic speaker, Mexico City abounds in things that delight the palate and the eye ("al gusto y a la vista deleitosas" [21]). The touristic poetic narrator professes to have devoured the city's attractions avidly. While certain other "cachopines," or gachupines, shrink from native foods or dances, he relishes them (21). In the sightseeing tour of the "Epístola," as in modern tourist advertising, Mexico is a pleasure palace that exists to be consumed.

To savor Mexico City to the fullest, the "Epístola" must touch on two of its major attractions, the marketplace and the plaza. Home to sensuous, consumable, harmless exotica, Cueva's marketplace duplicates that of Cervantes de Salazar point by point. The poem showcases fruits, flourishes their native names, touts their variety, and praises their delicious properties to the skies. Like Cervantes, Cueva dissociates the produce from its indigenous producers. His poetic "I" cares not a whit who cultivates the fruits, only how they taste. Yet in a plaza (presumably the Zócalo because it accommodates two thousand Indians) that Cueva equates to the marketplace as a site of the enjoyable visual exotica of the Indians' ritual dances, the poet discloses the not-unfamiliar motivation for his and Cervantes's dissociation of produce from producer. With undisguised scorn, Cueva states, "La gente natural, sí, es desabrida / (digo los indios) y de no buen trato" [Yes, the natives (I mean the Indians) are distasteful and intractable] (21). Cueva goes on to deprecate the Indians as drunken, slothful beings and to depotentiate them into a race that has bent to the yoke of defeat. They have traded their lances not for plowshares but for the "glasses of Castilian wine" that now accompany their tribal dances (22). The Indians praise Cortés and recriminate Malinche in songs resembling the epics of the Cortés cycle that creole authors began to write in the late 1500s. Cueva's portrayal of the Indians' dreary epic incantation ("es cansancio oílla" [22]) and peculiar dances to the beat of wine glasses caricatures their quasi-poetic endeavors. In the view of the Petrarchan Cueva, besides the Indians' exotic sheen only the "savage" love that according to his description can fell barbarian and Spaniard alike would qualify the natives as Spanish poetic subjects (22).

Perhaps in Cueva's eyes duly uninspired, his inaugural Spanish poem on the viceregal capital breaks little new ground. It complacently poeticizes Cervantes's Ordered City. Identity-erasing resemblances between Venice and Mexico City ("cual Venecia edificada / sobre la mar, sin diferencia alguna," built in the water like Venice, with not the least difference between them, 20) open the "Epístola," which then moves into difference-as-exotica, lightly embellished with mythological allusion. The "Epístola"'s hendecasyllabic linked tercets, together with its simple semantic rhymes, move the poem along in the brisk, limpid harmony that befits an Ordered City.

Rapid and catchy, the composition finds no shame in failing to engage with the rich texture of the city. Cueva declares his inability to come to verbal terms with the capital, as quoted above and as his relatively short sojourn might well warrant. Instead of making a good faith effort to describe the capital, he immediately taxonomizes it. With a middling display of poetic wit, in his only pathbreaking move of sorts Cueva coins a neat panegyric formula for the city:

> Seis cosas excelentes en belleza
> hallo, escritas con C, que son notables
> y dignas de alabaros su grandeza:
> casas, calles, caballos admirables, carnes, cabellos y criaturas bellas,
> que en todo extremo todas son loables. (20–21)

> [I find six things of excellent beauty, each starting with a C, which are notable and whose grandeur is worthy of acclaim: houses, streets, admirable horses, women with lovely forms and hair, all praiseworthy in all particulars.]

Unfortunately but understandably in view of their inaugural status and appealing simplicity, the six Cs of Cueva's touristic "Epístola" go on to have a tremendous afterlife, leaving a legacy of questionable merit. They pass into later works of all sorts, forming the bases of an urban literary tradition, and into literary histories. With the shorthand of the six Cs—a poetic act but an impoverished one—Mexico City attains literary manageability, a facile order.

Cueva's premature poetic codification of the Ordered City attempts, however reductively, to capture some of its distinctive features. In the last years of the century, Eugenio de Salazar y Alarcón's two poems on Mexico City devise a far more extreme response to the Ordered City. Born in Madrid around 1530 and educated at three Spanish universities, Salazar spent nearly twenty years in Mexico (1581–1598), where he occupied various important government positions.[32] Whatever particularized knowledge of New Spain Salazar had gleaned over the years barely impacts the two poems, given over as they are to the rehearsal of Renaissance literary modes confederated with overblown propaganda for Spain. Cervantes de Salazar applied his propagandistic impulses to a recognizable form of the city; Salazar y Alarcón prefers to dissolve the real city, purified by Spanish efforts, into a fully estheticized, sublimated paradise.

Salazar y Alarcón's relatively referential "Epístola al insigne Hernando de Herrera en que se refiere al estado de la ilustre Ciudad de México" [Epistle to the celebrated Hernando de Herrero, which reports on the state of the illustrious City of Mexico] (c. 1597; in Gallardo),[33] for instance, shares Cervantes de Salazar's view that education completes the direly needed rehabilitation of the New World ("which the devil had possessed" [354]) and escorts the reader through the Spanish curriculum. Nevertheless, the poem tropes more than tours both the university and the city. Writing to a famed poet whose friendship he abjectly courts, Salazar paints the ever more cultured Mexico City into a poem worthy of Herrera and *as* a poem shaped by the pastoral, mythological Garcilaso de la Vega whose poetry Herrera edited. Spanish education, Salazar writes, has managed to transform a paradise of nature into the home of the Muses: "La Nueva España: ya resuena en ella / El canto de las Musas deleitosas / Que vienen con gran gusto a ennoblecella" [New Spain now resounding with the song of the delightful Muses, who have come very happily to ennoble it] (355). In the conventional pastoral world of Salazar's Mexican Muses, lyres and fountains and sheep calls and poetry form a single harmonious chord when a panpipe "alien to malice" "arranges their sound into simple accord" (356). Salazar estheticizes the New World purposefully and with impunity. He contains it in Spanish literary structures. This is not a rendition of just any "prose of the world" in the poetic verse that its all-embracing harmony demands, but of the prose of the problematic New World and its city, now fitted into the rhyming universe of the Neoplatonists.

Triumphantly pastoral, it is barely a city at all. Here, and more extensively in the "Bucólica: Descripción de la laguna de Méjico" [Bucolic: Description of the lagoon of Mexico] (in Gallardo),[34] grand finale of the sixteenth-century Ordered City, Salazar effects a lovely, seemingly innocent coalition of sublime Renaissance literary modes and Spanish ideology. He employs the pastoral as a model not for the countryside of the New World but for the purified colonial city. Salazar's estheticizing of domination opens the gates to the urban pastoral, which will play a large role in New World city representation and in the Mexican Archive.

Why might so unlikely and oxymoronic a combination as the urban pastoral have gained prominence? Beyond the will to order and concert endemic in the sixteenth century, one detects in the urban pastoral of the island-based Mexico City nostalgic traces of the first, relatively uncomplicated and easily estheticizable "island phase" of Spanish exploration in the Caribbean. Columbus's and Pedro Mártir de Anglería's writings from that first phase bind the New World to pastoral images of fertility and innocence that have a biblical air and associate the pastoral New World with terrestrial Paradise or with a lost Golden Age.[35] A salable, pastoral nature comes to represent the benign aspects of the new in early writers like Oviedo, and, as we have seen, is next lodged in the city marketplace to palliate the category crises the New World entailed. It then involved only a small leap for colonialogical thinking to cast the incipient New World city wholesale as an emollient, utopian locus amoenus. Moreover, since the New World city aspired to nobility, it required an urbane, aristocratic, legitimating discourse. While the epic met the social and moral needs of city representation, heroic poetry could not fully serve the discourse of place. Despite its obvious inconveniences, the sublime, aristocratic, place-based Renaissance pastoral appreciably did. All told, one ends up with the paradoxical situation of an urban discourse wanting to be urbane and natural and thus taking recourse to the pastoral.

An operatic, sublime, imperialist extravaganza that culminates in arias to the "blancura" [whiteness] desired by the enlightened Ordered City, Salazar's "Bucólica" glosses over any difficulty that the transposition of city into pastoral space, or any transposition whatsoever, might present. Indeed, the lengthy (sixty-stanza) poem buoyantly presses referentiality, ideology, mythology, allegory, and the pastoral alike into the service of urban literary representation. The poem departs from a few factual aspects of Mexico City, notably the waterways that run through it and the mixture of sweet and salt water in the lagoon. These malleable facts, readily estheticizable properties of the city, become factoids that provide the scaffolding for the text's subsequent transpositions. The poem opens with an impassioned evocation of the wealthy and populous "Tenuxtitlan" as Moctezuma's preterite kingdom, home to sinful sacrifices yet source of wealth for Spain. It then proceeds quite graphically to submerge the actual city with the following sexualized allegory of flood and purification.

Tapping into the tradition of Spanish Reconquest poetry that represents the Moorish city as a beautiful woman whom the conqueror wishes to possess, Salazar has Neptune order his servant, the "Sur," or Southern Sea (the Pacific Ocean), to flood the beautiful Tenochtitlán for which the sea god yearns. The Southern Sea willingly obeys and transforms the city into the lagoon of the poem's title, a "paradise" (363). With a Christlike trident as his standard and attired in shining pearls, Salazar's Neptune cuts through the "most secret aqueduct" (362) that the Southern Sea had carved out from its floodwaters, "lovingly" to take possession of the "beautiful port" (363). Neptune tours his new kingdom not on foot but atop a huge, mother-of-pearl, stridently phallic whale.

A peculiar mixture of rape and redemption, the poem also mythologizes the ceremonial entries of viceregal figures into the city. The floodwaters that carry Neptune into the city and over *three* Aztec hills, have exiled evil, guaranteed the "health" of the city, and banished war (364). At this point, what started out as an allegory of conquest staged by mythological figures assumes the functions of an actual myth that purports to explain the fresh and salt water of Tenochtitlán's lagoon in moral terms. To purify the deep, salty waters of any properties that might strike terror in a "gallant lady" (364), Salazar's Neptune opens a vein of sweet water in them that leaves the lagoon light, transparent, shallow, and cleansed of sin.

While delighted nymphs hasten to occupy the sweet waters, Neptune takes command of his, that is, *the* New World. He erects an Ordered City in which elements familiar to us from other authors suffer outrageous esthetic and ideological modulations. As he fashions Neptune's city, Salazar outdoes his precursors, his successors (such as Sor Juana, in her *Neptuno alegórico* of 1680), and even himself. Salazar informs his readers that Neptune forbids any saltwater fish—read: rebellious heathen Indians—to enter the sweet waters, but that he does allow in less "importunate," feminized beings: "unos pesces blandos, delicados / Al gusto de las damas apropriados" [soft, delicate fish, suitable to ladies' tastes] (364). Neptune enlists the Indians in the very task of estheticizing the purified Tenochtitlán. "Hizo por eras un comunicable / Repartimiento entre la gente indiana" [he distributed the gardens equally among the Indians], so that "with wonderful order" they could cultivate "beautiful cornfields" in the lagoon for the enjoyment of all (364). The distribution, an echo of consigned Indian labor for the state in *repartimiento,* and fields thus incongruously figured yield the exact same products that have appeared in Cervantes's and Cueva's marketplaces. Yet in Neptune's sanitized waterworld, red and orange peppers have been bleached of their jarringly bright colors and beautified by the "agua dulce . . . que blanquea" [sweet water that bleaches] them into an "enrejado claro y puro / De blanca plata" [a shining, pure trellis of white silver] (364). With this, exotica lose even their exoticism. Salazar's end-of-the-century poeticized marketplace brings to a logical, if preposterous, terminus the sixteenth century's insistent recycling of the awe-inspiring new into ever less threatening forms.

Neptune goes on to complete the purged Ordered City. He sets up its tribute structures, obliges the winds to temper its climate into one of sheer "happiness," consecrates it to God, and invites women, whom he deems deserving of entry into his paradise because they materialize ideal beauty, to populate its waters. Then, to the "wonder" of all spectators (365), he disappears into the depths of the water, presumably to continue decontaminating them.

Like the divine Eucharist that restores the body of Christ, in Neptune's place arrive the viceregal couple qua shepherds.[36] The new Adam and Eve, named Albár (*alba* means "dawn") and Blanca [white] after Viceroy Álvaro Manrique de Zúñiga and Vicereine Blanca Henríquez, survey their perfectly pastoral empire of amorous nymphs, verdant grazing lands, pleasure, and play. Neither darkness nor danger, in the form of disruptive wolves, has any place in the light-filled world (365). Blanca and Albár's abstract peaceable kingdom, another New World performance by Salazar of Garcilaso de la Vega's Renaissance lyric, tenuously moors itself in New Spain by visiting Chapultepec. The viceroys turned shepherds, we read, have their sheepfold in the green pastures on the outskirts of the effaced pastoral city, in Chapultepec, which began as

Moctezuma's pleasure palace and became the playground of the creole elite as well as the water source for the city (Valle-Arzpe 161–168). Chapultepec, pleasurable supplement to the urban landscape, is now a metaphor of Mexico City, both coextensive and coterminous with it.

Salazar's ingenious mytho-logical mind plants atop the hill of Chapultepec a kind of capitol building construed as a temple to the god Pan, "the Eternal Pan who is singular and triple" (*pan* also means "bread") (366). There, fauns—presumably the regenerated Indian, half-man/half-beast—cavort with sylvans (366). Its mythological and biblical contortions aside, Salazar y Alarcón's poem has reinserted readers into Cervantes de Salazar's panoptic Chapultepec. Blanca and Albár stand on the hill, and the pastoral city lays itself out to their gaze: "Porque del cerro todo se descubre, / Que es eminente, y nada se le encubre" [because everything is revealed from the hilltop, which is prominent, and nothing is hidden from it] (365). Although in the "Bucólica" Mexico City has in effect *become* Chapultepec, Salazar's capital claims the epistemological transparency essential to Cervantes's Ordered City as seen in the dialogues *from* Chapultepec.

Transparency gives way to fetishized, hypertrophic whiteness in the last portion of the poem. Albár, the overseer of the shepherds (and the viceroy), occupies his sweet days in an undemanding world with thoughts of and songs to his beloved Blanca. His encomiums of her reach fever pitch in the following stanza:

> ¡Oh BLANCA, BLANCA más que blanca nieve!
> Blanca en la condición, blanda y sencilla;
> Blanca en el alma que en su Dios blanquea;
> Blanca en costumbres, blanca y sin mancilla;
> Blanca en la casta fe que a mí se debe.
> ¿Cuál blanca hay, BLANCA, que tan blanca sea? (368)

> [Oh BLANCA, BLANCA, whiter than snow! White in character, soft and simple; white in soul, which she purifies in her God; white in customs, white and untainted; white in the chaste faith that she owes me. Oh BLANCA, what other white is so white?]

Distasteful as it may be to approach this stanza, approach it one must in order to penetrate the last precincts of the Ordered City. The jarringly unsubtle stanza actually operates rather complexly, if still monologically.

Albár's ode to whiteness quite blatantly recapitulates the Spanish efforts to bleach and sanitize the Indians that have resulted in the effulgent pastoral city purged of all darkness. No less overtly, whiteness bespeaks purity. Albár imputes purity to himself, as one who will not abandon the virtue of the Old World and succumb to the enticements of New World riches or women, but much more so to his wife, Blanca. In a final act of resemblance he posits, and his shepherdess wife's concluding aria reaffirms, that Blanca will continue in the New World to be the same pure woman and faithful wife to him and to Spain that she had been in the Old. As white and pure as the Virgin Mary, Blanca will not go native. She will not surrender to the moral corrosions of tropicalization or to the inconstancies that allegedly characterize those of her sex.

Encomium of Blanca shades into a unique epithalamium, a song to the marriage of Old and New worlds. The epithalamium celebrates the union of a man who will preserve Spanish values in a dawning Mexico with a woman whose purity will cross the seas undiminished, and finally, the exemplary, faithful marriage of viceroy and vicereine. Encomium fuses with epithalamium and in so doing draws a portrait of the companionate marriage advocated by Renaissance thinkers like Vives and Luis de León. If Indians can be "bleached" and incorporated into the order and concert of the all-consuming Renaissance machine, so can women. Salazar's resplendent, apotheosized Blanca, as divested of peril and darkness as the Indians, furnishes a model for the Spanish women who by the end of the sixteenth century had also put down roots in the New World.

In the end, Salazar's idiosyncratic waterworld, a pastoral locus amoenus purged of fearsome depths and ruled by the shimmering, idealized, virginal Blanca, reminds us of nothing so much as Botticelli's *Venus*. We have come full circle to witness the unabashed consummation of the marriage between the sixteenth-century episteme and the Spanish project: the pastoral fully reborn as hegemonic discourse, as a wolf in sheep's clothing, if you will. With this it becomes clear that from start to finish the foregoing chapter has told a neat story, perhaps too neat for comfort or credibility. Yet the story's very neatness reflects the aims of the Ordered City and of the worldview from which it emanates. For, as we have seen, the sixteenth century spares no pains to keep its house in order, to absorb everything into its concert. A world which, in the words of Salazar y Alarcón's poem to Herrera, boasts a mathematics that "entiende / La inmensidad del orbe" [understands the immensity of the orb], a dialectics that "la resolución cierta comprehende" [comprehends the definite resolution], a moral philosophy that supplies "preceptos memorables, / Y reglas justas de costumbres bellas" [memorable precepts, and the just rules for beautiful customs], a physics that "descubre los notables / Secretos de las cosas naturales" (reveals the notable secrets of natural phenomena), and a music that "no consiente dura disonancia" (does not tolerate harsh dissonance) (355) will brook no untidiness. Much as the poetic theatrics of Salazar gesture toward the Baroque and toward the Spectacular City that shatters the cosmic housekeeping of the sixteenth century, the poet, like my narrative and the texts it treats, for the moment remains firmly wedded to the Ordered City.

FIGURE 3. Cristóbal de Villalpando (1639–1714). Central Square of Mexico City, 1695. Oil on canvas. Corsham Court, Wiltshire / The Bridgeman Art Library.

Three   BALBUENA'S "LA GRANDEZA MEXICANA" AND THE ADVENT OF THE SPECTACULAR CITY

> *Bosque ideal que lo real complica*
> *[Ideal forest complicated by reality]*
> RUBÉN DARÍO, *CANTOS DE VIDA Y ESPERANZA*
> [SONGS OF LIFE AND HOPE] (1905)

I. INTRODUCTION: "BOSQUE IDEAL QUE LO REAL COMPLICA"

In the Eighth Eclogue of Bernardo de Balbuena's pastoral novel *Siglo de oro en las selvas de Erífile* [Golden age in the forest of Erífile] (written in 1601, published in Spain in 1608), on his way back from the city to the bucolic forest of Erífile the shepherd Melancio makes a startling discovery. Not far from the road he encounters a cunningly crafted golden globe, an exquisite precursor of Jorge Luis Borges's universe-encompassing "Aleph." Sculpted, utterly implausibly, onto the incredibly small surface of Melancio's globe are *all* the places and things of the world, so throbbing with life that the land itself seems to be giving birth to them at that very moment. With artifice layered upon artifice to the point of vertigo, the top of the globe boasts a portrait of the god of love surrounded by a squadron of nymphs so tiny that they resemble "ants" (160). Some of the nymphs pester the god, others enter a cave. Every so often there suddenly issues from the cave—that is, in this mad *mise en abîme,* from within the cave that lies inside the portrait of Cupid that crowns the microcosmic globe—the "celestial voice" (161) of a god who has never before spoken to humans and who prophetically recounts parts of each person's life. Melancio views the "miraculous globe full of divine secrets" (161) as the golden apple of poetry for which the gods contended. On closer examination the globe proves to be made not of gold but of the metal of workaday cowbells!

His fellow shepherds ultimately concur that, despite its kinship with cowbells, Melancio's wondrous object is "worthy of not being held in rustic hands" (164). The shepherds awkwardly state a truth of epochal proportions and resonance. Although Garcilaso de la Vega's Renaissance eclogues display a certain fondness for objects that depict history such as urns and tapestries, the overwrought textualized objects crafted by Balbuena in *Siglo de oro,* of which the globe is but one, egregiously transgress the natural, limpid, Platonic space of the pastoral. Their wild imbrication and artifice contravene the esthetic and episteme that gird the Renaissance and sustain the Ordered City.

Though an impossible object, Melancio's microcosmic golden globe holds the keys to Balbuena's poetry and to the tropics of place of the incipient Spectacular City. Like the prophetic voice that emanates from Melancio's treasure, his globe itself augurs the advent of the Spectacular City in "La grandeza mexicana" (1604), caught as the incipient Spectacular City is between artifice and nature, the city and the countryside, the human and the divine, token and archetype, the reduced and the infinite, speaking and silence, the real and the ideal. And the object is, as it were, the thing, the early heart of the matter. In "La grandeza mexicana," a paean to mercantile capitalism, textualized objects at once execute and emblematize the disruption of the Renaissance Ordered City. Balbuena's poem traffics specifically in the luxury items endemic in the mercantile environment of seventeenth-century Mexico City. While unequivocally and self-righteously objects per se, Balbuena's fetishized commodities inaugurate the optic and texture of particularity and the overpowering demands of local realities that in his works and in those of subsequent authors will shatter the Ordered City, constitute the Spectacular City, and derail the hegemonic Spanish Baroque. Objects, in short, emerge as the agents of the real that complicate the ideal. They will take us from Melancio's globe (which I challenge anyone to draw) into the particularized world that appears in the visual epigraph to this chapter, Cristóbal de Villalpando's painting.

The Ordered City cleaves to archetypes, containment, knowability, and clarity. The Spectacular City, whether Balbuena's or Villalpando's or those to come, is all about unmanageable complexity. Similarly, to tell the story of the advent of the Spectacular City in Balbuena's paradigmatic poem draws us into a richly complex scenario. As but the second text published in Mexico in the seventeenth century (the first is lost) and as the first Hispanic poem to commit itself deeply to the texture of Mexico City, "La grandeza mexicana" has been acknowledged to represent the birth of "American poetry proper" (Menéndez y Pelayo 57). On the other hand, the degree to which "La grandeza mexicana" and Balbuena's other works resonate with the literary, political, philosophical, and epistemic tides of change asserting themselves at the beginning of the seventeenth century in Mexico City has largely gone unnoticed.[1]

As it carries out this location of Balbuena's works, the present chapter chronicles the crisis of the Ordered City together with the pluralized advent and energies of the Spectacular City. Section II of the chapter follows the trajectory of Balbuena's works from *Siglo de oro* to "La grandeza mexicana." It introduces the 1604 text and charts the emergence in it of the elements of the Spectacular City, particularly as they dovetail with the signature features of Balbuena's power-mongering poem. Section III surveys the breakdown of the Renaissance esthetic of order and harmony and the flailing of the New World Ordered City in the environment of the so-called second life-project of Mexican colonialism (Manrique, "El manierismo" 108). We then turn to the category crises bound up in Balbuena's prescient, fractured text. Sections IV and V delve into the texture of the Spectacular City and of Balbuena's city poem. They bring forth the disruptive particularity and the economically and ideologically driven literary protocols that engender in "La grandeza mexicana" a new New World poetics of the marketplace, which quite literally crowns the newly installed Spectacular City.

In endeavoring to offer an account of the many fascinating, monumental, and often unexplored aspects of "La grandeza mexicana" that bear on the Spectacular City, the chapter ranges over a broad territory. However, one unifying, if consistently destabilizing, strand will carry us through it: objects that speak volumes, shatter paradigms, break history, make imperialism, and in Balbuena's work, derange the Ordered City into the Spectacular City. Or, as the author writes in his epic poem *El Bernardo* (1624), objects whose language can shake "concert" to the point of madness and still hold the visionary poet, who understands it, delightedly in thrall, "a todas horas ocupado en ella" [at all times engrossed in it] (151–152).

II. FROM THE *SELVAS DE ERÍFILE* TO "LA GRANDEZA MEXICANA"

Siglo de oro en las selvas de Erífile inaugurates the literary production of Bernardo de Balbuena (1562–1627) with the mixture of conservatism and foresight that marks all of the author's works. Balbuena's pastoral text sidesteps the novelistic development that Jorge de Montemayor's *Diana* (c. 1559) had introduced fairly recently. Instead of fully devoting itself to telling a story, *Siglo de oro* revels in the incantatory creation of a sensuous, pleasure-filled world, as had earlier examples of the genre such as Jacopo Sannazaro's *Arcadia* (1504; Van Horne, *Balbuena* 144; Goic 383–384). There is more than a touch of desperation in *Siglo de oro*, written in the less-than-lyrical world of actual shepherding and real cowbells that was the Nueva Galicia (Jalisco) in which the radicado Balbuena grew up and from which he ardently wished to escape. The fledgling writer Balbuena undertakes to rescue the ideal by countering a paltry reality with the dreamy pastoral of *Siglo de oro*. Erecting an ideal, noble, fictional world and keeping it defensively running all around him, he indulges in a talismanic narration akin to the spellbinding tales of Scheherazade. In this sense a kind of *Künstlerroman,* from within its backward-looking, anachronistic space *Siglo de oro* tells a new, passionate, and polemical story. Balbuena builds his pastoral novel into a seminal treatise on poetry (Goic 383), one given over to contemplating the synergy of the new and the old and of the ideal and the real that lays the groundwork for the innovative poetics of the Spectacular City.[2]

The learned shepherds of Balbuena's virtual symposium live for poetry. They sing it and read it on tree trunks and luxury objects. And throughout the novel, they debate poetry in lively dialogues. What has become of the Golden Age of bucolic lyric? Are the remote forests of Erífile still the privileged abode of poetry? For some of the shepherds, Erífile remains the consummate poetic space where gods still commune with humankind. For others, it has decayed into a prosaic world contaminated by the real, nitty-gritty work of shepherding, infected with poverty poetic and real, prey to death and dangers. As the shepherds call for Erífile's renewal, they worry through the possibilities of regenerating the forest as a poetic space. Can the forest assimilate new currents? If or as it does, will it cease to be the fount of sublime poetic creation?

The currents invading Erífile are both exogenous and bizarre. Travelers like Melancio return to Erífile from their journeys with stories of "maravillas" (171) that fellow shepherds in the forest receive with frissons of fear and admiration. Even more dramatically, in the remarkable dream vision of *Siglo de oro*'s Fifth and Sixth Eclogues an angel guides the novel's narrator out of Erífile to a lagoon from which materializes "a proud and populous city," "that *Grandeza Mejicana* about which the world says such miraculous things" (132; emphasis added). Among the myriad marvels that appear before the narrator's eyes, an apparition of Mexico City as a Parnassus of students and learning where "the divine sublimity of poetry" (133) comes into its own sanctifies the capital as a source of positive poetic infusions for Erífile. A picture of the strange new poetry to which the forest must adapt comes into focus over the course of the novel. The new poetry will deviate from light songs of pleasure and consolation (173), from the "simplicity and naturalness" of poetry's "golden centuries" (66). It will be more artificial and more robust than Erífile's organic lyric, yet still full of "[a]uthority, valor, mystery, and finery" (214) and never low, comical, or satirical.

In the end, *Siglo de oro* reinvigorates and reclaims Erífile as the site of poetry. The bucolic space having been subjected to scrutiny and alteration, the final two eclogues of the text reconsecrate it. They decide that the renewed forest can indeed assimilate the currents of change and resemble the waters of the fountain from which the novel takes its name, waters described in the opening of *La grandeza mexicana* (I italicize the title when referring specifically to aspects of the text beyond the poem or specifically to the whole text) as a "living figure of human life which, like the fountain, has no resting point" (53). Erífile, in other words, has the ability to conjugate the perpetual motion of a river like Heraclitus's with the eternal Castalian spring of poetry. In a conservative, all-preserving stratagem, Balbuena has resolved that poetry may, but need not necessarily, be bucolic to live up to the sacred space of Erífile. The Golden Age of poetry can still be sited in the woods of Erífile but only after the pastoral space has broken its hermetic seal and regenerated itself, to become the permeable *selva,* or thick forest, that befits a synergistic, ductile poetry. The "selvas de Erífile" will finally live up to their name.

Siglo de oro abundantly alludes to the new poetry. However, the novel itself proffers only conventional Renaissance lyric and, at one point, an excruciating antimodel of poetic innovation, the "tangled verses" screaming with forced rhyme that a denizen of Erífile attributes to a false, female shepherd from the city (213). Rather than poetry, something else pleasingly assaults the "simplicity and naturalness" of Erífile and essentially fronts for the new esthetic the text champions. And that must be the magnificent objects like Melancio's globe in whose description the text delights and for which the shepherds avidly vie in poetry contests. The artifacts may be worthy of other than "rustic hands," but Erífile covets them. They provide a conduit from Erífile to another world, much as the dream vision of the Fifth and Sixth Eclogues renders Mexico City a fellow traveler of the bucolic poetic space. Both the fabulous artifacts housed in Erífile and the fantastical dream vision wending from forest to city introduce the enthusiastic cross-fertilization between nature and artifice that redeems Erífile and that will come to characterize "La grandeza mexicana."

Its forward-looking, regenerative aspects notwithstanding, *Siglo de oro*—no more or less than an enchanting diversion for Balbuena—stands at a significant remove from *La grandeza mexicana*. Monumental fantasy- and paradigm-shaking shifts take place in Balbuena's work when he engages with the city and its power dynamic and as the poet weds them to his personal interests. Balbuena, born in Spain the illegitimate son of a Spaniard and raised by his father in Mexico from an early age, wrote *La grandeza mexicana* from the Mexico City that he worshiped. He had studied there as a youth and perhaps subsequently. After spending years in Guadalajara as chaplain of its Audiencia and then as the priest of the isolated Indian mining town of San Pedro Lagunillas in Jalisco, which he frequently fled, the writer fervently desired to return to the capital permanently ("in Mexico City I am content," he writes in the poem [85]). Ambition for a more distinguished, central post and perhaps for the legitimation such a post entailed integrates the otherwise motley life of the illegitimate Balbuena, later the abbot of Jamaica and bishop of Puerto Rico.

The very genesis and packaging of "La grandeza mexicana," the forty-year-old Balbuena's first published work, reveals the author's anxious pragmatism. Balbuena originally intended the poem as a guide to Mexico City for a friend from Jalisco, the recently widowed Isabel de Tobar, about to take orders in the capital's Convent of San Lorenzo. Eager to publish the poem yet encountering obstacles to its publication, Balbuena elaborately reoriented his work. He deflected its principal addressee from Isabel de Tobar to the recently arrived archbishop of Mexico, García de Mendoza y Zúñiga, and, in a limited edition, to the Count de Lemos, president of the Council of the Indies in Spain.[3] Further, Balbuena embedded the poem in a bundle of texts. The meaningful, if extremely ungainly, full ensemble that is *La grandeza mexicana* includes (1) various short prefatory materials; (2) a poem of praise to the archbishop, incongruously dedicated to yet another personage, the archdeacon of Nueva Galicia; (3) an extensive prose gloss of the poetic elegy to the archbishop; (4) the poem "La grandeza mexicana" itself, which includes an extensive epilogue; and (5) the first outright treatise (as distinct from the novelistic exercises of *Siglo de oro*) on poetry to originate from the New World, the "Compendio apologético en alabanza de la poesía" [Apologetic compendium in praise of poetry]. José Carlos González Boixo remarks on the engorged published work: "doubtless, the use of poetry as social steppingstone explains this type of text" (23). That each component of *La grandeza mexicana,* even the defense of a transcendent Platonic poetry, must simultaneously serve its author and his masters primes the text for the overblown proportions of the Spectacular City that issue from it. Vested in the festive society of the spectacle, an elite and commercialized city, and a wealth-involved wonder, the Spectacular City will now make its debut.

Unlike most of the sixteenth-century works that we have examined thus far, the glossed elegy to Mendoza y Zúñiga and the poem "La grandeza mexicana" (henceforth abbreviated as "Grandeza") draw concrete and esthetic sustenance from a constituent feature of the Spectacular City, an actual and sumptuous festival. The spectacular ceremonial entry of the archbishop into Mexico City had taken place just eight days before Balbuena composed his prefatory materials. As would so many writers treating secular themes in the orthodox seventeenth century, the author opportunistically avails himself of the spectacle as a springboard for publication. Balbuena describes the festival as a "gorgeous theater of beauty" (33), replete with magnificent cloth hangings, arches, commotion, parading horses, music, and finery, and as a "spectacle" that incited the "wonder" [admiración] of the public (14). The author offers "Grandeza" as the poetic equivalent of the recent festival: "Que yo con la Grandeza Mejicana / coronaré tus sienes / de heroicos bienes y de gloria ufana" [for I, with my Grandeza Mexicana, will crown your brow with heroic treasures and proud glory] (16). And with an obtrusive, insufferable fawning, he plays into the power mongering that underwrites the spectacular festival. Balbuena's short poem to the archbishop and the exorbitant gloss that unpacks the elegy's hidden meanings in a truly virtuoso performance tender the most fulsome praise of their addressee. No less unabashedly than in the opening tribute to the archbishop does "Grandeza" go on to pay homage to the Spanish empire and its viceregal representatives. The poem devotes a full two of its nine chapters (7, 8) to the exaltation of church and state, disingenuously asking which is more admirable, and rounds off its would-be compact epilogue with a distended paean to Spain and to empire. Just two years later Balbuena set sail for Spain to petition for a better position in Mexico. *Grandeza* had paved his way.

If "Grandeza" extols the empire and its power brokers in no uncertain terms, it principally magnifies one of the Spanish empire's most illustrious New World cities, Mexico City, in truly spectacular fashion. The poem's more than two thousand lines, gathered into tercets, inscribe Mexico City in the classical panegyric. As does the traditional panegyric systematically canvass a city, "Grandeza" begins with a panoramic view of the site, or "asiento," of the capital and then broadens out to include in its encyclopedic purview chapters on the origins and greatness of the city, its elegant streets and customs, elevated culture and occupations, many recreations, pastoral beauty, illustrious government, and impressive religious and state institutions. Upon reaching the end of its totalizing survey, the poem actually restarts with an "Epílogo" that professes to revisit, in a "cifrado" (113), or condensed, form all the topics of the poem.

The fabulous exhibitionism of "Grandeza" that motivates the excessive epilogue and mirrors the theatrics of the festival also determines the rhetorical system of the poem. Balbuena marshals for city representation an elaborate set of inflated, urbane rhetorical devices that he utilizes to the point of tedium: superlative, hyperbole, aporia ("I cannot express"), the *brevitatis formula* ("I'll leave aside"), and synecdoche. Rather than the comparisons of similitude, for example, between Mexico City and Spain or Venice, that domesticated the New World for the Old, "Grandeza" invokes protracted lists of classical and contemporary European cities only to state that Mexico City exceeds them all (a technique known as *sobrepujamiento*).

The Baroque festival parades a city's wealth and eminence. To match the extravagant festival that provided him with a venue for publication, Balbuena composes a poetry of surpassing civic pride. The first apostrophe to Mexico City in the poem—as "centro de perfección, del mundo el quicio" [center of perfection, hinge of the world] (62)—marks the shift from pronounced but balanced Renaissance encomium, such as we saw in Cervantes de Salazar, into hyperbole. Balbuena introduces hyperbole as a rhetorical device in his gloss, saying, "this figure allows one to express the impossible" (20). Indeed, everything in the Mexico City of "Grandeza" is impossibly, hyperbolically, supremely superb. Balbuena, ever the architect of elevated worlds, now frames a sublime city devoid of negative aspects and characterized by "beauty," "nobility," "virtue," and "learning" (93). Its soaring towers fuse with the heavens (72). They share the ascensional dream of Gothic churches rather than the earthbound concerns of crenellated fortresses. For Balbuena, a postheroic climate abounding in all but war (81, 118) gives birth to the capital's heavenly tenor. The heroic world of the previous century cedes to a demilitarized city given over to pleasure, art, and culture. Such delights acquire their nobility and concomitant hyperbole from the humanist poetic tradition in which Balbuena anchors his poetic city, a tradition that regards the imperial city as a center of virtue, pleasure, civilization, and culture (Sabat de Rivers, *Estudios* 52, 75).

Only a sublime and noble poetry, Balbuena's own, suits so spectacular a city. In *Grandeza*'s "Compendio apologético en alabanza de la poesía," Balbuena expounds upon poetry at length, creating a treatise far more politicized and excessive than that of *Siglo de oro*. The "Compendio" justifies poetry as an activity appropriate to an imperial city and worthy of Balbuena's involvement, clergyman that he is: "My poetry, heroic and dignified in style, will treat the most noble, rich and populous city of this new America" (146). As Luis de Góngora y Argote (1561-1627, almost Balbuena's exact contemporary) did for the Hapsburg empire, Balbuena advocates an elevated poetic discourse of "dignity, honesty, sublimity and spirit" (145). Also like Góngora, Balbuena proudly gears his poetry to an elite audience: "may it succeed in satisfying the tastes of the cultivated reader, for whom it was devised" (6). Elitism goes hand in hand with the omnivorous erudition that Balbuena prescribes for poets and that he himself wastes no opportunity to display. The pedantic "Compendio" weaves together defenses of poetry by a vast parade of classical and contemporary authorities; the gloss contains approximately 159 references to authors or texts (Van Horne, *Balbuena* 124). Balbuena here steps into the lineage, seeded by Cervantes de Salazar, of the colonial intellectual who flaunts his or her erudition and exploits it as a vehicle for social mobility. At the same time, Balbuena raises the bar for erudition. He opens the new century with the overloaded pedantry that will reign supreme and run amok over at least the next one hundred years.

Erudition, authority, elitism, and nobility all conspire in Balbuena's larger project for the sublime city and for Mexico City per se. Again purposefully or not advancing Cervantes de Salazar's agenda, as a fulcrum of his civic pride Balbuena advertises and promotes the coming into culture of the New World. *Grandeza* repeatedly proves the dream vision that appeared in *Siglo de oro,* of Mexico City as a center of learning, to be a magnificent reality. Numerous passages in "Grandeza" confirm that as a mecca of education and the arts the city has achieved the heights of "Parnassus" (35), that poetry "must be something of a heavenly influence or particular constellation of this city, given how generally and felicitously its noble youth practice it" (36). With a nod to the Mirror for Princes, Balbuena urges the archbishop to support the cultivation of learning (22) as well as poets. Then in the "Compendio" Balbuena makes a stunning, self-serving case for the lyric as the prime mover of civilization (127), which case goes so far as to imply that the sublime properties of poetry have superseded proselytizing or religion as a tool for civilizing the barbaric New World (129). Less audaciously but equally incongruously, Balbuena rehabilitates an often-maligned writerly element of Mexico City, the notaries whose "gran legalidad" [great lawfulness] and "plumas y manos / llenas de fe" [pens and hands full of faith] (103) he acclaims. We see that "Grandeza"'s sublime city embraces the ciudad letrada, ennobling its bureaucratic elitism.

The poet's surprising absorption of the businesslike ciudad letrada into the divinely erudite city gestures toward the regeneration of commercial enterprise that constitutes the most unique aspect of "Grandeza"'s festival-allied civic pride. Balbuena's obsessive insistence on what he calls "interés"—a combination of mercantile dealings, self-interest, greed, and materialism—highlights its nature as a signature element that distinguishes his text from all others, including his own previous works.[4] Cervantes de Salazar set up the university as the antithesis of and antidote to materialism ("New Spain, hitherto known for its supply of silver, will be celebrated among other nations in the future for the multitude of its learned men" [36]). Throughout "Grandeza" Balbuena labors to dissolve such damning oppositions, anathema to the commercial, practical mindset he displays in reports on Jamaica and Puerto Rico (Van Horne, "Documentos") and injurious to his commercially alive Mexico City. He converts "Grandeza" into a hearty defense of the interés that the poet dubs the "señor de las naciones" [sovereign of nations] (70).

In a pathbreaking article that takes its title from the phrase just cited, Luis Íñigo Madrigal charts the theme of interés in "Grandeza" and establishes that Balbuena's defense of materialism flies in the face of emphatically negative classical, biblical, and contemporary treatments of the theme.[5] Challenging so weighty a tradition and playing to Spain's need for New World wealth, Balbuena sweepingly states, "que ya cuanto se trata y se pratica / es interés de un modo o de otro modo" [for now all dealings and practices involve interés in one way or another] (65). He tweaks interés into the battery of the New World, the improbable source of all of Mexico's positive aspects. "Grandeza" attributes to avid materialism the civilizing of the Indians (55); the wealth that produces every kind of pleasure, art, and virtuous charity; the nobility, splendor, and superiority of the viceregal capital to European cities; and so on. Balbuena skews chapter 1 of the poem, "De la famosa México el asiento" [About the site of the famous Mexico City], away from the traditional panegyric discussion of topography into a full-blown paean to interés that broaches many of the preceding themes. Despite the chapter's title, it barely touches on the city's physical location, for what Balbuena wants is to project the capital's location in the nascent capitalist order. And if, as subsequent pages of my chapter attest, materialism impacts almost every aspect of Balbuena's new Spectacular City, according to the poet the "concert" of the city, or maybe of civilization itself, now also depends on it: "Quitad a este gigante el señorío / y las leyes que ha impuesto a los mortales; / volveréis su concierto en desvarío" [strip this giant of its sovereignty and of the laws it has imposed on mortals and you will turn their concert into madness] (67).

The mercantilism Balbuena iconoclastically rehabilitates also begets the amazing commodities, from silks to foodstuffs to art objects, that populate Balbuena's literary Mexico City more palpably and conspicuously than people.[6] As a corollary to his reimagining of interés and extending the proclivity for objects found in *Siglo de oro,* Balbuena now purveys commercial goods as positive, sublime, and pleasurable. The poet, who seems often to polemicize earlier texts written on and in New Spain, recuperates as totemic objects the fabulous "counterfeits" that inspired Cortés's agitated fascination. Balbuena salutes the artisans of gold, sculptors, and painters who "consuelan / con sus primores los curiosos ojos / y en contrahacer el mundo se desvelan" [whose artistry consoles curious eyes and who labor without sleep to create counterfeits of the world] (66). Even religion appears largely as a mere spur for ornate ecclesiastical buildings, altars, vestments, and jewels (Domínguez xxx).

These proliferating material artifacts saturate "Grandeza" with a special form of wonder, the final key element of the Spectacular City. In its first chapter, in one breath, the poem promises to deliver the city's "strange things" and "wealth" (63). Balbuena's association of wonder and wealth leaves no doubt that, distinct from the sixteenth-century texts examined earlier, "Grandeza" deals less with the Renaissance emotion of *admiratio,* or "wonder reaction" (Bynum 5), than with wonders-as-objects (though wonder-as-object generally produces the wonder reaction).[7] As the poet's personal taste for extreme objects teams up with colonial writers' involvement in anatomizing and vaunting their reality to imperial powers, "Grandeza" leaves behind Oviedo's sensationalizing, boxed-in collection of natural exotica to become a living, vibrant, infinite wonder cabinet bursting with every conceivable sort of civilized pleasure, treasure, and marvel. Qua wonder cabinet, Balbuena's collection poem equates material objects to all of the cultural capital that *Grandeza* so ostentatiously promotes under the auspices of civic pride.

Stockrooms of capital real and symbolic, the actual wonder cabinets of the seventeenth century orchestrate and consolidate the picture of *Grandeza* that I have been building. In the privately owned *Wunderkammern,* precursors of modern museums, aristocrats amassed precious artifacts, including exotica. By the seventeenth century, cabinets of curiosities formed the "nodes of a thickly cross-hatched network" (Daston and Park 265). Diverse in function, wonder cabinets could operate as a laboratory for knowledge (a gathering place for scholars), a treasury (*Schatzkammer*), a locus for commercial dealings with merchants who supplied collectors with marvels from abroad, and a tool of statecraft intended to impress visitors with the owner's wealth and refined sensibility.[8] Each of these functions of the wonder cabinet—a public-pleasing exhibition as spectacular in its own way as the festival but permanent and always available—patently obtains in *Grandeza* as it memorializes the archbishop's ceremonial entry into the city.

Moreover, even the more hidden, personal designs of Balbuena for himself and his poem find their model in the wonder cabinet. For early modern Europeans collecting was a form of self-fashioning. To assemble a collection was to produce a personal identity, to estheticize and reify the self for public consumption. Lorraine Daston and Katharine Park maintain that from the Middle Ages onward wonder cabinets "were partly constitutive of what it meant to be a cultural elite in Europe" (19). Collected objects, "semiophores" divorced from their context and emptied of use value, gained exchange value as signs of their owner's connoisseurship and nobility.[9] In mounting his collection poem, the illegitimate, aspiring, supplicant Balbuena seeks the prestige entailed in the wonder cabinet. The poet eager to cut a large image on the scene becomes one more aristocratic, sublime object in his own museum, dwelling place of the Muses, *and* the aggregate of it.

III. LIMINALITY AND METAMORPHOSES

Early modern European wonder cabinets had their radar trained on the new. By virtue of the objects from far and wide that they assembled, wonder cabinets appropriated novelty and domesticated it. The later years of the Renaissance witnessed a shift in these barometers of change. Wonder cabinet collectors began to prize intricate objects that bore a remarkable similarity to Melancio's fanciful golden globe—objects that were the quintessence of artifice or that breached the boundaries between the natural and the artificial.[10] Collections, in other words, had begun to register the breakdown of the nature-oriented Renaissance esthetic that took place in Europe by the first half of the sixteenth century, and, as is less well known but equally important, in Mexico by the final quarter of the century. I refer to the liminal period and esthetic commonly, if loosely, designated as Mannerist.

I use the vexed, amorphous term "Mannerism" here, first, to denote the esthetic generally associated with the movement, including a penchant for experimentation, individualism, iconoclasm, disproportion, stylization, the abstruse, and the artificial. More broadly, I especially have in mind Arnold Hauser's understanding of the period as the crisis of the Renaissance, motivated in no small part by the burgeoning of capitalism. Hauser emphasizes that the rigid, confining lines of classicism and their consubstantial illusion of total knowability, which, as we saw in chapter 2, the Renaissance advocated and zealously safeguarded, could not hold. Too constraining to endure, they had to give way. Putting aside Hauser's problematic claims that historical Mannerism extends to the end of the seventeenth century and instead identifying the movement with the earliest shattering of a vulnerable Renaissance esthetic, one can embrace the German critic's valuable construction of Mannerism as a liminal period reacting against classicism. In essence, says Hauser, Mannerism perpetrates the "dethronement of aesthetic doctrines based on the principles of order, proportion, balance, of economy of means" (3). To identify Mannerism as an inaugural, transitional moment primarily devoted to dismantling actually lends more credence to Hauser's own axiomatic contentions that the essence of the movement resides in "the union of apparently irreconcilable opposites" (12), in paradox, and in the tension between classicisim and anticlassicism, traditionalism and innovation. Such indefinition could no more easily hold over the full course of the seventeenth century than could the hyperdefined classicism of the Renaissance.

For our purposes, the beauty of Hauser's sense of Mannerism and the beauty of Mannerism itself particularly lie in their shared, kinetic unseizability, their "opposition to the principles of order, proportion, and subservience to rules" (9). In this regard, Claude-Gilbert Dubois equates Mannerism both with the decomposition of unitary, centralized regimes and with the conflicted subjectivity of individuals marginalized by these regimes.[11] Mannerist minority writers and painters, Dubois argues, utilize intense stylization to voice and veil their distance from the dominant model (182–183). Undermining orderly definitions and order itself in ways that Dubois and Hauser together suggest, the conflicted, threshold Mannerist moment in Mexico to which we now turn harbors the breakdown of the way of life and esthetic of the colonial Ordered City, and the attendant schizophrenic impulses of "Grandeza."

During the final twenty years of the sixteenth century, colonial Mexico City was in the throes of transition to what the Mexican historian Jorge Alberto Manrique calls its "second life-project" ("El manierismo" 108), a transition accompanied by crises. The watershed period witnessed the demise of the militarized New Spain of the conquest and, in the postheroic climate that "Grandeza" celebrates, a string of momentous changes. The city had become the focal point of the viceroyalty, by 1580 housing approximately 26 percent of its Hispanic population (and 41 percent by 1630 [Hardoy and Aranovich 193]). The private encomienda system was giving way to the consigned Indian labor for the state that creoles bemoaned and to the large haciendas of outlying regions. Abuses of Indian labor and virulent disease, most recently the plagues of the 1570s and late 1590s, had reduced the native population to its nadir, from an estimated 6,300,000 in 1548 to about 1,075,000 at the end of the century (Phelan 92). With the decline in the labor force came a diminishing of the tribute and metal production that the beleaguered Spanish empire needed more acutely than ever.

Spiritually as well as economically, Mexico City was undergoing a crisis and paradigm shift. In his *Historia eclesiástica indiana* [Ecclesiastic history of the Indies] (written between 1595 and 1596, published in 1830) the Franciscan Gerónimo de Mendieta terms the era between the arrival of the first Franciscans in 1524 and the death of Viceroy Luis de Velasco the Elder in 1564 as the "Golden Age of the Indian Church" and 1564–1596 as the "time of troubles" for the new Church (Phelan chap. 4; Bacigalupo chap. 1). Over the course of the time of troubles, the viceregal government found itself increasingly at odds with the Franciscans and sought to limit their power along with that of the other original Mendicant orders, the Augustinians and Dominicans. These orders' common concern with fair treatment of the Indians ran counter to the exigencies of imperialism. The militant asceticism of the Franciscans, who personified the spirit of the Spanish Reformation, particularly rankled the state. And then, in 1572, the Company of Jesus entered Mexico City.

No single contextual issue holds greater import for the installation of a real or abstract Spectacular City in Mexico—and arguably for viceregal culture at large—than the sea change in this period from the Mendicant to the Jesuit orders that had fully made itself felt by 1604, the year of Mendieta's death and of *Grandeza*'s publication (see Lafaye chap. 5). The Jesuit presence instituted or at least accompanied a shift from the Reformation to the Counter-Reformation that transfigured a swath of Mexico City's aspects. As the Jesuits gained force, the Mendicants' devotion to proselytizing and to the Indians, their aspirations to establish in the New World a City of God or millennial kingdom that revived the pure foundational golden age of the Church, and their characteristic austerity, which had imprinted the city with the monumental architectural Forms elegized by Cervantes de Salazar, all slowly fell away.

In the place of these defining aspects of colonial Mexico's first lifeproject, the more worldly world of the Jesuits gradually achieved preeminence in the city.[12] The pragmatic Jesuits cultivated rather than scorned wealth, in their extensive commercial dealings in the New World and with the Orient (to which James Clavell's blockbuster novel *Shogun* attests), in the haciendas and company stores they held, in their courting of rich patrons, and in the great fortunes that the order managed. The Jesuits' wealth and ethos reoriented religious architecture, exterior and interior, toward ornament and display. Jesuit extravagance also fed a theatrics of seduction that included an emotional, dramatic iconography; emphasis on the supernatural marvelous; an elaborate ceremonial manifested in the sumptuous festivals that confraternities were formed to support; and actual theatrical productions. The geometric and segregated Ordered City remained in place but now served as the backdrop for the spectacularly theatrical city that Archbishop Mendoza y Zúñiga's ceremonial entry in 1604 epitomized.

Perhaps most pivotal of all, for the enduring consequences to which their activities gave rise, the Jesuits educated the wealthy creole youth who found themselves at loose ends in the postconquest period. Known no less for their excellent schools than for their adeptness in infiltrating the local milieu, the Jesuits quickly recognized the potential of the creoles as a source of revenue and as an emerging sector ripe for interpellation into their imperial mission. The Company of Jesus therefore almost immediately upon arrival in Mexico constructed for creole youths the Colegio de San Pedro y San Pablo, which by 1576 had a permanent home and the title of Colegio Máximo de San Pedro y San Pablo. Other educational institutions in Mexico City and Puebla, such as the boarding school of San Ildefonso in the capital, soon followed. In 1604 the creole Baltasar Dorantes de Carranza gives thanks to the Jesuits as gifts from heaven who rescued his compatriots from "the thousand disgraces that ignorance and the laxness with which they were raised occasioned" (104). Jesuit-trained creole youths, increasingly divested of the encomiendas that their conqueror fathers had enjoyed and generally shut out of the higher reaches of civil government, were able to rise to prominence in the order's ranks. The Jesuits fomented not just a unique social mobility but also the class consciousness and pride of the creoles. By the turn of the century the Jesuits Antonio Rubio (teacher of the creole apologist Juan de Cárdenas)[13] and Pedro de Hortigosa advocated a republic directed by a Spanish and creole aristocracy supported by Indian labor (Bacigalupo 86).

The Jesuit schools came to rival in curriculum and power the University of Mexico that we toured via Cervantes de Salazar in chapter 2. The development of humanism in Mexico at this point takes a significant turn away from the university, whose curriculum had congealed into the conservative scholastic lines that persisted throughout the seventeenth century. Prior to the arrival of the Jesuits, Cervantes de Salazar and his successor, interestingly, were the last professors of humanist letters in the increasingly orthodox university (Jacobsen 118). The broad, worldly, humanist curriculum of the Jesuits, called the Ratio Studiorum [Plan of studies], filled the void. Following St. Ignatius's affirmation in his *Spiritual Exercises* that one can find God "in the world," the minutely prescriptive Jesuit curriculum, with its 467 rules, incorporated the study of pagan classics into literature, philosophy, history, rhetoric, natural history, and so on (Gonzalbo Aizpuru 135).[14] Shortly after their arrival, for example, the Jesuits asked the viceroy's permission to print selections from works by Ovid, Cicero, Vives, and Virgil (including the pastoral *Georgics*) for use in their colleges (Gallegos Rocafull 211). In sum, by 1599, when the Ratio Studiorum reached definitive form, some 270 Jesuits had settled in New Spain, the Colegio Máximo in Mexico City boasted more than 700 extern students and the boarding school of

San Ildefonso more than 100. As Jerome V. Jacobsen concludes, "a true center for the spread of humanistic education had been built in the capital" (230).

Under the tutelage of the Jesuits, influenced by currents arriving from abroad, and at the crossroads of the second phase of Mexican colonialism, creoles began to enact a literary and artistic Mannerism in New Spain. It is an exciting, pregnant moment and avant-garde movement whose literary bravura we have already begun to sample in the operatic "Bucólica" of the radicado Eugenio de Salazar y Alarcón. Salazar's poem taps into an esthetic that, again according to the work of Manrique, emanated from local circumstances and pertained more properly to creole than to radicado writers. Manrique convincingly parallels the state of crisis in Counter-Reformation Europe that gave birth to its Mannerism with the late sixteenth-century "crisis of New Spain" (*Manierismo* 60) that we have just surveyed. He records an influx of European Mannerist artists, architects, and treatises such as Sebastiano Serlio's *Tutte l'opere d'architettura et prospectiva* [The complete works on architecture and perspective] into Mexico during the late 1500s and argues that the Mannerist sensibility easily took root in the troubled, transitional climate of New Spain.[15] Manrique imputes the inception in Mexico City of the pronouncedly secular and urban Mannerism to Jesuit-trained creole youths "anxious to be au courant in literature, culture and art" ("El manierismo" 110), who sought "in refined culture a substitute for their frustrations, a source of pride, the possibility of breaking into civil and ecclesiastic employment, and even a way to find explanations for a world that escaped their comprehension" (*Manierismo* 41). No other esthetic, Manrique asserts, could "more fully suit the concerns and circumstances of men of the times than Mannerism" (*Manierismo* 23).

Mannerism's characteristic foregrounding of the artist's individual imprimatur would appeal to the creole eager to make a mark. Serlio's entrancement with the complexities of perspective suited the embroiled political environment of colonial Mexico. His descriptions of the artifice of stage sets spoke to the increasingly theatrical cast of a state that, among other things, witnessed the installation of the first permanent theaters. Mannerism's other, generally iconoclastic, tendencies no doubt held equal allure for the anxious, disenfranchised creole writers who banded together and made common cause in literary academies.[16] It is not difficult to grant Manrique's assertions or to discern the imprint of Mannerism in passionate, extreme, almost incoherent creole works such as Juan Suárez de Peralta's *Tratado del descubrimiento de las Indias* [Treatise on the discovery of the Indies] (1589) or Dorantes de Carranza's *Sumaria relación de las cosas de la Nueva España* (1604).

The new poetics Balbuena heralded in *Siglo de oro* from Jalisco (be it or not in view of developments in the capital) and both theorized and implemented in *Grandeza* thus did not by any means stand alone as the isolated, idiosyncratic product of a singular mind. The original colonial world of the Ordered City and its initial colonialist esthetic were disintegrating all around him. And Balbuena had his finger on the pulse of the city. His poem evinces a parvenu's excited passion for the cutting edge as it chronicles the newest and best wonders of the city. It mentions local Mannerist artists (81) and Vetruvius (48), the subject of Serlio's treatise. Even the broad picture of "Grandeza" presented above supports the conclusion that characteristics of the newly installed Mannerism, including the penchant for novelty, disproportion, and iconoclasm, and for the abstruse and the artificial, had made their way into the poem.

Yet what most consummately renders "Grandeza" paradigmatic of its transitional Mannerist moment is the poem's profound, multidimensional involvement with liminality per se.[17] Digging more deeply into the poem, one discovers that "Grandeza" mediates extensively, intricately, and jaggedly between inimical elements, situating itself in the space of tension and category crisis. It thematizes metamorphosis and extols artifice, standard bearers of change. "Grandeza" struggles to preserve pieces of the still-enticing Ordered City, to make it as synergistic as the forest of Erífile. And yet, the poem dismembers the harmonious, univocal esthetic of the Ordered City. Thematically and discursively, in short, "Grandeza" dramatizes the breakdown of the Ordered City and the labored advent of the new. While Balbuena refers to an assortment of "monstrous" phenomena in "Grandeza," his poem ends up as the most monstrous phenomenon of all. It thrashes about like a furious monster and, in keeping with the seventeenth-century sense of the word, remains monstrously Janus-faced, an embodiment of the civil war between the entrenched and emergent forces that circulated in the poet's milieu.

Fitting to its changing context, the first classical text Balbuena cites in the protean *Grandeza* is Ovid's *Metamorphoses* (26). The *Metamorphoses* figures prominently in seventeenth-century European culture and in a surprising array of New World texts, from the Olympian *Grandeza* to scatological works such as Mateo Rosas de Oquendo's poetic satire of Peru in 1598. Ovid's works play the role of Hermes for the late early modern period.[18] They serve as guides between the past and the present and thus as mediators of change. They preside over the pluralized spaces that, as Renaissance humanism progressed, increasingly attempted to span nature and art, science and myth, the religious and the secular.

For its part, "Grandeza" introduces Ovid to New World literature in the poem's fascination with the artifice that represents the heights of civilization attained by Mexico City as well as the *nec plus ultra* of modernity. Like the wonder cabinet objects of the times, which themselves drew inspiration from the *Metamorphoses*,[19] "Grandeza" thrills to things artificial and/or metamorphosed from nature. The poem's fourth chapter, "Letras, virtudes, y variedad de oficios" [Learning, virtues, and variety of occupations], presents a veritable ode to both as it pays tribute to the "inventions and diverse artifices" (81) of the skilled workmen, artisans, and artists who transform metals into utilitarian objects and elaborate artifacts. An unlikely lyric subject, the "fragua," or forge, enters the poetic world as its new icon, appropriate to the *Metamorphoses,* Mannerism, and capitalism. Chapter 4 of "Grandeza," which features the most complex, anticlassical imagery and syntax of the entire text, launches the new protagonist together with a new modus operandi for poetry.

Often more transparently but still with innovative brio, throughout "Grandeza" the poet fixates on the metamorphosis of nature into the "beautiful artifice" in which art adds "great value" to raw material (82), thus implying that nature comes into its own only when revamped by human ingenuity. Horses decked out in showy livery and pantomiming the combat of bygone days march down the broad city streets as if the proud steeds were nothing more than mannequins born to parade their owner's commerce-begotten wealth on vast runways (82). The *desagüe,* or project to drain the naturally watery landscape of Mexico City, a project which "human ingenuity forges" at the behest of "art" and "desire," has caused the city's lagoon (we remember that Salazar's "Bucólica" had already sanitized it into transparency) now completely to recede and to leave the city "pleasant, illustrious, and wealthy" (67). Another established topic of Mexican nature, the exotic fruits that so captivated sixteenth-century authors, at various points in "Grandeza" appear as prepared food, the analogue of Claude Lévi-Strauss's cooked meat, mark of civilization. In a telling dual metamorphosis worthy of Góngora and with some outrageous punning, fruits become a "mina de conservas rica" [mine rich with preserves] and "metal" (92). Despite the transformation of nature that Balbuena shares with Cervantes de Salazar, this is no longer the Renaissance ideologue's universe, which sought to tame and cleanse the natural native world in and of itself. Rather, Balbuena lavishes attention on human-made objects or possessions that incarnate category crises and liminality. He situates his poem squarely in an empire of *things* that elaborate on, play with, reinvent, and triumph over nature.[20]

In Balbuena's representations of the urban environment, nature fully metamorphoses into the art worthy of the Spectacular City. "Grandeza"'s larger exertions to build an estheticized ideal city, on the other hand, cannot and will not so readily dispense with the nature that traditionally represented a *locus amoenus* and that Salazar y Alarcón's urban pastoral had claimed for the Ordered City. Rather than discard the Renaissance locus amoenus, "Grandeza" enters into tangled, redemptive bargains with it.

One set of bargains involves the countryside. The famous satire of provincial life in chapter 4 of "Grandeza" acerbically scorns the natural home of the pastoral, the countryside that Balbuena struggled to elevate in *Siglo de oro* and from which, as we know, he contrived to flee. "Pueblos chicos y cortos todo es brega, / chisme, murmuración, conseja, contento, / mentira, envidia" [Small villages where everything is strife, gossip, rumors, tall tales, satisfaction, lies, envy] (84): Balbuena portrays life in the countryside as an exile from the paradise of the city, a fall from grace visited upon individuals poor in resources and thus, given Balbuena's belief that material poverty equals spiritual poverty (28), lacking in virtue. Only horses truly need the countryside, but even they suffer indignities there (84). With these pronouncements, the only crass interlude in the poem, Balbuena passes a harsh judgment on the countryside. It is perhaps too harsh a judgment to suit his ulterior purposes. To avoid offending the archdeacon of Nueva Galicia or to avoid entirely demolishing the pastoral in its own territory, Balbuena appends to his satire a caveat laden with Mannerist code words. He grudgingly concedes that the countryside can contain generous individuals and some sweet flowers, but they are "bizarre influences," "miracles," "extraordinary," "a monster" (84). Balbuena, who has become a city writer, here avails himself of a cosmopolitan, avant-garde lexicon to keep somewhat intact the Renaissance pastoral that he himself had previously championed.

Scholars rightfully see in Balbuena's satire of the countryside an inversion of the Spanish Golden Age topic of "menosprecio de la corte, alabanza de la aldea" [disdain of the court and praise of the village] (Van Horne, *Balbuena* 131; Sabat de Rivers, *Estudios* 76). Nevertheless, the binary framework of the topic, or any neat binary, obscures what I consider to be the trademark of Balbuena's poem. And that is how, in the effort to construct a truly sublime space and its equivalent elite discourse, "Grandeza" dissolves oppositions and ruptures boundaries by importing pastoral topics into the city. *Siglo de oro* had a vision of the city briefly infiltrate the countryside that proved capable of accommodating it; Salazar y Alarcón's "Bucólica" cavalierly mutated the Ordered City wholesale into a pastoral landscape; the liminal "Grandeza" preserves its precursor's thrusting of the city toward the pastoral but commits itself to the representation of the city. Balbuena's urban pastoral venerates and reinflects the noble, ideal, entrenched mode of the Ordered City—first of all by deploying nature as the principal source of metaphor or simile for the city. Women are the city's flowers, the convents its gardens or "paradise," its varied way of life a twining ivy vine.[21] Virgil appears in "Grandeza" writing not pastoral poetry but the history of the capital's city council (103)!

Bending natural imagery to city representation feeds into "Grandeza"'s ambitious project for the urban pastoral of arrogating the exact pleasures associated with the locus amoenus unto the capital, now a "beautiful garden" (100), "delightful place" (88), "kingdom of contentment" (93), "mother of pleasure" (73). To make the city a locus amoenus while still (unlike Salazar y Alarcón's "Bucólica") keeping it unambiguously a city involves some striking, strained maneuvers. "Grandeza" conspicuously transports Luis de León's prototypically Renaissance, neostoical "vida retirada" [reclusive life] (from the poem of that title, 2:742) into the inimical world of "mundanal ruido" [the world's noise].[22] The agitated city of "Grandeza" dissolves into a "repository of good, untroubled by evil" (85) thanks to the infinite pleasures it offers, pleasures that anyone with money can enjoy with "honest living, reserved conduct" (89).

This virtuoso juggling act from chapter 5 meets its match or its breaking point in the explicitly pastoral chapter 6, "Primavera inmortal y sus indicios" [Immortal spring and its signs], oddly enough now the most anthologized chapter of the city-centered "Grandeza." Chapter 6 slips from the previous chapter's perfected but recognizably real Mexico City into an ideal pastoral space, a world of natural abundance and pleasure. As a slew of pastoral topics, including romping nymphs, tumble onto the scene, a basic question forms in the reader's mind. Where on earth or in Mexico does the pastoral activity depicted in the chapter take place? If on earth, the poet's previous disparagement of the countryside would rule it out as the seat of such unmitigated pleasures. Balbuena anchors chapter 6 in the time of spring and in the gentle climate that unites all Mexico, but in terms of space he makes only vague references to the "contorno mexicano" (95) [outskirts of Mexico City] and to a "real jardín" [royal garden] (99). Hence it appears that the nymph-ridden pastoral idyll does purport to occur in the real world of Mexico, in a domesticated nature and an exurban space that, like Salazar y Alacón's, becomes coterminous with Mexico City. Yet where the allegorical "Bucólica" draws the line at equating the bucolic countryside with the city, Balbuena infuses the city itself with pastoral attributes. Further, the Arcadian interlude of chapter 6 disturbs the pastoral by comparing its royal garden to those of Cyprus, a famed commercial center.

Seeing the Arcadian space adulterated, seeing it revamped into an exurbia (which, for its part, stands in for Mexico City), and seeing nymphs lay claim to a real existence, one realizes that Balbuena has pushed interchangeability and plausibility to the limits, to the brink of catachresis and incoherence. In devising a consummate pastoral space, he has written himself into a corner and incurred paradoxes that put stress even on an inherently kinetic Mannerism. When, toward the end of chapter 6, Balbuena describes the waves of the pastoral pool in which the nymphs bathe as "espejos quebrados alteradas" [broken altered mirrors], we therefore recognize that the line perfectly enunciates his liminal poetics. It beautifully captures Balbuena's break with the transparent, mirrorlike Ordered City together with his straining of Renaissance pastoral topics as they are forcibly lodged in the Spectacular City.

Balbuena, it is clear, is constantly involved in convoluted, staggering, almost self-defeating negotiations between nature and culture, city and countryside. What, if anything, tempers the schizophrenia of his discourse is the gold that permeates "Grandeza." Golden rooftops,[23] golden jewelry, golden coins, gold-encrusted liveries and clothing, gilded artifacts: now like Borges's "Zahir" rather than his "Aleph," gold is everywhere and everything in "Grandeza." Gold is the city and the countryside. It naturalizes the city into a pleasure world tantamount to the pastoral universe: "¿Quién con dineros / halló a su gusto estorbo ni intervalo?" [Who, having money, ever found his pleasure obstructed or interrupted?] (83). Gold bridges nature and culture. Whereas Bernal Díaz shows Cortés melting the troubling Aztec artifacts back into pure gold (203, 248), doggedly reclaiming gold for nature, Balbuena accentuates the infinite alchemy or lability of gold that can metamorphose nature into any kind of artifice. Golden is the luminous esthetic of the Renaissance and of Mannerism, with its taste for the artificial, extreme, and marvelous. Finally, despite its potential for corruption in the hands of greedy individuals, gold can represent for Balbuena, as it did for the Baroque in general, incorruptibility, divine wisdom through association with Solomon's mines, and the purity of God (Vargaslugo 109) that bathes the wealthy, mercantile city in a sublime, celestial nimbus.

The category-spanning, crisis-salving properties of a conceivably divine gold return us to Ovid and to the metamorphoses that Mexico City experienced at the end of the sixteenth century. Balbuena's first mention of Ovid relocates to contemporary Mexico City the Roman poet's idyllic and uncorrupted age of gold, which in Hesiod and in the *Metamorphoses* actually preceded the formation of cities. The New World poet writes, "When Ovid depicts the age of gold in his first Metamorphosis, he endows it with the same felicity that the arrival of your Most Reverend Lordship promises for this city" (26). This adulatory flourish, it turns out, signals the reterritorializing of more than Ovid's Golden Age. It signals the reconstruction of the Franciscans' golden age or millennial kingdom that "Grandeza"'s urban pastoral effectively accomplishes. Jacques Lafaye observes that Balbuena's pastoral chapter 6 "explicitly laid the foundations of a new Mexican utopia, called to replace the evangelical utopia of the *Iglesia Indiana,* which had collapsed" (54). Lafaye also notes that "Grandeza" describes a luxury society "whose tastes and aspirations had nothing in common with the militant asceticism of a Motolinía or his ideal of charity" (52).

Combining and polemicizing Lafaye's statements, I would say that the utopia of "Grandeza" has everything to do with *both* luxury and the collapsed original religious mission. The Jesuits' worldliness had demonstrated that luxury and spirituality could go hand in hand. Similarly, the category-conflating "Grandeza" undoes the antagonism between the pure City of God and the earthly city of Mammon that impelled the Franciscan millennial project—and redeems the materialistic city of Mammon. "Grandeza" lays out and ennobles a secular, materialist agenda based on interés that folds the sublime City of God into the city of Mammon attractive to the poet and to the Jesuits. Balbuena's urban pastoral, still nostalgic for a golden age past like that which his own *Siglo de oro* commemorated and revitalized, inescapably attracted to the Ideal, sings a swan song of the defunct Franciscan dream that absorbs its millennial utopia into a park, a city, a mercantile world. The urban pastoral of "Grandeza" wraps the pastoral golden age into the imperial age of gold. It builds a new, capitalist golden age, predicated on a literalized, all-emollient gold: "Fue la primera edad criada de oro / que sin apremio, con deleite y gusto / y sin leyes la fe se conservaba" [It was the first age created from gold, which, without constraint, with delight and pleasure, and without laws, upheld faith] (Balbuena, quoting Ovid, 26).

A whole band of ecological considerations, in sum, motivates the fracturing of Renaissance topics that patently inscribes "Grandeza" in a Mannerist mode. Nevertheless, multiple features of the poem arguably move beyond the pale of both Renaissance and Mannerist esthetics. "Grandeza"'s spectacularity, excess, elitist language, overburdened erudition, sense of overall design, rampant hyperbole, thick imagery, and at times intensely contorted syntax all overspill Mannerism and ally the poem with the repertoire commonly identified with the Baroque. The mention of Góngora in the "Compendio apologético" (141) and "Grandeza"'s Gongoresque squared metaphors, catachreses, vast verbiage expressing few ideas, lexicon of amazement, *horror vacui,* and wordplay equally betoken the Baroque. When, in the "Compendio," Balbuena prescribes the "delicate and beautiful displacements, the subtle, elegant and new forms of expression," which convey "ordinary and common things" "in a special, extraordinary way" and "extraordinary, new, and difficult things in an ordinary way" (131) that "Grandeza" itself institutes, seventeenth-century or even modern readers strongly sense that they have stepped into a radically new, more-than-Mannerist poetic world. Balbuena himself comments three times on the negative reactions to the poem of early readers who deemed it overly dense and contrived.[24] It appears that, to his dismay, the poetic innovator found himself in the same position as the false, female shepherd whose bizarre lyric Erífile mocked. "Grandeza" may thus present one final leap toward the future and a pointed contradiction that ensues from the oxymoronic urban pastoral. For Balbuena has maneuvered the traditional, natural pastoral universe into a space that rehearses the unparalleled artifice of the Baroque.

Mannerist or Baroque? On the one hand, on the basis of the above features scholars have credited Balbuena with the inception of the Baroque in the New World.[25] Given that the Mexican poet was unlikely to have known anything other than Góngora's early *romances,* if that (Schons 23), several scholars view Balbuena's Baroque as an autonomous and natural outgrowth of the complex, hybrid, restless New World environment. As Ross states, they perceive "in the very excesses and exaggerations of Baroque style the beginnings of an American idiom, a liberation from classical form that reflected the heterogeneity of colonial life" ("Historians" 111). I, too, maintain that Balbuena arrived at his *barroquismo,* or Baroque tendencies, independently and organically, for his proto-Baroque is deeply implicated in the spectacular practices of the viceregal colonial city, practices he avidly assimilates into his poem. Both the grandiose festival that the poem matches and the fierce power dynamics of the city to which the panegyric plays key into and fuel the birth in "Grandeza" of a homegrown Baroque or proto-Baroque that would link up with the Spanish Baroque as it made its way into New Spain in succeeding years of the century. The significance of Balbuena's achievements for colonial culture (no less than for the Spectacular City) cannot be overestimated.

On the other hand, to distinguish between Mannerism and the Baroque is invariably a difficult, if not impossible, call. Hauser, like most scholars, waffles notably on the matter (e.g., 20, 150–152) owing to the fact that in his interpretation both trends came into being simultaneously and "were anti-classical" and "the product of the same spiritual crisis; both expressed what had become an open split between the spiritual and physical values, on the harmony between which the survival of the Renaissance principally depended" (151). Sufficiently challenging in a European context, to differentiate between Mannerism and Baroque becomes an appreciably more formidable task in the colonial New World. Since the New World exhibits "the overlapping of intellectual frameworks and practices drawn from periods that tended to be regarded as organic and successive within the scheme of European history" (Higgins xi), European stylistic categories and periodization rarely obtained wholesale in the colonies.

Art historians of the colonial period have shown a fine sensitivity to the inadequacy of European categories for the New World milieu.[26] For example, in her superb *Art and Time in Mexico* Elizabeth Wilder Weismann asks, "Where else but in Mexico would the term *anástilo* have been seriously used—a category referred to as 'without style,' because it fits into none of the orthodox types?" (4). Somewhat paradoxically, anástilo aptly describes the will to style of "Grandeza," its pronounced, self-conscious performance of not one but a whole panoply of styles. And this imposing, flailing refusal to abide by a single style, I submit, constitutes "Grandeza"'s most portentous break with the Ordered City that labored so mightily to subjugate the New World to European norms and forms, to occlude its plurality and novelty. The anticlassical Mannerist tendencies of "Grandeza" likely metamorphose into an incipient Baroque. They certainly activate the breaking of schemes, binaries, and monolithic constructs or epistemes that is the very motor of the New World Baroque and of the Spectacular City.

IV. THE "ARCHITEXTURE" OF THE SPECTACULAR CITY

The absolutist yet multifaceted Baroque city that Lewis Mumford maps in *The City in History*, a source cited by Angel Rama in *La ciudad letrada*, supplies a blueprint for Balbuena's Spectacular City.[27] According to Mumford, it takes two vantage points to apprehend the topography of the Baroque city. First, an aerial view of the absolutist city reveals a neatly geometric, Apollonian metropolis laid out in broad avenues, an Ordered City. Second, the flâneur's view from the ground, immersed in the broad avenues, discloses the teeming Dionysian particularity of the streets that obscures their clean lines.

This dual focus both encompasses Mumford's Baroque city as a whole and encapsulates his Janus-faced, or "monstrous," concept of the Baroque:

> I long ago chose to use this term [the Baroque city]—originally contemptuous—as one of social description, not of limited architectural reference. The concept of the baroque, as it shaped itself in the seventeenth century, is particularly useful because it holds in itself the two contradictory elements of the age. First the abstract mathematical and methodical side, expressed to perfection in its rigorous street plans, its formal city layouts, and in its geometrically ordered gardens and landscape designs. At the same time . . . it embraces the sensuous, rebellious, extravagant, anti-classical, anti-mechanical side, expressed in its clothes and its sexual life and its crazy statecraft. Between the sixteenth and the nineteenth century, these two elements existed together: sometimes acting separately, sometimes held in tension within a larger whole. (Mumford 351)

It is of no small consequence that instead of incorporating Mumford's comprehensive mix of reason and rebellion against it, Rama's lettered city just centers on the aerial view. That is to say, Rama's lettered city populated with educated individuals subservient to the empire focuses only the hegemonic project of the colonial state. It tacitly accords that project absolute dominance over the colonial world. As commentators have pointed out, Rama does not account for the fact that the ciudad letrada was neither closed nor inviolable (Adorno, "La ciudad letrada" 23).[28]

Balbuena's Mexico City, we know, glorifies empire and absorbs the ciudad letrada. Here it will come into view that Balbuena, himself a proud member of the educated elite, tries to remain faithful to the episteme of the Ordered City, the aerial view, the hegemonic project. However, under the pressures of his own rhapsodic, materialist agenda the entranced flâneur succumbs to the sensuous, extravagant, rebellious side of Mumford's absolutist city. The real destabilizes and complicates the ideal. If despite itself, Balbuena's texturized or "architextural" Mexico City introduces the disruptive energies of particularity "in which architecture rebels against geometry" (to again quote Góngora's *Soledad segunda*) that by the end of the century will fill in the blanks of Rama's ciudad letrada and countervail the Spanish hegemonic project.

"Grandeza"'s conservative romance with the Renaissance, so apparent in its preservation of the Platonically inflected pastoral, assumes the contours of an absolute mania when it comes to the freighted issues of order and concert that had defined sixteenth-century contexts and texts. Time after time Balbuena refers to the order, concert, propriety, harmony, and peace of the city's religious and civil mechanisms and of its physical layout (e.g., 104, 107, 115, 119). As he does, the poet appears to pay homage to his literary precursors. In words that evoke Cervantes de Salazar's, he lauds the providential mission of the conquest. Balbuena writes in the "Introduction," "And once the serpent of idolatry had died ... new men were reborn in the baptismal font, which improved everything, and the city's buildings and streets then grew with such order and rhythm that they seemed to have been planted more by musical concert and harmony than by the plumbs and instruments of architects" (44). Again, one is struck by the intimate complicity between the Renaissance episteme and the conquest, a complicity that continues vigorously to hold fast in Balbuena's peaceful, poetic, self-statedly Pythagorean universe.[29] It could hardly be otherwise. Order and concert were undying desiderata that persisted into the Mannerism of a conflicted universe as what Hauser calls "wish-dreams" (6). Moreover, no apologist for Spain, and certainly not the ambitious Balbuena, could abdicate a position that provided so valuable a moral, philosophical, political, and esthetic basis for the colonial city.

As was the case with *Siglo de oro* but more momentously now, what "Grandeza" declares and what it enacts are two quite different things.

In *Siglo de oro* Balbuena expatiated on the new poetics but only modeled a timeworn Renaissance lyric. The converse occurs in "Grandeza" as it strives to meet the exigencies of representing the imperial city. Balbuena steadfastly and purposefully honors, even mythologizes, the old Ordered City but in fact produces a new, almost chaotic entity because each and every treasure in the wonder cabinet that is Mexico City demands expression. In "Grandeza"'s texturized particularity, or what I call architexture, the architectural, symmetrical chessboard of the Ordered City gives way to a maze that places in crisis the knowability, regulation, and neat definition of the Ordered City. "[Y]o no sé hacer mundos abreviados" [I don't know how to make abbreviated worlds] (114) confesses the poetic narrator of the epilogue: as the "I" verbally traverses the city, he is overwhelmed by the demands of its particularity. So overwhelmed, in fact, is the narrator that he shatters the essentialized Apollonian chessboard lines of the Ordered City with the plethoric Dionysian detail, the overflowing of received containers and containment, that will become a *hallmark of the New World Baroque and a benchmark of the seventeenth-century Spectacular City*. The Spectacular Cities of such texts as *El Carnero* abandon clean architectural lines and get bogged down in a dizzy particularity as they expose the abuses wrought by the viceregal regime in their local milieu. Balbuena, on the other hand, trips over his own imperial agenda and erects the unruly, architextural Spectacular City in an attempt to do justice to the infinite, superlative local realities that represent the glory of the Spanish empire.

The esthetic of the Spectacular City that would mature into an efficacious political tool begins in rhetoric, in the features that constitute "Grandeza"'s stylistics of particularity. Though the poem employs the tercets that are typical of narrative poetry (González Echevarría, "Colonial Lyric" 210), it describes more than it narrates. "Grandeza"'s fleshed-out descriptions (made up of adjectives, verbs, and nouns) themselves commonly degenerate into prolix, unabashed lists of various sorts: extensive comparisons, strings of adjectives or verbs, desiccated *recopilaciones,* or summaries, and chaotic enumerations worthy of Pablo Neruda. No reader of "Grandeza" could fail to notice that the poem has the general look and feel of an inventory, a dimension entirely absent from the pastoral *Siglo de oro*.[30] That chapter titles in "Grandeza" can bear but a tenuous connection to their actual subjects and that the epilogue far overruns its stated mission by introducing a new spate of topics and details further confirm that in "Grandeza" the contents of the urban world have commandeered the poetic word to the detriment of structure. The thick forest or jungle of Erífile has taken root in the city, but there, literally and literarily, one cannot see the forest for the trees.

Balbuena derives unstated but unmistakable authorization for his incorrigible listing from the theme of variety passed down to him by Oviedo and Cervantes de Salazar. The variety on which Balbuena so repeatedly comments is the true spice of life (pun intended, since the poet often associates variety with the infusion of goods from the Orient), now in the city rather than in nature, and to exemplify it occasions numerous inventories (e.g., 64, 66, 80, 107). Variety continues to represent the essence of the New World, but Balbuena cares little about the thorny issues of similitude or diversity that sixteenth-century authors broached under the protection of the humanist commonplace.[31] Rather, he cares inordinately about the things, places, and other phenomena that variety licenses him to detail. Chapter 2 of the poem delivers a near parable of the deconstruction of the Ordered City that in the grip of variety and detail "Grandeza" effects. The poet praises the majesty of the city's gridiron-pattern streets, "a las del ajedrez bien comparadas" [much like those of a chessboard] (70). Yet, rather than stabilizing one who walks through it, the chessboard induces vertigo: "¿Quién, puesta ya la mira en tantos blancos / y los débiles pies en esta altura, / irá sin dar descompasados trancos?" [Who, with sights now trained on so many white squares and weak feet poised on such heights, could walk without wavering?] (71). No longer does the blocked-out city yield an embodied experience of order. Amazed and unhinged by the plethora of the city, the flâneur loses his bearings, his compass.

Painfully aware of his out-of-control, aberrant tendency toward listing, Balbuena undertakes to limit and to take rhetorical ownership of it. At key points in the poem its author attempts to rein in "Grandeza"'s ungovernable particularity by means of what he calls "ciphering," the condensing or summarizing of plethora. The eight lines of the prefatory "Argumento" declare that they summarize both the whole poem and the whole of Mexico City, saying, "todo en este discurso está cifrado" [everything is condensed into this discourse] (59). The epilogue adopts this line as its title and proceeds to heap one reference to ciphering upon another: "¿quién alborota en mí nuevos cuidados / para cifrar lo que cifré primero, / pues todo es cifra y versos limitados?" [who incites me to new worries about condensing what I have already condensed, because everything here is condensed, the verses constricted?] (113–114, also see

6, 91). Though almost ludicrous here, ciphering brings into the poem the fairly recent discoveries of optics and perspective and thus possesses a certain cachet (Rama, "Fundación" 18). Balbuena so foregrounds his ingenious abridgments that they take their place alongside interés as one of the two major innovations that the poem self-consciously premieres and alongside order and concert as another of the poem's major obsessions.

And well they should take that place, for ciphering elicits the tension between a closed (archetypal, ideal, taxonomized, calculable) and an open (excessive, real, uncontainable, incalculable) design that Balbuena's watershed poem, like Mumford's absolutist city, nervously encloses. Balbuena's ciphering tries to camouflage or counteract the disruptive dominion that particularity has on the poem but at times fails and falls into aporia, such as, "Who can quantify the city's wealth . . . ?" (91). It wistfully summons unto "Grandeza" the magic of Melancio's golden globe, capable of abridging the whole universe into a small, manageable object. In the architexture of "Grandeza," however, the act of abridgment is but a compensatory mask, a pre-text, a souvenir from a bygone universe for an urban world that has moved into an infinite new space. As Roberto González Echevarría comments, "*cifrado* may well mean here 'subordinated to a numerological scheme beyond our grasp'" ("Colonial Lyric" 211).

Beyond one's grasp but warranting the closest attention, "Grandeza" stands in stark contrast to sixteenth-century renditions of Mexico City. The discrepancy between "Grandeza"'s detailed insider's representation of the city and Zorita's quantifiable entity, Cervantes de Salazar's airbrushed Forms, Cueva's shallow formulas, and the mythological haze in which Salazar y Alarcón envelops the city could not be more prominent or pungent. Each of the sixteenth-century writers engages with the city in a largely gestural manner and depicts it as a knowable, contained entity. To quote Octavio Paz, "The abstract, limpid form of New Spain's first poetry did not countenance the intrusion of American reality" (*Peras* 13). If Botticelli's *Venus* embodies the sixteenth-century literary city, the busy *Central Square of Mexico City, 1695* by the creole artist Cristóbal de Villalpando, with its more than twelve hundred minute figures (Maza, *Pintor* 168) buying, selling, and parading through the center of the city, conveys Balbuena's intensely texturized poetic world. Firmly tethered not to the pure, abstract Augustinian or Franciscan City of God but to the stuff of the earthly city, "Grandeza" enters a new economy both literary and real.

V. THE POETICS OF THE MARKETPLACE

I do not refer idly or metaphorically to the new economies bound up in "Grandeza." On the contrary: two main aspects of the Mexican economy, its mercantile relations and Indian labor, forcefully impact the text, spurring its paradigmatic innovations. In "Grandeza," the economic circumstances of colonial Mexico and empire reroute the exotic, rupture schemas, redistribute textual energies, and incur charged silences that infuriated later writers. As Balbuena carves out a new New World poetics of the marketplace, the economics of Mexico City derange and divorce "Grandeza" from the Ordered City in equal measure with the flâneur's rapt commitment to the particularity of his immediate surroundings.

Balbuena's love of fabulous objects feeds his portrayal of the Mexican capital as an emporium city, an insatiable consumer of luxury goods from abroad. The panegyrist touts his city as the nucleus of a transnational trade network, a realization of Cervantes de Salazar's once metaphorical image of Mexico as a microcosm of the universe: "En ti [Mexico City] se junta España con la China, / Italia con Japón, y finalmente / un mundo entero en trato" [You join Spain and China, Italy and Japan, and, ultimately, an entire world in trade] (91; see the whole second movement of chapter 2, 90–91). If, as the saying goes, the sun never set on the British empire, for Balbuena it never set on the trading partners of the Spanish empire (78). Balbuena waxes poetic but does not fictionalize. By the turn of the seventeenth century New Spain had indeed become a hub of international commerce, a global city in economic terms. Losing its monopoly on trade with the colonies, in the same year as the publication of "Grandeza" Spain began to curtail Mexico's commercial dealings (Israel 100). The Orient, in which the Jesuits had established several outposts, played a prominent role in those commercial dealings. In Mexico, the poet proclaims, one enjoys "the best of everything that the Orient begets" (91). Perhaps in homage to the Jesuits, surely for its sheen of luxury, the Orient looms large in Balbuena's poem.

From its real connection with the Orient, Balbuena's Mexico City derives an exoticism that breaks with and breaks out of previous containers. Radically distinct from sixteenth-century writers, Balbuena no longer vests the exotic in the Indian or confines it to the Indian zone of the city. Instead of spotlighting the consumerist pleasures of the exotic Indian marketplace, "Grandeza" surveys a series of nameless plazas and inventories their extensive wares (82, 92, 116). Tlatelolco has dropped off the map of shopping venues. In a parallel move, Balbuena resites the exotic in the wonder cabinet commodities, such as those arriving from the Orient, that he lists and lauds. He extends the exotic to the entire emporium city: "Es *toda* una riquísima aduana; / sus plazas una hermosa alcaicería / de sedas, joyas, perlas, oro y grana" [It is *all* a rich customshouse, its plazas a single bazaar with silks, jewels, pearls, gold, and scarlet cloth] (116; emphasis added). The real Orient has at long last completely supplanted Columbus's Indies-as-Orient yet continues to imbue the New World with an aura of exotic "Orientalism."

A seventeenth-century colonialist poet like Balbuena might feel free to decouple the exotic from the Indians because in his mind the native peoples no longer posed so great a threat or challenge as they had in the first life-project of New Spain. As mentioned earlier, by the end of the sixteenth century the Indian population had descended to its nadir and the imperial preoccupation with evangelizing had waned. Balbuena thus hails from a society that had to a considerable degree shifted its sights away from the generally pacified and converted, no longer novel Indian.[32] His wonder cabinet is a postconquest and postethnographic anatomy of a New World city no longer considered to reverberate with hostile otherness. None of this destigmatizing, however, means that *Grandeza* will not textually manage the Indians with great care and complexity. Given the dependence of the imperial economy on the native peoples and the problems with that dependence now making themselves felt, Balbuena's text simultaneously overdetermines and effaces the Indians, sharply provoking writers to come.

As did the segregated city and even more so the *congregaciones*, or dedicated villages (often far from the Indians' original homes), into which the government had begun to move the native peoples between 1593 and 1604 (Brading 288), Balbuena exiles the Indian to the margins of the civilized world and to the bookends of the text. In the prose introduction he refers almost Romantically to the "dreadful image and frightful figure of some savage Indian" from "these ends of the earth" that the conquest has awakened to the "dealings and advantages of human life" (55). Balbuena's opening melodramatics estheticize the Indian, though negatively so, into the wild man or monster, the sometimes specter of the New World on the European scene. In traditional pastoral literature the wild man or monster often disrupts the peaceful forest, and the contrast between the fearsome, violent monster and the environment on which he encroaches serves to accentuate the utopian charms of the pastoral world (see Ryjik; Mujica). Thus, whereas Salazar's utopian "Bucólica" brooked no monsters, only Indians happily bent to their conscripted labor, Balbuena exploits the newly depotentiated Indian as a monster who throws into relief the sublimity of his pastoral, Parnassian Mexico City.

Balbuena returns to the monstrous Indian in the penultimate stanza of the epilogue (124). He caps off the poem's cloying final paean to the Spanish empire, which harps on the vast wealth coming to Spain from the New World, with the infamous reference to the "indio feo" [ugly Indian] who devotes himself to offering the tribute that fills imperial coffers. Invisibly, from one bookend to the other, the Indian has been regenerated from frightening savage to payer of tribute. He is still, in Balbuena's construction, a monster, but now a tame, instrumental one. And what began as tendentious estheticizing ends in wishful, willful fictionalizing in that Balbuena finishes the poem with a chain of interlocking colonialist fictions. He has brought the devastated native population back to life (for, as he says, the plague that decimated them miraculously ceased with the arrival of the new archbishop [26]), set the Indians to offering tribute, set them up as the supporters of a Spanish empire also magically restored to health, and wiped away Spain's faltering monopoly on colonial trade. Spain will now astonishedly welcome ships coming across the Atlantic loaded with tribute goods (122).

The estheticizing, fictionalizing, and exiling of the native peoples that the bookends of *Grandeza* present merely symptomatize the obliteration of the Indian in the body of the poem. Chapter 2 of "Grandeza" declines at length to recount the epic deeds of the conquest and the history of the Indians (68–70). Its indigenous history sublimated, the city appears basically to have been born ex nihilo with the arrival of the Spaniards. Balbuena thus claims for his city the ahistoricity of the pastoral. Following suit and producing another tremendous studied silence, he imports to his urban Arcadia the pastoral's suppression of work, its myths of spontaneous production and leisure. That is to say, although the epilogue of "Grandeza" leaves the fate of the empire resting on the shoulders of the "indio feo," the poem itself never shows the Indian at work. "Grandeza" replaces the narrative of production—labor, history, remembering—with the decontextualized narrative of the collection.[33]

Balbuena's multiplex agendas clash in his staging of the Indian for the wonder cabinet collection that is "Grandeza." On the one hand, imperial economic necessities demand that he have the Indian pay tribute.

On the other, the wondrous pastoral, the festival theme of *Grandeza*, and colonialogic in general require an effacing of the labor force. The body of "Grandeza" chooses the latter course, of commodity fetishism, and erases the material circumstances that produce goods. In so doing, Balbuena follows in the hallowed footsteps of Pedro Mártir de Anglería's *Décadas* (1530). "Grandeza"'s predominantly work-free world perpetuates in the seventeenth century and for the city Mártir's exoticizing vision of the New World as an ideal, pastoral "Golden Age" (42) where the land produces its fruits spontaneously with no need of labor (182). Despite loaded appearances to the contrary, both Balbuena's and Mártir's avatars of the Golden Age ratify not the natural order but the economic and social orders, specifically the exploitative orders of the colonial world.

With regard to the economic and social orders of seventeenth-century Mexico, Enrique Semo argues that New Spain remained in the stage of embryonic or incipient capitalism owing to its dependence on the feudal labor of the Indians. John Beverley, for his part (chap. 3), examines a function of the seventeenth-century pastoral that pertains to "Grandeza," that of keeping visible and vibrant the myth of leisure, or *otium*, in the climate of incipient capitalism, or *negotium*, that the New World fomented. Balbuena's poem masterfully conjugates these two issues. Given its blatant glorification of interés and magnetic attraction to artifice, "Grandeza" does register the work of the merchants, artisans, and artists who execute the Ovidian metamorphoses of nature that the poem's fourth chapter details.[34] Their specialized, remunerated work is worthy of note, worthy of the capitalistic order. Yet the absolutely essential, still feudal work of the Indians remains hidden from view in *Grandeza*, obscured by colonialist representational practices that shroud indigenous labor in the mystique of commodity fetishism.

We are now ready to take a tour of "Grandeza"'s textualized marketplaces, whose nonnative commodities and commodity fetishism demolish the marketing practices of the Ordered City. "Grandeza," we already know, lacks both the Indian marketplace and its attendant management of exoticism through native foodstuffs. Balbuena may eschew Tlatelolco, but his sybaritic sensibility cannot forgo food. In chapter 5 he therefore inventories with surpassing sensorial vivacity the scores of edible delights for sale in unspecified plazas by vendors absent from the textual landscape. What in sixteenth-century works were emphatically native products bearing "outlandish" Nahuatl names, are replaced in Balbuena's non-Indian, international city by European fruits, the quince, apple, peach, and pomegranate (92). Indians do not produce exotica in

"Grandeza"; according to the poem, they do not produce anything at all besides tribute. As "Grandeza" substitutes European for Indian fruits, the foodstuffs that Salazar y Alarcón had already disinfected shed their remaining traces of exoticism. The fruits no longer shout their exotic and erotic (in Roland Barthes's sense) existence. Rather, Balbuena plies them as just another of the many variegated urbane entertainments that the chapter serves up for the readers' delectation.

Although "Grandeza" feeds off sixteenth-century textualized marketplaces and maintains their marriage of colonialist business with pastoral and sensual pleasure, from its postconquest and postethnographic position Balbuena's poem triumphantly disavows the ideological work of earlier textualized marketplaces. Cortés, Cervantes de Salazar, Cueva, and Salazar y Alarcón, all Spanish apologists, had at least accorded Indians the equivocal honor of recognizing them as agents potent enough to warrant delicate negotiations through foodstuff and medicinal herbs. Conversely, Balbuena has not only negatively estheticized, marginalized, and obliterated the Indians with impunity, he has refused even to acknowledge the natives as worthy opponents by troping them in the marketplace. As it breaks the containers that previously held the New World in careful check and redistributes textual energies, "Grandeza" releases the marketplace from its old job of merchandising and marketing otherness. In the mercantile wonder cabinet overflowing with delights edible or otherwise consumable that is "Grandeza"'s Spectacular Mexico City, things, for once, are richly, self-importantly, and militantly *just* things.

The blatant, unadulterated "thingness" of "Grandeza"'s verbal wares equates them ever more closely to actual merchandise and puts them to work for the bona fide marketplace. It stands to reason that textualized marketplaces, be they Balbuena's or others', can serve to advertise merchandise for sale in their real counterparts.[35] "Grandeza" obviously spares no pains in this regard. The work poeticizes, ennobles, and celebrates the merchandise of Mexico City in the inordinate detail that I have discussed and situated vis-à-vis the Spectacular City.

Now, let us consider the fact that "detail" derives from "retail," from the itemized invoice or catalogues of retail ventures (Campbell 183). This fact suggests that mercantilism makes deep inroads into the texture of "Grandeza," ridden as it is with lists, and that "Grandeza" does not limit itself to functioning as a billboard for select articles of merchandise. Indeed, and all told, "Grandeza"'s advertisement of objects devolves into a full-bodied poetics of mercantilism based on materialism and surfeit. Almost everything that disarticulates the text, that divorces it from proportion and coherence, ultimately articulates the new discourse. The poetics of mercantilism joins "Grandeza"'s proto-Baroque, monstrous excess and oversaturated space to the architextural inventories and particularity that reflect the sensuous side of Mumford's absolutist city, gathering them all into a single construct. "Grandeza" writes itself into and reifies the seventeenth-century's imperial, capitalistic economy of *crematistike,* according to Beverley (chap. 1) an economy recently divorced from landownership and resituated in money. As an economy of money, crematistike knows no bounds, no anchor, only (non-Petrarchan) desire. Balbuena's desiring, imperial, Baroque poem advertises and estheticizes commodities and "commodifies" esthetics into the mercantile poetics of crematistike. The text consecrates itself to the poetics of mercantilism as did the bard of *El Bernardo* to the speech of things, "at all times engrossed in it."

Balbuena's fervent investment in the poetics of the marketplace has one last job to do, perhaps its most important and all-inclusive. Although his and other textualized marketplaces hawk the goods of the real marketplace, what is arguably most vitally and singularly up for sale in "Grandeza"—to the crown, the Council of the Indies, or even the viceregal regime—is the market itself, the mercantile system per se. Rather than merchandising alterity, "Grandeza" markets the market. The goal of the poem vis-à-vis the empire merges with its original objective vis-à-vis Isabel de Tobar, namely, of winning her over to "la ciudad *más rica* / que el mundo goza en cuanto el sol rodea" [the *wealthiest* city that the world encircled by the sun enjoys] (61; emphasis added). Balbuena's iconoclastic signature theme of interés becomes a multifaceted service to the empire. Hoping for reward, the aspiring divine bard offers the financially ailing crown a seductive, sanitized, mythified version of the mercantilism that it so needed and desired. Perhaps knowingly, he counters attacks on the mercantile system such as Tomás de Mercado's *Suma de tratos y contratos* [Summa of trade and contracts].[36] In Balbuena's simultaneously sublime and mercantile Mexico City, Apollo, god of poetry, and Mercury, god of merchants, form "a single subject" (116). Accordingly, the poet exalts mercantilism and the city in one breath. Only the feudal labor of the "ugly Indian" disturbs their concerted capitalistic beauty, hence his absence from the market and from the body of the text.

And even he is folded into a sham gift economy analogous to that of the society of the spectacle's festivals. The Indian does not visibly work but does offer tribute, a gift: in the festival-allied "Grandeza," that gift economy masks and redeems commercial endeavors. Similarly (and identifying himself with the Indian in that both of them "pay" tribute [124]), Balbuena fashions the marketplace and Mexico City itself as a wonder cabinet that he, the encyclopedic poet, verbally possesses in full and gifts to the empire. Now a gift rather than the product of exploitation, now extensively metamorphosed from a potentially ignoble materialism into art, now an aristocratic possession removed from the bourgeois order, the wonder cabinet city Balbuena has constructed allows the empire to enjoy its new entity and economic order wholeheartedly, nobly. From the poet's gift of Mexico and mercantilism there accrue to the Spanish empire the pleasure and prestige of the collector, patron of the arts.

"Wealthy means the same thing as divine" (30), pontificates Balbuena, intent on rendering his mercantile Mexico philosophically and morally palatable as he gifts it to the empire. Beyond promoting riches as a vehicle of neostoical happiness and equating poverty with a lack of virtue, "Grandeza" spiritualizes actual money. Balbuena maneuvers money into a metaphor of virtue, telling his readers that the royal treasury contains not silver but faith and loyalty (103). He employs mercantile imagery to describe the Catholic Church as a "treasury of truths" (105; also 107, 110). While everything that Ovid's Midas touched and turned to gold eventually threatened to kill the greedy king, "Grandeza"'s ever-labile gold radiates sublimity and moral probity. Finally, Balbuena's superimposing of Ovid's pre-city age of gold onto the mercantile age conceivably salves the moral crisis of the transition from the ascetic Mendicant orders to the worldly Jesuits.

If in truth, as the poet has led his readers to believe, mercantile gold signifies virtue and the mercantile city has assimilated the pastoral millennial kingdom rather than annihilating it, then the City of God can and does coexist unproblematically with the city of Mammon. Imperial Spain can reign over its golden, blissful, pastoral metropolis with no remorse for a lapsed asceticism, no moral compunctions. This last piece in Balbuena's redemption of Mammon crowns an esthetic and ideological program that has reclaimed the real for the ideal while still allowing it to flourish and proliferate monstrously, destabilizing the geometric Ordered City and creating the complex Spectacular City.[37]

Four   BALBUENA'S
SPECTACULAR CITY
AND THE CREOLE CAUSE

At the heart of the heart of present-day Mexico City, near the center of its Zócalo, stand the remains of the Aztec Templo Mayor, excavated in the late 1980s. The Templo Mayor breaks the vast sweep of the second largest city plaza in the world and claims a powerful place for Aztec culture in the value system of contemporary Mexico. Viewing the Zócalo as a living cultural text, compare, if you will, the present-day plaza with Cristóbal de Villalpando's pictorial rendition of it from 1695. In Villalpando's spectacular masterpiece, on the very ground under which the Templo Mayor still lay buried, not one but two market installations monopolize the Zócalo. One bounded by walls, the other an array of stalls, both are symmetrical and glisten with goldtones. The enclosed marketplace, the new Parián for which Viceroy Galve (who commissioned the painting) wished to be remembered, bears on its golden entry arch the words, "Plaza mayor de México." If the marketplace metonymizes the city's main plaza and the plaza to some degree metonymizes colonial Mexico, then it becomes inescapably present to the viewer that the mercantilism for which Balbuena's poem served as a passionate advocate had become a commanding force in seventeenth-century New Spain. So much so, in fact, that as the twelve hundred miniature figures of the painting converge on the marketplace from all walks of life, they appear as mere cogs in the mercantile machine, magnetically drawn to it.

Curiously enough, while Mexican creoles launched Balbuena's Spectacular City into activism, they themselves played a quite vexed role both in the earliest activity of the omnivorous mercantile machine on Mexico City and in its early textual embodiment, "La grandeza mexicana." Chapter Four probes this fraught situation. It reframes Balbuena's poem, wresting it from the imperial project and situating it in the orbit of the creole program. In its new frame the resounding defense of mercantilism that allied "Grandeza" with the appetites of the empire proves to signal the text's principal disjunction from the cause of the seignorial creoles. Yet a kind of poetic justice quickly prevails. Creole or creole-allied writers almost instantly recognize the splendid availability of Balbuena's work for their purposes and extort from it an unexpected afterlife. In other words and crucially, the Spectacular City, whose three elements *Grandeza* fully incarnates for the first time, immediately demonstrates its volatility and "great" potential for the colonial subject who would exploit it in ever-different ways over the course of the entire seventeenth century. This chapter, a gateway to the full-blown work of the New World Baroque, will therefore afford a first glimpse of the implosive, political potency of the Spectacular City as it seduces satirical, programmatic, and festival writings alike.

In something of a coda to the preceding chapter we will here enter the early wake of "Grandeza." To lay out the tangled, deliciously ironic story of "Grandeza"'s surging aura, what follows tracks the poem's relationship to the creole platform, the productive instability of "Grandeza"'s hyperbolic esthetic, and the specific appropriations of the text by the creole colonial subjects to whom, on the face of it, Balbuena's grand poem does no great service. Each of these arenas holds exceptional importance for the creoles and for Spectacular Cities to come.

I. CREOLES, MERCHANTS, AND "LA GRANDEZA MEXICANA"

The creoles of colonial Mexico's second life-project increasingly resented the crown's forceful efforts to divest them of the encomiendas they considered to be both their birthright and the bedrock of their pretensions to aristocracy. This group, its livelihood and status based on agriculture, had a particular quarrel with merchants. As a center of international trade, Mexico had given rise to a wealthy merchant class that flaunted its affluence and, on the strength of that affluence, claimed membership in the aristocracy. In an ardent entreaty from 1599 that the crown retract the "two lives" encomienda policy and other practices that disenfranchise his brethren, the conqueror's son Gonzalo Gómez de Cervantes writes, "it is clear that wealth lies in the power of merchants and traders, not in the hands of leading and noble citizens" (126), a state of affairs that leaves those worthy scions of the conquerors "poor, dejected, disfavored and abandoned" (94). Clearly, by the end of the sixteenth century, merchants had become a thorn in the creoles' sides. Following the lead of Hernán Cortés himself, some creoles did begin to engage in commercial activity (Liss 102). Rather than change with the times, however, creoles more generally assumed the "intransigent seignorial stance" (Liss 102) that galvanized and defined sixteenth-century criollismo. Mercantilism remained inimical to the would-be noble creoles, and the nouveaux riches merchants remained the rivals of the conservative New Spaniards, who complained heartily of their increasing impoverishment. In 1623 the creole-allied Arias de Villalobos wrote, "Tarde llegaron los conquistadores / A aprender de la abeja y la hormiga; / Pues la prosperidad se les fue en flores" [The conquerors learned too late from the bee and the ant, for they squandered their prosperity] (264).

That Balbuena not only extols commerce but also thoroughly thrashes poverty as a moral failing pits him sharply against the creoles. The same can be said of several other aspects of "Grandeza," since Balbuena either eliminates or gives short shrift to key points in the creole program. The phantasmagorical "indio feo"—always overdetermined in "Grandeza," through his presence or absence—does double disservice to the creole cause. His presence in "Grandeza" as a payer of bountiful tribute underscores the financial demands of the empire that burdened and angered the creoles. The absence of the Indian as a labor force eliminates from the text the encomienda that the feudal creoles desired above all else. Significantly, Balbuena dismisses the Indians' history and the epic history of the conquest with the same *brevitatis formulae* and in the same passages (68–70). He brings up but begs off detailing both issues together (though his brevitatis formulae are more copious with regard to the conquest), saying, "Esto es muy lejos" [This is very remote] (70). No less significantly, Balbuena shunts off the commemoration of epic deeds to *El Bernardo* (69; begun in 1592, published in 1624), in which epic poem he regales his audience with the Old World, purely Spanish feats of Roncesvalles. By shortchanging the Mexican conquest, "Grandeza" flies in the face of creole literary efforts of the time, centered as they were on the Cortés cycle of epic poems that memorialized the deeds of the creoles' fathers and thereby bolstered petitions for encomiendas.[1] Balbuena's studied discounting of this epic material would not ingratiate him to creole authors or their readers.

On other fronts "Grandeza" enters into a more slippery, sinuous relationship with the creoles. Balbuena commends the devotion of Mexican youths to learning and *lettres,* yet mentions no creole poets in the

"Compendio." He lauds both the city council dominated by creoles and the Spanish auditors whom they hated (103). He alludes to creole litigiousness in referring to the "great swarms of honorable petitioners to the court," yet mutes the creoles' complaints into a testimony to the tribunal's efficacy and "decorum" (103). The cautious, canny Balbuena, who strives to keep his text sublime, will enter into the particulars of Mexico's greatness but not those of its politics. Unwilling to alienate any power centers, he hedges his bets.

However, by striving to keep his options open, Balbuena tacitly limits them. Be they the Cortés epics with their melodramatic Mannerist bent, the scientific apologetics of Juan de Cárdenas and Baltasar Dorantes de Carranza, or the impassioned petitions of Dorantes and Gómez de Cervantes, creole self-defenses were anything but subtle. Anyone not overtly for the creoles might well be taken to be against them. At most, therefore, "Grandeza" had distanced itself from the creoles' project on two levels, by statement and by default. At the very least, "Grandeza" had placed itself in an equivocal position vis-à-vis their concerns. Either scenario makes Balbuena's text, republished several times in Spain shortly after the wars of independence as evidence of the merits of the colonial regime (Van Horne, *Balbuena* 120), an unlikely weapon in the creole arsenal.

Balbuena's position does dovetail with that of the creoles at one vital pressure point. No less than Balbuena, though for different reasons, creole writers praised the empire. In what Yolanda Martínez-San Miguel views as their oscillation between different centers of legitimation and authority (35–36) and Anthony Higgins terms their ambiguous situation "between different discourses and investments" (3), creoles at odds with the local regime appealed to a higher authority. They would dissociate themselves from and berate the viceregal regime but vaunt their allegiance to the glorious empire that included Mexico. Creoles revolting against Viceroy Gelves in 1624, for example, shouted, "Long live the king, down with bad government" (Pagden, "Identity Formation" 63). Balbuena of course acclaims all aspects of the empire, local and international, in overblown terms. The common ground of praising the empire that the imperialist "Grandeza" shares with creole discourse holds out a lure to the local constituency with whom the text has an otherwise disjunctive or equivocal relationship. More specifically, the no-holds-barred hyperbolic cast of "Grandeza"'s praise of the empire—and especially of the jewel of the empire that was the creoles' own New Spain—sets the text up for appropriation by creole writers and thus for an exorbitant afterlife and performativity that run counter to the poem's original intent. In a truly exquisite irony, the spectacular elements of "Grandeza" that purport best to serve the empire backfire and engender fissures that make the text available as a tool in the cultural nationalism that bit by bit eroded the stranglehold of Spain on its colonies.

II. EXORBITANCE AND STRUCTURES OF FEELING

"Exorbitant" derives from the Latin *ex-orbitare,* to go off track. The exorbitant praise Balbuena lavishes on imperial New Spain lives up to the word's etymology, first of all, by incurring *ex*oticism. Balbuena's Mexico City rejects its Aztec past, surpasses the classical world, and aligns itself with the exotic Orient. For Balbuena, Mexico City's affiliation with exotic Orientalism and with the Orient itself assigns the New World metropolis a pivotal place on the globe. A nucleus of far-flung commercial dealings, the Mexico Balbuena had described in his introduction as ex-centric ("these ends of the earth, last to be discovered and ultimate extremes of the great body of this earth" [55]) obtains an apocalyptic centrality. Balbuena states: "México al mundo por igual divide / y como a un sol la tierra se le inclina / y en toda ella parece que preside" [Mexico divides the world in half, and the land bends toward it as if toward a sun, and it seems to preside over all land] (79). So central is the Mexico conveniently situated near the equator that the poet audaciously implies that New Spain displaces even Spain: "¡Oh pueblo ilustre y rico, en quien se pierde / el deseo de más mundo, que es muy justo / que el que éste goza de otro no se acuerde" [Oh Mexico, illustrious and rich, where one loses the desire for any other world, for it is very fair that anyone who enjoys this world will forget all others] (76). The Orientalism of Balbuena's Spectacular City has imploded and spun off its axis both geographically and rhetorically. It has, if unwittingly, wrested exoticism from its entrenched function as a technology for the colonialist management of the New World and primed it for the contestatory *self*-exoticizing that, as we will soon see, the creole Dorantes de Carranza begins to enact, and that subsequent creole writers perform in service of their various personal and political goals.

The implosion of exoticizing in "Grandeza" carries particular pungency given the already substantial history of that tactic in colonialist New World discourse. At the same time, aspects of New World discourse that "Grandeza" inaugurates reap an exorbitant performativity for the text. Marcelino Menéndez y Pelayo locates the birth of a genuinely American poetry in "Grandeza" due precisely to Balbuena's enthusiasm for and veneration of Mexico (57). "Grandeza"'s zestful particularity confederated with inflated encomium, I submit, could not help but magnify the creole subject's sense of place and self and thereby foment creole patriotism. Just like the festival that the text replays and immortalizes, and to no less indeterminate an effect, "Grandeza" purveys an ideal, spectacular representation of the colonial Mexican world. Edmundo O'Gorman, author of the pathbreaking *Meditaciones sobre el criollismo,* thinks that creoles took such representations to heart: "One believes what one wants to believe, but even more firmly in what one needs to believe" (28). In fueling with its overswollen civic pride and proto-Baroque rhetorical excesses a local patriotism that was the first step toward Mexican nationalism, the imperialist "Grandeza" acquires a double edge, a volatility. Its imploding esthetic subverts the imperial project without subverting. Together with the poem's exorbitant exoticizing, "Grandeza"'s inflated praise mobilizes and positions toward the future what are quite literally, quite palpably, creole structures of *feeling.*

Rare and compelling proof that the structures of feeling generated by "Grandeza" were indeed so excessively favorable to Mexico as to have been felt with resentment by some of its first readers appears in two poems from the period: the "Romance a México" [*Romance* to Mexico] and the "Sátira que hizo un galán a una dama criolla que le alababa mucho a México" [Satire from a young man to a creole woman who praised Mexico City highly]. The two pieces form part of the "Cartapacio de diferentes versos a diferentes asuntos compuestos o recogidos por Mateo Rosas de Oquendo," a notebook of probably unpublished poems of or by Rosas de Oquendo that Antonio Paz y Meliá encountered in the National Library of Madrid; both Paz y Meliá (in 1907) and Alfonso Reyes (in 1939) published some of the notebook's poems. In their themes, style, and structure, the "Romance" (Reyes 52–54) and the "Sátira" (Paz y Meliá 159–163) are strikingly similar. They also match other poems written by Rosas de Oquendo, a Spanish expatriate and loyalist turned biting satirist of the New World (to whom we owe the *Sátira hecha por Mateo Rosas de Oquendo a las cosas que pasan en el Pirú, año de 1598* [Satire by Mateo Rosas de Oquendo of the things that happen in Peru, 1598]). Whether written by Oquendo or by one of his contemporaries, the two poems display considerable spleen toward Balbuena.

The first-person poetic voice of the "Romance a México" describes just having read a "great discourse" that praises Mexico City, its gentlemen, ladies, merchants, and literati, a discourse that elevates Mexico above Rome, Spain, Italy, and France. From the abundance of quotes and topics of Balbuena's text in the "Romance," it becomes obvious that the narrator has just read "Grandeza." The "Romance" discredits "Grandeza"'s praise of Mexico and satirizes Balbuena's signature theme of interés with the refrain "lo que no alcansa el amor / todo el ynterés lo alcanza" [whatever love does not attain, interés does] (quotations from the "Cartapacio" poems here reproduce their interesting orthography). It blasts interés as the "evil poison" of Mexico City's inhabitants, who live without faith, God, law, and soul (the above quotes come from Reyes 53–54). The "Sátira que hizo un galán," in turn, broadens and intensifies the critique of Mexico City. It mocks the city's lack of truth and wonders, its absurd natural products, and unscrupulous merchants. By all lights issuing from the same pen and spirit as the "Romance," the "Sátira" also contains smaller but still unmistakable traces of "Grandeza."[2]

When, as the preceding evidence warrants, one reads the two poems as a continuum, the "Sátira"'s barbed criticism of Mexico's pretensions to rival or even surpass Spain leaps off the page and into direct combat with "Grandeza"'s claims to this very effect. The "Sátira" first states, "Dírame que es Nueva España, / yo reverencio tal nombre, / mas niego que en los efectos con España se conforme" [You tell me that it is New Spain; I revere the name, but deny that its assets match those of Spain] (Paz y Meliá 160). More pointedly, it later exhorts, "España abundante y rica, / fuerte patria de leones, / tesoro de la nobleza," "*Castiga a este reino loco* / . . . / que quiere competir contigo / y usurparte tus blasones" [Rich and abundant Spain, stalwart homeland of lions, treasury of nobles, *punish this mad kingdom,* which wants to compete with you and usurp your coats of arms] (Paz y Meliá 163; emphasis added). The "Sátira" then attacks the architecture of Mexico and gainsays both its reputed splendor and Mexico's exoticism: "Mas yo no he hallado en ellas / muros, piramis ni torres / de Babilonia ni Exito" [But I have found in them neither the walls, pyramids, nor towers of Babylon or Egypt] (Paz y Meliá 163). Despite the enigmas of their authorship, both "Cartapacio" compositions succeed in performing the two extraordinary tasks of establishing reader response to a seventeenth-century text and of supplying pungent evidence that his contemporaries perceived Balbuena to have crossed an unwritten line in his exorbitant praise of Mexico.

III. TOWARD THE MEXICAN ARCHIVE: DORANTES DE CARRANZA

A text from the archives of seventeenth-century Mexican creole historiography less shrouded in mystery than the "Cartapacio" delivers a willful reading of Oquendo and precisely the opposite reading of Balbuena. One finds unimpugnable proof of "Grandeza"'s serviceability for the creole cause in the *Sumaria relación de las cosas de la Nueva España con noticia individual de los descendientes legítimos de los conquistadores y primeros pobladores españoles* [Summary account of the things of New Spain with individual information on the legitimate descendents of the conquerors and first Spanish settlers] by Baltasar Dorantes de Carranza, son of the Andrés Dorantes who participated in Alvar Núñez Cabeza de Vaca's expedition. Written in 1604, the same year "Grandeza" was published, the *Sumaria relación* is an archive unto itself, the prime inaugural manifestation of the creole-constructed Mexican Archive. As such, the *Sumaria relación* carves out a genealogy and a "position of space and authority within colonial society" for creoles (Higgins xii) by incorporating not just Balbuena and Oquendo, but also a range of contemporary poetry into its fevered prose plea that the creoles receive the gains supposedly due to them. Dorantes's *Sumaria relación* offers extensive chunks of, among others, epic poems on the conquest by Francisco de Terrazas (indeed, his epic poem survives only in Dorantes's work) and Alonso de Ercilla y Zúñiga, both fully favorable to the creole cause.

The archival *Sumaria relación* also houses texts that present some problems for its platform, reproducing only the portions of them that meet the needs of creole discourse. For example, Dorantes's work includes poems explicitly attributed to Oquendo, poems recognizable as extracts from his 1598 *Sátira* of Peru (which had circulated in manuscript) but with small changes adapting them to Mexico.[3] Exercising its selective creole optic on the contrarian Oquendo, the *Sumaria relación* reprints only the fragments of Oquendo's work that attack Spanish gachupines, which fragments illustrate Dorantes's own thesis that the foreign upstarts have arrogated unto themselves "false titles and honors, with a thousand scams that help them rise to grandeur in this land, while complaining about it and obliterating those who are truly deserving" (233). Similarly, as the reference to the "grandeur" just cited might suggest, Dorantes avidly embraces Balbuena's assessment of New Spain. Along with numerous references to the greatness of Mexico, Dorantes cites in full the eight-line opening "Argumento" of Balbuena's text that ciphers the whole poem and epitomizes its praise of Mexico's grandeur (*Sumaria relación* 116; "Grandeza" 59). If Oquendo abets the critical bent of the *Sumaria relación,* Balbuena serves its sublime mission of exalting Mexico.

On the same page in which he quotes the "Argumento" Dorantes also hastens to stretch and bend "Grandeza" to his agenda, affording a concrete, elaborate performance of the poem's malleability by and for the creole. The sequencing and montage of this important, self-statedly "labyrinthine" section of the *Sumaria relación* reveal Dorantes's proclivities or skill as a bricoleur. First, he offers a long tirade on the disenfranchisement of the creoles that encapsulates the thesis of the entire *Sumaria relación,* then a satirical poem with echoes of "Grandeza" attributable to Oquendo that lambastes the sad state of affairs in the New World ("Minas sin plata" [Mines without silver], also in folio 77 of the "Cartapacio"). After this overture, Dorantes launches his defense of Mexico with a paraphrase of Balbuena's declarations that Mexico rivals the best cities of Europe.[4] Immediately ensuing upon the citation of "Grandeza"'s "Argumento," Dorantes stakes out his own territory, predicated on but edging away from Balbuena's. In a remarkable passage, he says of Balbuena and "Grandeza,"

> He writes only of this Mexican *city,* with the majority of the kingdom escaping his notice despite its many grandeurs and great wealth, its fruits, trees, magueys and peanut plants, fowl and birds and the medicinal herbs that aid our health and constitution, all of which inspire wonder and make this a paradise. Were he to come back to life, Pliny would certainly praise these, the world's most novel and monstrous natural phenomena. But how could he praise or even describe the cacao and its benefits? (116; emphasis added)

This passage, which introduces Dorantes's principal defense of Mexico, could scarcely be more intertextual or loaded. It segues from the city to nature and there invokes, as I will demonstrate, not just Balbuena but also Cárdenas, Cervantes de Salazar, Columbus, Pliny, and Oviedo. Each of Dorantes's gestures, compounded in other pages of the *Sumaria relación,* consolidates a Mexican Archive and saturates it with wonder.

Dorantes, who greatly admires the Jesuits, anchors his defense of Mexico and its creoles in the *Primera parte de los problemas y secretos ma-*

ravillosos de las Indias (1591) by the Jesuit-trained Juan de Cárdenas. Like Dorantes a flamboyant apologist for the creoles, Cárdenas utilizes the scientific approach of his times to argue that both the inhabitants and natural phenomena of the New World profit from its beneficial climate, the utter antithesis of the antipodes. In chapter 1 we heard Cárdenas's climatological defense of the creoles; the autodidact Dorantes repeats it, expands on it with jittery erudition, and further racializes it by often referring to the skin color that distinguishes the creole from the allegedly inferior, darker-skinned Indian.

While Dorantes and Cárdenas concur that creoles possess a marvelous intelligence, for both authors the most "marvelous secrets" of the Indies lie in the New World's natural assets. Cárdenas rests the bulk of his case for Mexico on celebrating the cornucopia of wonderful products New Spain has brought to the fore: chocolate, prickly pears, cassava, tobacco, corn, peyote, and so on. Echoing his mentor, Dorantes freights his history of the conquerors' heirs with several lengthy discussions of natural phenomena that do the same ideological work for which Cárdenas had conscripted them. Both authors, in other words, execute a major refunctioning of the native Mexican products that have figured so prominently in sixteenth-century writings like Cervantes de Salazar's *Dialogues*. Even the worms that Cervantes de Salazar nastily linked to the Indians now appear as tasty ingredients of a certain bread (67). Thus do the *cacao, maguey, guacama,* and scores of other plants and trees native to Mexico— that is, all of the products absent from Balbuena's Europeanized marketplaces and plazas—reappear as the fundamental ingredients of Dorantes's and Cárdenas's creole apologetics.[5]

Colonial Mexican writers, along with other Latin Americans, would discover the spirit of their land "through the internalization of an external reality, the landscape" (González Echevarría, *Celestina's Brood* 140).[6] Hence, although Dorantes's opening invocation of "Grandeza"'s city keeps the grandeur of the strictly urban environment alive in his text and weds it to the wonders of nature, Balbuena's marvelous pastoral city proves most apposite to the *Sumaria relación*. Balbuena's pastoral construction of the city in chapter 6 of "Grandeza" resurfaces in the thick of Dorantes's tribute to Mexico's climate, flora, and fauna: "What city in the world has more lovely and graceful means of entry or egress, is more full of beautiful fields and fragrant meadows, full of flowers, including carnations, and trees, and refreshing waters and bullrushes, with the fowl and birds that live among them forming a pleasant murmur of great happiness and *wonder* . . . ?" (125; emphasis added). Dorantes has reclaimed Mexican nature from its various unnatural renditions in colonialist texts and regenerated it as the heart of his defense of a Mexican paradise that joins forces with Balbuena's "Immortal Spring."

Together with the sublime qualities of Mexico, its abundant earthy pleasures inspire transports of wonder in Dorantes. For instance, redeploying Cárdenas's or Balbuena's storied "grandeza" with an almost comic prosiness, he says of a delightfully corpulent hen, "what can one say of its grandeur, flavor, and plumpness? Certainly a whole crowd could feast on a single rooster or wild hen. Oh how this would impress Castilla la Vieja or La Montaña!" (123). The *Sumaria relación*'s rapturous depictions of hens, roosters, iguanas, crocodiles, cacti, herbs, and numerous other wonders indigenous to Mexico (and, occasionally, Peru) signal that, as had Cárdenas, Dorantes inserts his text in the lineage of Oviedo's *Sumario*. Though Dorantes, manifestly eager to put his personal stamp on the Archive, never mentions Oviedo, he inundates his *Sumaria relación* with the Spaniard's trademark elements. These include emphases on empiricism, the senses, variety, medicinal utility, and gustatory delight, and on the novelty and difference of the New World. Countering Cárdenas's medicinal, scientific bent, Dorantes reverts to the theological stance championed by Oviedo, that of the "Natural Magician" who unearths the living world's secrets and gives praise to their Creator. In so doing, Dorantes reminds his reader that the smallest natural object should prompt one to venerate God's greatness and marvels (126).

Most of all, Dorantes adopts from various predecessors the supremely efficacious criterion of the marvelous, expedient as it was on theological and ideological grounds for a defense of the New World. Like Pliny, Oviedo, and Cárdenas, Dorantes writes natural history in function of the marvelous. He categorically concludes that everything in the Indies is "marvelous" and "miraculous" (138). Dorantes brings Balbuena into the act by constantly tagging New World nature as both great (surpassing Old World nature) and wondrously strange: "There are strange birds, fish and animals in the Indies, strange in their grandeur and richness . . . and in everything else" (138). As one can gather, there lurks in Dorantes's words, and in his overall criterion of the marvelous, another efficacious conjunction—of Oviedo's and Balbuena's exoticizing of the New World. A long, self-declared digression in the *Sumaria relación* on Columbus's providential, lucrative discovery of the New World, for example, literalizes Balbuena's Orientalism. In a total departure from Cárdenas's ahistorical natural history, Dorantes argues that the New World does not merely resemble India enough to have fooled Columbus, it actually *is* India. Providing a hefty list of the exotica common to the Indies and India (59–61), Dorantes identifies the New World as "the furthest part of the real India," the "ultra or extra" branch of the Ganges (59).

European historiography from the times of Pliny to Columbus's era lends credence to the existence of fantastic creatures like monsters in faraway places like India and Africa. Further, we know from Hieronymus Bosch and Antonio de León Pinelo that Paradise, with which Dorantes metaphorically or concretely identifies the New World, breeds all manner of fabulous beings. This logic would make the *Sumaria relación*'s Indies-India-Paradise the natural breeding ground for the monstrous properties Dorantes attributes wholesale and superlatively to the New World ("the world's most novel and monstrous natural phenomena"); Dorantes here inserts the monstrous into Cárdenas's own words on Pliny.[7] Integrally related to the marvelous and the exotic, the monstrous pervades the *Sumaria relación*. Hallucinated imagery in a Mannerist or proto-Baroque mode of the land as an animal,[8] monstrously large nuggets of gold, and horrific sea beasts crop up in the text. Perhaps owing to the shared esthetic climate, the *Sumaria relación* falls in line with the "frightful figure" of the "savage Indian" (55), the monstrous "ugly Indian" who disrupts pastoral serenity, and the "monstrously" intelligent Mexicans (86) of Balbuena's *Grandeza*.

Yet all told something larger, something in which literary currents play but one part, would appear to be coming to life in Dorantes's Mexican Archive. Just when Balbuena's exorbitant, seductive, imperialist poem arrives on the scene, a rebirth of European exoticizing in another vein, to other purposes, accompanies it. While teaming up with Cárdenas, Dorantes has worked the reputed exoticism of the New World more historically and profusely than his direct forebear. Concomitantly, Dorantes has parlayed the tropes of heterogeneity such as the wonder cabinet and monstrosity with which Europe managed the New World into outright creole advocacy for the New World. In a textbook enactment of mimicry, he has appropriated exoticizing modes and consciously staged the marginality of the New World to its benefit rather than to its disadvantage.[9] That is to say, the old and new texts that dynamically commingle in Dorantes's archive give rise to *creole self-exoticizing*. As Octavio Paz writes, "the criollo breathed naturally in a world of strangeness because he was, and knew himself to be, a strange being" (59). Further, Dorantes's blazoning of the New World's favorable difference militates against the identity-numbing similitude of historiographic syncretism and of palliative efforts (including Balbuena's) to reduce Mexico City to an idyllic, unthreatening, pastoral entity.

Paz has also remarked that "the unique esthetic of the Mexican Baroque corresponded to the historical and existential uniqueness of the criollo" (59), a statement that well applies to the creole activism whose first stage Dorantes exemplifies at the start of the seventeenth century and the Mexican Baroque. In the *Sumaria relación,* acrimonious creole complaint and vehement denunciations of a colonial environment taken over by Spanish upstarts catalyze the wild words of disillusionment I cited in chapter 1. Dorantes adds to those images of lies and deceptions such inflamed statements as "Oh Indies! Snare of the weak, house of madmen, compendium of malice, conceit of the wealthy, vanity of the arrogant" (113). The air one breathes in Dorantes's text is indeed a strange one, stranger than that of Balbuena's "Grandeza," more akin to the air churning with chimeras and horrors of Francisco de Quevedo's quintessentially Baroque *Los sueños,* subtitled *Sueños y discursos de verdades descubridoras de abusos, vicios y engaños en todos los oficios y estados del mundo* [The dreams: dreams and discourses on truths revealing abuses, vices and deceptions in all the professions of the world] (1627). Dorantes's conflicted interactions with his troubled environment, it emerges, have propelled him beyond Balbuena's Baroque-sounding, happy hyperboles and into the Baroque heart of darkness. The wild words of the *Sumaria relación* thereby introduce the specifically denunciatory Baroque self-exoticizing of the colonial New World's ills by creoles, which we will rejoin in chapter 7.

IV. DISARTICULATIONS: ARIAS DE VILLALOBOS

Dorantes de Carranza takes up "Grandeza" at its moment of publication, weaving it incrementally and patently into his text. A couple of decades later, one finds in the compass of creole discourse a no less patent but far more problematic rearticulation, or disarticulation, of Balbuena's text. Celebrations commemorating the centenary of the conquest of Mexico, appropriately enough, beget the final and perhaps the most telling chapter in the story of "Grandeza"'s immediate productivity for the creole milieu. I refer to Arias de Villalobos's *Canto intitulado Mercurio* (1623), whose subtitle reads, *Dase razón en él del estado y grandeza de esta gran Ciudad de Mexico Tenoxtitlan, desde su principio, al estado que hoy tiene; con los príncipes que le han gobernado por nuestros reyes* [Song entitled Mercury: which gives an account of the state and grandeur of this great city of Mexico Tenochtitlán, from its beginnings to its present state; including the princes who have governed it for our kings].[10]

Starting with its genesis and extending into its body, most everything about Villalobos's *Mercurio* is remarkably convoluted. A dramatist whose plays have all disappeared, a poet, and a festival chronicler celebrated in his times but now almost entirely forgotten, Villalobos received commissions for literary works from both the viceregal Audiencia and the creole-dominated city cabildo.[11] One commission from the Audiencia, on the occasion of Philip IV's ascent to the Spanish throne in 1621, led to the *Mercurio*, published two years later. The *Mercurio* has two addressees: principally Juan de Mendoza y Luna, third Marquis de Montesclaros, viceroy of New Spain from 1603 to 1607 and of Peru from 1607 to 1615; also, as the text's epilogue establishes, the Council of the Indies.[12] To make matters even more interesting, the *Mercurio* contains two texts, which do *not* correlate to its dual addressees. The first, rife with wonderizing verbal theatrics, is a bulky epic poem similar to Terrazas's *Nuevo Mundo y Conquista* [New World and conquest] that celebrates and spiritualizes the conquest of colonial Mexico in ways equally pleasing to creoles and the crown. The second is a forty-six-stanza poem in octaves that takes a site-by-site tour of Mexico City. It professes to be the ekphrastic reading of a tapestry that depicts Mercury guiding Montesclaros through the capital's landmarks on the day of the viceroy's festive 1603 entry into the city, "best in the world" (279).

This intricate second text of the *Mercurio*, which clearly embodies the three elements of the Spectacular City, warrants close attention. Given that Villalobos's poem, written in 1623, anachronistically narrates an event that took place in 1603, it makes special sense that the *Mercurio*'s Spectacular City is shot through with elements from the "Grandeza" published in 1604.[13] Villalobos's city tour in fact draws so extensively on "Grandeza" that Méndez Plancarte terms it a "new version" of the poem (*Poetas, Segundo siglo* 1:xlii). The *Mercurio* revisits scores of topics from "Grandeza," employs Balbuena's incipient Baroque idiom, and replicates Balbuena's disposition to sublimity as well as his penchant for art over nature and for inventories. As does Balbuena, Villalobos pays tribute to a city whose institutions, political and religious and artistic figures, public works, architectural achievements, and gold have converted it into the jewel of the Spanish empire (279). By the same token, to the conceivable consternation of whoever wrote the "Sátira que hizo un galán," Villalobos does not refrain (266) from echoing Balbuena's praise of Mexico as superior to Spain. "Esteem Mexico," urges Villalobos, "que hay mucha causa / Para hacer de su grandeza, estima" [for there are many reasons to esteem its greatness] (279).

The *Mercurio* translates Balbuena's signature theme of mercantile interés into an unrelenting emphasis on wealth. Wealth underwrites Mexico City's public works, charity, and the numerous charitable institutions of the capital such as hospitals, shelters, and Jesuit confraternities. Wealth emanating from the copious mineral resources of Mexico showers forth onto the recently arrived Spanish gachupines. It is in the domain of this loaded topic of wealth, the very core of "Grandeza"'s and the *Mercurio*'s city, that Villalobos will install his own creole-allied complaint, effectively disarticulate both Balbuena's and his own texts, and ultimately betray Balbuena.

Like Balbuena, Villalobos was born in Spain (in Jerez de los Caballeros de Extremadura, c. 1568) and raised from an early age in Mexico. Unlike Balbuena, as a seventeenth-century tribute to Villalobos states, the later poet "lies honorably" and claims as his own his adopted homeland of Mexico (Méndez Plancarte, *Poetas, Segundo siglo* 1:xl). Hence, according to José Joaquín Blanco, Villalobos's work evinces a "belligerent criollismo" (*La literatura* 203), and ties both thematic and stylistic to the procreole Jesuits. The melodramatic, epic version of the conquest effected by the first part of the *Mercurio* confirms Villalobos's close relationship to the Jesuits and the creoles. In stark contrast to the heroic poem and certainly intended to rouse the sympathies of the Council of the Indies, at the outset of the text's second part Villalobos directly voices the tragic, impoverished situation of the creole heirs of the conquerors. He initially frames the creole complaint through the parable of the bee and the ant quoted at the beginning of this chapter, which ends with the words, "Vino el Invierno y fuése la encomienda" [Winter arrived and the encomiendas went away] (264). As did Dorantes and Oquendo, here and elsewhere in the second part Villalobos satirically decries the financial sway that upstart gachupines have gained in a New Spain that he deems "Tan madre natural de los extraños, / Que echa a los [que] parió, por los rincones" [So natural a mother to foreigners that it casts its own children aside] (264). Similar to Dorantes and Cárdenas—but, quite significantly, embedded in a segment on a marketplace that sells "Grandeza"-inspired luxury goods rather than the native products that his predecessors' apologetics celebrated—Villalobos sets forth a robust defense of the creoles, who are favored by the planets, underrated in their homeland, intelligent, learned, and virtuous (265). The praise of Mexico City's creole artists and their accomplishments that follows soon shades into a lengthy riff on the capital's wealth and charitable institutions. There, in strong alignment with the preceding lament of creole poverty, Villalobos interjects a disruptive satirical punch line: "Tanta demanda añal perpetuamente, / Que no hay fisco sin Dios que tal sustente" [Such a great annual demand, perpetually, that without God no treasury could meet it] (267). Villalobos here asserts that no one but God, and certainly not the impoverished creoles, can afford to subsidize the greatness of Mexico City.

With this satirical flourish, a kind of "smoking gun," Villalobos both punctuates his creole platform and substantially reinflects the role of "Grandeza" in the *Mercurio*. On Balbuena's very own turf of city representation, Villalobos has plugged "Grandeza"'s sublime, spectacular, proto-Baroque metropolis into creole complaint. He has put pressure on Balbuena's universally, ideally wealthy city by reaching out to the historical, economic, and social reality of that wealth, enjoyed by some, mourned by others. As he strains Balbuena's one-sided poetics of capitalism (another telltale sign of the earlier author's remove from the creoles), Villalobos laces "Grandeza"'s absorption into the *Mercurio* with a corrosive edge. Read in tandem with Villalobos's thrust toward the creoles, any reference in the *Mercurio* to Balbuena's pivotal theme of Mexico's wealth-dependent greatness inevitably summons up those to whom it is denied, those who for reasons deplorable or perhaps partially deserved have been stripped of economic power. The *Mercurio*, in other words, maneuvers "Grandeza" into an ironic counterpoint to its ideological platform as it implies that all of the wealth standing at the heart of Balbuena's poem eludes creoles in 1623. Villalobos says that a poet who purports to celebrate the city's site, construction, and climate will either sing well or weep ("Que si no canta bien, llora quien canta" [263]). Analogously, in the end the ever-imploding "Grandeza" has furnished the *Mercurio* with the raw material for both the serenade and the lament that inhere in creole discourse.

Villalobos's more inclusive, intensely local, particularized poem has thus conspicuously articulated and surreptitiously corroded or disarticulated its own matrix, "Grandeza." As one surveys the entirety of the *Mercurio*'s second part, its disarticulation of "Grandeza" assumes more tangible and far-reaching proportions. Villalobos's in truth more mediocre poetic effort by design or default dismantles the would-be neat taxonomic structure of Balbuena's poem, the *Mercurio* becoming, to its detriment, nothing *but* architexture. The *Mercurio*'s sometimes heterogeneous stanzas jump around Mexico City. They allude to rather than name the places they visit. Villalobos himself included thirty-nine footnotes intended to make the poem's confused, confounding tour intelligible to the Council of the Indies. Also careening on the brink of incoherence and betraying Balbuena's uniformly exalted text, satire and sublimity coexist in the *Mercurio*.[14] Distinct from the manner in which the prose of the bricoleur Dorantes mediates between satire and praise, effectively harmonizing them, the two modes coexist awkwardly and disjunctively in the *Mercurio*. The *Mercurio*'s inability or refusal to decide between sublime song and acidic lament, the ineptness of its "inferior lyre" (263) in fusing the two modes, rend the text—rendering it irremediably schizophrenic. Whereas the Mannerist alchemy of "Grandeza" laboriously bridges all sorts of inimical elements, the *Mercurio*'s incomplete chemistry results in an undissolved, uncategorizable mix. Only the imaginary conceit of the tapestry illustrating the viceroy's festival tour of the city imparts cohesion to the jagged, aleatory body of the *Mercurio*.

Maladroit, incoherent, riven, devastating "Grandeza" at every turn: in and of themselves these problematic characteristics of the *Mercurio* make meaningful, weighty statements. Articulating an era, the very ruins that constitute Villalobos's poem inadvertently frame a consummate portrait of the multiple, conflicting investments of creole colonial subjects at the centenary of the conquest. In 1623 the schizophrenic body of the *Mercurio* lays bare the divided body or loyalties of the creoles, torn as they were between bitterness toward and fawning on the colonial regime, serenade and satire, a recent heroic past and a reduced present, and in fledgling ways between Spain and Mexico. The *Mercurio*'s awkwardly rent nature catches these unnegotiated tensions without resolving them. Analogously, and just as retrospectively, the body of the *Mercurio* emerges as another important creole archive. It houses not just "Grandeza" but also shards of various texts written in the Mexican milieu. As one might expect, the uncontrolled energy of a flailing identity that disarticulated other aspects of the *Mercurio* also penetrates and dismembers its archive, distinguishing the work from Dorantes's less cynical enterprise. For Villalobos's intertextual gallery gestures fitfully and parodically to its sixteenth-century forebears.

Another visit to a marketplace—staple of the Ordered City, a crucial site for Balbuena's Spectacular City, the mother lode for creole polemics—affords a sense of Villalobos's disruptive archive and closure to this chapter. As is fitting for a tour led by Mercury, god of commerce, Villalobos's text alights several times on marketplaces. Rather than transacting alterity as they did in Cervantes de Salazar, the *Mercurio*'s marketplaces become emporiums of textual goods. The poem's first commercial stop, mentioned above, tenders the defense of the creole's nature, learning, and virtue indebted to Dorantes. Villalobos lodges that defense in a textualized marketplace said to cater to the absurdly refined needs of "ladies," which thus mocks Balbuena's obsession with luxury goods (264–265). A subsequent trip to a marketplace in the *Mercurio* features not one but two passages overloaded with the *C*s of Juan de la Cueva's glib poem (272). Villalobos's second shrieking *C*-passage skews the majestic avenues of Mexico City from Balbuena's runways for nobly decked-out horses into the venue for carts of sewage (273), thus also deranging such insidiously sanitized worlds as those of Cervantes de Salazar and Salazar y Alarcón.

Villalobos had begun his ultimately conflicted intertextual relationship to "Grandeza" with a reference to New Spain's centenary: "Haber que se ganó, ciento y dos años, / Y hoy ser Babel y emporio de naciones" [It was conquered 102 years ago, and today is Babel and an emporium of many nations] (264). Itself a degraded emporium of textual wares, the retrospective, fractured *Mercurio* has taken on some Babelic contours of its own. As the poem's early Spectacular City decenters and deranges its predecessors at the hundredth anniversary of the conquest, it brings to a giddy peak and into dark focus the first act of the Mexican creole drama. The late seventeenth-century texts of Carlos de Sigüenza y Góngora, Agustín de Vetancurt, Sor Juana Inés de la Cruz, and others to whom we turn in chapters 5 and 6 give voice to the next milestone development in the colonial Mexican creole "subject-in-process."[15] They carry Balbuena's Spectacular City, and the Spectacular City in general, to their plenitude and partial dissolution. Departing from their creole forebears writing at the centenary, even as they maneuver within the constructs of the Spectacular City these fin-de-siècle seventeenth-century works erect a new, Indian-based platform for creole discourse. They contest and attenuate Balbuena's text by filling in the blanks of "Grandeza," conveying it to places far beyond its ken, and reconfiguring both its ideological and philosophical bases.

Yet, as the members of the fully Baroque Spectacular City hark back proudly to an origin of the Baroque on Mexican soil, Balbuena's poem remains a shifter and enabler of creole discourse. Phoenix-like, "Grandeza" will be reborn from the ashes and its ruins in Villalobos to serve a new generation of creole writers. Each, in his or her own highly distinctive way, will perpetuate the volatile productivity that Balbuena's imploding imperialist Spectacular City yielded for its contemporaries.

FIGURE 4. *Felipe Guaman Poma de Ayala (fl. 1613). Drawing 372. The city of Cuzco, principal city and royal court of the twelve Inka kings of this realm, and bishopric of the church.* El primer nueva corónica y buen gobierno. *Courtesy the Royal Library, Copenhagen.*

Five   ENGAGING PLURALITY

Baroque Plenitude and the Spectacular City in Mexico

> Plus ultra! ¡Más Mundos hay, / y ya venimos de verlos!
> [Plus ultra! There are more Worlds, and we have just seen them!]
>
> SOR JUANA INÉS DE LA CRUZ, *LOA* TO *EL MÁRTIR DEL SACRAMENTO, SAN HERMENEGILDO* (1692)

I. SEVENTEENTH-CENTURY PLURALITY AND PLENITUDE

In protesting Spanish abuses of the Indians, *El primer nueva corónica y buen gobierno* [First new chronicle and good government] by the Peruvian Yarovilca Indian Felipe Guaman Poma de Ayala relentlessly impresses on its readers that there are many more worlds in the New World than Balbuena and his cohorts admit. Completed around 1615, nearly the same time that the Inca Garcilaso de la Vega published his *Comentarios reales* in Spain, the *Nueva corónica* transcends the similitude that largely runs the Inca's text to embrace in its plenitude the dynamic multiplicity of the Western world's most racially and ethnically complex society. As chapter 33 of the *Nueva corónica* (from which the visual epigraph to this chapter is taken), "Chapter on This Kingdom and Its Cities and Towns," travels through the Spanish viceroyalties of South America, its words and pictures map out a world in which nothing is singular. The Indian author systematically registers each space's multiple history, indigenous and Spanish, and its multiple racial or ethnic composition, a melting pot generally including Spanish, African, and Indian populations. Guaman Poma's pluricultural, irremediably heterogeneous cities are all contact zones, the essence of lived syncretism, spaces configured by cultural mixture, juxtaposition, exchange, fluidity.

And, as even the stylized and communocentric picture of Cuzco attests, along with plurality comes the intense, unseizable particularity of architexture. Busy and labyrinthine, Guaman's Cuzco confounds the eye. The proliferating, irregular forms of its monuments crowd together. Their crosshatching throws them into relief and endows them with restless movement. Surveying the jumble of asymmetrical shapes, the viewer's eye seeks a center and finds two, one a festival plaza (*hasicay pata*), the other what appears to be a marketplace. The modern viewer strives to make sense of the bustling, imbricated picture and runs up against shibboleths: coded iconography and almost opaque identifying captions in Spanish and Quechua that obstruct interpretation of the drawing according to the conceptual distributions of pictorial space that scholars have identified in Guaman Poma's work.[1] Yet two things are certain. First, Guaman Poma's Cuzco, littered with courts and jails, bespeaks Spanish efforts to police boundaries. Second, emblematizing an era, his Cuzco has left the uniform, monolithic, intelligible Ordered City far behind.

The *Nueva corónica* opens up another vista in Villalpando's masterpiece and leads into the Mexican Baroque Spectacular City. A fresh look at Villalpando's painting through Guaman Poma's optic liberates its twelve hundred minute Mexican figures from the mercantile machine, individuating them. The dark faces of Indians swathed in ponchos and rebozos as well as those of acculturated Indians in sober European garb come forcefully into view. The Indians mingle with tradespeople who ply their wares, bewigged courtiers arrayed in finery that befits the French court, swarms of women and friars shrouded in black. Villalpando's painting vibrates with the energy of the assorted individuals who converge upon and pluralize the very center of Mexico City at the end of the seventeenth century, with the Baroque in full force.

This new view on Villalpando's view of the Zócalo drives home the fact that by the end of the seventeenth century the racial and ethnic composition of Mexico City had risen to dizzying heights. As the creole Agustín de Vetancurt writes in the last years of the century, "There are thousands of Blacks, Mulattos, Mestizos, Indians, and others of mixed race who fill the streets, throngs of common folk" (2:191). True to Vetancurt's assertion, the African population of the capital had surged over the course of the seventeenth century. While castas and creoles were the fastest growing populations, Spaniards of every class and corporation now resided in the city. Further, ever-swelling trade circuits vastly enhanced the melting pot aspect of the city, realizing Balbuena's most excessive rhapsodies. Propelled by trade, compounded by missionary activity in the Orient and Africa, especially that of the Jesuits, it is the first era of globalization.

In such a world it was virtually impossible for any sector, hegemonic or counterhegemonic, to fail to contend with plurality. "This was the main drama of the seventeenth century: civilizing and cultural mixture [*mestizaje*]," Bolívar Echeverría states unconditionally (32). In seventeenth-century Mexico one therefore finds the pluralized city (or cities, as secondary cities come onto the stage), pluralized historiography and philosophy, pluralized creole discourse, and pluralized culture. Creole discourse reaches a new peak amidst this drama, burgeoning into creole patriotism.

"¡Mas Mundos hay, / y ya venimos de verlos!," writes the creole Sor Juana Inés de la Cruz, who died the same year that Villalpando painted Mexico City. Especially in the macaronic *ensaladas,* or hodgepodges, that she composed for numerous festivals, Sor Juana voices the plurality of her world.[2] Sor Juana's comic pieces, intended to provide some relief at the end of the long public religious festivals, bring parodic renditions of Afro-Hispanic dialect, Nahuatl, Spanish, and Latin into entertaining play, and bring their speakers on occasion into temporary dissent with the Catholic Church. Sor Juana's wonderfully dialogical, plural medleys have acquired enormous currency in recent literary studies.[3] Despite their parodic nature, scholars celebrate them as epitomizing her "American" loyalties and, no less, for catapulting the would-be monolithic Spanish literary Baroque into a vehicle for the complex, hybrid, kinetic environment of New Spain at the end of the seventeenth century. Sor Juana's ensaladas, it follows, embody the manner in which the New World Baroque overflows metropolitan containers and reaches plenitude—in the word's dual sense of fullness and fulfillment.

Chapter 5 makes common cause with the plenitude and "plus ultra" will to plurality of the New World Baroque incarnated in Sor Juana's comic festive pieces, which resonate with the indomitably multiple world of Guaman Poma. And Sor Juana will have an important place in our present inquiries. However, here we will move quite emphatically beyond her and any comical renditions of New Spain's multicultural society into works that engage its plurality with the gravitas the subject demands. Confronting plurality intricately and profoundly, the creole works we will examine bring to rich fruition the Baroque Spectacular City of Mexico in all its diversified complexity.

They do so, as "Engaging Plurality" will bear out, both seriously and sinuously, by interacting explosively with the very structures that the Spanish hegemony employed at least in part to manage heterogeneity: wonder, festivals, the Baroque, and historiographic syncretism. The creole satellites of the viceregal regime are pulled into the arduous mix of heterogeneity and hegemony, and push back at the latter. The early Mexican patriotism that runs through all of the creole texts studied here depends profoundly, and often in previously undisclosed ways, on the infrastructure of hegemonic culture. Therefore, at the same time as it showcases creole texts, the present chapter necessarily treats hegemonic negotiations with plurality in some detail.

Above all, the chapter traverses the pluralized landscape, nerve center, and *differentia specifica* of the Baroque era in Mexico, definitive rupture with the monolithic Ordered City. Section II introduces a little-studied purveyor of Mexican multiplicity. Section III probes the imprint of the strange bedfellows, hegemony and heterogeneity, on seventeenth-century Mexico City and its guided culture. Section IV then considers the discursive management of plurality in the seventeenth century, through the Baroque and the historiographic syncretism that originated in the Old World. Having assembled a toolkit for their texts, the central portion of the chapter turns the stage over to creole writers (principally Carlos de Sigüenza y Góngora and Sor Juana), to see how they engage plurality, erect their own platforms from received forms that they shake to their core, and enact the plenitude of the Baroque Spectacular City in a spectrum of festival texts.

II. AGUSTÍN DE VETANCURT AND MEXICAN MULTIPLICITY

Substantial as they will prove to be, neither Sor Juana's nor Sigüenza's efforts match Agustín de Vetancurt's extravagant, sustained commitment to the plurality of Mexico, a small sample of which we heard above. This creole historian, whom modern scholars inexplicably neglect, was born in Mexico City and took orders as a Franciscan in Puebla.[4] Vetancurt taught philosophy and theology at the university in Mexico City and in 1673 published a work on Mexican Spanish. For over forty years he served as priest and chapel vicar of the oldest Indian parish in Mexico City, the Curato de San José. In 1681 Vetancurt accepted a commission to chronicle the activities of his order from 1600 onward, which resulted in his four-volume *Teatro mexicano* [Treasury, or Theater, of Mexico; *teatro* had both related meanings], published in Mexico between 1697 and 1698. Materials lent to Vetancurt by his close friend Carlos de Sigüenza y Góngora significantly shaped the *Teatro mexicano:* Vetancurt's text shares with those of Sigüenza a concern for their country's history and heightened patriotic sentiments. Hence, beyond detailing the missionary work of the Franciscans in New Spain, Vetancurt's totalizing *Teatro* chronicles every aspect of Mexico, including natural history, Indian history, religion and culture, and the colonial regime. The third part of the *Teatro* also includes a separate treatise on Puebla and another on the City of Mexico (vol. 2 of the modern edition). Entitled "Tratado de la Ciudad de México; y las grandezas que la ilustran después que la fundaron españoles" [Treatise on the City of Mexico, and the grandeurs that ennoble it after the Spaniards founded it], it affords an almost delirious experience of late seventeenth-century Mexico City's greatness and plurality.

According to Vetancurt's depiction, it is indeed a spectacular city, unparalleled in its festivals and wealth (2:192–194). As the treatise's title implies, Vetancurt reduplicates and reinvigorates Balbuena's hyperbolic enthusiasm for Mexico City. Punctuating his extensive praise of Mexico City's charity, parks, climate, diversions, piety, and the inevitable "C-things" (2:193, lifted from Villalobos), the Franciscan exclaims, "to classify [*singularizar*] the grandeurs of Mexico would take several whole volumes, because its grandeurs exceed those of much of the Christian world, and Mexico stands shoulder to shoulder with the best of the world" (2:299). However overtly Vetancurt appears to invoke "Grandeza," his list of sources nonetheless conspicuously omits Balbuena. Instead, it does publicity for Villalobos's poem, which Vetancurt oddly calls the *Poema de las grandezas de México* [Poem of the grandeurs of Mexico] (1:xxi).

The migration of allegiance from Balbuena to Villalobos, also found in Sigüenza's *Teatro* (203), reflects Balbuena's equivocal relationship to the creoles *and* signals a paradigm shift.[5] For, like Villalobos but with infinitely greater zeal and breadth, Vetancurt puts pressure on the unidimensional city that Balbuena had restricted to the wealthy and the white. While Vetancurt carries Balbuena's trademark particularity into his work's minute descriptions, he shatters the apartheid to which "Grandeza" had subjected Mexico City. Vetancurt's *Teatro* systematically and consistently attends to all sectors of society. The text devotes itself equitably to the wealthy and to the poor and even the insane, to the creole and the Indian and the gachupín and the African and the mestizo, to the plebeian and the noble, to women of all social stations. Underscoring the diversity of the actors he places on the stage of Mexico City, Vetancurt punctiliously identifies their race, ethnicity, class, and gender, or some combination thereof. The good Franciscan of course has much to say about religious festivals and Indian participation in them.[6] Yet most striking is how the ecumenical *Teatro* projects the defining feature of the New World festival, multiethnicity, onto its every depiction of Mexican society.

The topography of Vetancurt's Mexico City similarly fills in the blanks left by Balbuena as it ranges over the whole city, including Indian precincts and marketplaces. Well informed by Sigüenza and other sources, Vetancurt both historicizes and verbally restores the Indian spaces of Mexico City. When he notes that the city cathedral stands on the space previously occupied by the Aztec Templo Mayor, Vetancurt also salves the wounds left by Cortés's origins-erasing *Cuarta carta-relación*. The Franciscan's treatise eventually veers from the heart of the capital to its suburbs. It amalgamates the city and proximate countryside, for example, by utilizing the title of Sigüenza's work on a convent in the heart of Mexico City, *Parayso Occidental* [Western paradise] (1684), to describe the fertile lands of the aristocracy's villas (2:190). The source of Sigüenza's trope, Balbuena's familiar, originary "Immortal Spring,"[7] enables Vetancurt to insinuate that by virtue of the year-round harvesting and selling in greater Mexico City of agricultural products from Spain, Castille is constantly being reborn and eclipsed by the vitalized New World capital (2:190). As Mexico City absorbs Spain and all of nature, it becomes clear that truly Vetancurt has been unable to "singularize" the grandeurs of México.

Vetancurt thus steeps his Mexico City in multiplication, the new math of the New World—and I speak more than metaphorically because the Franciscan often backs up his statements with grand statistics. The new math, a quantum leap beyond Alonso de Zorita's reductive sixteenth-century geometry, does not cease to prevail when the *Teatro* treats subjects other than Mexico City. Rather, it permeates all facets of the encyclopedia, rendering the text a comprehensive stage for heterogeneity. The *Teatro*'s New World contains New Spain, New Galicia, New Granada, New Mexico, and so on; it possesses not one but many climates; its Indians must be parsed out into their diverse tribes, with their many languages and forms of pictorial representation. Drawing on information from several zones of the New World, Vetancurt goes so far as to deploy the new math on previous tropes of heterogeneity such as alterity and abundance. He maintains that the otherness of the New World metamorphoses Spanish immigrants into new men with new blood, new humors, new minds (1:32), and he identifies every product of the New World's natural abundance with its native name. Each of these moves establishes an unmistakable and, in fact, chartable kinship with Guaman Poma's text. Vetancurt knew the Franciscan Buenaventura de Salinas y Córdoba and drew on his *Memorial* (1630), a work so allied with the inflammatory *Nueva corónica* that it had sent Salinas into exile in Europe and Mexico.[8] Although Vetancurt, as we will see, is no Guaman Poma or Salinas with regard to defending the Indians, we have now arrived at the point in which a Mexican creole insider takes up the reins of plurality.

Finally and most broadly, Vetancurt theorizes New World multiplicity along characteristically Baroque philosophical lines. A stunning suite of passages from chapter 5 of book 1, "On Why It Does Not Rain Here at the Same Time as in Spain and Why a Small Area Can Have Different Climates" (1:24), outlines the metaphysics of a world so shifting and plural that it is unknowable, except by God. The first passage, reminiscent of Gracián's *Agudeza y arte de ingenio,* transports Renaissance wonder and order and concert into the new cosmography: "Changes in the climate of the land, and the nature and spirit of people inspire great wonder, for they result from Divine Providence's intervention in the world, and the more one contemplates them the more one wonders at the harmony, and mysterious order and concert with which God arranged natural phenomena. Exhaustively as man scrutinizes them, it seems impossible to understand them" (1:28). In the second passage, Vetancurt reworks the topic of variety rife in New World writings, tethering it to mutability. He lists a skein of continuities that begins with the "variety and mutability" of the heavens, which stretches into and determines the "earth's climates" and the "constitutions of people" as well as their souls, corroborated by the fact that "nations have mutated and varied, and are not what they were before" (1:29). The Baroque has infiltrated Vetancurt's epistemology to radical effect for similitude, even more radical than in Gracián's poetics. Although Vetancurt's universe still nostalgically arranges itself into the old unbroken chain of similitudes, the affinities that the phenomena share are themselves now comprised of an unstable variety and a mutability that implicitly but deeply complicate the new math.

III. HEGEMONY AND HETEROGENEITY IN THE BAROQUE SPECTACULAR CITY

The mercurial heterogeneity that Vetancurt's *Teatro* presses on its readers and, far more important, that had become the *differentia specifica* of the New World, posed enormous challenges for the hegemonic viceregal regime. How to manage heterogeneity so as to ward off heterodoxy? How to escape, much worse yet, falling into the chasm that lies just beyond heterogeneity, a very real heterotopia? Heterotopia—the total breakdown of similitude and society, a disorder "without law or geometry" (Foucault, *Order* xvii)—must be avoided at all costs. Absolutism needed vitally to engage the plurality of the New World, and engage plurality it did. Consistent with the all-pervading nature of hegemony,[9] the state's efforts to manage heterogeneity profoundly impacted the realpolitik of the Mexican Spectacular City. Wrestling with heterogeneity and attempting, as in Guaman Poma's drawing of Cuzco, to police boundaries, the hegemonic state bent the city, wonder, and the festival to its designs. Its efforts reverberate into and ricochet in creole works of the time.

The City: While smaller cities like Querétaro and Puebla (treated in section IV below) began to come into their own in the seventeenth century, Mexico City maintained and reinforced its position as the economic clearinghouse and hub of the viceroyalty, the center and showplace of viceregal power. Given the city's prominence and diversity, the state exerted strenuous efforts to regulate it into a segregated Ordered City. Extensive measures were taken to give physical reality to a conceptual "republic of the Spaniards" and "republic of the Indians" and to keep the two entities separate.[10] The viceregal regime consigned the Indians to their own districts in the city, and these districts, which Mendicant orders like the Franciscans tended, had their own political organization. Instrumentalizing difference, the state set Indian nobility up as their brethren's chiefs.

Primordially, however, the apartheid depended on the so-called *sistema de castas,* or caste system, a racial ideology that translated into a social hierarchy maintained through administrative fiat. Positioning Spaniards and creoles at the cusp of the hierarchy, people of mixed race (the specific meaning of *castas* at the time) in the middle, and Indians and Africans at the bottom, the viceregal government of Mexico sought to control the diverse masses by dividing and regulating them. It forbade Indians and individuals of mixed race to carry arms, ride horses (hence, perhaps, Balbuena's insistence on the "noble" beasts), hold certain offices, and enter into legal contracts. It subjected them to sumptuary laws, prohibited their drinking of *pulque* [maguey brandy], and mandated that if they resided outside their prescribed districts, they live with a known master. Nonetheless, the evasion of administrative control that I detailed in chapter 1 continued tenaciously. Though power and stratification were concentrated in the capital, to a significant degree the city remained the mixed, contested terrain of Villalpando's Zócalo. Its own organic vitality overwhelming efforts to impose an Ordered City, the capital represented what María Alba Pastor Llaneza terms a "new Baroque order" "that attempts to relax codes, establish new everyday relationships . . . erase social barriers, and weaken the rules and levies by means of which the crown, in segregating the 'republic of the Indians,' attempts to impede confluence" (190).

Wonder: When it proved impossible to manage multiplicity thoroughly by administrative fiat, the viceregal state resorted to more symbolic and ostensibly benign measures to discharge the task. The indirect social control that a guided culture exercises now attains its full force and majesty, with decisive consequences for wonder. Aspiring to overtake all sectors of society, the guided culture wrenched wonder from its former homes in the elite wonder cabinet, textualized luxury object, and aristocratic city. Baroque cultural shaping, we recall from chapter 1, deployed wonder as a means of acting upon the emotions of both the elite and the masses. Seventeenth-century official wonder (*asombro, lo raro, maravilla*) was therefore built of drama, shock, splendor, extravagance, excess, sensoriality, and novelty. It aimed to inspire the wonder reactions of dazzlement and total surrender. As Sigüenza suggests in saying that an event of the festival he chronicles in *Glorias de Querétaro* left its spectators "extáticos" [ecstatic] (38), Baroque wonder purported to expel or suspend the will of its subjects, leaving them standing outside themselves, ex-static, and freed up to be filled up with the state's objectives.

Festivals: Festivals of every ilk played a starring role in the dissemination of wonder and in the larger efforts of the guided culture to interpellate all constituencies. Residents of late seventeenth-century Mexico City could enjoy a nearly ceaseless flow of celebrations, more than ninety a year. Festivals generally culminated at the ritualistic, monumental urban space of the Zócalo, which accommodated some forty thousand individuals (Curcio-Nagy 7). There, the society of the spectacle's celebrations brought together and into a living, idealized whole the groups that the state itself had torn asunder. Through festivals the hegemonic state gathered into its embrace and forged into an illusory and temporary collectivity all sectors of the otherwise motley, compartmentalized society. In a show of power and pleasure that mixed popular with elite entertainments, satisfying the tastes of each group singularly and collectively, festivals enticed the city's variegated residents into enacting a unified imagined community. The magnificence of the imagined community to which the festival gave palpable form impressed upon participants the grandeur of their city, homeland, and the Spanish empire.

With such acts of "social magic," festivals endeavored to impose on all constituencies the values and history necessary for the survival of the greater society (García Canclini 24, 135). The manner in which official festivals entangled subalterns in the performance of a "shared" historical patrimony holds particular interest. Linda Curcio-Nagy's outstanding study of colonial Mexican festivals asserts that, perhaps lured by the opportunity to mingle with the elite, Indian and African participants alike fell party to performing "in a highly choreographed and scripted fashion" the identity the state had assigned them (42). To personify the complete vassal, acculturated, predominantly Spanish-speaking Indians, often of the ruling nobility, would appear in festival pageants speaking Nahuatl, clad in stylized native garb, and thus reracialized. For their part, free blacks dramatized not their African but their Hispanic allegiances by wearing Afro-Mexican dress and tacitly advertising the somewhat liberal manumission policies of the viceroyalty (42, 58–66).

Moreover, as one reads in numerous chronicles, festivals embroiled the Indians in performing a sanitized, providentialist version of their own history. Indians attired in traditional ceremonial regalia—sometimes thousands of them from scores of tribes—led the processions, followed by viceregal personages, and ultimately the highest dignitaries. The ascending hierarchy of the procession staged Indian history as a teleology that culminated in Spanish rule. By the end of the parade or festival, Indians manipulated into festive complicity with an alien, problematic version of history invariably offered their homage and gifts to the viceroy, the crown, and the church. The autocratic cultural politics of the festival thereby propagated an originary myth that effaced Mexico's authentic origins. In simultaneously absorbing and reimagining Mexico's past, festivals perhaps betrayed New Spain's history more violently than the studied silences of Balbuena's "Grandeza."

IV. VEHICLES OF PLURALITY: RUINS AND RIFTS

As they strain to manage plurality, Mexican festivals effect a "travesty of dialogue" (Debord 113), a counterfeit of authentic involvement with indigenous culture and history. The festivals thus fan into and bolster received notions of the Baroque as an era of hegemonic monologue, compared to the more dialogical Renaissance. Chapter 2 above has already problematized the dialogical nature of the Renaissance, at least in terms of the New World; at this point a broad look at the logic of the Baroque and its historiography, as respectively harboring ruins and rifts, will do some damage to the allegedly monological nature of seventeenth-century discourse. Considered irreverently and somewhat counterintuitively, the Baroque and its historiography reveal themselves as potential instruments of plurality, poised to do the disruptive breakout work for which creole writers mobilize them.

The Baroque: While one cannot deny that the Baroque of absolutist Spain aspires to monologue, certain of its fundamental mechanisms position it as a vehicle for dialogue or multiplicity, despite itself. That aftershocks of the New World are likely to have affected the Baroque in barely perceptible but formative ways dynamizes it from the start.[11] Seventeenth-century Spain, further, recoiled from the new and fell into a conservatism that has several remarkable implications for epistemology on both sides of the Atlantic.

As is well known, Counter-Reformation Spain stepped back from the apertures of humanism. Its retrenchment from humanism entailed an approach to knowledge quite distinct from that of the Renaissance. To summarize a complex situation one can say that Renaissance humanism critiqued and purified ancient sources (classical and biblical), essaying to separate fable from fact and newly valorizing empirical experience over tradition. On the grounds of his sensorial, firsthand experiences in the New World, for example, Oviedo refutes Pliny and other ancients; with regard to sources, the humanist José de Acosta exhorts, "in Holy Writ we need not follow the letter that killeth but the spirit that quickeneth" (24, *24*). Quite distinctly, seventeenth-century Spanish thinkers retreated from humanism into the modus operandi of the medieval Catholic scholasticism that had coexisted with humanism in the previous century. Under siege from the Reformation, "Catholic scholastics insisted that the whole traditional armament of their profession should not be only staunchly retained but fiercely defended" (Grafton 34). This defense in effect entailed reversion from direct experience into a sclerotic, hidebound respect for written authority and for abstract a priori categories. Methodologically, it involved a predilection for formal, syllogistic, authority-based dialectics over a living "logic of discovery" (Popkin 673). Much vilified by Renaissance and modern scholars alike, scholasticism could degenerate into an arid argumentation more concerned with its own internal logic than with plausibility or truth.

And yet the epistemological landscape of the Baroque emerges as vast and as tremendously, intrinsically heterogeneous in its own special way. Whereas Renaissance scholars subjected received knowledge to acute scrutiny, critiquing it, Baroque intellectuals tended to accumulate information, to pile up and weave together information from the most varied sources so long as it did not clash with Christian doctrine. Inimical to the critical spirit of the Renaissance and to the Cartesianism and New Science of Francis Bacon that was infusing the rest of Europe with radical skepticism, the Baroque modus operandi accepts and stockpiles multiple knowledges. Rather than forging new paradigms, Baroque scholarship amasses older ones, a profusion of them. As myth rejoins fact, medieval scholasticism, which is Aristotelian in form and content, fuses with hermetic Renaissance Neoplatonism and with revivals of Skepticism, Stoicism, Epicureanism, and so on to form the eclectic, heteroglossic territory of seventeenth-century Spanish thought. Analogously and imperiously, from within the prisonhouse of the Counter-Reformation, the intransigent Spanish Baroque wants to arrest all knowledge. It hypervalorizes erudition: as Gracián writes in his *Agudeza,* arguments lacking erudition "are dry, sterile, and pall" (2:217). It fosters the totalizing impulses that inform Vetancurt's *Teatro* and other encyclopedic, holistic works of the times. In partnership with the broad Jesuit curriculum, it conjoins pagan, classical, and Christian learning.

The possessive, epigonic Baroque, clinging fast to old paradigms like order and concert, sets up a discursive playing field comprised of ruins. Walter Benjamin describes the kind of mobility that such a playing field affords writers:

> That which lies here in ruins, the highly significant fragment, the remnant, is, in fact, the finest material in baroque creation. For it is common practice in the literature of the baroque to pile up fragments ceaselessly, without any strict

idea of a goal, and, in the unremitting expectation of a miracle, to take the repetition of stereotypes for a process of intensification. The baroque writers must have regarded the work of art as just such a miracle. . . . The legacy of antiquity constitutes, item for item, the elements from which the new whole is mixed. Or rather: is constructed. (178)

If miracles could result from new ensembles of ruins or "*disjecta membra*" (198) in European Baroque discourse, Benjamin's predictions have particular relevance to the colonial setting.[12] Inherently a mosaic of foreign and indigenous cultural remnants, operating under a regime that mandated conservatism, the colonies constituted a fertile space in which the always already multiple, additive Baroque could flourish. We meet here at its very heart José Lezama Lima's celebration of the New World Baroque, with its emphasis on how elements of native culture enter the mix, as symbolizing that the New World had "attained its form in the art of the city" (51). Lezama Lima and more recent Neo-Baroque writers (as well as Ultra Baroque artists) revive the seventeenth-century Baroque, permeable and ductile as it was against all odds, as a vehicle for their depictions of a hybrid, plural Latin America.[13]

Historiographic Syncretism: The Neo- and Ultra Baroques of recent times tease a multiplicity out of the New World Baroque that tacitly partners it with another discourse trained on plurality, early modern historiographic syncretism. We know from chapter 1 that the Old World did confront the plurality of the New World or of the world at large more frontally than through the coded mechanisms of the Baroque, and that for more than a century historiography engaged plurality in a syncretic mode that grappled head-on, albeit problematically, with precontact indigenous history and culture. Though forbiddingly voluminous, convoluted, and erudite, syncretic histories lead a vibrant, magnetic life in the seventeenth century. From the launching pad of similitude they dig deeper than ever into indigenous history and cultures, destabilize stereotypes, incur unknowability, acquire their own multiplicity as a genre, and galvanize creole writers.

Most important for our concerns, I will argue here that syncretic histories hold the keys to the plurality or hybridity of Mexican Baroque creole works. Lezama Lima and others have motivated modern readers to seek out traces of Indian culture and history in New World Baroque texts, and on the basis of them to acclaim the hybridity and difference of the New World Baroque. However, in my view a missing link, another dynamic, needs to be factored into the situation: New World texts frequently derive their hybrid nature from a middleman, that is, from the mediating force of historiographic syncretism. Eminently Baroque in their erudition, availing themselves of ventures that recuperate Mexico's past, creole texts such as Vetancurt's and Sigüenza's *Teatros* and Sor Juana's famous introductory short play, or *loa*, to *El Divino Narciso* [The Divine Narcissus] signify upon historiographic syncretism. Baroque creole texts that appear to be *enacting* hybridity or syncretism, in short, are frequently, subtly, and disruptively *interacting* with historiographic syncretism (which I will again abbreviate to "syncretism").

This is a large and basically new claim. To bear it out and see it through into the creole projects one needs an anatomy of salient currents in seventeenth-century syncretism. Although the tangled currents of late syncretism, like the texts that contain them, resist streamlining, the cumbersome work of anatomizing historiographic trends is worth the effort because it can transfigure our understanding of several protonationalist Mexican projects. I will therefore map out as succinctly as possible the terms of syncretism's engagement with a pluralized world, terms that the creole texts of the Spectacular City purposefully mix and match.[14]

A lightning rod for creole writers, the Franciscan Juan de Torquemada's *Monarquía indiana* (1615) begins to challenge the colonialist imaginary of the New World to which syncretism had greatly contributed. Born in Spain around 1557, Torquemada spent the majority of his life in Mexico. He professed allegiance to his adopted homeland (Brading 291), allegiance that took the form of activism for the Indians. Torquemada learned Nahuatl, revived the declining school for Indians at Santiago de Tlatelolco, and incorporated indigenous sources such as native informants, codices, manuscripts, and evidence from archeological sites into his splendidly inclusive writings. As a stated apologist for the Indians ("my being so fond of these poor people and wanting to exculpate them" [1: "Prólogo general" n.p.]), Torquemada modifies the role in the founding of the New World that previous texts like Acosta's had assigned to the devil. Torquemada regards the Indians' precontact religious practices not as diabolical parodies of Christianity but, similar to the Inca Garcilaso's more positive outlook, as harbingers and prefigurations of the true religion. The *Monarquía* maintains that guided by natural reason the Indians instinctively inclined toward the One God.[15] Torquemada concedes that the devil led them astray, yet limits Satan's sphere of influence by placing him on the scene only with advent of the Mexica and their human sacrifices. Despite his liberal leanings, like Acosta and the whole syncretist contingent, Torquemada could not fail to invite the devil into his cosmology and thus at once to uplift indigenous culture and to debase and subalternize it.

Syncretism's reliance on the devil to explain both the similitudes and disjunctions of the New World vis-à-vis the Old meets its match in the huge theological polemic around the origins of New World peoples that dominates the historiography of the times. That for the Christian world the polemic involves nothing less than the origins of humankind (Huddleston 12) means that it must confirm biblical doxa and thereby disallow the New World any autonomous origins or, by extension, unique cultural achievements. However foregone its conclusions, the charged site-of-origin theory focuses the multiplicity of later syncretism, its proliferating hypotheses and internal divisions. Predicated as it is on any and all perceived similarities between the Old and New worlds, syncretism's inveterate logic would inevitably engender multiple origin theories. By the seventeenth century, this logic devolves into a contested terrain brimming with conjectures.[16] Consubstantial with its efforts to unify the world under the aegis of similitude, syncretism itself manufactures dissonance and heterogeneity.

As syncretism assumes the Baroque's special covenant with multiplicity, it often indiscriminately weaves together biblical, classical, mythological, and historical sources. From such ruins or, to borrow William Faulkner's words, the "rag-tag and bob-ends of old tales" (243), it crafts the host of frequently tenuous genealogies for the New World that compete for protagonism on the syncretist stage. Some theories maintain that the Indians descended from the Ten Lost Tribes of the Jews. The fact that the Indians of the Yucatán practice circumcision and that the name "Yucatan" resembles the biblical "Yectan" (Acosta 52, 45) or Joktan, remarkably enough, fuels a persistent association with the Jews of dubious advantage, from a Counter-Reformation standpoint, to the Amerindians.[17] Or perhaps, as one of the most widely held and equally problematic theories would have it, the brown Indians sprung from Noah's treacherous son Ham, stigmatized with dark skin for having exposed his father's drunken state (Gen. 9:22–25). Or perhaps they hailed from Solomon's treasure-ridden Ophir; or from the island that Carthaginian merchants had founded in the Atlantic beyond the pillars of Hercules; or from the sunken island of Atlantis, as many believed Plato's *Timaeus* to suggest. Origin theories abound and continue to multiply, with the landscape further enlarged by growing Hispanic familiarity with the Indians' own cosmogonies (generally discredited) and accounts of their wanderings (often accepted, in support of the Ten Lost Tribes hypothesis).

The burning question of the Amerindians', or humankind's, origins creates the fault lines that fracture the otherwise unified field of syncretist historiography. Jesuit syncretism has the most individualistic profile. As the Jesuits occupy the furthest reaches of the earth, they elaborate a truly global philosophy that rationalizes the gradual unfolding of Christian revelation in the world arena. Incongruous as it might sound, the Jesuit Christian system gains sustenance from the magical conjurations of the Neoplatonic hermeticism revived in Florence during the early Renaissance. Neoplatonic hermeticism modeled a syncretism capable of assimilating the pagan classics so dear to the Company of Jesus together with esoteric notions akin to those of the ancient national religions the Jesuits encountered in their global missions. Hermes' Egypt has a special purchase on the esoteric systems the Jesuits imported into their syncretism and into the New World. Hermeticism anoints Egypt as the originary fount of universal wisdom, the *prisca theologia*. Last of the great Jesuit polymaths (Godwin 5), the fabulously learned German Athanasius Kircher believed that Hermes Trismegistus had foreknowledge of Christianity (Yates 416) and explicitly associated Hermes and hermeticism with Mexico. His *Oedipus Aegyptiacus* [Egyptian Oedipus] (1652–1654) posits an Egyptian origin for ancient Mexico. Writing from the Vatican, Kircher contemplates the deep pertinence of Mexico, with its pyramids and hieroglyphs, to Cairo.

The brand of syncretism Kircher captains stands apart from others owing to its Neoplatonic methodology and investment in Egypt. It stands at a notable remove even from the syncretism of his fellow Jesuit Acosta, which, less esoteric, attracted more followers than that of Kircher. Acosta's approach to the origins of the New World constitutes the final and most definitive divide in syncretism: a divide between those who display a certain skepticism toward origin theories and those who tend to accept a panoply of them.[18] Acosta's end of the sixteenth-century history exemplifies the first course. Partaking of the Renaissance critical spirit, Acosta brings a posture of doubt to bear on the pantheon of origin theories he reviews. His ironclad logic and empirical observations deriving from ten years in Peru (and one in Mexico) lead Acosta to scorn fanciful philological proofs like Yectan–Yucatán and to reason through popular theories of the New World origins until they collapse.[19]

Extremely influential, Torquemada again deserves separate mention.

While Torquemada distances himself from Acosta in terms of the devil's activities, the Franciscan's sputters of skepticism about any given theory ally him with the Jesuit. So does Torquemada's express "absolute" rejection of so major a matter as the Ten Lost Tribes hypothesis (1:26). The *Monarquía indiana* declares itself a legal deposition, or "probança" (1:32), and it concludes that the origins of the New World are not yet known (1:30-32). Torquemada's New World advocacy equates the Indians with the problematic Ham only through skin color, not by dint of shared moral failings (1:30).

In unequivocal contrast to Torquemada and Acosta, Gregorio García's *Origen de los indios del nuevo mundo* (1607) showcases all extant origin theories and magnanimously validates them. The first book exclusively devoted to New World origin theories, García's history rejects "all the theories separately" and then "affirm[s] them all collectively" (Huddleston 74). García ratifies theories outlandish and recondite, plausible and popular. Having done so, he arrives at the conclusion, shot through with multiplicity, that the New World's peoples "proceeded from various nations," by sea and by land, in successive waves of migration (315). Lee Huddleston observes with some dismay that after the mid-seventeenth century, Spanish historians opted for García's credulous eclecticism over Acosta's relatively enlightened methodology (78); he ascribes the predominance of García's modus operandi to Spain's growing intellectual isolation from the mainstream of (rationalist) European scholarship (79). One can hardly dispute Spain's intellectual solitude, which results in the veneration of authority that characterizes syncretism. I do, however, take some exception to Huddleston's discomfort with García's eclecticism. Despite García's excessive credulousness, his text and its successors prove themselves willing, in the propitious mode of the Baroque, to countenance multiplicity and indeterminacy. With this, their resolute plurality, they ended up being more forward looking as well as more accurate than their more discriminating counterparts.[20]

V. CREOLE PLURALITY

We now have the tools to unlock a number of signal creole texts from the late seventeenth century. The writings of Vetancurt, Sigüenza y Góngora, and Sor Juana negotiate with syncretism and plurality. Concomitantly, they bring into play key developments in creole discourse. Mature and multiple in its tactics, Mexican creole discourse ramifies into cultural nationalism and worship of the Virgin of Guadalupe. It penetrates history, chronicle, and literature. It appropriates the official discourse of city festivals and, in risky flights, lifts the pluralized, paradigm-shattering Baroque Spectacular City to its apogee.

Vetancurt and Creole Cultural Nationalism: Agustín de Vetancurt, who explodes the singular city, similarly exploits the pluralism of colonialist syncretism. He exploits it to the maximum and, following either a cautious or a deceptive course, stealthily. As he did with Balbuena's "Grandeza," Vetancurt fails to place a pivotal source on the seemingly comprehensive stage of his *Teatro*. This time he fails to cite García, from whose text Vetancurt unmistakably lifts his historiographic methodology and philosophy. Silently quoting or simply stealing from the prologue to the first book of García's text, Vetancurt outlines the four principal ways of knowing.[21] According to Vetancurt, none of them, including "divine faith" (1:208), settles the thorny matter of Indian origins. The inadequacy of epistemology, be it that of the *Orígenes* or any established epistemology, licenses Vetancurt to repeat the eclecticism of the early seventeenth-century García. Vetancurt rehearses all the major theories without critiquing them (1:189-207), only to conclude, like García, that "those who populated the new world of the Indies did not come from one people or nation, but from many" (1:209). "Agreeing with all opinions," Vetancurt declares that "at diverse times" the Indians derive from the Jews, the Carthaginians, Ophir, the Spaniards, the Hesperides, the Romans, the Tartars, and so on (1:210). The Baroque preservationist Vetancurt, disposed to multiplicity, stockpiles theories and defaults on resolving them.

Vetancurt does temper García's sweeping credulousness by adducing an empirical proof. He backreads from the diversity of his present-day Mexico to the diversity of its origins: "I find the basis for this [the diverse roots of Mexico] in the fact that here one finds such variety of customs, rites, ceremonies, dress, and languages that people say they originated in various countries" (1:210). His empirical proof, together with the locutions of diversity that crowd into each of the above-quoted statements on origins, remind one that no matter how much Vetancurt poaches García's earlier methodology of 1607, the fin-de-siècle *Teatro* occupies a different space. For Vetancurt, plurality has broken out of its confinement in methodology to become the prime characteristic of Mexico itself.

Vetancurt manipulates historiographic syncretism with equal stealth to the gain of Mexico. He operates by statement and, cleverly, by omission. The *Teatro* echoes Acosta's script on the devil mimicking Christian sacraments, yet Vetancurt will not credit Satan with founding Mexico. Instead, he puts forth the exceptional proposition that Mexico was populated before the biblical Flood (the general title of the section reads, "On the Inhabitants of New Spain Before the Universal Flood" [1:185]), by the giants mentioned in Genesis 6:4. He goes on to agree with tradition that the lineage of the world after the Flood issues from Noah. Undiscriminating as he was toward origin theories, Vetancurt here displays keen discernment. Although, he says, the Bible informs us that all humankind derives from Noah's sons, "it does not tell us from which son the Indians derived" (1:209). At no point in its laundry list of origin theories does the *Teatro* buy into the evil Ham story. Through a calculatedly selective, sometimes invisible eclecticism, Vetancurt has exonerated both ante- and postdiluvian Mexico from the stain of sin.

Vetancurt's treatment of origin theories indexes his ardent patriotism, which also informed the *Teatro*'s depiction of Mexico City. The roster of Mexico City's grandeurs offered just a small taste of the pride in Mexico that the *Teatro* vigorously espouses, among several ways, by revealing New Spain to be the biblical Earthly Paradise (1:48), surpassing Balbuena in extolling Mexico's supremacy over all peers, and placing Mexico center stage in the world arena. At the heart of Vetancurt's laudatory efforts lies his biological theory of Mexican superiority. Again without attribution, Vetancurt builds on the humoral vindication of Mexicans that Juan de Cárdenas devised in 1591. Cárdenas praises the "sanguine" disposition, hot and humid, of those born in Mexico, which enlivens their wits (1:59–62). Vetancurt concurs and alleges four robust explanations (climate, humors, abundance, wealth) of why in Mexico "minds are more vigorous, and physical strength less vigorous" (1:30). After this oblique but transparent justification of creole membership in the intellectual elite rather than in the ranks of physical laborers, Vetancurt finesses Aristotelian apologetics into a zone for creole pride-cum-complaint. He laments that the creole citizens of the Baroque intelligentsia lack due recognition. Like some New World plants, Vetancurt states, creole intellectuals wither prematurely, either because of the climate "or because they find their studies so little rewarded" and "learning held in such low esteem" (1:34–35). The new creole polemics of the *Teatro* has little of a positive nature to say about the contemporary Indians.[22] It does, however, lay the blame for the Indians' purported sloth and rampant alcoholism on the loss of the just, homegrown law that guided them before the conquest as well on Spanish neglect and abuses (1:410).

Vetancurt, minister of diversity, has clearly not relinquished his class prejudices or interests. Though the superintendent of an Indian parish, he has pleaded the cause of the creole intellectual still, at the end of the seventeenth century, handicapped by the glass ceiling that makes advancement into high office difficult if not impossible. The subjugated, ambitious, educated creoles of New Spain whom Vetancurt supports constitute a fertile breeding ground for the brand of nationalism known as cultural nationalism. Its defining aspects suit cultural nationalism both to a colonial situation and to the creoles of New Spain. Cultural nationalism can serve as a form of activism separate from or actually undercutting political, statist nationalism; it can oppose the nation, as conceived by a special interest group, to the state. Thus, when "the state is regarded with suspicion as a product of conquest," cultural nationalism can step in with its defining contention that the "glory of a country comes not from its political power but from the culture of its people and the contributions of its thinkers and educators to humanity" (Hutchinson 124).[23] Capitalizing on their particular skills, the intellectuals and artists who customarily spearhead cultural nationalism enshrine and propagate their culture's distinctive traits, with attention to the select moments of the historical patrimony that lend themselves to mythmaking.

Creole writers who by the end of the seventeenth century had become "increasingly conscious of themselves as a class and of Mexico as their patria" (Keen 188) present an early modern instance of the cultural nationalism just described. They find a rich, ready-made playing field for their endeavors right at hand. The indigenous history that, often to its glory, Spanish and radicado syncretist writers had reincarnated in the name of providentialism beckons to the creoles as an apt foundation for what Sigüenza openly calls "nuestra nación criolla" [our creole nation] (*Teatro de virtudes* 181; *Libra* 250), as a highly usable past. Read selectively, ancient Indian civilization could provide the traditional cornerstone of cultural nationalism, a bygone golden age. To the established topics on which an ideological creole nation could be premised—climate, biology, fertility, the great Mexico City and its refined viceregal culture—later creole writers therefore add indigenous history. As has often been noted, they appropriate indigenous history for creole patriotism.[24] José Joaquín Blanco, for one, observes that creoles seek "an identity of their own, distinct from (even opposing) that of the Indians and Spaniards, but shaped by peculiar and frequently grudging borrowings from both cultures" (*Esplendores* 16–17). The turn to another sector, to Indian history, pluralizes creole discourse. Yet, as Blanco's statement corroborates, the pluralizing of creole discourse harbors the class tensions manifested in Vetancurt's appraisal of the latter-day Indian.

The alliance between creole discourse and Indian history carries other inherent limitations. Confederated with syncretism, the creole historical project generally upholds historiography's hegemonic providentialism. Balancing the cultivation of a New World identity with the embracing of metropolitan paradigms, later creoles perpetuate the conflicting investments Villalobos had jaggedly reified. Cultural nationalism, too, both enables and constrains by fostering a retreat into history that does not readily lend itself to the formulation of the superstructures integral to instituting change. The putative creole nation that the literati contrive to birth into existence therefore goes only so far. Creole writers neither propose a precise revolutionary platform nor agitate for a separatist state. Their nationalist impulses remain firmly implanted in the patriotism that Vetancurt and our next subject, Sigüenza y Góngora, advocate so fervently. Although it has invaded history and engaged plurality, creole discourse still rests more on structures of feeling than on superstructures.

Sigüenza y Góngora and the Cities of the Margins, 1680: Vetancurt extols his fellow scholar Carlos de Sigüenza y Góngora as warmly as he does his homeland, calling his friend a "diligent investigator of ancient texts," "eager to discover, and publish, the grandeurs of this new world" (1: xviii). He rues that "Learned Men" have never "sufficiently celebrated" Sigüenza (2:269). Vetancurt's comments neatly catch three forces that unite to drive Sigüenza's writings. First, Sigüenza, who compiled his own archive of original Indian texts, delves into history. Second, by means of its history, Sigüenza exalts his homeland. He chooses Pegasus as his literary persona, for the mythological horse "represents man, who almost always trains his soul on the sublime, to benefit his homeland" (*Teatro de virtudes* 174). On the same page, Sigüenza notes that "the beautiful love of virtue should not be sought in foreign models; praise of domestic matters moves the soul." Third, animus spurs Sigüenza's efforts. Sigüenza, Lezama Lima's quintessential "Señor barroco," in fact lived out his days surrounded by poverty as lay chaplain to the Mexico City hospital for venereal diseases and as the archbishop of Mexico's almoner. Always seeking a patron for his secular writings, he often bemoans the lack of recognition and difficulties of publication that plagued him.[25]

While thirst for his due ("I value my reputation [*fama*] as much as my very life" [*Libra* 251–252]) could easily underwrite Sigüenza's conspicuous patriotism, a less personal resentment no doubt incites him. He wars against the ignorant scorn of Europeans, who, Sigüenza sarcastically remarks in his *Libra astronómica* (Book of astronomy) (1681), barely acknowledge either the Indians or the creoles as rational beings who walk on two feet (312–313). Sparked to action, Sigüenza styles himself as something of an organic intellectual, at the helm of the creole nation. Described as a "proprietor of the past" (*Glorias* xi), Sigüenza employs the tools of his trade to model an agenda for his class.

State and religious festivals, which covet the chronicles that guarantee their immortality, allow Sigüenza unique access to publication and to the public domain. In 1680, the year in which Sigüenza especially takes up the mantle of the organic intellectual, he seizes the bait and runs with it. Sigüenza's chronicles of two festivals that took place in 1680, *Glorias de Querétaro* and *Teatro de virtudes políticas que constituyen a un príncipe: advertidas en los monarcas antiguos del mexicano imperio* [Treasury of the political virtues that constitute a prince: noted in the ancient monarchs of the Mexican empire], published in rapid succession that same year, recreate the events in consonance with his agenda. Sigüenza avails himself of the festival chronicle to regale the public with his versions of various syncretisms, of the city, wonder, and, primordially, the Indians and their history. His chronicles and other contributions to the festivals succeed in erecting for posterity a pluralized Querétaro and Mexico City that claim the Spectacular City for the margins.

Glorias de Querétaro relates the efforts of a marginal city to establish a temple to the Virgin of Guadalupe, efforts that culminate in a week-long inaugural celebration during May of 1680.[26] Sigüenza's narrative shines a spotlight on a rather odd figure marching down the streets of Querétaro to broadcast the poetry contest that caps the celebration: "a tiny black man" so small that even the "Pygmies would dwarf him" (61). Given the Baroque taste for oddities, the man's "unfortunate smallness" "was the very thing that suited him to call attention to the event" (61). It is, in ways that fan out to encompass all aspects of *Glorias,* an emblematic moment. A small city in a viceregal colony relegated to the backwaters of modernity, Querétaro itself qualifies as a dwarf amidst somewhat bigger pygmies. Founded in 1537 by Spaniards and Otomi Indians, Querétaro developed into an agricultural region, a way station to the upper mining regions, and the base of operations for Franciscan evangelizing campaigns to the north. Though Querétaro was granted the status of city in 1556, it did not yet rival Mexico City or Puebla, the second most populous metropolis of New Spain. Puebla had been established by Franciscans in 1530 to entice Hispanic settlers to abandon their indolence and actually work the land; in contrast to Puebla, intended for creoles, Querétaro had a markedly Indian cast. A frontier zone from Toltec times on and now a fluid contact zone, Querétaro boasted a large, nonsegregated population of Indians who retained their languages and customs.[27] The state settled in Querétaro domesticated Indians like the Otomis and Tarascans, hoping they would bring the still-unpacified neighboring Chichimecas into the fold.

In 1680, the relatively small, "otherly" outpost of Querétaro opened its doors to a central enterprise that cut a huge swath at the time, an outsized issue that *Glorias* would have to tackle. The church of the Virgin of Guadalupe inaugurated that year implicates Querétaro in the Guadalupan cult that had overtaken Mexico City after the midcentury. Catching fire in Baroque times and extending to ours, Guadalupanism has perpetually aimed to knit Mexico's "increasingly heterogeneous population of white, mestizo, Indian, and black into a single spiritual cloth" (Kagan 152). The Virgin of Guadalupe, of course, held appeal in the colonial period for both Indians (through her appearance at Tepeyac, home to the Aztec goddess Tonantzín) and Spaniards (Guadalupe being the most venerated Marian image in Spain). The Jesuit Miguel Sánchez's Guadalupan treatise published 1648, which proclaimed Guadalupe the first creole, ignited a creolization of the icon that consolidated the Virgin as a syncretic, unitary symbol for the bulk of Mexico's plural, sharply divided constituencies. As the title of the Jesuit Francisco de Florencia's treatise of 1688 indicates, the Virgin of Guadalupe had become *La estrella del norte de México,* Mexico's guiding star.

Creole-allied Jesuits like Florencia and Sánchez took a leading role in promoting the cult that so dovetailed with the avid syncretism of their order. Sigüenza, for his part, had been expelled from the Jesuit seminary in Puebla as a consequence of some youthful folly. He nevertheless swore a debt to the Jesuits who had taught him, a debt "that I would pay back with the lifeblood that runs through my veins" (*Libra* 247). Throughout his life Sigüenza toiled to win the Jesuits' approval by supporting their concerns, including the Guadalupan cult to which he first paid homage at the precocious age of sixteen in his poem *Primavera indiana* [Spring of the Indies] (republished in 1680).[28] The inauguration of a Guadalupan temple in Franciscan Querétaro boded well for the Jesuits, and it fell to Sigüenza to capitalize on that promise.

In chronicling the vastly important Guadalupan activities and festivities of little Querétaro, dwarfed in resources as well as size by Mexico City, Sigüenza also faced the radical asymmetry and daunting challenge that the title of *Glorias*'s chapter 3 exemplifies: "Attempts to Form an Ecclesiastical Congregation in Honor of the Most Holy Virgin; Mexico City Grants Permission and Madrid offers Royal Consent for the Founding of a Church, Which *for Lack of Resources Is Reduced to a Small Room*" (15; emphasis added). The chapter title frames a contrast—between the glorious, internationally renowned Virgen of Guadalupe and her humble home in a tiny Querétaro room—so asymmetrical as to be comical. Yet, as the second "Approbation" of *Glorias* tells us, "*Nihil iucundius, quam veritas*" (xi), nothing true can be laughable. The endearingly true-to-life scenario expressed in the title in fact encloses the quite serious solution that Sigüenza devises to the fraught problem of how to transmute the small and humble into the glorious, large scope demanded by the festival chronicle's divine, syncretic subject. He meets the rhetorical and ideological challenges Querétaro poses, as he does in the chapter title, by embracing an entirely anticlassical disproportion. Through a series of interlocking initiatives, Sigüenza pungently contrasts *and* jolts the SMALL into the LARGE, the marginal into the central and great. Siguenza's strategy of disproportion and permutability reaches articulation toward the end of the text, when he attributes to the influence of Mexico's archbishop and viceroy, Payo de Ribera Enríquez, the "small beginnings, great progress, and gigantic perfection" of the church's construction (72). The aspiring author dedicates the text to Payo de Ribera, but the clever alchemy his chronicle achieves redounds to the credit of all concerned.

Sigüenza works his compulsory transformative magic on the wearisome trajectory of events ("the work advanced in Pygmies' strides" [26]) that led up to the inauguration of the church. Querétaro obtains from Mexico City a mere copy of an image of the Virgin of Guadalupe, installs it in a private home, and then transfers it to a chapel in the Hospital de Nuestra Señora, "no less modestly than the limited means of those who worshipped her allowed" (11). This least magnificent of temples, with its "none too costly altar," says Sigüenza, only allows the image to shine all the more brilliantly (11). After securing permission for the church from the grand imperial centers of Mexico City and Madrid, the citizens of Querétaro muster the little room mentioned above. It turns out to be much too small for their inordinately large devotion to the Virgin, who "by turns inspired fervent, gigantic flames of devotion in her disciples" (15). The citizens then transport the copy of the image to yet another modest room on the grounds of the future church. As humble spaces proliferate in a text that sounds alarmingly like satire, Sigüenza comes up with a redeeming spiritual justification for them. He observes that the Virgin's unworthy homes replicate her infinite affection for "smallness of mankind" (20). Finally, owing to the "singular prodigy" of Juan Caballero y Ocio's donation of land, the pious fathers of Querétaro lay the foundations for the church ("all spacious and grand") but have to halt the labor due to lack of funds (24).

Vexed, prodigious, giant-sized in its spirituality: Sigüenza's Guadalupan Querétaro is nothing if not, in literary terms, a Baroque city. As he details the church's trajectory, and throughout the text, the author rallies the resources of the ever-malleable Baroque to the cause of the peripheral Querétaro. From the *brevitatis formula,* aporia, chiaroscuro, penchant for the grotesque, mythological references, recondite metaphors, emotional melodramatics, *tremendismo,* or exaggeration, *horror vacui,* and extreme erudition intrinsic to the Baroque repertoire, Sigüenza derives a monumentalist rhetoric that magnifies the provincial city beyond all due proportion. The fabulous aggrandizement of Querétaro's Guadalupan travails feeds into Sigüenza's thoroughly Baroque objective for the text of projecting the minute events in Querétaro onto a huge, cosmic canvas. He depicts the laborious steps toward founding the church allegorically, as battles in a war waged by Divine Providence in the blessed arena of Querétaro to vanquish evil and to honor the Virgin (13–14, 16, 24, 26, 30). And when Divine Providence or the Divinity intervenes, the miracles so dear to the Baroque sensibility of the Jesuits cannot help but follow. A modest smattering of humble miracles, as sweet and earthy as a church patron falling down stairs without suffering major injury (55), therefore punctuates the narrative. Minor as they are, the miracles of *Glorias* return Baroque wonder to its origins in the divine supernatural. Rhetorically, emotionally, and theologically, everything is always overspilling its small container in Querétaro.

Glorias de Querétaro would hardly live up to its title and Sigüenza hardly satisfy his patrons' expectations had the text neglected the wonders of the city itself. Chapter 1 of *Glorias* does the job in abundant detail. Sigüenza begins his portrait of Querétaro with its glorious Indian past, noting that the first Moctezuma won it over to the Mexicas and fortified it as the frontier outpost of his empire (2). Although Querétaro can take pride in its indigenous history, Sigüenza decides that a description of the present-day city "will most appropriately attest to its grandeur" (2). With this, the text unexpectedly enters the terrain of "La grandeza mexicana." Sigüenza once wrote a no-longer-extant history of Mexico City from its Indian origins up to his day, evocatively titled *Teatro de grandezas de México* [Treasury of the grandeurs of Mexico City] (*Libra* 245). In *Glorias,* he relocates the topics of Balbuena's poem to Querétaro, as signposts of the town's grandeur and glory.

Chapter 1 of *Glorias* does its best to transmute Querétaro into a wondrous and great city. Sigüenza underscores the fertility and moderately dry climate of Querétaro (better, one infers, than the humid, flooded Mexico City); its fine houses (perhaps a bit squat but fully possessed of "capaciousness and grandeur" [4]); its commerce and economic self-sufficiency; the traffic of the obligatory "carriages and coaches that ennoble the city" (5); the elevated culture with which the "supreme intelligence and abilities of those born in the city" endow Querétaro (5); its lofty festivals, churches, religious orders, and so on. As he transplants "Grandeza" into Querétaro, Sigüenza reactivates another topic on which Balbuena had already laid hands, "disdain of the court and praise of the village." The would-be spectacular cityscape of *Glorias* essays to convince its readers that the small, agricultural city boasts the best of the city and of the countryside.

Sigüenza assigns the pastoral and utopian chapter 6 of "Grandeza," so appropriate to the agrarian Querétaro, a cascading job in *Glorias.* He variously attaches the floating motif of Balbuena's "Mexican paradise" ("Grandeza" 94) to the convents, new church, and city of Querétaro in toto. Likewise, the flowers for which Querétaro is justly renowned qualify it as a "vestige of Paradise" (10) that enjoys "Grandeza"'s immortal "spring" (53). Pastoral imagery once again lodges itself in the city, but the city has changed from Balbuena's. We have entered a Guadalupan city, where a rose is no longer just a rose. Now roses are attributes of the Virgin of Guadalupe, and Sigüenza's celebration of the flowers transparently suggests Querétaro, rather than Tepeyac, to be her natural home. Indeed, the extraordinary artificial mountain of Tepeyac concocted for one of the Guadalupan galas, which Sigüenza describes as astonishing and "suspending" the public (37-38), physically installs Tepeyac in Querétaro. The pastoral imagery, metaphorical and real in its references, has taken off from Balbuena's paradise and immortal spring and progressed inexorably to roses, to the Virgin of Guadalupe, and finally to a Querétaro conflated with Tepeyac. In keeping with its cosmic designs, *Glorias* has inch by inch effected a typological reading of "La grandeza mexicana."

Nonetheless, Sigüenza's ulterior motive in superimposing "Grandeza"'s spectacular metropolis on the provincial one is to set Querétaro up as a city that rivals or conceivably outdoes the great Mexico City. He announces unabashedly that the gardens, churches, and generosity of Querétaro match those of the capital (4, 7, 71). Yet Mexico City is not world enough for Querétaro and thus, akin to the centrality on the world stage that Balbuena assigned the capital, Sigüenza goes on to align the small Querétaro with the large centers of Europe. Now, in "Los funerales de la Mamá Grande" [Big Mama's funeral], Gabriel García Márquez has the pope step out of the Vatican directly into the obscure, remote Macondo (142); Sigüenza similarly blurs the boundaries between Europe and Querétaro by highlighting the ways in which Querétaro's Guadalupan efforts encroach on Madrid and Rome. The last pages of *Glorias* proudly announce the success of the Querétaro Jesuit Juan de Monroy in obtaining honors for the church from the Vatican, thus ensuring the good name of "the creole nation" (76) of which Querétaro now appears to have become the benchmark. In a final homage to the metamorphoses that Balbuena's text artfully executes, Sigüenza has rendered the frontier Querétaro not just highly permutable but also limitless.

Even "La grandeza mexicana," it turns out, is not world enough for Sigüenza's Querétaro. At crucial points in *Glorias,* its author abandons the Balbuena who refused to have commerce with the axiomatic issues of Sigüenza's agenda, the past and the Indians. Sigüenza's description of Querétaro veers away from Balbuena to pluralize the city. His verbal tour of Querétaro, dramatically different from either Balbuena's or Cervantes de Salazar's of Mexico City, leads off with the Indian district that houses "Indians, blacks, mulattos and mestizos, of which there are many" (3). Sigüenza takes pains to register that the body of the city's "republic" is composed "not only of common folk who answer the call of abundance with all the skills that it requires to achieve its full grandeur," but also of merchants, aristocrats, and immigrants from Spain (4). The natural abundance that employs the workers whom Sigüenza esteems produces the custard apples, avocados, plums, and many more fruits that, he says, appeal to the "creole," as well as "celebrated and much-craved peaches" for the Spanish "gachupín" (4). In the same breath that regenerates the colonialist topics of the marketplace, Sigüenza definitively materializes Querétaro into a fac*simile* of Vetancurt's inclusive Mexico City.

Beyond advertising the now-widened, intensely particularized wonders of Querétaro, it falls to Sigüenza to recount the two Guadalupan festivals the town mounted in honor of the church. One can hardly envision more ideal raw material for Sigüenza's political imagination than the two celebrations in which Chichimeca, Tarascan, and Otomi Indians play an enormous role, epitomizing the plural New World festival.

Predictably, then, Sigüenza discharges his task with zest. He infuses the spectacles with the locutions of marvel and awe that the festival itself provokes in its spectators and crafts a verbal portrait of the galas so minute that he "did not fail to mention even the tiniest blemish, perhaps because the more true to life the narrative, the better it expresses the pleasure of the celebration" (xi). The protocol of minutiae that festival chronicles warrant entitles Sigüenza to emphasize the aspects that fit his agenda, to interject editorial commentary, and to narrate his favored subjects in such inordinate, tremendous detail that they loom large in the text, conceivably larger than they did in real life.

Sigüenza's chapter 7 relates the indigenous masquerade with an array of telling details that cast it as a veritable primer of the author's cultural politics vis-à-vis Indian history. He informs his readers that the governor of the Indian community organized the masquerade to demonstrate "the singular affection of the natives for Our Lady [of Guadalupe]" (50). Willingly or not, the Indians' contribution to the festival takes the shape of a parade that replays a providential, Spanish view of their history. At its head (the least privileged position) stride the "disorganized tumult of wild Chichemeca" Indians (50). Half-naked, their matted hair adorned with drooping feathers, "almost a vestige of the legendary satyrs," the "barbarous" Chichimecas inspire horror and terror (50). Sigüenza, author of the now-lost work *Imperio de los chichimecos* [Empire of the Chichimecas] (*Libra* 245), continues the demonizing of the Chichimecas perpetrated by Acosta and by creole apologist Cárdenas (179). The residue of European scorn for Indian barbarity has come to rest in the wild northern Chichimecas, scapegoated and subalternized even or especially by creole writers.

Sigüenza's version of the masquerade then pans from the Chichimecas to the more pleasing sight of a hundred Indian boys decked out in Spanish finery. They march with admirable discipline, which proves that acculturated Indians are entirely capable of "order" and "concert" (50). *Glorias* next alights on the line of gorgeously attired Indian nobility who impersonate ancient indigenous rulers in a chronological sweep of Indian history that culminates in the Spanish king, Charles V, represented by an Indian. The spectacular pageant of a domesticated Indian history prompts Sigüenza to argue that it would be a "monstruosidad censurable" [reprehensible monstrosity] for the Indians to avail themselves of an alien esthetic since their own, while "pagan and barbarous," does not lack the "grandeur" that the occasion demands (51).

Having recruited order, concert, grandeur, and the Baroque's beloved monstrosity for the Indians, Sigüenza interprets the allegorical floats accompanied by native music and dances. Principal among them is the float bearing the image of Guadalupe. Prostrated at the feet of Guadalupe, surrounded by angels, kneels an Indian girl clad in native finery "who symbolized all of America, and, even more so, these Septentrional Provinces of it, which the pagan Indians called Anáhuac" (52). The young Indian protagonist of the syncretic festival carries a heart, "the heart of all" (53), and dispenses incense that bathes onlookers in perfume, palpably and sensuously binding the variegated Mexican crowd into a single community.

Chapter 8 of *Glorias* shifts from plebeian entertainments to the celebrations of the elite. Sigüenza reports on the sermons and plays and especially the poetry contest, "which rewarded Learned Men (with no involvement of the masses)" (63), in painfully exorbitant detail. There is a method to his maddening tediousness. Siguenza wishes to leave no doubt that the elite entertainments comprise a second heart of his festival chronicle, tantamount to the first. The author equally wishes to impress on the reader that he himself won the poetry contest, with the mediocre poem that the protocol of the minute entitles him to reproduce in its woeful entirety. Excruciatingly slight in esthetic merit, the poem nevertheless cements one of the two LARGE goals of the already busy text. The first is personal: the whole virtuouso performance of jolting the small into the large that Sigüenza has pulled off with an elaborate display of Baroque artifice validates him as a key player in the elite intelligentsia. Only a master of the Baroque could have accomplished such a feat. The only missing piece for full membership in the select corps was the poetry that any intellectual worthy of the title could produce in a heartbeat.

The author's extraordinarily large, ideologically driven, second goal for both his text and Querétaro overruns his personal interests. Sigüenza has aimed to decenter or at least to pluralize the map of New Spain by divesting Mexico City of its monopoly on the urban front and by advancing Querétaro as a new center for a syncretic Mexico. In ancient times a frontier and in colonial times a dwarf among pygmies, the contact zone of Querétaro bursts into new prominence and positionality as the standard-bearer of a plural yet unified Mexico. Renovation of Mexico comes from the provincial margins, from a Querétaro that has incorporated both its Indian past and the Indians themselves. Sigüenza's pluralized Querétaro also edges creole Puebla off the map as it incarnates the mission of the Virgin of Guadalupe, mother and symbol of all

Mexico. Querétaro, "this communal mother" (4), ascends to the large status of fitting flagship for the Virgin of Guadalupe. It has eclipsed the segregated Mexico City that houses the patriarchal institutions of the viceroyalty to become the all-welcoming Mother City. Thus does Querétaro, by virtue of Sigüenza's contrivances, overcome its multiply marginalized smallness to bear the mantle of Mexico's glory and greatness.

Sigüenza delivers the glories of Querétaro directly unto Mexico City in his contributions to the grand festival that marked the arrival of the new viceroy, the Marquis de la Laguna, in November of 1680. The author returned to Mexico City in May, and in October, the glories of Querétaro still fresh in his mind, accepted the charge from the creole city cabildo of composing for the ceremonial entry a triumphal arch together with an explanatory text. As is well known, the creole Metropolitan Cathedral Chapter bestowed the same honor on Sor Juana. Sor Juana's arch stood in the center of the city in front of the still-unfinished cathedral, Sigüenza's at the traditional entry point of dignitaries and the home of the Inquisition offices, in the Plaza de Santo Domingo.[29] The freestanding wooden arch that Sigüenza designed rose to ninety feet. Corinthian pillars supported its three levels, which contained sixteen niched pedestals. Here Querétaro begins to invade Mexico City.[30] For, exactly like the Indian masquerade and employing the "grand" Indian esthetic Sigüenza had admired in Querétaro, twelve of the Mexico City arch's pedestals bore portraits of ancient Aztec rulers, arranged chronologically. Echoing the providentialism of the Querétaro parade, which culminated in Charles V, the other four pedestals of the arch boasted portraits of figures from Mercury to an Indian girl welcoming the viceroy and vicereine. The emblems or "hieroglyphs" (188) that surrounded the portraits stated the virtues Sigüenza intends each Aztec ruler to model for the incoming viceroy.

Thus, not only Querétaro enters the capital. The arch brings the Indians that the state had relegated to Mexico City's margins out of exile and enthrones them in the very center of the city, pluralizing that bastion of power. Thanks to Sigüenza's arch, for a few days the heretofore marginalized Indians would dominate Mexico City. Yet long after his arch was razed the text that accompanied it would endure. Sigüenza's *Teatro de virtudes* eternalizes the ephemeral city of the margins together with the special pleading for Indian history that his arch brazenly foists on the solemn state occasion.[31]

That *Teatro de virtudes* takes its cue from a recent, real festival only heightens its audacity. In a *mise en abîme* of theatricality, Sigüenza's appropriately named *Teatro* layers one festival on another, instrumentalizing both of them. Pulsating behind the Indians of the text whom Sigüenza presses into allegorical service lie the real Indian actors of Querétaro. And although Sigüenza makes no reference to the matter, *Teatro de virtudes* forcibly bears the creole, Jesuit, Guadalupan platform of the recent *Glorias* in its aura. The author's protestations of creole patriotism and defense of homegrown models cited earlier reinforce the Guadalupan platform and form the linchpins of the apology for the text's daring, to which Sigüenza devotes his wildly protracted preludes. In the second prelude, Sigüenza calls on the Baroque taste for "the extraordinary" and the tradition of civic pride to legitimate his text and safeguard it from the "precipice" of extreme "risk" (172).

Venerable as they are, the safeguards cannot defuse the text's volatility. For it is precisely in the space of tradition that Sigüenza takes the greatest risk by playing a game of double jeopardy with the genre of *speculum principis* customary to festival celebrations. In the Mirror for Princes festival panegyrists outline the ideal qualities of a ruler, qualities that the ruler whom the festival honors presumably possesses. Flying in the face of convention, Sigüenza vests the ideal qualities in Aztec leaders. He then utilizes the Indian personages as smoke screens by means of which to set his cherished project for the creole nation in circulation. Sigüenza proclaims that the ideal ruler of the creole nation should exercise patience, tolerance, pacifism, piety, generosity (especially to intellectuals), audacity, and tenacity when provoked by adversity. The ruler should govern democratically, accepting good counsel. Further, Sigüenza filters several inflammatory insinuations through his descriptions of the Aztec leaders. Citing Villalobos, he characterizes the Aztecs as a *gentum expectantem* (180–181), a people in waiting (for their messiah Huitzilopochtli, not Christ). A passage full of pathos recounts the trials of the Aztecs, "a people broken to pieces by defending their homeland and broken by poverty, terrible in their suffering, as a result of which one can find no people who bear affliction so patiently, always hoping for a solution to their misery though everyone always beats them down" (180). Sigüenza praises freedom as the paramount value, "for there is no greater prerogative than freedom" (200). It is incumbent upon the good leader, he says, to throw off the yoke of servitude (225) and upon the collectivity to remember that its leaders must act for the common good (207–208). Sigüenza's loaded, forward-looking insinuations negate the suspended atemporality of the hegemonic festival and lay paths for the future.

They do so along the lines of cultural nationalism, by looking backward. Sigüenza's deliberate archaism invites spectators into history. On the hegemony's most prized cultural stage, the festival, *Teatro de virtudes* reinforces cultural memory. It replaces the false originary myths that colonialist festivals propagate with more authentic origins, albeit equally mythified ones. I refer to the fact that in his most audacious move yet, Sigüenza, "proprietor of the past," remythologizes Indian history. One by one, *Teatro de virtudes* rehabilitates the eleven Aztec rulers into exemplars of nonviolent, clement, generous leadership. Sigüenza maneuvers the Aztec god of war Huitzilopochtli into an avatar of the Christian Messiah for having led his people to their motherland, Mexico. Hazardously, Sigüenza regenerates the storied Aztec leaders who directly thwarted the conquerors. Moctezuma II comes to symbolize absolute monarchy, majesty, generosity, and affability, the sum total of the greatness of Mexico that derives from its Aztec past. Sigüenza christens Cuauhtémoc, who resisted the Spanish to the last, a martyr and a "steadfast soul" in the face of adversity (228).

From Huitzilopochtli to Cuauhtémoc, Sigüenza's revisionary Aztecs salvage the ancient past—and, to a degree, the recent present. In contrast to Querétaro's festivities, which dealt the Indians Manichean identities (bad Chichimecas, good Tarascans, etc.) and inveigled them into paying providential homage to the emperor, Sigüenza reinvents the allegorical Indians of *Teatro de virtudes* as models for the viceroy. The Mexico City festival and its text continue to sustain providentialism, but *Teatro de virtudes* disarms the identity-squelching machine of the festival. The text's Indians, though mythified and allegorical, are at least in this regard more authentic than those of *Glorias*. However, Sigüenza's *Parayso Occidental* (1684) and *Alboroto y motín de los indios de México* [Uproar and revolt of the Indians of Mexico City] (1692) make it clear that for him the glorious, more real Indian lives only in history. Like Vetancurt but more fiercely, Sigüenza condemns the vice-ridden, degraded state of the contemporary Indian.[32]

Firmly tethering the glorious Indians to the past entails confronting their textualization in prior works. That *Teatro de virtudes*, with its specific commission to interpret the festival arch, can circumvent some of the business of a full-fledged history does not keep Sigüenza from dealing extensively with syncretist historiography. In order to construct the golden age past integral to cultural nationalism, Sigüenza approaches history with a revisionary optic that rejects its crass aspects. He reads history selectively and, breaking with syncretic tradition, defaults on similitude: "One need not always seek similarity" (175). Sigüenza first contends with Torquemada's *Monarquía indiana*. Torquemada's reliance on Indian sources commends him to Sigüenza, who borrows the Franciscan's Spanish translation of Indian names. Debunking at several points all previous writers on the Indians except the *Monarquía*'s author (e.g., 208, 214), Sigüenza adopts him as his chief source on the matter and as a stand-in for his own kindred but still-unfinished work on the Indians. Yet then he locks horns with Torquemada on the issue of Mexico City's origins. Sigüenza opposes any demonizing of his messianic Huitzilopochtli, including that of Torquemada, and so whereas Torquemada views the Aztec war god as the devil's "magician," Sigüenza elevates him into a beatific miracle worker (196).

The third prelude of *Teatro de virtudes* takes on syncretism's thorniest issue, the origins of the New World Indians. Ostentatiously entitled "Neptune Is Not the Imaginary God of the Pagans but the Son of Mizraim, Grandson of Ham, Great-grandson of Noah, and Father of the Indians of the West," the prelude is one of the most astounding, challenging, and unusual texts in the entire corpus of syncretist historiography. Sigüenza intends it as such. To whet readers' appetites for his work in progress on the subject, he blazons his tantalizing Mizraim theory as totally new (183).[33] The author employs the rhetorical topic of "I bring new things" that resonates with the Baroque emphasis on novelty, and his Baroque text in no way disappoints. Sigüenza marshals an imposing army of biblical, classical, mythological, and contemporary sources. He assembles the battery of sources into outwardly coherent but ultimately fantastical ratiocinations, which will take the epigonic, conservative Baroque discourse to an extreme. This Pegasus aims his extreme games at one unique, spectacular goal: to establish, through Mizraim and others, the Egyptian origins of Mexico and of Mexico City. In the milieu of New Spain, only the creole author Juan Suárez de Peralta had hinted at Mexico's Egyptian origins, and he based his argument on comparisons none too flattering to either party.[34] Familiar or not with his predecessor's treatise, Sigüenza travels in a different direction from Súarez de Peralta and from Vetancurt, toward a source outside Mexico: Kircher.

In his *Oedipus Aegyptiacus,* Kircher had looked to the New World as a possible source of information on the prisca theologia, Egypt. Believing that the progeny of Egypt's originator, Ham, had founded Mexico, Kircher attempted to reconstruct the ancient religion of the pyramid-

and hieroglyph-laden Mexico, remote from him in time and space but less so than ancient Egypt. His association of Mexico with the prestigious Egypt, among other things, won Kircher several disciples in New Spain (our next chapter elaborates on this). Sigüenza's last will and testament reveals that his library contained all but four of Kircher's writings (Findlen, "Jesuit's Books" 346), writings that *Teatro de virtudes* references with great fanfare to support each bizarre wrinkle of its Egyptian origins argument.[35] Sigüenza needs to profit from Kircher's currency but to boost his own cannot merely echo the German Jesuit. *Teatro de virtudes* therefore forges a startling, labyrinthine, two-stage proof of Mexico's Egyptian provenance, as follows.

Joining the tradition of Salazar y Alarcón, both Sigüenza and Sor Juana portray the incoming viceroy (the Marquis de la Laguna, meaning "lake") as Neptune taking possession of the watery Mexico City. Whereas Sor Juana works the viceroy-Neptune theme mythologically, Sigüenza chooses what purports to be a more concrete, historical course. Through multiple philological and biblical sleights of hand too lengthy to recount, he twists Neptune into Naphtuhim, son of the Mizraim who in Sigüenza's view founded Egypt. The conundrum of establishing Naphtuhim and Neptune as one and the same person visibly strains even the erudite Sigüenza. He comes up with the astonishing solution (178–179) of making the Egyptian goddess of wisdom, Isis, whose mystical name means "varón varón" [man-man], either androgynous or a man. She literally *is,* he states, the male Mizraim whom the Bible equates with wisdom. Since classical texts consider Neptune the very figure of wisdom, Neptune then *is* Naphtuhim, son of Mizraim/Isis.

Sigüenza pushes the already attenuated Baroque logic to the breaking point because much is at stake. He intends to prove that Neptune was not a "chimerical king or fantastic deity but a person who actually lived, under the excellent circumstances of having been the father of the Indians of America" (177). In other words, while syncretist historiography might content itself with drawing analogies between Old and New World civilizations or with proposing multiple hypotheses of New World origins, Sigüenza will not rest until he has linked Mexico to Egypt historically (Keen 192) and definitively. To that end, he next brings to mind that Neptune founded Carthage and, on the authority of García together with others, that the Carthaginians founded the New World (179).

At this point, Sigüenza takes a sharp detour that initiates the second stage of his proof. "But if truth be told," he confesses, "the [theories involving] Carthaginian or African sailors have never satisfied me" (179). Rejecting Carthaginian origins, with Kircher (181–182) he lists the similarities between ancient Mexican and Egyptian civilizations and proceeds to historicize the communalities at length.[36] This, the pièce de résistance of his polemic, holds that after Atlantis sunk its survivors went on to establish Egypt, and from there to originate the New World. Interestingly enough, Sigüenza's crowning syllogism predicates itself less on the mountains of undiscriminating information the Baroque has accumulated than on the fissures and imponderables that accompany them. To locate Neptune in the Atlantis–Egypt–Mexico scenario, the author rummages through the huge warehouse of Baroque erudition and ferrets out the empty places, that is, the gaps in contemporary knowledge of Neptune. Gaps abound, and Sigüenza turns them into the cornerstones of his polemic. He fills the voids with fragments of received knowledge and streams of logic that ultimately confirm the sea god as ruler of the island Atlantis/the Atlantic Ocean and thus as progenitor of America. The fact that the first founders of Mexico had the Egyptian Naphtuhim–Neptune as their guide (181) appoints a second figure to the new pantheon of messiahs that *Teatro de virtudes* has devised from the radical fringes of syncretism. A regenerated Huitzilopochtli, founder of Mexico City, and a historicized Neptune, father of Mexico, now stand side by side as the messiahs who replace European syncretism's (including Kircher's) iniquitous Ham and notorious devil.[37]

Still, Sigüenza singles out the Egyptian argument of *Teatro de virtudes* as the means by which he pays his debt to the Indians for "the homeland that they gave us" and to heaven for the favors it has conferred on Mexico (183). His point is well taken. The Egyptian connection, which distinguishes the Jesuit-leaning Sigüenza from the Franciscan Vetancurt, benefits Mexico on several levels. In allying Mexico with the prestigious prisca theologia, it imbues New Spain with a grandeur more spectacular and transcendent than in "Grandeza" or ever before. Conversely yet advantageously, it freights Mexico with the political connotations of Egypt: home of the Jews oppressed by the Pharaoh and kept from the Promised Land. Last but not least, under the protection of the Vatican's Kircher, the affiliation with an exotic Egypt in effect distances Mexico from the Catholicism that the conquest had visited upon it. Jesuit-sanctioned hermeticism straddles the line between Christianity and paganism, the totem and the taboo. When enlisted for creole patriotism, it endows the creole nation with a distinctive sacred scripture. Hermeticism offers the creole nation an alternative quasi-religion and Sigüenza a stellar role, as its high priest.[38]

Sor Juana: Crisis, Syncretism, and Festival Cities: In her passionately serious contributions to the Mexico City festival of 1680 and onward, Sor Juana Inés de la Cruz sets *herself* up as a high priestess. She fashions a unipersonal "religion" with a pantheon of its own, contrived to buttress her unique, precarious situation as a famed female intellectual. Sor Juana's "religion" feeds into a vast special pleading that trades on her specific talents, intellectual proclivities, and circumstances. Ultimately, it surpasses her personal situation to speak for womankind and humankind, the intelligentsia, the colonial subject, and her fellow creoles. Our next chapter follows Sor Juana's treatment of these large issues to some of their highest levels of abstraction and implication. There, her themes, together with the Baroque Spectacular City in Mexico, reach their peak and their breaking point. On the path toward that critical moment, the nun-writer composed two festival works for and about specific places on which I will concentrate here. Her official festival pieces of 1680 and 1689 constitute Sor Juana's major public debuts for Mexico City and Madrid, respectively. Driven by their author's personal exigencies and envisaged as vehicles to catapult her into the sanctuary of stardom, the two festival pieces draw on the abundant field of syncretism to spectacularize and pluralize their host cities.

Only her second published text, and one that would reappear as the final crowning jewel in the first volume of her complete works (*Inundación castálida* [Overflowing of the Castalian Spring] 1689), the *Neptuno alegórico* (OC:4) Sor Juana composed for the festival of 1680 embodies the pressures and literary tactics that would radiate into her subsequent writing life. The commission that the Metropolitan Cathedral Chapter of Mexico awarded to Sor Juana for the festival catalyzed extant, paradigmatic tensions around the fledgling writer, goading her severe Jesuit confessor, Antonio Núñez de Miranda, into adversarial action.[39] That the Cathedral Chapter, with the support of the incumbent viceroy and the archbishop, had selected Sor Juana as bard of the supremely prestigious public event may well have ignited Núñez's jealousy. Why Sor Juana and not him, renowned for his festival contributions, spiritual advisor of viceroys, officer of the Inquisition, appointed by the Company of Jesus in Spain as provincial of the Mexican Jesuits in February of that very year (Robles 1:275)? Pablo Brescia speculates that this may have been "the first time the monster of envy" had "reared its ugly head" (48) in her confessor. Núñez appears to have reacted with umbrage to the commission and, as Sor Juana reports in her so-called "Autodefensa espiritual" [Spiritual self-defense] (written around 1682), he publicly slandered his protegée. In the letter, Sor Juana asks her confessor why he had to malign her "publicly before everyone" (English version included in Paz's *Sor Juana;* 501), thereby setting off what is arguably the first major crisis of Sor Juana's career.

By the date of the "Autodefensa," Sor Juana felt so empowered that she dismissed Núñez as her confessor. Her opening act for the new viceroy and vicereine in the festival of their entry had helped win her the leverage with them that would afford Sor Juana the most productive, free stretch in her career. Cognizant in 1680 of the high stakes, Sor Juana forges the machinery of her festival contribution exquisitely and from the ground up. She designs the festival arch, conceivably supervises its construction from her convent apartment, writes a poetic explanation of it to be recited on the day of the event, and later expands and further glosses the original arch and poetic text in a prose version also published separately in Mexico City.

The arch that the *Neptuno* textualizes gave Sor Juana her first and only opportunity to help construct a real physical edifice. She responds by fabricating an artifact as absorbing and intricate as Balbuena's fabulous objects, an otherworldly world unto itself painted on a huge façade that stood in front of the cathedral's western portal. Brightly colored, richly detailed columns in various classical styles divided the façade into eight sections. Each section contained a canvas with an allegorical scene that illustrated the virtues of the new viceroy in the person of Neptune, accompanied by an epigram that articulated the painting's message. On the lower of the two central canvases appeared an almost prurient, Botticelliesque scene of a naked Neptune and his wife posed on a seashell, a male/female couple echoed in the top left-hand portrait of Neptune and Minerva.

From the twin portraits of the arch that train the eye on magnificent female figures to the whole of the *Neptuno,* Sor Juana takes the festival as a personal stage on which she will present herself and her concerns to the incoming viceroy. Collaborating with Sigüenza on her festival pieces, Sor Juana brings her subaltern—not the Indian but woman—to the fore of the festival and the heart of the city. The poetic explication of the Minerva/Neptune scene flirts with danger to call the vast festival audience's attention to Sor Juana's agenda. It recounts the competition between Neptune and Minerva, "Great Mother" and "inventor of arms and knowledge" (408), to name the city of Athens. As did Sor Juana in the "magnificent contests" (408) to which earlier Viceroy Mancera had subjected her to certify her prodigious knowledge, Minerva emerges from the contest as "most beautiful and wise victress" (409).

Minerva's victory over the viceroy/Neptune advances Sor Juana's self-portrait and her feminism, but it leaves the author in a situation no less hazardous than that of Sigüenza with his Huitzilopochtli and Cuauhtémoc. The nun cuts through the Gordian knot none too cleanly by parlaying Neptune's defeat into an indirect victory. Sor Juana portrays Neptune as a belligerent, armed brute vanquished by a Minerva adorned with the "tokens of peace" (408); however, since Sor Juana casts Minerva as the daughter of Neptune rather than of Jupiter, Minerva's victory allegedly reactivates the inborn wisdom of Neptune and erases his former brutality, all of which augurs the new viceroy's own peaceful reign. Sor Juana not only pushes the figuration of the viceroy close to catastrophe, she also rewrites as a feminist fable the story of the competition found in one of the *Neptuno*'s stated sources. St. Augustine's *City of God* (which Sor Juana cites on page 361 of her text) has Neptune bitterly resenting Minerva's victory and her female supporters eventually abhorring the goddess.[40]

The official entry of the viceroy, we see, has become a forum for Sor Juana and Sigüenza's extreme signature issues as well as a spectacle of marginality stationed in the power centers of the capital. Tempering their mutual daring, to curry the viceroy's support both authors showcase their exemplary, superlative erudition and place it at the ruler's disposal. In *Teatro de virtudes*, Sigüenza calls the festival commission a "[g]lorious reward for my studies" and gratefully acknowledges "the opportunity good fortune has granted me," which allows him to prostrate himself at the feet of the viceroy (167). Sor Juana coyly allies her knowledge with the viceroy's power, making herself present on the very day of the occasion in the poem that refers to her triumphal arch as deriving more from "el estudio de amor / que no el amor del estudio" [more from the study of love than from the love of study] (403). The exorbitant erudition that had acquired such prestige in Baroque times qualifies the disgraced former Jesuit Sigüenza and the beleaguered, illegitimate Sor Juana as icons of culture worthy of the viceroy's much-desired patronage.

Given the goals and scholarly tools for achieving them that Sigüenza shared with Sor Juana, it comes as no surprise that the nun also seizes upon the Mirror for Princes tradition or that she construes it similarly to her fellow creole intellectual. Of value to them both, and to the colonial intellectual in general, the program Sor Juana proffers in her assorted festival contributions of 1680 advocates that the viceroy incarnate liberality, pacifism, prudence, a collaborative spirit, and a benevolent, nonpunitive attitude toward the weak.[41] Preemptively, prematurely, she terms the viceroy "optimal protector" (374, in Latin). Speaking directly to the viceroy in the poem, she thrusts her definition of leadership on him: "you are the greatest sanctuary for learning" (407). Sor Juana does not fail to note in the prose text, with a fine pragmatic cynicism, that the structures of patronage actually oppress the colonial intellectual, "for the beneficiary never has the right to act freely" (386).

If her prescriptions relevant to the colonial intelligentsia reverberate with the sometimes querulous creole platform put forth by Sigüenza and Vetancurt, the exalted vision of Mexico City that runs through Sor Juana's whole festival ensemble foments unreserved creole civic pride. Along with Sigüenza, who lists and quotes New World works that sing the praises of New Spain's capital (203), Sor Juana compares the "imperial" Mexican city to Delos, birthplace of the gods, and to Rome (378–380 *et passim*). Her repeated exhortations that the viceroy complete the cathedral (which the poem calls an "Imperial Mexican Marvel" [410]) and drainage of Mexico City suit both creole civic pride and activism. The *Neptuno* engages the cityscape of the capital more fully and with more particularity than any other work in Sor Juana's repertoire.

As might be expected in view of their commonalities, Sigüenza praises Sor Juana's arch extensively in the *Teatro de virtudes*. He also insinuates at the beginning of his prologue on Neptune as founder of Mexico (176–177) that, compared to his effort, hers remains rather innocuous. Sigüenza does Sor Juana no injustice. Aside from (and all the more effectively to highlight) her brash riff on Neptune and Minerva, the nun largely takes shelter in safe, conventional topics on the day of the celebration. In keeping with Sigüenza's not-unreasonable comments, scholars tend to play up the differences between the published *Teatro de virtudes* and the *Neptuno*.[42] Nonetheless, the two authors exchanged manuscripts as they prepared their texts for publication, and their final texts share some distinctive, idiosyncratic arguments. Both works argue that Neptune actually existed (*Teatro de virtudes* 177, 183; *Neptuno* 359), feature the same outré etymology of Isis's doubly masculine name, and the same genealogy of Isis, Neptune, and Mizraim.

As the mutual references to Isis imply, both authors also overlay their explanations in prose with wonderfully exotic, Egyptian, Kircherian dimensions completely absent from either of their original festival contributions.⁴³ Sigüenza, who acquired his first book by Kircher in 1672 (Trabulse, "*Itinerarium*" 33), lards his prologues with quotations from the *Oedipus Aegyptiacus* and other of Kircher's texts. At this point in his career Sigüenza is clearly immersed in Kircher. On the other hand, Sor Juana opens her prose text with references to the Egyptian hieroglyphs (355–356) that Kircher purportedly deciphered in his *Oedipus*, to my knowledge her first references to Egypt ever. Although nowhere in its vast stock of references does the *Neptuno* cite Kircher, in constructing her Isis, Sor Juana patently relies on the engraving of the goddess found in the *Oedipus*.⁴⁴ Why, beyond wanting a profile of her own, might Sor Juana play such hide-and-seek with Kircher? A possible answer to the question lies waiting in the sonnet Sor Juana writes to Sigüenza about their festival collaboration. The sonnet's first-person speaker praises Sigüenza's erudition and mentions her respectful ignorance of an undisclosed matter ("mi fe reverencia lo que ignoro" [Soneto #204, OC:1]). Sor Juana's praise of her collaborator's knowledge combined with her reluctance to cite Kircher outright strongly suggest that in 1680 Sigüenza has just introduced Sor Juana to the Egyptian scenario and Kircherian thought that, as my next chapter explores, will greatly affect her subsequent works.⁴⁵

Reflecting Sor Juana's possible status as a novice Kircherian and/or purposely setting itself apart from Sigüenza's temerity, the *Neptuno*'s foray into Egyptology skirts full-fledged engagement with historiographic syncretism. Nowhere in the *Neptuno* does Sor Juana declare Mexico's Egyptian origins. She keeps the connections between Mexico and Egypt more metaphorical than real (e.g., Mexico City compared to, rather than as, Delos). She lets the manifest, presumptuous syncretism of Sigüenza's *Teatro de virtudes* both camouflage and authorize her own operations. Still, like the patriotic Sigüenza, Sor Juana avoids the miscreant Ham and the devil. And Isis so dominates her text as to suffuse it with an Egyptian, syncretic cast.

Tempered or extreme, the two authors' Egyptianizing, Kircherian syncretism pluralizes Mexico City, coating it with a veneer of the exotic. Their sequel to Balbuena's and Dorantes's self-exoticizing delivers an Egyptian Mexico City replete with the wondrous, glittering spectacularity that festival city texts demand. Sigüenza expressly applies to Kircher because he has elucidated Mexico's awe-inspiring origins, a task that, in the view of Sigüenza, organic intellectual, Mexicans themselves should assume but have not (*Teatro de virtudes* 181). He registers the mistakes in Kircher's work, attributing them to the Jesuit's lack of native informants. Since, as Sigüenza well knew, other Mexican intellectuals had already entered into correspondence with Kircher, it would seem that he and Sor Juana take it upon themselves to set the then cutting-edge, exotic Kircher into official circulation, claiming his cachet for themselves.[46]

Their mutual appeal to Kircher, an unconscious epitaph for the recently deceased German Jesuit, also surreptitiously seeks a new life for Sigüenza and Sor Juana.[47] By means of Kircher, the two creole authors could at once placate the local Jesuits with whom they had clashed and transcend localisms. Sor Juana and Sigüenza tacitly, or maybe quite obviously for their milieu, pit the intellectually wide-ranging, universal, Vatican-sanctioned Kircher against the more constraining Núñez de Miranda and other Mexican Jesuits of his ilk. As does the soul shed the material body and take flight in Sor Juana's *Primero sueño* [First dream], so do the two intellectuals positioning themselves to skyrocket into fame via the new regime subtly slough off repressive local Jesuits in favor of the universal Kircher and his Egyptian syncretism.

Sor Juana's particular involvement with syncretism in the *Neptuno*, it should be understood, has just as much to do with herself and with the devising of a unipersonal religion as it does with the above matters. One can easily imagine the nun at this early, agitated moment in her career, scanning history for a female icon who could publicly authorize her exceptional existence and maybe even rate her private veneration. Isis meets Sor Juana's needs precisely because of her supremely multiple, syncretic nature.[48] The cult of Isis arose at the dawn of civilization; as it spread to the Greco-Roman empire, the Egyptian goddess acquired the attributes of other primitive and local deities. Plutarch, cited in the prose *Neptuno* (361–362), mentions that "receptive of all manner and shapes and forms," Isis "has been called by countless names" (¶53). Along with Plutarch and Kircher, and Kircher's source, Apuleius's Isis-worshiping *The Golden Ass* (which Sor Juana references on 364–365), the nun-writer dwells on the multiplicity of Isis, "to whom writers have given a tremendous variety of names" (365). They have identified Isis, says Sor Juana, with Minerva, Venus, Diana, Ceres, Persephone, Juno, the Earth, the Moon and, primordially, as the embodiment of wisdom (365–366). Sor Juana thus encounters in Isis an all-purpose, sublime model. Moreover, the Egyptian figure's consecrated syncretism supports the quirky, bold syllogism toward which the prologue of the *Neptuno* builds. Namely, Sor

Juana argues that all goddesses converge in Isis, ergo all are goddesses of wisdom, the exact profile the erudite *Neptuno* wishes to procure for its author.

The syncretic, all-purpose Isis, finally, helps crack the code of a major enigma. I refer to Sor Juana's apparently scant devotion to the Virgin of Guadalupe, hallmark of the plural Mexico, nucleus of creole cultural nationalism, rallying point of the festival city. Although Sor Juana resided in a creole-dominated convent; although her order, the Hieronymites, had long maintained the shrine of Guadalupe in Spain; although Viceroy Marquis de Mancera and, subsequently, Archbishop Francisco de Aguiar y Seijas pledged themselves to Guadalupe, the nun explicitly dedicates only one composition to the Mexican icon (Soneto #206, OC:1). Almost obsessively, though, Sor Juana does write about the Virgin Mary, often invoking her as a paragon of knowledge and hence as an idealized self-mask. She most frequently confers on Mary the attributes of Guadalupe that Sánchez's treatise had expanded and popularized.[49] Once chaplain to Sor Juana's convent, Sánchez syncretically conflated the Mexican icon with the devil-banishing Woman of Patmos (Rev. 12), whose iconology of moon, sun, stars, eagle, serpent overlaps with Guadalupe's. Interestingly enough, venerable depictions of Isis, including Kircher's, endow her with the very same attributes. (Tradition also represents Isis, like the Woman of Patmos and Mary, with her boy-child.) That Apuleius has the roses carried in a festival procession play a signal role in bringing Lucius to the transformation from ass to man masterminded by Isis, and that in the portion of the 1680 text on Isis Sor Juana quotes a poem penned by Góngora for the Spanish shrine of Guadalupe (369),[50] continue to align the Virgin of Guadalupe with Isis and the *Neptuno*.

Incredibly complex and perfectly Baroque, the genealogy of Isis–Mary–Guadalupe indicates that Sor Juana does in a myriad of texts obliquely invoke the creole-championed Virgin of Guadalupe, albeit once again outleaping the local. Further, the genealogy indicates that the nun's pantheon of self-serving female icons, with its profound reliance on amalgamation and transubstantiation, takes its cue from the exotic, syncretic Isis inaugurated in the festive *Neptuno*. The multiplex Egyptian goddess is Sor Juana's first, most paradigmatic heroine. Yet, like the Virgin of Guadalupe, Isis ends up dismembered and submerged. At Sor Juana's worst crisis point in 1691, after being reprimanded for the *Carta Atenagórica* [Letter worthy of Athena] and creating a storm with the *Respuesta a Sor Filotea de la Cruz* [Reply to Sister Philothea of the Cross], she orchestrates her debut in Oaxaca around the pronouncedly

Egyptian, learned St. Catherine of Alexandria, associated with Isis's Nile (Villancicos #312–322, OC:2). Given that Isis and her female-centered cult, a thorn in St. Paul's side, could represent "whatever Christianity was to stigmatize and attack as idolatry" (Witt 59),[51] it probably does not escape Sor Juana that the Isis whom the *Neptuno* idolizes was too heterodox to stand its author in good stead against the hegemonic forces that bore down on her.

In spectacularizing Isis as well as other female figures, Sor Juana's *Neptuno* effectively rivals the audacity of Sigüenza's Aztec-oriented *Teatro de virtudes* (Arenal 176). Sigüenza's syncretic *Teatro* takes existing creole patriotism to an extreme, but Sor Juana's syncretic Isis fronts for a feminist cause that formed part of no established or acceptable Mexican agenda whatsoever. The nun's creations of 1680 inject the unwonted, unwanted element of women into the festive city. They disrupt the ideal, imagined community of the festival, pluralizing it in wayward directions. Ironically or predictably, Sor Juana's anomalous, basically irrelevant efforts won her greater advantage on a personal level than Sigüenza's politically inflammatory chronicle did for him. Whereas she obtained enormous patronage from the viceregal couple, he still struggled to publish his works and ended up doling out alms for the misogynist Archbishop Aguiar y Seijas.

The profits the *Neptuno* reaped for Sor Juana spurred her to work Baroque public statecraft whenever the opportunity presented itself. With the fame that soon accrued to her, opportunities presented themselves in abundance. For instance, Sor Juana became the principal Marian poet of Mexico City festivals. The explosive renown that afforded her increasing access to public venues also exacerbated the tensions that 1680 first brought to a boiling point. Sor Juana retaliates, among many ways, by directing her self-defensive campaign to the metropolis, to Spain. She cultivates European contacts and has her work published in Spain. As Frederick Luciani notes, "The beginning of the nun's descent from the height of favor in the Mexican capital virtually coincided . . . with her entry onto the transatlantic literary scene" (23). Sor Juana's transatlantic game plan, like her negotiations with Jesuit syncretism, straddles the line between the local and the universal. It skillfully twists the often conflictive dual investment of the creoles, torn between Mexican and metropolitan loyalties, into a positive. In works like her Romance #37 to the Portuguese duchess de Aveyro (OC:1) and those discussed below, Sor Juana capitalizes on the in-between status of the creole to broker Mexico to Spain.[52] The more Spanish the audience, the more "Mexican"

Sor Juana would be. On "alas de papel frágil" [wings of fragile paper] (Romance #37) she fashions herself as a bridge between two worlds.

A bittersweet opportunity for Sor Juana's transatlantic agency, which would again prompt her recourse to the world-bridging syncretism, arose in 1688. The viceroy and vicereine, the Marquis de la Laguna and Countess de Paredes, were called back to Spain, leaving the nun bereft of her strongest supporters. In consolation, the viceregal couple transported to Europe Sor Juana's complete works, which the countess would have published in 1689 as the *Inundación castálida*. The oeuvre Sor Juana sent to Spain included the Eucharistic drama *El Divino Narciso* and its introductory *Loa* (OC:3). Sor Juana had written the festival ensemble at the behest of the vicereine shortly before the countess left Mexico, "to be taken to the court in Madrid so that it could be performed there" (513), presumably at the Madrid festival of Corpus Christi in 1689. *El Divino Narciso* did not attain publication in the initial edition of *Inundación*, reaching print only in subsequent Spanish volumes of Sor Juana's works.[53] The play itself emits signals that Sor Juana intended it as a debut piece for her largest Spanish audience to date, arguably as a kind of advertisement for the publication of her complete works shortly to follow. Nevertheless, as far as we know neither the Eucharistic drama nor its loa was ever performed in Madrid or in Mexico (Sabat de Rivers, *En busca* 266). Sor Juana, it appears, had grievously mismanaged her Spanish debut.

Interacting more profoundly and critically with historiographic syncretism than any other work in her oeuvre, Sor Juana's loa gives strong indications of why the would-be debut misfired.[54] A creole broker, Sor Juana decides to represent Mexico's and by extension her own uniqueness by bringing Mexican history, specifically the Aztec city of Tenochtitlán, to Madrid. Her daring loa orchestrates the Aztec ceremony of *teocualo*, which means "God is eaten," as described in Torquemada's *Monarquía indiana* (2:71–73). According to Torquemada, Aztec priests gathered in the Templo Mayor at the center of Tenochtitlán to celebrate Huitzilopochtli. From seeds and the blood of sacrificed children they fashioned a statue of the war god, which they paraded around the city and subsequently ingested. Torquemada recounts the festival with the high drama and exoticism that engrave Tenochtitlán in the reader's mind as a spectacular city. While Sor Juana's loa takes place in a "Royal City" (4) that remains a fairly abstract, disembodied space, the play spotlights the spectacular Aztec festival. Transplanting the spectacular city of Tenochtitlán to Madrid and translating it into the festival of Corpus Christi, the loa equates the Aztec ceremony with the sacrament of the Eucharist. Sor Juana subscribes to Torquemada's conviction that the Indians' natural reason inclined them to God, and in concert with the *Monarquía*'s author, she represents the ceremony of the "God of the Seeds" as a prefiguration of Communion.

To a significant degree Sor Juana plays back for Spain its own discursive and ideological management technique for the plural New World, syncretism. Like Torquemada, she concedes the diabolical nature of the teocualo. Following Acosta et alia and betraying her *Neptuno*, she grants that the devil implanted the correspondences between Aztec and Christian rituals. The allegorical character of Spanish Religión exactly voices the Acostan script:

> ¡Válgame Dios! ¿Qué dibujos,
> qué remedos o qué cifras
> de nuestras sacras Verdades
> quieren ser estas mentiras?
> ¡Oh cautelosa Serpiente!
> Oh Áspid venenosa!
>
> . . . .
>
> ¿Hasta dónde tu malicia
> quiere remedar de Dios
> las sagradas Maravillas? (13)
>
> [Heaven help me! What kind of outlines, imitations, or ciphers of our sacred truths do these lies purport to be? O cautious Serpent! O poisonous Asp! How far will you go in imitating the sacred Marvels of God?]

Religión repeats the words of St. Paul to the Athenians on the "Unknown God" whom heathens worship in the form of their own deities (Acts 17:22–23; *Loa* 13–14) that Acosta and other syncretist historians frequently applied to New World religion.

Sor Juana's adherence to the providential aspects of syncretism is undeniable but also gestural and proleptic. Under the guise of the most consecrated syncretism, authorized by the Baroque desire to shock, she strikes at the heart of the Spanish colonial mission. Her loa depicts Spanish efforts to convert the Aztecs to Christianity, and its second scene cuts right to a nerve as it dramatizes an internecine conflict over methods of conversion. Spanish Religión and Spanish Celo, or Zeal, war over which form of conversion, peaceful or violent, is more efficacious. Celo initially has his brutal way. In a scene remarkably akin to Pedro de Alvarado's massacre of the Aztecs during the initial phase of the conquest, Celo attacks the Indians as they celebrate the God of the Seeds. Sor Juana's Religión accuses Celo of waging an offensive of punishment, terror, and revenge on America. The allegorical character América verbally assaults Celo as well, calling him a "barbarian" and a "madman" who has disrupted the calm the Indians enjoy in "serene peace" (9).

Celo's aggression only occasions Indian resistance to Christianity. Hence, the latter part of the loa counters physical violence with a rational, syncretic form of conquest that successfully persuades by elucidating the similarities between Indian sacrifice and the Catholic Eucharist. Thinking with, rather than in opposition to, the Indian worldview, Sor Juana's Religión portrays Christianity as an organic outgrowth of Aztec practices (Christ as sacrificial victim, the Host as Christ's body and blood, and so on). Religión's measures allow "divine inspiration" to enter the Indians and sway them toward Christianity (17). Concomitantly, they bring the Spaniards into an exceptional understanding and appreciation of Indian religion. By the end of the loa, Sor Juana has in essence modified Acosta's construction of Indian religion as devil-inspired imitation of Christian ritual to posit Aztec worship as a meaningful system in its own right. Hence all, Spaniards and Indians alike, implausibly exit singing, "¡Dichoso el día / que conocí al gran Dios de las Semillas!" [Blessed was the day I encountered the great God of the Seeds!] (21).

The ways in which the loa superimposes Tenochtitlán on Madrid, chides Spain for its violence, and dignifies Aztec religious practices all militate for Mexico and against the success of Sor Juana's would-be brilliant international debut. The resulting inadequacy of Sor Juana's transatlantic campaign, the fact that the bridge between two worlds had become another problematic agile platform, manifests itself not only in the troubled publishing and performance history of the loa but also toward the end of the nun's life.

Romance #51 ("En reconocimiento a las inimitables plumas de la Europa, que hicieron mayores sus obras con sus elogios: que no se halló acabado" [OC:1], [To the matchless pens of Europe, whose praises only enhanced her works, lines found unfinished] [#36]), reputed to be her last composition, finds Sor Juana laboring mightily to disabuse herself of the European praise that has earned her nothing but misery in Mexico. Since the 1693 arrival there of the second volume of her complete works published in Europe had aggravated her already dire situation at home, Romance #51 undertakes to defrock, so to speak, the praises of her that the volume contained. In the poem, Sor Juana strenuously denounces its exogamous tributes to her person.

Further, she disabuses herself of the role of literary bridge between worlds that she had strived to win by conveying Mexican knowledge to Europe in works like the loa, and European literary culture to Mexico in works like the *Neptuno* and numerous others. The creole broker Sor Juana, who sidestepped and internationalized the Virgin of Guadalupe, had in effect positioned *herself* to occupy that figure's continent-spanning place. To wit, in the frontispiece of her *Fama y obras póstumas* (Fame and posthumous works) (1700), Sor Juana appears in the central place between Europe and America that Guadalupe should by all rights occupy. Yet now, with a truly fraught sweep of her pen, the nun terms European writers "inimitables." Romance #51, all told, can be construed as Sor Juana's renunciation of her European project, on the wings of ever more fragile paper. The piercingly conventional penitential documents (#408–410, OC:4) of her alleged conversion to orthodoxy and the reunion with her strict Jesuit confessor date from the period in which she wrote the *romance*.

The net failure of Sor Juana's transatlantic campaign has stinging implications for the issues examined in this chapter. It unmasks the fraudulence of hegemonic Baroque plurality, the dangers it held for those who would take it quite literally at its word. No matter how much the colonialist Baroque surface engaged or incarnated plurality, no matter how universalizing Baroque syncretism purported to be, the colonial New World remained at heart absolutist, its pressures local.

There are some saving graces. From a Spanish perspective the anti-colonialist static of Sor Juana's loa may have derailed her Madrid debut, but the loa has delighted present-day scholars in equal measure with her comic medleys as evidence of her commitment to the sociopolitical realities of Mexico. Although our perusal of Sor Juana's festival texts has brought out the boundaries, personal motivations, and distinctive profile of her "Mexican" leanings, it has also confirmed the congruence of her texts with then-contemporary patriotic discourse, belying David A. Brading's conclusion that Sor Juana "did not contribute to the growth of creole patriotism other than to figure in her own right as a cultural icon, since both her ambition and talent found expression and fulfilment within the universal tradition of Spanish literature" (373). Particularly thanks to her engagement with pluralizing syncretism, Sor Juana's spectacular cities join those of Sigüenza, high priest of creole patriotism, and Vetancurt, strident messenger of multiplicity.

By the same token, when set alongside her compatriots' works the loa that Blanco considers to have broached "the most scandalous theological theme imaginable" (*Esplendores* 49) loses its problematic uniqueness (if not its potential for scandal). Purposefully convulsive and shocking, Sor Juana's loa emerges as eminently imaginable within the landscape of its time and place. No less than her compatriots' writings, Sor Juana's extreme loa is a natural scion of the wonder-packed yet conservative Baroque, historiographic syncretism, and spectacular festivals that derive from the Old World as well as of the cultural nationalism and disrupting of received paradigms that issue from the New. The colonial Baroque plenitude that emanates from Guaman Poma's and Villalpando's pluralized New World cityscapes throbs with the "plus ultra" dynamism, immanence, and complexity to which Sor Juana and her fellow creole authors give verbal form. Writers on the brink, emissaries of a people in waiting, they have forged their Spectacular Cities from the very building blocks that the hegemony's spurious "concierto barroco" (Sarduy 102) places at their disposal to the viceregal regime's own peril. The case of Sor Juana makes it painfully clear that writers who activate the opportunities rife in Baroque discourse also do so to their own peril. Yet our next chapter bears witness to the ways in which legions of creole writers eagerly avail themselves of these esoteric opportunities to make their way up the social ladder and, at times, toward a knowledge of the All that stretches beyond the plural, if profoundly circumscribed, bounds of the Baroque.

Six   "TO KNOW THE ALL"

The Spectacular Esoteric City in Mexico

Nothing is more beautiful than to know the All.
ATHANASIUS KIRCHER, *ARS MAGNA SCIENDI*
[GREAT ART OF KNOWING] (1669)

Plato said, "Nothing is more divine than to know everything," sagely and elegantly, for just as Knowledge illuminates the mind, refines the intellect and pursues universal truths, so out of love of beautiful things it quickly conceives and then gives birth to a daughter, Wisdom, the explorer of the loftiest matters, who, passing far beyond the limits of human joy, joins her own to the Angelic Choruses, and borne before the Ultimate Throne of Divinity, makes them consorts and possessors of Divine Nature.
ATHANASIUS KIRCHER, *ARS MAGNA SCIENDI*

I. TWO CITIES

Over the course of the seventeenth century, a prosperous Mexico City experienced a veritable orgy of construction and renovation that rendered it indisputably spectacular in material terms. Agustín de Vetancurt remarks with awe in 1698 that more than twenty sumptuous churches and thousands of buildings had recently been constructed, that practically every street boasted houses either being built or refurbished (3:193). Scores of new monasteries, convents, and schools ringed the Zócalo. Previously low city structures reached for the sky, growing new levels, balconies, cupolas, and domes. Gilded rooftops crowned highly adorned buildings fashioned out of gray quarrystone (*cantera*) and contrasting bright hues of the rosy *tezontle* that another seventeenth-century observer called "an exquisite reddish stone, a great oddity" (Maza, *Ciudad* 14). The Baroque esthetic had already left its grandiose mark on the Solomonic portals of the ever-evolving Metropolitan Cathedral, the luminous Baroque murals of its sacristy painted by none other than Cristóbal de Villalpando, and especially on the astounding altarpieces of the city's churches. Baroque stage sets designed to inspire divine reveries, the reredos' gold, polychrome, and endless involutions dazzled and interpellated spectators no less than the city's festivals. Spectacular church altarpieces and Baroque festivals met their match in the ready supply of actual theater. Venues for theatrical performances burgeoned. The theater-crazed city, whose royal palace sported a Sala de Comedias, offered all citizens the opportunity to experience religious and secular entertainments at the public theater in the Hospital Real de Indios founded in 1638 (Maza, *Ciudad* 25).

In the dramatic Baroque city, poetry became a performance art. Performances of abstruse, almost unintelligible Baroque compositions in poetry contests that helped anoint a Mexican literati mushroomed into major public occasions, with a lavish pageantry of their own. Weeks before the tournament, a parade far outstripping that of little Querétaro would march through the city to announce the literary competition.[1] Mexico City festooned itself as if for a viceroy's festive entry. Crowds lined the streets to gape at the long line of brilliantly clad religious and secular officials avid to be included in society's prime cultural event. When the contest finally took place, the city's elite—the viceroy himself often among them—mingled with poets who performed their offerings in sumptuously decorated halls replete with tables of glittering, costly prizes. The event lasted for hours, taxing even the most literarily inclined but confirming the surpassing value that colonial Hispanic subjects attached to stratospheric poetry.

"What extravagance, what magnificence!" comments Carlos de Sigüenza y Góngora of a poetry contest held in conjunction with a Marian festival (*Triunfo* 55). The display and prestige that poetry competitions commanded speaks to the extraordinary force in late seventeenth-century Mexico City of a body that hovers over and animates the real city of tezontle, gilded rooftops, and altarpieces. I will call that thriving, peculiar body the *esoteric city* and define it as an entity composed of the rarefied cultural practices of late seventeenth-century Mexican intellectuals—an entity that, like any city, has its own citizens, laws, and life. The improbable currency of the esoteric city derives from the entrenched view of high culture as sublime and ennobling that Bernardo de Balbuena had compellingly articulated at the outset of the century. Baroque society, now at its dizzying, complex peak, values and promotes recondite intellectual practices all the more. Under such circumstances the esoteric, intellectual city flies high, yet, as the poetry contests suggest, it maintains an unshakable connection with materiality. The colonial esoteric city constantly interacts with the material city, from its wonderful objects to its festivals. Though by definition elite, in impacting public culture the esoteric city extensively affects Mexican society.

The social and epistemological constraints of that society have driven its intelligentsia to esoterics, adherence to mysterious or secret doctrines. Cryptic Baroque style plays a starring yet debased role in the efforts of creole poets to overcome social and economic obstacles. Maneuvering within Baroque bounds, the most ambitious movers and shakers of the esoteric city endeavor to surmount them. The sweeping, omnivorous compass of Baroque epistemology discussed in chapter 5 raises the divine, sublime hope of knowing "everything" or "the All" that Kircher expresses in the epigraphs above. The hope to know the All sometimes galvanizes the members of the esoteric city, which thoroughly transcends the merely bureaucratic corporation of Rama's "lettered city." Explorers "of the loftiest matters," those who spearhead the esoteric city aspire to the celestial realms of ether, the upper regions of space outside the phenomenal world that afford a totalizing view of Kircher's "universal truths."[2] They soar into ether on the wings of philosophies so spectacularly totalizing, so intensely dependent on wonders, that they could gain credence or viability only in a Baroque "colonial echo chamber" (Harss 17) at the apocalyptic end of a confining century.

Our present investigation reconstitutes salient aspects of the esoteric city, from its central social and epistemological dimensions down to its very furnishings. The chapter takes the pulse of the esoteric city by probing the rarefied, totalizing modes of thought that at the end of the seventeenth century had obtained a vibrant life in creole writings by virtue, to no small degree, of Kircher's influence. As it contemplates philosophical and festival texts, less distinguished writers, whose works expose the innersprings of the esoteric city, will stand side by side with luminaries like Sor Juana Inés de la Cruz and Sigüenza y Góngora.

Concluding our chronological inquiry into colonial Mexican literary culture, the chapter pays special attention to endings, that is, to the remarkable extremes, endpoints, and breaking points that the Spectacular City's mainstay elements reach in late seventeenth-century Mexico. Section II locates Baroque creole authors vis-à-vis the esoteric city. Section III turns to the wonders that under the sway of Kircher acquire new life as epistemological objects. Section IV examines how Sor Juana and Sigüenza mount a literary fin de siècle, which conveys the Mexican Archive to an Olympian peak. Sor Juana also carries the intellectual city to its downfall. Dramatizing in the *Primero sueño* [First dream] the clash between St. Augustine's earthly and divine cities, she etherealizes the festival and the city from real into philosophical, metaphorical constructs and lays ruin to Baroque epistemologies, including Kircher's. Section V then reveals Sigüenza's *Alboroto y motín de los indios de México* [Uproar and revolt of the Indians of Mexico City] as a twisted festival chronicle that holds the epistemological *Primero sueño* in its conflicted embrace. Thus the platforms of the Spectacular City all volatilize at the end of the century into the stunning ethereal, cerebral constructs that the esoteric city both ordains and produces, creating the Spectacular Esoteric City.

II. CREOLES AND THE ESOTERIC CITY

Belying Balbuena's premature triumphalism, Vetancurt and Sigüenza extol their own times as a realization of his dreams for Mexican literary culture. Vetancurt draws not only on Balbuena but also on a full century of local biological apologetics for the superior intelligence of those born in the Indies to laud creoles as "extremely intelligent and well versed in all fields of knowledge" (2:192).[3] In his *Triunfo Parténico* [Parthenic triumph], a chronicle and anthology of a spectacular festival poetry contest held at the university in 1683, Sigüenza quotes Cervantes de Salazar's and Balbuena's virtually inescapable panegyrics to Mexico's cultural primacy. The esoteric city now in full bloom, notes Sigüenza, owes its achievements to the exceptional devotion of Viceroy Marquis de la Laguna to the university. It turns out that the viceroy's sponsorship of Sor Juana fed into his larger mission of propelling colonial Mexico to its cultural apogee.

When Sigüenza, ever the organic intellectual and champion of the creole intellectual city, composed in 1690 the life story the Puerto Rican Alonso Ramírez had recounted to him, the Count de Galve had assumed office as viceroy of New Spain (in 1688). Shaping his early testimonial narrative entitled *Infortunios de Alonso Ramírez* [The misadventures of Alonso Ramírez] into a paean to the esoteric city, Sigüenza positions the tale to cajole the viceroy into continuing the Marquis de la Laguna's commitment to intellectual endeavors. Hence, at the end of *Infortunios* Ramírez finally receives recompense for his misfortunes in what Sigüenza portrays as an ideally enlightened, intellectual Mexico City. The addressee of the text, the new viceroy to whom Sigüenza attributes knowledge of geography and hydrography, munificently grants Ramírez the rights to his beached frigate. In the reader's last glimpse of Ramírez, he is departing for Veracruz to rescue the ship, accompanied by Juan Enríquez Barroto, "an excellent youth, well-informed in hydrography, learned in the mathematical sciences" (71, *105*) and therefore the alter ego of Count de Galve and of the count's new twin, the learned Sigüenza—all exemplars of the esoteric city.

This final snapshot of Ramírez in Mexico City caps off a text that harbors a subtle polemic of knowledge versus faith and Mexico versus Puerto Rico, designed to promote both knowledge and the Mexican intellectual. The erudite Mexican Sigüenza, possessing many titles that "have a ring to them but are of very little real value" (71, *104*), has committed to writing the oral tale of the uneducated Puerto Rican Ramírez. In their collaborative venture, *Infortunios,* Sigüenza strives to gain some heft for his empty titles. He courts the viceroy's patronage by flaunting, once again, his erudition. Going overboard, Sigüenza so burdens the text with learned quotes and dense Baroque wordplay as to sap the lifeblood from an intrinsically exciting tale of a trip around the world to exotic locales. Further, the encyclopedic *Infortunios* subtly and successively filters Ramírez's tale through almost all of the literary discourses current at the times, including the picaresque novel, the Byzantine novel, the shipwreck tale, and early chronicles of the conquest. Alongside the ostentatious, anxious, literary performances of *Infortunios,* Sigüenza blazons the utility of his knowledge to the viceroy and the crown. Maps in hand, the cosmographer superimposes on the apparently vague narrative of Ramírez precise scientific cartographic and navigational coordinates. Such knowledge could lead the crown to the pirates and heretics who increasingly threatened the Spanish empire; the Count de Galve had particularly undertaken to purge New Spain of pirates (*Alboroto* 97, 213).[4]

In contrast, according to the text what saved Ramírez was his faith. The mother from whom Alonso takes his sole last name (Irizarry suggests that his father may have been a convert to Christianity [38-43]) had imparted to him the only gift an impoverished parent could provide, Christian faith. Ramírez's devotion to God and to the Virgin of Guadalupe reportedly rescue him from several dire situations: "I believe my liberty would have been impossible if my mind and affections had not been continuously on the most Holy Mary of Guadalupe in Mexico whose slave I will ever be for what I owe her" (48, 52). The emotional, timid, resoundingly medieval Ramírez buffeted by fate ends up as the spiritual leader of his company, as a martyr to faith.

"The tears of joy for liberation were followed by tears that could have been of blood, at the memory of our past ordeals" (48, 53), *Infortunios* relates, Sigüenza no doubt retooling Ramírez's diction into elegant phraseology. Ramírez has suffered tremendously, maybe inordinately. Why? The text pointedly insinuates that much of Ramírez's suffering stems from his ignorance. For example: "The reader should not be shocked at my ignorance about where we were in those islands because I left my country at a tender age and never learned what islands were close by and what their names were, nor did I take the trouble to do that later" (54, 67). A plaintive "no sé" [I don't know] becomes Ramírez's theme song. He has no knowledge of geography and cannot discern the pirates' route. As the dazed pilot of his frigate, he has only a rudimentary command of navigation and constantly loses his way. He wounds himself twice by accident. Ramírez's faith has sufficed to rescue him but not to avert his suffering.

Masterminded by Sigüenza, *Infortunios* has doubly "framed" Ramírez. It has set forth his embryonic story (27) so effectively as to earn Ramírez the reward he seeks. And, while presenting itself as an equal collaboration between members of the popular and learned cities, *Infortunios* has also clandestinely set Ramírez up as the protagonist of a moral tale that exposes the inadequacies of faith when it is not partnered with knowledge. The collaboration of Ramírez with Sigüenza in Mexico City remedies the Puerto Rican's deficiencies after the fact and completes the dialectic. Ramírez has traveled from his home to a Mexico City that he initially praises, saying, "It is a great pity that the magnificent grandeur of such a superb city should not spread through the world engraved by a glazier's diamond on plates of gold" (33, *12*). After a hallucinated journey around the world and through the provinces of Mexico, each space rife with Baroque deceptions, Ramírez returns to the capital and to stability. There, thanks to the learned Sigüenza and the viceroy, he secures the boon that certifies the benefits of knowledge as well as the Mexican capital's superiority over San Juan, bled dry by the conquerors (31, 8–9) and left solely with the faith that sustains Ramírez. The symbolic configuration that closes *Infortunios,* in which a man of faith marches off with a man of science, asserts that only a commitment to the intellectual city for which the text has made a covert yet strong case will guarantee "the magnificent grandeur" of the viceregal capital.

Who actually was Alonso Ramírez? Scholars have found in *Infortunios* the historical specificity that would derive from an eyewitness and stylistic features that unequivocally indicate the presence of two voices in the text (see Irizarry, Sacido Romero), yet no one has succeeded in identifying the historical figure Alonso Ramírez. There does exist, however, considerable information about a quite literary Mexican named Alonso Ramírez de Vargas, a creole aristocrat, a poet, and a close friend of Sigüenza.[5] Profusely lauding the poet who won seven prizes, Sigüenza includes more of Ramírez de Vargas's poems in *Triunfo Parténico* than those of any other author. While certainly not the Ramírez of *Infortunios,* Ramírez de Vargas had attained such standing as a festival poet that the name of the text's protagonist would certainly have struck the knowledgeable public as a double entendre, one which gestured away from the illiterate Puerto Rican and toward the esoteric city Sigüenza zealously promoted.

Among Ramírez de Vargas's poems in *Triunfo* one encounters the extreme, extremely repugnant conceit of Apollo's birthplace, Delos, as an archipelago vomited up by a scaly whale (159). If the whale found the archipelago hard to digest, the public would doubtless have the same problem with the convolutions of another poem on Delos by Ramírez de Vargas. His prizewinning composition reassembles disparate verses of the already esoteric Luis de Góngora into a far more abstruse new poem (221–223; the kind of poem known as a *centón,* or cento). Alarmingly similar to those of Sigüenza and Sor Juana published in *Triunfo,*[6] Ramírez de Vargas's contributions demonstrate the simultaneously highflying and degraded nature of poetry contest works. The artifice-ridden works, abounding in bricolages, acrostics, cryptograms and anagrams, echoes and double echoes, and reversible lines, paid odd homage to Góngora and Francisco de Quevedo by perverting the authors' techniques into the frippery of occasional, eminently forgettable poetry. As long as it adhered to the contests' prescribed themes, the more spectacular and esoteric the poetry, the more likely to be rewarded. Vehemently denounced by Irving A. Leonard as "meaningless jumbles of artificial expressions and numbing Latinisms" (147), this epigonic poetry of poetasters served many ends and masters, but it hardly fulfills the expectations for an enlightened, profound intellectual city that *Infortunios* raises. Yet such poetry, not worthy, substantive works like Sor Juana's *Primero sueño*, was the representative stuff of that city in Mexico City itself. Put simply, the esoteric city that Sigüenza venerates in point of fact often consisted of very bad poetry, elaborate parlor tricks.

The disappointments and splendors of the more representative esoteric city raise a couple of fascinating issues. First, the question of the relatively dead middle (in literary terms) of the seventeenth century, populated as it was largely by poetasters. At least as it has come down to us, except for Guadalupan works the midcentury shows little notable literary production. On the other hand, in literary histories outstanding works, from Balbuena's to Sor Juana's, cluster insistently at the beginning and the end of the century. Later pages of this chapter will establish the impression of loaded bookends that the century presents not just as a historical phenomenon but as the masterful handiwork of Sigüenza and of Sor Juana herself.

Second, the intellectual city's exorbitant investment in Gongorism unleashes some truly bewildering paradoxes. How could the dissident, secular poetry of Góngora that, according to Jaime Concha, "emerges as a heterodox deviation from the dominant religious ideology of the Counter-Reformation" in Spain (44) have become so destigmatized in the severely orthodox New Spain? After all, the libertine Góngora had proclaimed, "I am not a theologian" (Concha 44), Quevedo had denounced him as a convert to Christianity, and the Inquisition banned the first commercial edition of his works in 1627 (Beverley 79).[7] Moreover, how had Góngora's dense, transgressive poetry metamorphosed into common currency and into the official currency of New Spain, into works bent to the flattery of church and state? José Joaquín Blanco astutely notes with regard to Mexico that Gongorism flourished there during the second half of the century for reasons and in texts that Góngora himself would have despised (*Esplendores* 23). Re-viewing the Baroque as an instrument and product of the colonial New World warrants consideration of these paradoxes.

The Jesuit educational program that had shaped so many young creole minds goes a long way in explaining New Spain's travesties of Gongorism. Jesuit humanist pedagogy co-opted Góngora's poetry and converted it into a tool for the formation of a creole elite. The avowedly elite character of Góngora's poetry (he shamelessly declared, "it gives me honor not to make myself clear to ignorant people, for such is the mark of distinction of a learned man" [896–897]) so suited the Jesuits' purposes that they had young students memorize and recite long passages of the Spanish poet's works (Concha 46). Jesuit pedagogy also turned the writing of poetry and theater into routine, ordinary activities. If, as the colonial playwright Fernán González de Eslava remarked, Mexico possessed "more poets than horse dung" (Rodríguez Hernández 58) and if, as Sigüenza reports in *Triunfo*, its poetry contest received more than five hundred submissions (139), then one can attribute the deluge of poetry in no small part to the Jesuits. Their humanistic program bred many versifiers but few poets (Rodríguez Hernández 57). By the same token, the Jesuit curriculum's domesticating and naturalizing of the most rarefied poetic currents bred flocks of writers who versified with relative ease in the forbidding Gongorine mode.

Proof of Gongorism's new life in the New World and proof that a superannuated Gongorism also took other parts of the viceregal world by storm appears in the Peruvian Juan de Espinosa Medrano's belated defense of Góngora, his *Apologético en favor de don Luis de Góngora* [Apologetics for Don Luis de Góngora] of 1662.[8] Trained by the Jesuits, Espinosa Medrano repeatedly vindicates Góngora's elite poetic diction with arguments like: "What Don Luis frequently employs so felicitously is not hyperbaton, nor synchesis [the confusion of words in a sentence], but merely the arrangement of elegant words . . . , a genuine feature of the Latin language and so natural to the art of prosody that his verse forms were never known as hyperbatons nor as any other poetic trope, but instead as utterly ordinary language" (39). In other words, Espinosa Medrano characterizes Góngora's language not as a vice, perversion, or affectation but as the utterly natural language into which colonial culture had effectively transformed it.

One still wonders why the demipoets clamored to broadcast their mediocre compositions. The rich prizes blanketing the tables of poetry contest venues represent one enticement to performance for struggling creoles. Sigüenza's *Triunfo* lists the prizes with a fetishistic precision: trays of silver, a silver filigree rose, an elegant porcelain pocket watch, pairs of polka-dot silk stockings, a five-stone ring, and so on. A mini-wonder cabinet, the table of objects Balbuena would have coveted solely for their exquisite rarity offers poets the wherewithal to cut a large swath in society. Nonetheless, the benefits of a poetry that absorbs into its own *cre-*

matistike verbal texture the esthetic of luxury prizes extend beyond the mere acquisition of social signifiers.

As the case of the illegitimate Sor Juana's meteoric rise in society makes quite clear, esoteric Baroque poetry accorded creoles a means of ascending the social ladder. More habitually than in Cervantes de Salazar's time, and involving literary techniques far more elaborate and therefore more impressive than those of the Renaissance, Baroque poetry could shatter colonial barriers to advancement.[9] The ability to wield the complex technical instruments of the *conceptismo* and *culteranismo* that conquest export culture had insouciantly purveyed to the colonies and that had acquired unprecedented prestige in Mexican literary culture cohered into a shibboleth, an instant passport to eminence. One can now fathom New Spain's tendency to construct metropolitan Baroque poetry as a bag of tricks, for with relative ease poets could master the mechanical devices and formulas to which it had been reduced. The canned hyperestheticism of Baroque poetry yielded a quick, public, highly effective means of achieving elite status. It left an indelible impression on the religious and secular officials who gathered at festive events, adulated them as hyperbolically as only the overblown Baroque could, and won authors publication. Enshrining the names and deeds of powerful personages in society's most prestigious, sublime verbal mode snared poets an endless parade of favors.

The creole intellectual city whose sublimity and practicality the preceding discussion has brought out again unsettles Angel Rama's notion of the ciudad letrada, prompting one final meditation on his important concept. In earlier chapters I have interrogated such matters as Rama's construction of the ciudad letrada as a monolithic, hegemonically oriented entity, a matter which the incipient, pugnacious cultural nationalism exercised by the creole intelligentsia that Chapter 5 described particularly places in question. Given the intimate connections between creole advancement of a quite concrete nature and the arcane Baroque poetry just discussed, Rama's view of the educated community as manipulating a hermetically sealed world of pure signs to the singular advantage of the ruling forces becomes more problematic yet. While it remains indisputable that creole writers corrupt esoteric Baroque poetry into an organ of the state, we see that they often do so not in complete surrender to hegemony but out of a hierarchy defying self-interest. Colonial writers grow the pure poetry of Gongorism, which began as an end in itself and which Rama characterizes as totally closed in on itself, into a uniquely Baroque means to an end.

III. TO KNOW THE ALL: KIRCHER IN MEXICO

However pressing the reasons for the transformations colonial writers wreak on metropolitan Golden Age lyric, their will to performance can still strip poetry of philosophical transcendence, of real sublimity. Other intellectuals feel the lack and break ranks with this intellectual bankruptcy. Taking at its word the Counter-Reformation's quest to arrest all knowledge, they seek to know everything, the totality. The outreaching minds of colonial intellectuals find magnificent sustenance in the end of the Baroque, totalizing, marvel-studded projects of the polymath Athanasius Kircher. Kircher has already entered our purview extensively in function of his syncretic Egyptology. More fully to establish Kircher's key place in the Mexican esoteric city, at this juncture we need to pan out to the broad contours of Kircher's undertakings that held such allure for colonial thinkers, and to the broader circle of Mexican writers who adopted him as their guide to the All.[10]

In 1633, the Jesuits summoned Kircher to Rome to help palliate the crisis in knowledge unleashed by the Copernicanism of Galileo, who had been tried and condemned as a heretic just months before. The Company of Jesus charged the prodigious, maverick German scholar with the mission of reconciling church doctrine and the scientific method (Rowland, *Ecstatic Journey* 31). Kircher spent the rest of his life, forty-six years that yielded some thirty-eight massive lavish books, enjoying the patronage of grandees as he fulfilled that mission. Descartes famously said of Kircher, "The Jesuit has a lot of tricks; he is more charlatan than scholar" (qtd. in Findlen, "Last Man" 22). The anti-Jesuit Descartes may exaggerate maliciously, but he does not lie. An inventor of cunning contraptions, an impresario of knowledge who cast his net to the four corners of the earth and deep into the past, Kircher opened up new fields without breaching—on the contrary, by magnifying—Catholic orthodoxy. His astonishing projects endowed the orthodox and the old with the enticing luster of the heterodox, the exotic, and the new. Kircher's always shifting and pioneering, often scientific investigations gave the unmistakable impression of cutting-edge knowledge. His gorgeously produced works seduced a large readership as they held out tantalizing flares of an imminent, proscribed modernity that the projects themselves in essence sought to usurp by ultimately confirming a conservative Christian worldview. Their scholarship sometimes flawed, their claims often outlandish, Kircher's works so met the needs of the Catholic Church that the Jesuits allowed him to publish with little obstruction (see Siebert).

"Unity is the essence of God," wrote Kircher in his *Oedipus Aegyptiacus* (qtd. in Findlen, *Possessing Nature* 82). Fortified by this belief, Kircher undertook to bundle all knowledge into a Godlike coherence. He wished not only to know everything that there was to know, but no less to insert everything in a totalizing system that would make sense of it all, of the All itself. Thus throughout his works and crystallizing in the *Ars magna sciendi,* Kircher channeled the pansophy on which he had set his sights into the familiar Renaissance model of Pythagorean concert and harmony. Craving, as Paula Findlen states, "a grand unified theory of absolutely everything" ("Last Man" 8), Kircher literally finds his salvation in the "prose of the world," with its God-given sympathies and correspondences, Great Chain of Being, harmony of the spheres, and "Natural Magician" able to read hidden correspondences. According to Kircher's resulting *ars analogica* (Findlen, *Possessing Nature* 82), Mexico resembles Egypt, Egyptian hieroglyphs contain all knowledge and predict Christianity, Confucianism is not inimical to Christianity, and so on. In essence, for Kircher all religions mesh, predicting and culminating in Christianity. Anachronistically but with the same full-bodied vigor as its Renaissance enactments, resemblance rules Kircher's seventeenth-century imagination.

The persistence of the Renaissance episteme into the late Baroque ensues from the needs and disposition of the seventeenth-century Catholic culture. Sacred and sanctified, the Renaissance model was needed to harmonize a world that by the seventeenth century was, if anything, more manifestly heterogeneous than before.[11] And certainly more throbbing with tensions and crises in the Old World (constant warfare, Cartesianism, heliocentrism, the Spanish empire's economic woes, the rifts of Christianity, and so on), some issuing from the New World (intermittent rebellions and failures of evangelization there, the increasing economic independence of the colonies, European inflation due to the New World bullion that flooded the market, and more). In the bounded, cautious, scholastic world of the Counter-Reformation, no new all-embracing paradigm had fully succeeded in supplanting the order and concert that, for instance, still palpably underwrites historiographic syncretism. Although Aristotelian dialectics dominated scholasticism, Baroque texts toiled to reaffirm the harmonious Neoplatonic cosmos in a world under acute stress. As Gracián's *Agudeza* exemplified in a desiccated form, the Baroque wants to massage catachresis into a near-miraculous harmony.

So it was that seventeenth-century Spain and other parts of Europe saw a resurgence of the patristic, apologistic genre known as hexameral writings. Alban Forcione defines hexameral writings as "a spectacular literary-ideological effort to defend orthodoxy from ascetic, nominalist, and Protestant currents," "concerned with apologetics and reassurance, taking up and refuting challenges to orthodox conceptions concerning the order of things and its providential designs" (17). The "hexameral speculative reassurance" (35) that texts from Luis de Granada's *Introducción del Símbolo de la Fe* [Introduction to the symbol of faith] of 1583 (which in chapter 1 we heard propound the trope of the world as a book) to Guillaume de Salluste Du Bartas's *La sepmaine* [Creation of the world] (1578) undertake to supply redeems a threatened "universalist image of integration, pacification, coherence and unity" (18), the rhyming Pythagorean universe that bolsters Catholic orthodoxy. Gracián's own *El criticón* [The critic] (1651–1657) problematizes that universe only to validate it.[12] Although not poetic texts, Kircher's investigations fall into line with the hexameral projects, specifically with their commitment to order and concert, to anachronistic but still vital paradigms.

The heteroglossic, accumulative cast of seventeenth-century Counter-Reformation thought, together with its encyclopedic impetus, further feeds the Baroque afterlife of the Renaissance model Kircher vivifies. Findlen notes that Kircher belonged "to an era that combined rather than divided" ("Last Man" 8). She registers his determination "to absorb every old and new philosophy that came his way in order to subsume them within his great synthesis of knowledge" (*Possessing Nature* 80). Often considered an intellectual dinosaur (Godwin 5), Kircher quintessentializes the all-preserving disposition of the Baroque I discussed in chapter 5. We can thus begin to appreciate the peculiarly Baroque profile of the beauty to which the maxim Kircher inscribed on the frontispiece of his *Ars magna sciendi* refers: "Nothing is more beautiful than to know the All."

The public museum Kircher mounted at the Jesuit College in Rome, one of the first of its kind, concretized and spectacularized the beautiful "prose of the world." Kircher's museum, a would-be microcosm of the world, monumentalized his grand philosophical design and sold it to the public as an assemblage of wonders. Kircher filled the museum with the Egyptian, Oriental, and American exotica he had diligently collected from a far-flung network of contacts. The museum that Kircher curated gathered and classified the secrets of nature to which Oviedo's museumizing natural history had many years earlier given verbal form. Kircher's Baroque wonder cabinet, however, encompassed both nature and artifice. Roman statues, Greek vases, Etruscan bronzes, and scientific apparatuses communed in the museum with ostrich eggs, fossils, and narwhal horns as well as with the scholar's own ingenious scientific inventions (Rowland, *Ecstatic Journey* 6). While the Balbuena who shared Kircher's taste for marvels of all sorts implicitly projected himself in his collection poem as yet another of its sublime artifacts, Kircher physically assumed that role. At the entrance of the Roman College he installed a brass trumpet and behind a statue in the museum a megaphone, both of which acted as intercoms that connected visitors to Kircher's study (Rowland, *Ecstatic Journey* 6). Visitors flocked to see and consult Kircher, crowning exhibit of his own spectacular museum. They plied the scholar with questions on sundry intellectual matters that he gamely essayed to answer (Malcolm 299).

Centerpiece of the Muses' dwelling, oracle and visionary thinker, Kircher acquired fame throughout the Catholic world. Thanks to his own assiduous efforts in corresponding with more than seven hundred individuals and to those of the Jesuits who promoted him around the globe, Kircher impacted the New World, especially Mexico. A spate of fine studies (by Findlen, Kramer, Osorio Romero, Trabulse) tells why and how. The why should already be self-evident. Kircher's prestige, orthodoxy, novelty, predilection for the wonders that stood in for modernity, mediation between old and new knowledge, and the promise of omniscience contained in his totalizing world as a book all beckoned irresistibly to the denizens of the isolated Mexican intellectual city. Philosophy had so stagnated in Mexico that in the seventeenth century no new works were published (Gallegos Rocafull 348) or, perhaps more accurately, were allowed to be published there. Alejandro Favián, a creole who corresponded with Kircher in Latin and in Spanish from Puebla during the third quarter of the century, declares time and again that absolutely no one in his environment writes, thinks, experiments, or invents like the German Jesuit.

Favián, a fanatic New World Kircherian to whom we will return shortly, may appropriately have concluded that no one in New Spain matched his idol, but the Mexican creole knew that others had tried. First in Puebla as confessor to its bishop and after 1663 in Mexico City, where he served as prefect of the Jesuit Colegio Máximo de San Pedro y San Pablo, Francisco Ximénez had read and corresponded with Kircher; it was Ximénez, erstwhile friend of Favián, who first commended him to Kircher. However, Kircher-mania had spread remarkably. Together with Ximénez, it had captivated several creole luminaries in the upper echelons of the Mexican capital. The two previous occupants of Sigüenza's chair in mathematics and astrology at the Mexico City university, Diego Rodríguez and Luis Becerra Tanco, subscribed to Kircher's thinking. The same held for the celebrated Jesuit missionary Eusebio Kino, whose stay in Mexico provoked the debate on comets that Sigüenza immortalized in his *Libra astronómica* (1681; Trabulse, *Círculo* 87), and for the Jesuit Francisco de Florencia, to whom Sigüenza owed the approbation of *Triunfo Parténico*. This roster of eminent figures contextualizes Sigüenza's fervent adherence to Kircher's thought. More important, it corroborates Ignacio Osorio Romero's hypothesis of 1993 that a relatively liberal, open-minded circle of Jesuit thinkers flourished in late seventeenth-century Mexico City, competing with and raising the hackles of hardline Jesuits like Sor Juana's confessor, Antonio Núñez de Miranda.[13]

The approval of a well-situated local coterie, Osorio Romero also contends, must have facilitated the penetration of Kircher's somewhat risqué works into such tightly guarded bastions as Sor Juana's convent (see section 5 of Osorio Romero's introduction). Indeed, under the auspices of the Vatican scholar's prestige, Sor Juana herself, as well as Favián, rides Kircher to his and *the* limits. Notably less gifted than Sor Juana, even a caricature of the learned nun and of Kircher, owing to those very aspects Favián exemplifies in pristine form the ardent desire for esoteric knowledge that could grip the colonial intellectual. Despite the vast discrepancies between Favián and Sor Juana, Kircher enabled both colonial seekers to stretch the bounds of knowledge. As they do so, the two overreaching questers extensively traffic in and etherealize the wonderful objects on which Kircher set such store.

Alejandro Favián adulated—and, ultimately, exploited—Kircher beyond any rightful measure. Kircher filled the restless creole's thoughts and propelled his life, which knew true glory when Kircher dedicated the *Magneticum naturae regnum* [Magnetic kingdom of nature] to him in 1667. From Puebla, between 1661 and 1674, Favián voraciously consumed Kircher's works, trying to reproduce their scientific experiments. He fashioned and preposterously fancied himself as Kircher's New World twin. In 1661, Favián wrote to Kircher, "I believe that you and I have the same nature and the same temperament, and so we will agree on everything" (Osorio Romero 16; all quotes from Favián derive from this text). The voluminous works by Favián that his correspondence heralds, none of which have come down to us or may ever have been completed, similarly modeled themselves on Kircher's. Favián's putative five-volume, many-thousand-page masterwork aped Kircher's dialogue on the nature of the universe, the *Itinerarium exstaticum* [Ecstatic journey] (1656),[14] which inspired Sor Juana's *Primero sueño*. The extreme title of Favián's work, *Tautología extática, Universal dialogística, cosmimétrica* [cosmimetrics, the art of measuring the universe], *hagiográphica, physiológica, philosóphica, geográphica, hidrográphica, topothésica* [toposthesia, the description of imaginary places], *chímica* [chemistry], *subterránea, astronómica, aritmética, óptica, machímica* [mechanical chemistry?], *Musi-armónica* [musical harmonics], *Mística* (149), leaves no doubt that he purported to compose not merely a sequel to the overarching *Itinerarium* but a new, encyclopedic, totalizing book of the world. Having depleted his inheritance by founding a congregation for Jesuit priests, Favián seeks symbolic restitution for lost fortune and honor in the holistic, divine omniscience Kircher proffered.

If the *Tautología*, like Kircher's *Itinerarium*, "encompasses all the above sciences and arts," when Favián states that his work contains "an immense number of other extraordinary, curious, new, odd, and unheard-of things" (150) he calls to mind the exchanges of wonderful commodities that more than anything else define his relationship with Kircher. For several years the neophyte and, in equal measure, the master, engage in a mutually profitable association that revolves around objects valuable in themselves but far more valuable for their symbolic capital. Favián and Kircher enter into a prolonged volley of goods that trades on and confirms the currency of wonders-as-objects for Baroque cities in the Old World and the New.

Favián bombards Kircher with unrelenting, exorbitant requests. To conduct his investigations, Favián wants the All: all of Kircher's amazing works, all the written sources that inform them, all the new scientific instruments Kircher employs in his experiments. Favián's Baroque tastes especially thrill to curiosities of every ilk. He begs Kircher for score on score of rare objects, the most recent mechanical marvels, fantastic inventions. Were Kircher not to send them, says Favián as he stoops to intellectual blackmail, "we [in the New World] would forever lack such wonderful things, profound secrets and prodigious experiences" (28). Son of a merchant, Favián goads Kircher into serving as a frontline merchant of marvels for the New World. Favían then mines the wonders' symbolic capital by erecting in his own house a Kircherian museum. Counterpart to the spectacular festival but permanent rather than transient, Favián's museum breeds a festive atmosphere. Hordes of Puebla's citizens, among them the society's elite, swarm to view the collection that incites "inexpressible wonder" (23). Favián reports to Kircher, "to this day my house has constantly been full of people who come to satisfy their desire to see and understand Your Reverence's marvels" (23–24). As visitors read and supposedly understand the prose of the world compacted into Favián's Puebla wonder cabinet, the creole's prestige skyrockets.

That Kircher required wonderful objects to keep his own cherished prestige afloat makes some sense of his almost incomprehensible compliance with Favián's outrageous demands. The Mexican curiosities Favián sent Kircher graced the Roman museum and greased the machines of patronage (as when Kircher requests a feather portrait to give to Pope Alexander VII [58]). For his part, Favián cannily recognizes that he could reap a profit from Kircher and Europe's marked tendency to view the New World as a locus of exotica. Favián therefore promises that if Kircher will stock his Puebla museum with wonders, he will adorn the Vatican museum with the "most extraordinary things that I can find here" (47). Favián starts with the obvious, chocolate and bits of silver, but then scrambles to come up with other local novelties that might strike Kircher's fancy. Though Ximénez had warned Favián that Mexican curiosities hold no interest for Europeans (36), commerce in the brilliant feather portraits referred to above and in natural *mirabilia* follows. Favián supplements the actual goods with extravagant verbal descriptions that pitch his wares to Kircher as high marvels.

Favián, however, eventually lapses into sending *only* words for the goods he receives from Kircher. While his requests to Kircher escalate into the solicitation of a bishopric, Favián's recompense to his benefactor increasingly shrivels down to praise of the Jesuit luminary that emphasizes the ethereal, intellectual value of their commerce in marvels. Ximénez steps in to put an end to the uneven exchanges. Scornful of Mexican creoles, Ximénez begins around 1661 to caution Kircher that Favián delivers nothing of a material value equivalent to that of the expensive gifts. Ten years later, Ximénez scathingly indicts what he considers to be Favián's typically New World chicanery of wheedling expensive objects out of others while returning only flattery and verbal "vain wisps of gifts" (169). That Kircher, ignoring Ximénez's sharp warnings, persists undeterred in his generosity to Favián shapes his commerce with the creole into a weighty "object lesson." Not even full awareness that Favián had exploited him in material terms, one surmises, could shake Kircher's avidity for goods of inestimable epistemological value and cachet.

Unlike Favián, when Sor Juana frames her most fervent, outright appeal to Kircher, in the *Respuesta a Sor Filotea de la Cruz* [Reply to Sister Philothea of the Cross] (1691; OC:4), she has more at stake than epistemology or cachet. Sor Juana's deployment of Kircher in the *Respuesta,* while sincere and significant on intellectual grounds, sets his conservative Baroque project to work for her. She calls on Kircher to help rehabilitate her besieged person. For, as is well known, Sor Juana's *Carta Atenagórica* [Letter worthy of Athena] (1690; OC:4), with its critique of a forty-year-old sermon by the Portuguese Jesuit Antonio de Vieyra (a particular favorite of Archbishop Francisco de Aguiar y Seijas), had sent shock waves into the religious community. The *Carta,* which the bishop of Puebla, Manuel Fernández de Santa Cruz, published for reasons that still remain open to lively speculation, included an admonishment to Sor Juana. Under the pseudonym of Sor Filotea de la Cruz, the bishop directed Sor Juana to train her intellectual sights on religious rather than secular matters.

In the *Respuesta,* then, an unnerved Sor Juana attempts to curry favor with Kircher's order, the Company of Jesus. She chooses a means of placating the Jesuits so obvious that it leaps into view despite the fact that it has not, to my knowledge, yet been articulated: Sor Juana's intimate account in the *Respuesta* of her lonely, autodidactic, seemingly idiosyncratic manner of study appropriates the methodology of the Jesuit Ratio Studiorum, sine qua non of the colonial intellectual and engine of the esoteric city.[15] For what, if not Jesuit humanism, guides the course of Sor Juana's study, as it purportedly clambers from "the human arts and sciences" "toward the eminence of sacred theology" (447, *213*)? And what, if not Jesuit syncretism, authorizes Sor Juana's statements that her mind exercises itself on various disciplines, be they secular or sacred, which end up illuminating and supporting one another (450, *216 et passim*)? Any reasonable individual, Sor Juana perhaps (mis)calculated, would grant that the deep and broad erudition of the *Respuesta* could only do honor to the Jesuits whom the *Carta* may have alienated. The nun-writer writes herself as—and, ironically enough for the Jesuits, was—the highest realization of their intellectual project.

As was Kircher. In the admonishment Sor Filotea had given Sor Juana a prompt to discuss Kircher by mentioning Egypt as the most learned but most barbarous nation (OC:4, 695; *201*). Since Sor Juana could also take Sor Filotea's reference as rebuking her Egyptian *Neptuno,* and since she often calibrates the *Respuesta* to the topics raised in the admonishment, she walks through the door Fernández de Santa Cruz had opened to enlist Kircher in the letter's pro-Jesuit campaign. If the *Respuesta* of 1691 revives her own and Sigüenza's tactical and practical conscription of the Jesuit Kircher from 1680, the nun-writer now presses into service the broader knowledge of his work she has obtained in the interim.

The Kircherian concepts Sor Juana invokes in the *Respuesta* (450, *216*) look backward, to a safe, wondrous space. When she details her haphazard wanderings from text to text in search of the "variations and occult connections," Sor Juana allows that sometimes, despite her unworthiness, they almost miraculously do emerge for her. They emerge, she says, because the "wisdom of their Author so put them in place that they appear correlated and bound together with marvelous concert and bonding." She then relates this "universal chain" to the Great Chain of Being, to Kircher, and through Kircher to the late medieval Nicholas of Cusa's aphorism that "all things proceed from God, who is at once the center and the circumference from which all existing lines proceed and at which all end up." Sor Juana has just rapidly sketched out and endorsed several facets of the time-honored Pythagorean, Neoplatonic model that Kircher and the hexameral poets strive to preserve.

Moreover, Sor Juana invokes the Neoplatonic model and displays its Kircherian pedigree all the better to arrogate to herself the positive connotations both entailed. Kircher had silently modified Plato's statement that "nothing is as sweet as knowing everything," replacing "sweet" with "divine" (Osorio Romero xliii).[16] Probably unaware of Kircher's not insignificant modification, Sor Juana certainly had much in mind the divine thrust of Kircher's epistemology. Kircher's *Obeliscus Pamphilius* [Pamphilian Obelisk] (1650) emphasizes that the "Natural Magician" who ferrets out the hidden correspondences of the universal chain walks a godly path. "[I]t would be welcome and acceptable" to God, writes Kircher, "that those genuinely desirous of true wisdom should investigate His hidden mysteries along secret paths, and proceed to uncover the secret sacraments of His holy doctrine by this underground way" (qtd. in Rowland, *Ecstatic Journey* 16). Arguing repeatedly in the autobiographical portion of the *Respuesta* that God bent her incorrigibly toward knowledge, Sor Juana mines her alleged association with God by disposing readers to acknowledge her as a divinely inclined visionary seeker endowed with an exceptional ability to investigate hidden mysteries (Luciani 102).[17] The numerous intricate examples of "marvelous concert and bonding" between seemingly disparate disciplines that she adduces in the document confirm her as a proprietor of privileged, secret knowledge akin to Harpocrates, whom Sor Juana adopts from Kircher. And he or she who grasps the hidden connections also comprehends the whole, the unity in diversity. Sor Juana's old Pythagorean math of unity in the *Respuesta*, so different from Vetancurt's new math of diversity and, as we will see in due course, from the *Primero sueño*'s critical appraisal of the German Jesuit, positions itself to reap the rewards inherent in Kircher's philosophical model.

To further bolster the image of herself as high priestess of a Kircherian "religion" or of the esoteric city who possesses an exceptional capacity to unearth secret knowledge, Sor Juana sites the temple of that religion in the unlikely space of the convent. The *Respuesta* reads the Kircherian book of the world as it materializes in the convent, her personal laboratory of knowledge: "although I did not study from books, I did from everything God has created, all of it being my letters, and all this universal chain of being my book. I saw nothing without reflecting on it; I heard nothing without wondering at it—not even the tiniest, most material thing" (458, *224*). Implicitly marrying the Jesuit practice of requiring students to perform menial domestic labor with St. Teresa of Jesus' affirmation that "God also walks among the cooking pots" (75), Sor Juana's text interrogates the quotidian. Humble phenomena—spinning tops, childrens' games, eggs frying in oil—all yield cosmic knowledge, metaphysical and scientific, when subjected to the author's gaze. As Sor Juana etherealizes the prosaic, the diffuse and particularized material world coalesces into a sublime geometry of Trinity-like triangles and circles reminiscent of Solomon's ring (459, *225*). Sor Juana presents her discoveries as being completely personal, empirical, and unmediated. Yet they have a "bookish cast," evidencing similarities to works by Aristotle, Kircher, and others that she likely read (Luciani 122; see 113–123). Generally keen on exhibiting her erudition, Sor Juana perforce banishes other voices from this portion of the *Respuesta*. The privileged seeker that the nun-writer professes to be must stand alone and singular as she extracts from the unpromising confines of the convent a host of wonders.

Above and beyond the *Respuesta,* Sor Juana wrests outsized, esoteric knowledge from her circumscribed world. The intellectual revelations the *Respuesta* recounts stem from almost random quotidian occurrences. In contrast, Sor Juana intently outfits her convent apartment as a space to know and be the All, where, in the lovely words of Jean Baudrillard, her "subjectivity can fulfill itself without let or hindrance" (16). Object by object, she converts her cell into a wonder cabinet, a Kircherian museum.[18] The miniature museum of curiosities she builds turns the objects, whose muteness the *Respuesta* had deplored as a negative, into an enabling positive. Construed as ingredients of a Kircherian collection, objects shed their alienated apathy and begin to speak, as did Melancio's Aleph-like globe. They become the stuff of a discourse that the collector herself can fashion at will and wield with impunity. An autonomous world in which the imagination can roam freely and an imaginary unto itself, the collection stands as "a universe peopled with strange beings and objects, where anything could happen, and where, consequently, every question could be posed" (Pomian 77). Steeped in the Baroque culture of curiosity and in a Kircherian mindset according to which "an experiment made in a room *could* reproduce the effects of the celestial influences on man" (Camenietzki 318), Sor Juana fashions a spectacular room of her own that has more than the proverbial implications.

In public, in private, and on paper, Sor Juana communes with the objects of her wonder cabinet. Her comedia, *Los empeños de una casa* [Trials of a noble house; OC:4] (1689), as housebound as the nun herself, signals that she clings fast to her material surroundings and that they stimulate all manner of literary musings. The wonderful objects that, inspired by Kircher, Sor Juana assembles in the rooms of San Jerónimo occasion a corpus of lyrical compositions, the *Primero sueño* among them. In other words, paraphrasing Kircher, Sor Juana's love of beautiful things that give birth to wisdom generates what can be understood as her *collection poems*. The collection poems constitute some of Kircher's deepest and most lively effects on the nun's writings as well as her deepest involvements with wonder. So let us peruse Sor Juana's Kircher-inspired, intensely material "scene of writing" and the poetry it begets.

Sor Juana crafted her rooms into a reification of the esoteric city. The eighteenth-century portraits of Sor Juana in her convent cell by Miguel Cabrera and Juan de Miranda attest specifically to the works, including Kircher's, contained in the library that the bibliophile amassed. Several verbal portraits inform about the other objects she collected. Legal documents recording her strenuous efforts to purchase new convent rooms in 1692 indicate that Sor Juana was acquisitive. Her first biographer, Diego Calleja, suggests the extent and fruits of her acquisitive tendencies. He reports, incurring widespread skepticism, that she willingly relinquished to Archbishop Aguiar y Seijas, for him to sell, books and "also the Musical and Mathematical instruments, of which she possessed many, all precious and exquisite. The jewels and charms and other goods that people attracted to her famous name sent her, even from very far away—he converted them all into money" ("Aprobación" to Sor Juana's *Fama,* n.p.). A later inventory of Sor Juana's possessions discloses that she managed to retain two splendid, jewel-encrusted religious statues. Like Favián and Kircher, Sor Juana prizes luxurious, unusual, spectacular curiosities, select Baroque arcana.

Sor Juana's poetry fleshes out the actual inventories.[19] It reveals an incessant flow of objects back and forth between the nun, her admirers, and her patrons. Jewelry, roses, pottery, rare foodstuffs, exquisite items of clothing, portraits, and mechanical devices: all were worldly objects, treasured or expendable, in the nun's possession. Sor Juana cultivates a gift economy in which she barters objects and poems-cum-objects for favors, and sends poems on objects as object-substitutes in return for presents she had received but could not reciprocate in kind. She revels in her role as broker of extraordinary objects, presenting herself as a collector. Décima #122 (OC:1), for instance, gleefully wrings conceits from a clock the nun sends to a person of authority. Clock and poet assume a Kircherian tone: "Raro es del Arte portento / en que su poder más luce, / que a breve espacio reduce / el celestial movimiento" [Rare marvel displaying the full power of Art, for it compresses the movements of the heavens into a small space]. While the poetry of Sor Juana's gift economy trades on the objects of her collection, in the first-person Romance #49 (OC:1) the poet goes so far as to portray herself, the famed Mexican Phoenix, as a grotesque object on exhibit. To avoid being paraded around as a "Giant's Head" that "those who love novelties" pay to see, Sor Juana's poetic speaker decides to withdraw from view.

Romance #49 may spurn the task Kircher all too happily took on in Rome, but Sor Juana's collection poetry accomplishes the fundamental philosophical job Kircher envisioned for his museum. A would-be microcosm of the world, the museum aspired to compress total or at least large knowledge into a reduced space. *Omnia in omnibus* (Camenietzki 318). This Kircherian notion, raison d'être of his museum, would have impressed upon Sor Juana that a limited space like her convent cell or, for that matter, a small object like any in her collection, could contain the All. Consequently, Sor Juana's poems on objects speak volumes. From the small things that they describe and read, they tease out large object lessons on the author's and the Baroque's privileged themes.

Among her many verses on painted portraits, a principal holding of Sor Juana's personal museum or material version of the esoteric city, are two probing, ingenious compositions (#126, #127, OC:1) devoted to a genuine wonder cabinet artifact. While Sor Juana's general fondness for portraits as substitutes for people leads her to write poems that speak to portraits, that make portraits speak, and that are themselves ekphrastic portraits, here she takes on the smallest of all such objects, a miniature of the Countess de Paredes that the poet herself painted on a ring. Mimetically, the tiny portrait gains poetic expression in tiny ten-line compositions, *décimas*. Yet the doubly miniature poems go large, for they reflect on the representational power of miniatures. And, as befits the aura of the objects in Sor Juana's wonder cabinet, the poems accord miniatures exceptional representational power. In Décima #126 the poetic speaker declares that she has copied the emotions of her heart onto a portrait set in a ring. Her emotions, equated to an archetype ("such extreme perfection" [53]), overflow the tiny space allotted to them. The ring nevertheless proves capable somehow of representing them. Borne on a finger, the ring will serve as an "index"—in Sor Juana's word but in the full Peircean sense of the term—of the heart's sentiments.

Another cluster of Sor Juana's collection poems (e.g., #128, #129, #133, #147, #148, #158 in OC:1) celebrates the rose, a natural marvel entrenched in the Baroque literary imaginary as an exemplum of beauty's deceptive ephemerality. Sor Juana therefore has at her disposal a ready-made repertoire by means of which to textualize the rose, "concepto florido" [flowery conceit] (Décima #129). Soneto #147, "En que da moral censura a una rosa, y en ella a sus semejantes" [In which she visits moral censure on a rose, and in it on fellow humans, #31], activates and complicates the whole cast of tropes. The sonnet rapidly explodes the small, singular, material rose into its conventional philosophical connotations: embodiment of divine beauty, semblance of human life, union of cradle and tomb. Yet even as the poem moves ineluctably toward the traditional "moral censure" of the rose's ephemerality, it lingers on the flower's proud daring, thrice noted. The two colors of the poem's rose, red and white, presage the sonnet's mixed message, its half-hearted condemnation of the rose and wholehearted praise of Sor Juana's beloved Phaethon-like daring. Protectively evoking the consecrated red and white roses of the Catholic rosary (red for martyrdom, white for purity), the flower has become a true meditational object for the poet. As such, it emits an arc of connotations too complex to be contained in univocal object lessons.

Sor Juana's roses impart their most profound message in the *Primero sueño* (written at an unknown date before the *Respuesta,* published in 1692; OC:1). There the rose joins the other wonders, ancient and modern, that the Soul ponders during her long journey. They include the Pharos of Alexandria ("glassy marvel, unique protection" [l. 268, *178*]), the pyramids of Cairo ("be they miracles or marvels" [l. 413, *180*]), and Kircher's inherently marvelous magic lantern (ll. 873–886, *193*). Sor Juana may have possessed a magic lantern. She may also have contemplated in her apartment one of the then-popular maps depicting the wonders of the ancient world along its borders. In any case, the *Primero sueño* weds the wonder cabinet, wonders, and the collection poem, carrying them all to their maximum philosophical expression by means of objects as vast as the pyramids, as minute as the rose.

The *Primero sueño* (henceforth, *PS*) embeds the rose in a sweeping meditation on the Aristotelian possibilities of knowing the All. Having regrouped her[20] forces after the failure of the Platonic attempt to attain total knowledge by means of an all-encompassing "act of intuition" (l. 592, *186*), the Soul proposes to mount the ladder of Aristotelian philosophy (forerunner of the *Respuesta*'s Jesuit ladder). Her—or, as Sor Juana unusually writes, "my"—mind (l. 617, *186*) will ascend its steps one by one, in the hope of incrementally obtaining knowledge of the lowest to the very highest forms of creation. An insurmountable obstacle soon arrests her progress. The Soul realizes that she, who "aun la más pequeña, / la más fácil parte no entendía / de los más manuales / efectos naturales" (ll. 708–711) [who failed to understand the very smallest, the easiest part of those effects of nature, *189*], can scarcely presume to scale the heights. Herein follows a first example of a natural phenomenon the Soul professes to be incapable of understanding, the stream. The unknown course (l. 713, *189*) of the stream, personified in Arethusa as she courses through the underground in search of Persephone, teems with secrets too complex to fathom.

Sor Juana's meditation on the stream, however, takes a strange turn. It pauses to redeem the female seeker and to acclaim the knowledge that she did, in fact, succeed in obtaining. Arethusa, "clara pesquidora" [bright seeker] who exercises "útil curiosidad" [useful curiosity], returns to Ceres with the "noticia cierta" [true word] of the "rubia" [golden] earth goddess's lost daughter (ll. 722–725; cf. *189*). For a moment the dark nightworld, scenario of the Soul's intellectual journey, gleams with flashes of light that crown the visionary seeker who protagonizes the *Respuesta,* honor her secret knowledge, and contradict the Soul's lament that the most minute phenomena of the world defy her understanding.

Into this setting Sor Juana inserts her quizzical, entranced reading of the rose. Of all the things of beauty with which Sor Juana stocked her mind and masterpiece (Trueblood 22), the rose is one of the most beautiful, the *PS*'s passage on it one of Sor Juana's most ravishingly sensual. The rose, identified as the flower of Venus, comes alive with flirtatious flounces and vibrant hues that threaten to outshine the Father Sun. Withal, as she did in Soneto #147, Sor Juana here lays out competing, conventional images of the rose. For the *PS*'s rose also emblematizes the doubly noxious tricks of female beauty, deceptions and a poisonous cosmetic powder. Having rendered the rose both surpassingly beautiful and, once again, contradictory and thus unseizably complex, Sor Juana deems the Soul's attempt to comprehend it a failure. Infinitely smaller than a stream, small enough to fit in the nun's apartment and to commune daily with the poet, the rose escapes her intellectual grasp. The *PS*'s rose, shot through with allusions to blood, wounding, and death, ends up as a memento of the Soul's failure to know the All, a failure made all the more poignant by contrast to Arethusa's foregoing triumphs.

A blend of nature and artifice, the overdetermined rose of the *PS*, finally, puts one in mind of Balbuena's liminal, overwrought objects. Indeed, Sor Juana's textualized objects as a whole stand in telling relationships to those of her early seventeenth-century forebear. Sor Juana's Kircher-inspired collection poetry situates itself in the very territory Balbuena had staked out, the world of objects. The nun's collection poems, however, transmogrify objects into icons of the late seventeenth-century esoteric city, of its lofty, abstract aspirations. Balbuena's textualized luxury objects retain and flaunt their material value; Sor Juana's etherealize into epistemological vehicles. Balbuena provisions his wonder cabinet poem with material objects on which he bestows economic and social prestige; Sor Juana's Kircherian wonder cabinet features objects that acquire intellectual capital. Exploiting commodity fetishism, Balbuena tenders a sham gift economy to the crown; Sor Juana's gift economy, with its fungibility between gifts and poems, is just that. Balbuena declares himself incapable of framing "abbreviated worlds" (114); for reasons personal and philosophical, Sor Juana compresses the world into her cell, laboratory of knowledge, and into microcosmic objects. "Oh Mexico, illustrious and rich, where one loses the desire for any other world [*más mundo*]" ("Grandeza" 76): whereas Balbuena would content himself with possessing the city's goods and pleasures, his late seventeenth-century avatar desires possession of the intellectual city. The wholly Baroque Sor Juana does want "más mundo," she wants to know the All.

IV. TO KNOW THE ALL AND THE FIN DE SIÈCLE

From the Olympian peak of the esoteric city, Sor Juana's textualized objects appear to gaze down derisively on those of Balbuena. In other ways, though, Sor Juana looks benignly upon the Balbuena who wrote "Grandeza" for a woman about to enter a sister Hieronymite convent (Muriel 300). Kindred to Sor Juana in his love of fabulous, speaking objects, Balbuena had also willed to her literary culture the inestimably vital tools of the Baroque, Neoplatonism, and Pythagoreanism as well as a sublime concept of poetry.[21] Such notions deserve, and win, the nun-writer's active respect. Her project of possessing the intellectual city, of knowing and writing the All, disposes Sor Juana toward the "all" of Mexican literary tradition, the Mexican Archive. And as Sor Juana surveys the intellectual city from her distinctive vantage point at the end of the seventeenth century, she folds Balbuena and other early seventeenth-century creole contributors to the Mexican Archive into her works.

That Sor Juana was heavily invested in the creole Mexican Archive stands to reason. She would have easiest access to works by these Mexican authors, works published and sanctioned in New Spain. Her creole-dominated convent would welcome the writings of its brethren, and the nun's literary involvement with Mexican creole texts would vouch for the allegiance of the suspect transatlantic Sor Juana to her local context. More important, the locally prestigious Mexican texts legitimate Sor Juana's own audacious, innovative writing. More personally, the familiarity of the local milieu with the texts commended the Mexican Archive to Sor Juana as a playing field for all sorts of fine, coded politics, not the least of which we sampled in the interactions between the loa to *El Divino Narciso* and Torquemada's *Monarquía indiana*.

Improbably, the Mexican Archive, a coded Mexican politics, and a retrospective impulse all saturate Sor Juana's festive Corpus Christi *auto sacramental* or Eucharistic drama, *El Divino Narciso* (OC:4; henceforth, *EDN* or *auto*), conceivably written around the same time as the *Primero sueño*. I say "improbably" because, on the face of it, *EDN* would seem to have nothing whatsoever to do with these matters. In stark contrast to its loa, grounded in the conquest, the ethereal *auto* rewrites the myth of Narcissus's self-love into an allegory of Christ's devotion to his mirror image, Humankind. Thus, whereas the loa works with history and addresses New World issues, the *auto* apparently works with an allegorical atemporality and addresses universal issues.

No less virtuoso a weaver of disparate phenomena than Kircher, Sor Juana mitigates the radical discrepancy between the two works and lays tracks that will culminate in the hidden Mexican dimensions of the *auto*. Among the elements of the Spectacular City that play a role in the puzzle, Baroque wonder and its desire to shock come to the fore, shaping Sor Juana's maneuvers in the *auto* vis-à-vis Mexico and Spain. The potential to shock that above all else unites the two parts of Sor Juana's festival contribution involves the fact that *EDN*'s shocking, riveting portrayal of the egotistical Narcissus as none other than Christ displays the same brinkmanship as the loa's portrayal of the conquest. In *EDN,* Sor Juana tempers her extreme gambit for attention by constantly emphasizing harmony, starting with the harmony between the Old and New worlds. At the end of the loa, the character Religión promises that the *auto* will introduce Mexico to Spain in the abstract form of allegorical figures that can pass easily between worlds (20). *EDN* fulfills the promise by taking as its motor the same harmonizing capabilities of historiographic syncretism that had fueled the loa and multitudes of other works. The *auto* exalts mirroring and similitude through the person of Narciso/Christ. It synthesizes mythological, Old Testament, and New Testament master narratives. A grand Augustinian machine of prophecy and prefiguration spins all three into consonance: "pues muchas veces conformes / Divinas y Humanas Letras, / dan a entender que Dios pone / aun en las Plumas Gentiles / unos visos en que asoman / los altos Misterios Suyos" [often working together, Divine and Human Knowledge intimate that God may even place glimmers of His lofty Mysteries in Pagan Pens] (26). The incredibly thick, far-reaching intertextuality of the New World author's play, with its many echoes of Spanish masters, likewise harmonizes disjunctive worlds.

"Escucha la armonía / de las canoras aves / que en coros diferentes / forman dulces discantes" [Listen to the harmony of the melodious birds, whose different choruses form sweet concerts] (46), sings *EDN*'s own Eco, the devil, as she tries to seduce Narciso/Christ with her dowry of nature's bounty. Eco's aria binds the loa's and the *auto*'s harmonizing, syncretic mechanisms to the harmonious pastoral, their rightful landscape and the landscape in which much of *EDN* takes place. Constantly resonating with the Song of Songs, the *auto* installs itself masterfully in the territory of the pastoral lyric and novel. Rightful and skillful as the play's pastoral is, it represents a departure from Sor Juana's previous works. For, beyond ruminations on roses, Sor Juana rarely writes about nature. That she here grapples with it for one of the few times in her career, revealing herself as an instant past master of the bucolic mode, compels one to ask why Sor Juana chose the occasion of her desired, proxy debut in Spain to try her hand at the pastoral.

A two-pronged answer comes to mind. On the one hand, the pastoral novel had exceptional cachet in seventeenth-century Spain. Considered sublime, just one step removed from the Bible, the pastoral had become the genre of choice and preponderance for authors wishing to establish themselves on the Spanish literary scene. Both Lope de Vega and Cervantes, for instance, had inaugurated their literary careers with pastoral novels. On the other hand, the pastoral has a long and fraught history in Mexican urban literature. By Sor Juana's era, that history included Guadalupan narratives like that of the creole Miguel Sánchez, who portrayed the exurban Tepeyac as an earthly paradise, the Promised Land, a land of milk and honey. It also appears that even Archbishop Aguiar y Seijas wrote a pastoral.[22]

One begins to intuit that it was not by chance or lacking in significance for both Spain and Mexico that Sor Juana stages a pastoral for the Madrid festival. Overtly, she plays out for an elite audience in Spain an elite Spanish genre, brandishing her mastery of it. Covertly, as a matter of national pride—perhaps hoping that the literati of the Spanish audience or expecting that a potential Mexican audience will grasp her allusions—Sor Juana activates the most ingrained, defining aspects of the literary Mexican Archive. With her sortie into the pastoral mode, the transatlantic Sor Juana concretizes the greatest point of convergence between Mexican and metropolitan literature. She exhibits one of Mexico's principal claims to Spanish literary fame. And as Sor Juana infuses the Eucharistic drama with vivid echoes of two pastoral novels from her milieu, she further "Mexicanizes" the *auto,* yoking it to the patently Mexican loa and molding both components of *EDN* into performances of the Mexican Archive.

Reading *EDN* through the lens of the Mexican Archive brings to light two earlier works that contain several of the play's signature elements:[23] Balbuena's *Siglo de oro en las selvas de Erífile* and the creole Francisco de Bramón's delightful early Baroque pastoral novel *a lo divino,* or in a divine mode, *Los sirgueros de la Virgen sin original pecado* [Heralds of the Virgin, exempt from original sin] (1620), created for a festival most dear to the Jesuits, the Feast of the Immaculate Conception.[24] Bramón's novel interacts with Balbuena's. Together, they constitute the first Hispanic novels written in and on Mexico, which fact reconfirms the currency of the pastoral in New Spain.

Separately and conjointly, the two authors Mexicanize the pastoral in ways that would appeal to Sor Juana as important for her *auto* to carry in its wake or with moves that directly enter her play. Balbuena and Bramón reterritorialize the pastoral novel by splicing pieces of Mexican reality—specifically, of Mexico City—into their works, be it the dream vision of Mexico City in *Siglo* or references to the university in *Sirgueros*. Bramón concludes his novel with another striking piece of Mexicana. The festive scene of "Mexican Rejoicing" in which the pastoral text culminates features an Aztec dance, or "tocotín," that manifests quite specific kinships with the loa to *EDN*.[25] Additionally and crucially, Bramón teams up with Balbuena to introduce Ovid to the New World, which lays the groundwork for Sor Juana's metamorphoses-ridden *PS*. Most vitally arguing for the influence of the two novels on Sor Juana's *auto*, their Ovidian inclinations lead them to showcase the myth of Echo and Narcissus. They spotlight the fountain crucial to the myth and to Sor Juana's *auto*, whose axial moments transpire around a fountain that one of the play's refrains commemorates: "Applaud Narciso, Fountains and Flowers!" (see act I, scene II). Bramón's interpolation of a Marian fountain into the myth directly portends Sor Juana's and authorizes her otherwise shocking, catachrestic version of the myth. The Mexican Archive has served her in good stead.

Although, as I have documented elsewhere,[26] many other aspects large and small implicate the early seventeenth-century pastoral novels in the dense weave of the nun's 1689 *auto*, more interesting for our purposes is the big picture toward which the presence of Balbuena's and Bramón's work in *EDN* points. In both the *auto* and its loa Sor Juana looks back to the beginning of the seventeenth century. From previous pages we have come to recognize the beginning of the century as a time of foundations at once literary (Mannerism, Baroque), religious (consolidation of Jesuit activity), political (tensions between creoles and Spaniards as well as intrareligious ones), and historiographic (García, Torquemada)—and as a rich period for the Mexican Archive, which Dorantes and Villalobos initiated in those very years. When Sor Juana gazes backward in *EDN*, she largely overleaps the "dead middle" of the seventeenth century. Instead, she gathers the bookends of the seventeenth century into her literary glance, conjugating them. The imprint on the *auto* of Balbuena and Bramón, as authors who inaugurated the currents that at the end of the seventeenth century Sor Juana conceivably epitomizes and brings to Spain, coordinates the beginning with the end of the century.

In doing so, Sor Juana surreptitiously builds not only a Mexican literary genealogy for herself, but also a portrait of the emergent Mexican intellectual city for Spain and New Spain. Balbuena's and Bramón's presence in the *auto* effectively regroups the two parts of *EDN,* the loa and the *auto.* It splits them, *not* into the Mexican loa versus the universal *auto* but into mise-en-scènes of two phases of New Spain's cultural history. In this scenario, first, we have the loa, which replays the conquest as filtered through Torquemada's influential beginning-of-the-century syncretism. Second, we have the *auto.* By recouping in 1689 the early pastoral novels of the Mexican Archive, the *auto* emerges as a gestural portrait of the colonial, largely creole Mexican culture that ensued from the initial clash of the conquest, an elite culture that first flowered at the turn of the seventeenth century and reached fruition at its end (in Sor Juana's own hands?). The pastoral and syncretism furnish threads of continuity that join the two stages and place them on a continuum as constituent elements of the Mexican Archive.

Altogether, it comes into view that for her festival debut in Madrid, with the bicentennial of the "discovery" and the end of the century fast approaching, the creole Sor Juana has mounted a veritable fin-de-siècle retrospective of Mexican colonial culture. Her sinuous, loaded festival performance of the Mexican Archive, a bona fide theatrical revue, bears a special message for Spain. Like Balbuena's inaugural *Siglo de oro,* Sor Juana's *EDN* calls for a renewal of the original (in her case, the metropolitan) poetic space. Balbuena wrote in his novel, "Who could place in memory .... a single concern and a single history?" (32). The dense cultural politics of *EDN* pressure Spain to recognize that European cultural memory must now accommodate more than a single concern, more than a single history, another intellectual city. As the "Tenth Muse" brings the Mexican Archive home, as it were, to Spain, she urges the motherland to extend to New World literary culture the same pluralistic spirit that syncretism had visited upon New World historiography.

The foregoing big picture leads to another, namely, the implications of the fin de siècle for the esoteric city in Mexico. Sor Juana's Ovillejo #214 (OC:1) situates its poetic speaker at the end of the century, from which perspective the speaker passes judgment on the literary challenges the century faces. "Oh unfortunate and destitute century," the poem exclaims, "in which we find that everything has already been used"

(321). Ovillejo #214 proclaims Sor Juana's belief that she stood at the terminus of an era. More momentously, it bespeaks her attempts both critically to assess her century from its endpoint and actively to produce a literary fin de siècle. Sor Juana's attempts culminate in the *PS* and, as the final section of this chapter will bear out, Sigüenza shares them. Two of the most accomplished, overreaching intellectuals of the time, both writers thread their texts with iterations of the Mexican Archive. In building retrospectives of the intellectual city, they manufacture a literary fin de siècle that advances cultural nationalism and install themselves as its captains. Received notions of the seventeenth century's dead middle and loaded bookends now come into focus as phenomena that its authors themselves to some degree contrived.

From its overviewing perspective outside time, space, and boundaries, the ethereal *Primero sueño* convokes all the energies of the fin de siècle. As Rafael Catalá's pathbreaking study from 1987 demonstrates, the poem marshals the Mexican Archive. Catalá's *Para una lectura americana del barroco mexicano* ["Toward an American reading of the Mexican Baroque"] elucidates the influence on the *PS* of Mexican works from Aztec mythology to Villalobos, Torquemada, Francisco de Castro, and many more. For example, in his fourth chapter Catalá details the multiple valences of the eagle who introduces the *PS*'s so-called "Intermezzo of the Pyramids" and thus the poem's first epistemological inquiry (ll. 327–339, *179*). According to Catalá, Sor Juana's eagle at once evokes Tenochtitlán and Huitzilopochtli (the founding of the Aztec city), Jupiter (eagle as bird of divine majesty), Cuauhtémoc and Juan Diego (both of whose Nahuatl names relate to the eagle), and the Virgin Mary of Revelation 12:14. By the same logic, the poem's epistemologically inflected rose would conjure up the Virgin of Guadalupe's flowers as well as the rosary. Catalá's examples, together with Sor Juana's renditions of the Virgin of Guadalupe herself, disclose the modus vivendi of the nun-writer's literary allusions. Diffuse, impossible to pin down, her imagery inhabits multiple worlds.[27] Sor Juana writes in the interstices of Western and Mexican literature, keeping open her mobility between them. Thus, the literary fin de siècle that the *PS* convenes radiates out in ever-expanding waves.

The omnivorous, climactic *PS* stretches outward, but primarily it surges upward, toward total knowledge. Diego Calleja's summary of the poem catches its totalizing design: "It being night, I fell asleep; I dreamed that I wanted to understand totally and instantly all things of which the universe is composed" ("Approbación" to *Fama,* n.p.). Questing for total knowledge, the Soul roams an apocalyptic landscape, essentialized distillation and apotheosis of the Spectacular Esoteric City. In the central portion of the poem she takes an awed journey through a purely ideational dreamscape. By turns astonished, exhilarated, and aghast, the Soul interpolates herself into a spectacular parade of epistemologies—no more or less than an ethereal festival of epistemologies, as illusory as a festival's imagined community. She first tests out the Platonic or intuitive method and then the Aristotelian or discursive method of scholasticism. Both methods' abstract principles attain a breathtaking corporeality in epistemological objects like the rose, the pyramid, and the ladder. That these vivid icons augur little more than the failure of the quest underscores the dramatic pathos of the *PS*. The poem conveys the intellectual city to its apotheosis only to devastate and raze it.

In that devastation lies the core of Sor Juana's fin-de-siècle project, an indictment of her century infinitely more cutting than that of Ovillejo #214 because it targets the prevailing epistemologies of her milieu. Unchained from the body, the epistemologically questing Soul of the *PS*'s dreamer soars into space. Her "vuelo intelectual" (l. 301) [flight of intellect, *179*] takes place outside the world, literally in the space of ether. A terra incognita, a chimeric realm rife with perils, the space of the Soul's intellectual investigations hardly qualifies as a city, not even as a utopian one. Against all odds, though, the outer space of the *PS* does share the coordinates of a particular city, an appropriately abstract one. Scholars have compared the *PS* to Christine de Pizan's *City of Women* (1403–1404) and related it to María de Ágreda's Marian *Mystical City of God* (1670). Valuable on their own terms, such comparisons also direct attention to a vital missing link. St. Augustine's *City of God,* the ur-text for Pizan and Ágreda's allegorical cities, proves to be an untold determining source for the *PS* as well as the powerhouse of its fin-de-siècle critique.[28] The *PS* pits one intellectual giant, St. Augustine, against an array of others, including Plato, Aristotle, and Kircher. St. Augustine triumphs, but it is a Pyrrhic victory for all involved.

Unusual or speculative as the preceding claims may sound to modern ears, for Sor Juana's philosophical poem *not* to have contended with St. Augustine would have been far more unusual, a conspicuous shortcoming. Little escaped the scrutiny of St. Augustine, who puzzled through everything from minutiae like the fingernails of angels to the attributes of utopias and the whole span of human history. Therefore, writers as fundamental to Sor Juana's milieu and as diverse as Gracián, Kircher, Las Casas, Mendieta, Sahagún, Sánchez, and St. Ignatius had relied on the *City of God,* as had Eiximenis in city planning and Sor Juana and Sigüenza in their festival contributions of 1680.[29] The nun's order was named after St. Jerome but followed Augustinian rules. Naturally, then, Sor Juana cites St. Jerome and St. Augustine more than any other Church Fathers (Paz 252). Many of her central themes also originate in St. Augustine. Since no one could have labored as hard and earnestly to know the All as St. Augustine, Sor Juana looks to him for guidance on matters theoretical and concrete. As *EDN* indicates, Sor Juana embraces the grand Augustinian machine, with its motor of prophecy, its intermeshing of history, myth, scripture, and science. The "book of the world" that has its origins in St. Augustine engenders an approach to material things—it "almost seems," he writes, "as if they long to be known, just because they cannot know themselves" (462)—that could easily undergird Sor Juana's collection poetry.

In dire need of a patron saint for its risky philosophical and feminist business, the *PS* places itself under the protection of St. Augustine's *City of God* (henceforth, *City*). Although one often cannot ascertain when Sor Juana cites St. Augustine directly, when she activates Augustinian notions that came down to her diffusely, or what parts of the *City* she read, its book 18 seems to have been a particular lightning rod for the nun. Book 18 contains a whole cluster of Sor Juanian topics that make their way into the *PS* as well as into other of her texts: Egypt, Isis, Minerva, Harpocrates, astronomy, dreams, prophets and poets, syncretism, birds, metamorphoses, Circe, Bacchus, Babel, perspectivism, persecution, and more.[30] Principally, St. Augustine's crucial book 18 takes as its subject the history of the "earthly city," starting with the Flood and ending with the coming of Christ. Engraved in the minds of Sor Juana's orthodox readers, this too is the principal terrain of the *PS*. With a special predilection for book 18, Sor Juana's poem engages the major constructs of the *City of God*. St. Augustine's earthly and (to a lesser degree) Heavenly cities, each with its attendant form of knowledge, shape the *PS* in ways that the following account can only begin to discern or unpack.

The *City of God* divides the human race into two branches and, "speaking allegorically" (595), identifies the endeavors of one human society with the Heavenly City and the other with the earthly city. Members of the first society live by the "standard of the spirit," the second by the "standard of the flesh" (547). Those who live by the standard of the spirit will ultimately gain entry into the promised kingdom, the Heavenly City proper, where they will dwell with God. There peace, serenity, harmony, order, proportion, and light reign supreme. (Almost needless to say, the Heavenly City informs the innumerable evocations of order, concert, and harmony that we have witnessed over the course of this book). Inhabitants of the Heavenly City will partake of God's knowledge, a wisdom perfect and complete, incorruptible and unchanging, multiplicity reduced to divine singularity:

> it is said in the holy Scriptures that the Spirit of Wisdom is "multiple" [Wisd. 7:22], in that it has many qualities in itself; but the Spirit's being is identical with its qualities, and all those qualities are one Person. For there are not many wisdoms, but one Wisdom, the storehouse, we may say, of things intelligible, of the riches which are infinite and yet confined to that Wisdom. And in that storehouse are contained all the invisible and unchanging causes of things visible and changing, which were created by the operation of Wisdom. (442)

When the Soul is set free for all eternity it will imbibe God's changeless, plenary Wisdom.

The second coming of Christ will definitively fuse the earthly and the Heavenly City. Until then, in the ways, times, places, and persons that the *City* extensively chronicles, the Heavenly City transitorily graces the lesser sphere: "the City of the saints is up above, although it produces citizens here below, and in their persons the City is on pilgrimage until the time of its kingdom comes" (596). Or, as book 17 states, "God's City lives in this world's city, as far as its human element is concerned; but it lives there as an alien sojourner" (761). If the blessed "alien sojourner" finds its model in the city of Jerusalem, Babylon/Babel signifies the inferior, degraded earthly city. St. Augustine bases himself on the account of Babel in Genesis 11:1–10. A tower founded by arrogant men, an effigy of their prideful desire to appropriate the heavens, Babel incurred God's wrath. God confused human languages, whence the fact that Babel, archetypal dreaded heterotopia, means "confusion" (*City* 657). Self-love rather than the love of God, the flesh rather than the spirit, and passions rather than serenity rule the Babelic earthly city.

As one can imagine, the earthly "city of confusion" (833 *et passim*) obtains only an imperfect knowledge. Chapters 37–42 of book 18 define that ungodly knowledge initiated by the Egyptian Isis as multiple and self-contradictory, more a matter of ingenuity than of genuine wisdom. St. Augustine berates the philosophers and rulers of the earthly city for accepting diverse opinions "without discrimination and without passing any judgment" (818). Proliferating uncontrolled, unregenerately multiple, the earthly city's knowledge stands at a far remove from God and from God's perfect, unitary wisdom. From this perspective of the earthly city, one can see another of Sor Juana's important epistemological poems, Romance #2 (which begins, "Finjamos que soy feliz / triste Pensamiento" [Let us pretend, sad Thought, that I am happy], published in 1689 [OC:1]), as fundamentally Augustinian. The poem confronts the disheartening multiplicity of human knowledge: "Todo el mundo es opiniones / de pareceres tan varios, / que lo que el uno que es negro, / el otro prueba que es blanco" [The world is full of such diverse opinions that what one person calls black, another will prove to be white] (ll. 13–16). Adumbrating the same example of the Stoics versus the Epicureans that St. Augustine employs (book 18, chap. 41), in Romance #2 Sor Juana expounds on human knowledge's irremediably relative, multiple, and ephemeral qualities.[31]

So does the *Primero sueño*. In her *silva,* a metric form related to a thick woods, or *selva,* and to confusion (Carreño 228, 235), Sor Juana critiques the Spectacular Esoteric City of her times by equating it to St. Augustine's earthly city. The prelude to the poem introduces an ensemble of female mythological figures transformed into terrifying birds as a "frightful punishment" (l. 49, *172*) for trying to steal knowledge. Their cacophonous, fearsome night chorus ("no canora" "capilla pavorosa" [ll. 56–57, *173*]) immediately flies in the face of the harmonious Heavenly City. Conversely, the poem's first movement, on the process of falling asleep, sketches out a picture of the balanced, machinelike, hierarchically ordered natural world, of God's handiwork: "que la Naturaleza siempre alterna / ya una, ya otra balanza" (ll. 160–161) [Nature is always shifting weight, from one side of the balance to the other, *175*]. Here the *PS* takes a hexameral stance only to corrode it from within.[32] In an abrupt chiaroscuro, when the dreamer whom St. Augustine had stigmatized (430) herself falls into sleep and night, the poem proceeds utterly to dismantle the neat, natural world, distancing itself from any hexameral aims.

For once freed from the body, the Soul shifts her ill-fated intellectual journey into a nocturnal outer space that—perhaps counterintuitively for the modern reader but quite logically for the early modern reader—assumes the qualities and contours of the *City of God*'s earthly city. The emotional landscape of the *PS* seethes with wonder and other disordered passions inimical to the serene Heavenly City. Similarly, the poem textualizes the earthly city through a poetics of contingency and confusion. The ambiguity, contradictions, nonlinear digressions, and Ovidian metamorphoses that configure the nightworld of the *PS* emanate organically from St. Augustine's corruptible, Babelic earthly city. His earthly city, in other words, organically invites the convolutions of Baroque poetry.

As an earthly city, the *PS* basks but little in the light of God and enjoys only presentiments of the Divinity's knowledge. The "Eternal author" (l. 674, *188*), in fact, encroaches on the poem largely as the author of punishments for Icarus, Phaethon, and for the retreating Dark Empress of the nightworld with which the text concludes. Sor Juana endows the poem with a rightful fear of God, with professions of humility and unworthiness of divine knowledge. She thus poises the transgressive *PS* to be read as a statement of Augustinian orthodoxy that culminates in the obligatory defeat of the Dark Empress, the arrival of the Father Sun, and the restitution of the Sun's "luz judiciosa / de orden distributivo" (ll. 969–970) [judicious light in orderly distribution, *195*]. The awakening of the dreamer whom the poem's final lines at long last name as an "I" (quickly stating, "quedando a luz más cierta / el Mundo iluminado, y yo despierta" [leaving the World illuminated by a more certain light, and I awake]) flickers with fideism, the sense that true knowledge can derive only from God. The *PS*'s more theologically problematic aspects also profit appreciably from associations with St. Augustine. For example, his belief that the Heavenly City has a fugitive life on earth lays the groundwork for the incongruous illumination, in the midst of the Soul's failures, of the pyramid (ll. 373–374, *180*) and of Arethusa's "feminine" knowledge. Or the baffling ambiguity of the poetic speaker's final truncated awakening (to what? by what grace? for how long?), which still incarnates the earthly city's poetics of contingency and mutability.[33]

Read through the shadow script of St. Augustine's *City*, which molded so much doctrine, the failure of the Soul's quest for total knowledge is a foregone conclusion. This preordained, orthodox outcome limits and liberates. In the *PS*, it frees Sor Juana to take a pioneering, enthralling journey through the earthly intellectual city, a journey which extensively dramatizes, interrogates, and critiques its multiple, inevitably flawed, often secular philosophies. As the Aristotelian inquiries into the rose exemplified, the philosophical investigations of the *PS* scintillate with epistemological insight, ardent emotion, and spectacular imagery. For their part, the Platonic portions of the *PS* vividly stage and adjudicate the earthly city's brand of knowledge by combining an emotive, humanized Soul with the magnificent image of the pyramid, as follows.

Throughout the *PS*, Sor Juana vests the Soul with strong (in Augustinian terms, somewhat wrong) emotions that personify her and safely personalize her defeat. Contradictory, spectacular emotions collide at the climactic moment of the Soul's attempt to apprehend the world by means of a single, overviewing glance like that of Platonic archetypes. She looks down from the awesome mental pyramid that symbolizes human yearning for knowledge (ll. 400–411, *181*):

> En cuya casi elevación inmensa,
> gozosa mas suspensa,
> suspensa pero ufana,
> y atónita aunque ufana, la suprema
> de lo sublunar Reina soberana,
> la vista perspicaz, libre de anteojos
> . . . .
> libre tendió por todo lo criado. (ll. 435–440; 445)

> [At this almost limitless elevation, jubilant but perplexed, perplexed yet full of pride, and astonished although proud, the sovereign Queen of this sublunary world let her probing gaze, by lenses unencumbered range unrestricted over all creation.] (*182*)

Behind the smoke screen of none too praiseworthy "feminine" emotions, Sor Juana has crowned the Soul queen. Under the same shield, she goes on to expose the inherent flaws of the Platonic method. In a passage that recalls Hernán Cortés's acknowledgment that his eyes could see but his mind not comprehend the splendor of Tenochtitlán (131, *102*), Sor Juana writes,

> y por mirarlo todo, nada vía,
> ni discernir podia
> (bota la facultad intelectiva
> en tanta, tan difusa
> incomprehensible especie que miraba
> desde el un eje en que librada estriba
> la máquina voluble de la Esfera,
> al contrapuesto polo) (ll. 480–487)

[and trying to look at everything, saw nothing, unable to discern (the intellective faculty gone blunt in the face of so diffuse a quantity of species beyond its grasp, that stretched from the axis on which is poised the revolving mechanism of the sphere to the opposite pole)] (*182*)

The slippage of the passage, from the individual to the general ("bota la facultad intelectiva"), distributes the onus of failure between the Soul and the method per se. From either vantage point, the world is too complex to be subsumed into Platonic archetypes.

Earlier on in the *PS* (ll. 414–422, *181–182*), its "Intermezzo of the Pyramids" had rather jarringly affiliated the shining pyramid with the tower of Babel. This anomalous move sets the stage for the crises of Platonism and Aristotelianism as depicted in the *PS*. Sor Juana orchestrates the breakdown of the earthly city's philosophical methods in stunning, parallel *tableaux vivants* of Babel, with its chaos, confusion, and unruly complexity. The Soul, who "asombrada / de la vista quedó de objeto tanto" (ll. 540–541) [astounded by the sight of such a mass of objects, *184*] and "aun no sabía recobrarse a sí misma del espanto"(ll. 543–544) [as yet found recovery impossible from the portentous shock, *184*] of her Platonic travails, has only managed to assimilate:

> de un concepto confuso
> el informe embrión que, mal formado,
> inordinado caos retrataba
> de confusas especies que abrazaba—sin orden avenidas,
> sin orden separadas,
> que cuanto más se implican combinadas
> tanto más se disuelven desunidas,
> de diversidad llenas— (ll. 548–556)

[a rudimentary embryo of muddled discourse, one so shapeless that from the confusion of species it embraced, it formed a picture of disordered chaos—associating species in no order, dissociating them in none, so that the more they mix and intermingle, the more they come apart in disarray from sheer diversity—] (*185*)

The ordering grid of the Platonic method has broken down and disintegrated into category crises, into a spectacle of ruins that evokes Walter Benjamin's characterization of the Baroque.

More softly because treading on the more dangerous territory of scholasticism, the poem again alludes to unbearable complexity at the end of its meditations on the rose. The Soul's astonished ("asombrada"), frightened mind, unable to process a singular object, quakes at the thought of taking on the "terrible, unendurable burden" of Nature's full machinery (ll. 757–780, *190*). Aristotelian categories, which Sor Juana, in terms pregnant with ambiguity, had earlier called "artificiosas" [artificial or artful] "mentales fantasías" [purely mental constructs] (ll. 581, 585; *185*), now reveal their intrinsic fallibility to the eminently, purposefully, fallible Soul. Were the world not upheld by God, Sor Juana writes, the machinery of the universe would prove no less formidable a challenge to understanding as that of nature (ll. 773–780, *190*).

In both of the above cases, the competing vehicles to knowledge collapse, and the nightworld that is already a swirling, disorderly version of the orderly diurnal world rushes toward Babel. As the order-endowing grids of the two earthly philosophies crash and burn, the finely tuned machinery of the world degenerates into an unknowable complexity, counterface and mockery of the Ordered City. Similitude, finally and fittingly, gives way to the Babelic chaos always latent in the Ordered City. Hexameral apologetics and "mentales fantasías" give way to an anti-Platonic nominalism.[34] And when the Soul confronts the category crises that threaten to plummet the world into a primal chaos, she reacts with a cosmic horror. Her joyful wonder at the top of the pyramid or when faced with the rose cedes to the paralysis of "espanto" and "asombro," shock and astonishment. There will be no Baroque miracles here, no more joy, just catachreses and dissonance. The horrified retreat of the Dark Empress at the end of the poem, as Father Sun routs her, replays and consolidates the nightworld's scenes of Babel. Fleeing without "concierto" (l. 952) or "orden" (l. 956) and "en sus mismos horrores tropezando" (l. 953) [stumbling over her native terrors, *195*], the Soul seeks refuge from the punitive, ordering Author of the World.

It takes little imagination to recognize the foregoing scenes of Babel as an assault not only on Plato and Aristotle but also on Kircher's project of knowing the All and of fitting the All into the divine order and concert of Neoplatonism. "Piramidal, funesta, de la tierra / nacida sombra, al Cielo encaminaba" [Pyramidal, lugubrious, a shadow born of earth pushed heavenward]: from its first two lines on, the *PS* pays tribute to the Egyptologist Kircher and to his master plan while simultaneously spelling out the doom of that plan. A Kircherian spirit of intellectual quest and interdisciplinary analogy drives the fated pursuits of the *PS* as a whole; Sor Juana layers her poem with evocations of the master. Kircher's Egypt, Harpocrates, Isis, underground waterways, *his* tower of Babel (*Turris Babel*, 1679), magic lantern, and so on, all crop up in the *PS*.[35] As Findlen writes, "Sor Juana's dream was not simply an ecstatic journey taken from the peak of Kircher's pyramid, but a voyage that allowed her to travel across his books" ("Jesuit's Books" 355). Journeying retrospectively through Kircher's works, the *PS* fits them into its fin-de-siècle project and subjects them to critical scrutiny.

Literally above all, the *PS* plants itself and its critique squarely in the territory of Kircher's cosmic *Itinerarium exstaticum*. Theodidactus, protagonist of the work and a transparent mask for Kircher, proposes to "rise now and go about the *heavenly city* in the streets," seeking God in His works.[36] In the dream voyage that ensues, Theodidactus receives a divine revelation from Cosmiel, minister of God. Cosmiel lays bare the whole divine system of the heavens and planets to the privileged eyes of Theodidactus. What Theodidactus, whose name means "taught by God," sees, however, deviates from the system espoused by God's early modern ministers on earth. The usually orthodox Kircher here treats Theodidactus to a vision of the universe that "dispelled nearly every tenet of the Aristotelian cosmology that Kircher was bound by the Jesuit curriculum to teach as accepted fact" (Rowland, "Athanasius Kircher" 194). The problematic *Itinerarium* incarnates Tycho Brahe's tempered heliocentrism, combats Aristotle's notion of a fluid outer space composed of ether, suggests the heretical existence of multiple worlds, and more (also see Rowland, *Ecstatic Journey*). Cognizant of its dangerous edge, Kircher couched the 1660 edition of the work as an "ingenious fiction" (Rowland, *Ecstatic Journey* 75), but his contrivances did not exempt the *Itinerarium* from the censors' criticism (see Siebert).

Sor Juana would therefore have considerable motivation both to adopt and to challenge Kircher's *Itinerarium*. She contests it on grounds personal and orthodox. The gendered/generic seeker in the *PS*, hurtling through the same outer space that brought Theodidactus his revelation, meets no divine messenger (Paz 366) and merits no enlightenment, altogether a sad fate for Sor Juana's "daughter," "explorer of the loftiest matters." Sor Juana reproduces the landscape of the *Itinerarium* and then defiles it by contriving her outer space not as the Heavenly City that Theodidactus proposes to walk but as St. Augustine's earthly city. The earthly city of the *PS* militates against basically everything Kircher held dear: harmony, correspondence, unity, knowledge, the visionary seeker, even God. Findlen aptly observes that in "the end, we must see Sor Juana's

Primero sueño as a respectful, admiring, but ultimately devastating critique of Kircher's own intellectual assumptions" ("Jesuit's Books" 353).

We can now understand why successfully executing an Augustinian critique of Kircher or of his fellow intellectual giants was a Pyrrhic victory for Sor Juana: it entailed sacrificing her own revered intellectual goals, as expressed in the *Respuesta,* along with theirs. Vetancurt, immersed in the Baroque unknowability of the world, accepts all earthly theories. Sor Juana, "sirtes tocando / de imposibles" (ll. 828–829) [brushing the shoals of impossible things, cf. *191*], accepts none. The *PS* leaves the secret searcher reeling in a void, in a bankrupt intellectual city. It also leaves her "esforzando el aliento en la ruina" (l. 962) and "segunda vez rebelde" (l. 965) [plucking courage up from her very ruin; rebelling once again, *195*], that is, still seeking. Whether the celebratory appraisal of Kircher and of hexameral projects akin to his found in the later *Respuesta* constitutes a new and happier phase of that search or more of an expedient strategy on Sor Juana's part remains open to question.

One last critique, which will specifically implicate the Mexican Baroque, arises from the Babelic multiplicity that has been the crux of Sor Juana's deliberations on Kircher and his fellow thinkers. The *PS,* as we have observed, dramatizes the ways in which human understanding ceaselessly aspires to the singularity and unity of divine knowledge but invariably falls into multiplicity and plurality. With multiplicity and plurality comes the *excess* that the *PS* Baroquely textualizes in its immoderate digressions as well as repeatedly thematizes. The Soul's bid to compress knowledge into clean archetypes succumbs to a chaotic, abhorrent profusion. Overflow and surplus—"la inmensa muchedumbre / de tanta maquinosa pesadumbre," "un mar de asombros" (ll. 470–471, 478) [the immense agglomeration of a congeries so weighty; a sea of astonishments, *183*]—capsize the seeker. She then shifts gears and pursues Aristotelian order ("más juzgó conveniente / a singular asunto reducirse" [ll. 576–577], considered more appropriate restriction to a single subject [*185*]), by means of the earthly city's own operating principle, excess. Utilizing a scientific method found in book 11 of *City of God,* the Soul undertakes to redirect a negative into a positive. Since "excess produces opposite effects" (l. 500, *183*), when meted out by degrees the excess of light may heal the *PS*'s seeker.

We already know that the Soul's second stab at order, centering on the rose, erupts yet again into excess. And we know that the wondrously imbricated rose of the *PS* implicitly or directly enters into a complex relationship with Balbuena's wondrous liminal objects. At this point, the energies of excess in the *PS* open up a final web of connections between Sor Juana's and Balbuena's Baroque masterpieces, definitely a tacit web but an illuminating one for our endings. The unmanageable excess of the city in "Grandeza," we remember, generated Balbuena's proto-Baroque. Excess unnerved and destabilized the poem's *flâneur* ("¿Quién, puesta ya la mira en tantos blancos / y los débiles pies en esta altura, / irá sin dar descompasados trancos?" [71]). The engrossing particularity or architexture of Balbuena's Mexico City placed the knowable, symmetrical Ordered City in crisis. No less did the excesses of that architexture provoke a rhetorical crisis in "Grandeza"'s author. Especially in the poem's epilogue, Balbuena worries through the dynamics of ciphering, abridgement, and containment. At times unequal to the task of imposing some order on his wayward text, Balbuena can fall into aporia.

The *PS* provides an epilogue to Balbuena's epilogue. From the tiny rose to the view of the universe atop the pyramid, all the phenomena of the *PS* resist containment and comprehension. They duplicate and immeasurably exacerbate Balbuena's dilemma of abridgment, his struggles with indomitable particularity. When the Soul, "entorpecida / con la sobra de objetos, y excedida de la grandeza de ellos su potencia / —retrocedió cobarde" (ll. 450–453) [dazed by objects in such profusion, its powers surpassed by their very magnitude, turned coward and drew back (*182*)], she recoils in aporia at an excess, an outpouring of architexture, that has swelled from Balbuena's early Baroque moment into a fin-de-siècle metaphysical crisis.

That metaphysical crisis eventuates precisely from the state of knowledge in the Mexican esoteric city. The conservative, omnivorous Baroque that stockpiles information without admitting new paradigms has produced an exorbitant pileup of knowledge, again in Benjamin's terms, an ensemble of ruins and fragments. Concomitantly, the Baroque has endeavored to subdue and naturalize the heterogeneity of the New World through such conceptual controls as historiographic syncretism. While elsewhere Sor Juana is by no means above exploiting the mobility of the Baroque playing field, in the *PS* she shifts into skepticism and unmasks the Baroque on both counts. Wedding epistemological breakdown to overflow, Sor Juana assesses Baroque knowledge as excessive *and* inadequate. When the *PS* destabilizes the orderly world and then swirls it into epistemological chaos, Sor Juana caricatures the Baroque's spurious attempts to effect harmony. All told, in consummately deploying the Baroque against itself, Sor Juana has erected what Paz terms a "baroque poem that negates the baroque" (381).[37]

V. RIOT AND DISRUPTIONS

The metaphysical *PS* trenchantly and suggestively affronts the esoteric city, but to all appearances it steers clear of the physical city, the actual Mexico City of the times. In contrast, Sigüenza's epistolary chronicle of riots that occurred in 1692, *Alboroto y motín de los indios de México,* meets the real Mexico City head-on, albeit when it is going up in flames. Sigüenza's report on the rebellion tackles the city at its most earthly worst (or heroic best, if one does not share his perspective), at the point in which the tensions that had accumulated over the course of two centuries boil over and convulse in actual revolt. Under these disruptive conditions, Sigüenza takes up the reins of manufacturing a fin de siècle. He delivers an apocalyptic, spectacular vision of a Mexico City rocked by the "gigantic revolt of the whole of Mexico City" (131, *269*), which unwittingly previews Mexican insurgent movements to come and purposefully passes review on the Mexican Archive in its literal and literary embodiments.

Quite wittingly and overtly jockeying for fame in Spain, Sigüenza writes a long letter on the events of 1692 so that the court and citizens of Madrid "may know on good authority what others have probably written with not so much personal and real information" (135, *227*). He addresses the formal letter-chronicle to Andrés de Pez, his former companion on an expedition to Pensacola who then resided in Madrid. Sigüenza regales his friend with the "bad news" of "our misfortunes" (95, *210*). The bad news that *Alboroto* will melodramatically impart centers on the food riots of 1692, colonial Mexico City's first wholly plebeian rebellion (Cope 125). Torrential rains and floods together with an outbreak of plant blight had ruined the wheat and corn harvests, inflated the price of grain, and caused a food shortage the Indians and castas refused to tolerate. Sigüenza recounts that the Indians then hatched a plot to unseat the Spanish regime by killing the viceroy and the corregidor and burning the city's official buildings.

They realized part of their plans on the night of June 8, interrupting the Corpus Christi festival in Mexico City. When an Indian woman was trampled in the marketplace, citizens carried her body to the archbishop's palace in a failed effort to rouse him and the viceroy to action. Consequently, that night some ten thousand insurgents set fire to the Palacio Real as well as to surrounding public buildings, shouting, "let us go joyfully into this strife. If God wills that the Spaniards be wiped out in it, it does not matter if we die without confession! Isn't this our land? Then what do the Spaniards want in it?" (123, *257*). The rebellious crowds, their patriotism of outrage a far cry from the cool refinement of creole cultural nationalism, went on to wreck and loot the marketplace of the Zócalo. At first ineffectual, government troops eventually overcame the rioters. The revolt had lasted one long night, after which, Sigüenza maintains, the city promptly returned to order.

An eyewitness to the riots, Sigüenza assures Andrés de Pez that he reports them transparently rather than through "a green glass" (96, *211*). Sigüenza silently quotes Sor Juana's Soneto #152 ("Verde embeleso de la vida humana" [OC:1], Green allurement of our human life, *33*), a denunciation of tinted, tainted perceptions. Yet, deny it as he will, Sigüenza's letter strays egregiously from objective observation. First, Sigüenza contorts the text into a ferocious diatribe against the Indians and castas. In a regrettable rebirth of Balbuena's monstrous Indian, Sigüenza here steps down from the abstract intellectual position that produced the glorious historical Indians of creole cultural nationalism to tongue-lash their living counterparts. He excoriates the Indians who instigated the riots, calling them "the most ungrateful, thankless, grumbling, and restless people that God ever created" (115, *244*). Narrating the riots that a mixed populace instigated allows Sigüenza again to break into Vetancurt's signature terrain, the irremediable diversity and multiplicity of Mexico City. Stating that the Indians allied with "mulattoes, Negroes, *chinos,* mestizos, lobos, and exceedingly vile Spaniards, both gachupines as well as creoles"(127, *263*), Sigüenza repeatedly emphasizes how all races comprising the "vile rabble" (113, *240*) banded together in the odious rebellion. Diversity descends into raging excess as the imagined community of the festival strikes back.

More in keeping with the spirit of the Corpus Christi festival, the author depicts the viceroy punctiliously ministering to all of the society's constituencies and to all of its religious orders (111, *236*). That Sigüenza emphasizes the viceroy's ecumenical liberality reveals the second and principal bias of *Alboroto*. Sigüenza's account scapegoats the mutineers and exculpates his patrons, Archbishop Aguiar y Seijas and Viceroy Galve, of blame for the riots. *Alboroto* flatters the archbishop, whose alms the author himself distributed and who had named Sigüenza chaplain of the Hospital de Amor de Dios in 1685. Yet Sigüenza especially gears his text to vindicating the viceroy, by 1692 an active supporter of the author. Mexicans less favored by Galve than Sigüenza had accused the viceroy of buying up the grain harvests and manufacturing the food shortage to inflate the price of his stores. As Iván Escamilla González writes, "It can be stated with almost absolute certainty that *Alboroto y motín* was written for publication in Spain and as part of a campaign that the Count de Galve orchestrated to safeguard his political reputation, which the uprising had seriously jeopardized" (194). Therefore, in what amounts to a commissioned work, Sigüenza lists the achievements of Galve's regime, a "Golden Age" (96, *211*) of military conquests, security, new buildings, and so on. Sigüenza's official story of the riots, excruciatingly similar to twentieth-century coverups of the massacre of students in Tlatelolco and of rebellions in Chiapas, downplays the government's brutality.[38]

More slanted than transparent, Sigüenza's chronicle at heart meets its definition in lines of Sor Juana's Soneto #152 that deride those who have green lenses in their spectacles for seeing everything just as they desire (OC:1). And because Sigüenza's desires often run toward self-promotion, he paints himself into the Spain-directed *Alboroto* as one of its heroes, as redeemer of the esoteric city that the insurgent city is about to immolate. At their most fascinating, the autobiographical aspects of the letter tell a tale of two cities, a tale that starts with a clash between the intellectual city and the real, rebellious one.

As the outside world shatters around him, at first Sigüenza keeps to himself, happily ensconced in intellectual pursuits: thrilled with the chance to study a solar eclipse (108) and oblivious to the beginnings of the food riots "because I was at home, poring over my books" (123, *256*). Finally jolted out of his house by the din of the food riots, Sigüenza goes off to do his duty by the archbishop, the viceroy, and his country. He counsels the two leaders and administers holy oil and confession to the wounded and dying. He then happens on a remarkable opportunity for heroic action. The Palacio Real that housed all the signal institutions of the viceregal regime is aflame, and with it the actual bureaucratic archives as well as Sigüenza's cherished historical archives of Mexico. Sigüenza loses his earlier fear, and, "freely and spontaneously without regard to my rank or for reward[, w]ith a bar and with an axe I cut beams and pried open doors by my own efforts and not only some apartments of the Palace but whole halls and the best archives of the city were rescued from the fire" (130, *268*). The writer thus rather spectacularly informs his readers that he has saved the physical plant of the intellectual city.

Sigüenza's rescue of the Mexican archives hardly stops here. Instead, it penetrates the very texture of *Alboroto*. The author of *Alboroto* saves the intellectual city in deed and in word—through a retrospective

Mexican intertextuality akin to that of Sor Juana's *EDN*. As Kathleen Ross's indispensable article from 1988 has brought out, *Alboroto* signifies upon Cortés's *Segunda carta-relación* at various points. Ditch-diggers under Sigüenza's guidance discover gruesome clay figurines of Spaniards, sprinkled with blood and pierced by knives; they extract the figurines from the waters below the "Alvarado bridge" over which, Sigüenza notes, Cortés fled the city on the famous Night of Sorrows (*Alboroto* 116–117, 246). In Sigüenza's explanation, the figurines connote the Indians' ongoing hatred of the colonizers, which foreshadows the present disturbances. When the Indians and others riot in 1692, they mock the lack of leadership in present-day Spanish troops, "exhorting each other to have courage since there was no longer any other Cortés to keep them in subjection" (123, 257). Rioting leads to looting, and Spaniards, Indians, and castas alike flee the Zócalo loaded down with stolen merchandise, as had Cortés's troops (128, 265). Amidst the panic and the vestiges of Cortés's text, in *Alboroto* Sigüenza takes the conqueror's place. Axe in hand, like Cortés, he batters away heroically at the obstacles. As Ross concludes, "Sigüenza's 'I,' in fully identifying itself with that of Cortés, executes the latter's feats, but as a man of letters rather than as a man of arms" (185).

Along the way, the man of letters has also built into his text remnants from the indigenous archive of the conquest such as that which he battled to save. Sigüenza's disquisition on Santiago de Tlatelolco, home of the Indians most intent on the present riot (117, 247), silently draws on the text that Miguel León-Portilla has dubbed *La relación anónima de Tlatelolco* [Anonymous account of Tlatelolco], a description of the Tlatelolcans' fierce resistance to the original Spanish conquest of Tenochtitlán. In stressing the cosmic portents that anticipated the food riots (floods, eclipse, earthquakes), Sigüenza also duplicates the apocalyptic climate of omens that according to Bernardino de Sahagún's native informants at the celebrated Franciscan college in Tlatelolco predetermined the downfall of Aztec empire. The author of *Alboroto* capitalizes on his acquaintance with native texts and with the natives themselves (117, 246) to style himself as the bearer of secret, privileged knowledge like Kircher's Harpocrates.

A tabernacle of esoterica, *Alboroto* recalls another of Harpocrates's manifestations in the Mexican Archive, the hermetic *Primero sueño* published that same year (Sigüenza could easily have had an advance copy). Repository of past and present knowledge, pinnacle of the contemporary esoteric city, a cryptic text that only the most learned literati could decipher, the spectacular *PS* would glimmer with attractions for Sigüenza. I believe those attractions pulled him in. Scanning *Alboroto* for resonances of the *PS*, one unearths powerful correspondences between the two works.

These correspondences powerfully impact Sigüenza's dealings with the Mexican Archive and the esoteric city, both of which he salvages *and* ultimately disrupts. They suggest that the Sigüenza who had maneuvered Alonso Ramírez's tale into an encyclopedia of current discourse does incorporate Sor Juana's avant-garde poem into *Alboroto*, crowning his renditions of the Mexican Archive and fin de siècle. Filtered into *Alboroto*, the *PS* would imbue Sigüenza's ostensible mere letter with the dimension and cachet of a supreme literary work. And it would allow the same pages that communicated the monstrous depths to which Mexico City had in Sigüenza's opinion fallen to transport the best of the Mexican creole intellectual city to Madrid. The correspondences between the two works further suggest that, having encountered in the *PS* latent parallels to the riots, Sigüenza adopted the nun's masterpiece not as just one among *Alboroto*'s welter of intertexts, but as an arcane, sublime, secret model for his text. If, as what follows should establish to a reasonable certainty, *Alboroto* bears the *PS* in palimpsest as its secret model, then Sigüenza has told more than one tale of two cities and, mutatis mutandis, set the esoteric *PS* in a relationship to the real-time state of Mexico City.

Alboroto's lengthy lead-in to the narration of the food riots reprises the lugubrious opening sections of the *PS*, anchoring them in reality and adding to them a new moralistic twist. An air of doom hangs over *Alboroto*'s Mexico City, concretized in a series of natural disasters and "pestilences" (109, 233). A dance of death that has a leveling effect parallel to that of sleep in the *PS*, the plagues affect and equalize all sectors of society (*Alboroto* 102, 221). Where there is plague, there must be the sin and punishment that dominate the prelude to the *PS*. Sigüenza decries both in Mexico City, branding the fatal events as punishments sent by God. Rather than for the theft of knowledge imputed to the *PS*'s birdwomen, in Sigüenza's interpretation Mexico deserves divine punishment for various sins of its history. Early on, attributing the conjecture to the populace, Sigüenza suggests that God has taken revenge on Mexico for the excesses of its festivals ("divine punishment for the recent festivities" [102, 222]). The root sin of Mexico finally surfaces much later. Completely dissociating the ills of Mexico from its viceroy's actions, the author ascribes Mexico City's divine castigation to the diabolical sacrificial practices of the Aztecs (134, *274*). With this, Sigüenza cinches a text that has located the epistemological *PS* in a biblical and historical framework.

The *PS*'s distinctive progression from order to disorder to chaos explains some of its purchase on *Alboroto*, since all three elements inhere in the events on which Sigüenza reports. *Alboroto* gyrates between the three, identifying order with the viceroy and archbishop, and disorder and chaos with nature and the populace. As an official story, the text must heartily acclaim the measures that viceregal officials took to impose order. The neat, hierarchical, hexameral world that the *PS* quickly sketches out consequently looms large in *Alboroto* as Sigüenza spotlights the order that obtains in the midst of chaos thanks to the viceroy and archbishop. He lauds the viceroy as a minister of God (120, *251*), a God known to readers of the *PS* as the order-endowing Father Sun. Companion and helpmeet of both officials, Sigüenza associates himself with the elite guardians of order.

Disorder and chaos, the nerve center of the *PS*, nonetheless prevail in *Alboroto* and pronouncedly align Sigüenza's report with Sor Juana's esoteric poem. In the *PS* the rebel Soul moves from a twilight land-based world into watery nocturnal one, laden with references to the sea, rivers, and navigation and textualized in an equally flowing, liquid fashion. Floodwaters play a major part in *Alboroto,* correlating it to the *PS*. They liquify Mexico City, dematerializing the capital into "shifting grounds and loose stone without any foundation" (107, cf. *230*). These unstable, crop-destroying grounds impel and serve as the backdrop for the nocturnal, nightlong uprisings of the seditious populace. Emboldened by drinking pulque, that night the Indians erupt into an irrational, oneiric force that hurls itself into "all sort of iniquities and senseless things" (115, *244*). By virtue of their nightmarish actions, Mexico City, like the nightworld of the *PS,* careens from instability into irrational chaos. The uncontrollable riots that blaze through the night match the spectacular breakdown of the *PS*'s order-endowing epistemological grids, the difference being that in *Alboroto* the unruly populace, instead of knowledge, defies containment. Yet the protagonists of both works, populace and Soul, ruthlessly test the limits, structures, and adequacy of order and concert in a multiple, Baroque world. In both cases, the tensely amalgamated center of the Ordered City has not held.

Sigüenza displays somewhat more than his usual middling literary skill when he forges *Alboroto*'s awesome, Babelic scenes of the disordered city. The author insistently enlivens his narrative with acoustic effects by means of direct discourse and descriptions of the plebeians' shouts, such as, "the birds in flight falling, dogs howling, and women and children shouting" (108, cf. *232*), "raised such sorrowful and raucous cry that it reached Mexico City" (111, *235–236*), "raucous din heard in the streets" (131, *259*). As Sigüenza makes horrifying acoustic effects a leitmotif of his text, one cannot help but think of the frightful, cacophonous night chorus of the *PS*'s birdwomen. Uncannily similar to their night chorus, *Alboroto*'s wailing Greek chorus captures the predominant emotion of the tumultuous city: "At the very moment that the doors were closed and the rabble found itself without any opposition, it raised such a uniformly raucous and frightful howl that it struck terror [*espanto*]" (124, *259*). Like the Soul's reaction to breakdown, the Babelic Mexico City in full disarray elicits the negative side of wonder, the "espanto" of the crowd and the reader.

Among the many possible lures of the *PS* for Sigüenza, none would recommend it more to his purposes or receive a more disruptive and problematic treatment in *Alboroto* than the poem's matriarchal bent. Whereas the *PS* indelibly engraves women in the Mexican Archive, *Alboroto* accords them an unforgettable place in Mexican history. For according to Sigüenza, women dominated the iniquitous rebellion. A trampled Indian woman ignites the violence, Indian women parade her body through the town and to the palace, taunt the viceroy to his face, catalyze the riots, and lead ferocious attacks on the Spaniards. Sigüenza vents his anger on the female protagonists of the riots as he had on the collective "rabble." Satirizing a tradition that runs from Columbus to Sor Juana, he characterizes the women as Amazons, here as brutal, inhuman Amazons who overpower men. In typical Baroque fashion, Sigüenza accuses the women warriors of evil schemes and theatrical deceptions.

The ghastly matriarchal world of *Alboroto,* we see, has everything and nothing to do with the *PS. Alboroto* correctively debunks Sor Juana's heroic female world, with Sigüenza no doubt intending to please the misogynistic Aguiar y Seijas (on whose paranoia regarding women the author remarks [119, *249*]). If, as I am arguing, Sigüenza did plot his text as a fac*simile* of Sor Juana's, thus reversing the master-pupil relationship of their collaboration in 1680, then he also exercises some censorious spleen on the Sor Juana who had angered Aguiar y Seijas. He flatters the nun by adopting her poem but chastises her by disrupting its heart and soul. One hears in *Alboroto* reverberations of the Sigüenza who, to our knowledge, did not defend Sor Juana precisely at this, her time of troubles.[39]

Women on top, a world upside down: Sigüenza has ample material in the riots further to disrupt the Mexican Archive by skewing it toward the carnivalesque. Satirizing female Amazons, *Alboroto* infuses the *PS*'s heroines with Rabelaisian dimensions. Furthermore, *Alboroto* inscribes itself in and radically complicates the long-lived, exalted, and exalting genre of the festival chronicle. *Alboroto* begins by invoking the joyous, righteous festival of May 1692 in which Mexico City honored the marriage of Spain's Carlos II. An "august stage" for demonstrating fidelity to Spain (95, *210*), the May festival glaringly contrasts with the insurrection that occurred the next month on a most holy Sunday of the holy Corpus Christi festival (120, *251*). As the riots executed by the collective castas parody the ideal imagined community that official festivals strive to advance, in Sigüenza's words they discharge a "monstrous undertaking" (119, *251*). The officially desired collectivity thus turns into a hydra-headed monster, a fearsome *tarasca*, or festival dragon, that throws into a carnivalesque bedlam everything that hegemonic spectacles seek to fortify.

The tumults that overthrow official strictures and structures rescript *Alboroto*'s Mexico City from Sigüenza's treasured esoteric city into a shocking carnivalesque entity. Bodily needs for food, rather than yearnings for the divine Eucharist that Corpus Christi celebrates, kindle the riots. Hunger trumps and deposes all other concerns (much in the way it shuts down the intellectual voyage of the *PS*'s Soul). Pulque, instead of food, fuels the rebels' bodies and leads to the city's undoing. The *pulquerías,* or taverns that dispense intoxicating brandy, become a template for the disordered city at large. Breeding ground for transgressive activity that upends the established order, a site where diverse ethnic groups fraternize to the default of social regulation, the pulquerías emblematize the Babelic Zócalo of the riots. As the uprisings reduce the regulated space of the Zócalo to carnival, they restore the city center to a natural state: fluid, unregulated, holistic, and diverse. And as the citizens' cacophonous shouts ring throughout the plaza, they install a new, carnivalesque language in the city. Their threats, vulgar curses, mockery, and jeering laughter dethrone the elite, arcane language of the Baroque esoteric city.

R. Douglas Cope notes that for its plebeian participants, "the riot was a liminal, almost festive event, a moment of sudden and sharp reversal but one that could not last" (160). No more than Sor Juana's nocturnal derangement of epistemology, the Mexico City "carnival" certainly did not last. Day breaks and, as Sigüenza hastens to observe, the viceroy reinstates order. He comes out of hiding in a Franciscan convent to join other dignitaries in a proper Corpus Christi parade (133, *273;* Robles 2:260), dispatches soldiers throughout the city, has Indian ringleaders arrested and killed ("without resort to any torture at all" [134, *275*]), and outlaws pulque. All of this squares both with Sigüenza's official perspective and with the very last lines of the *PS,* but *Alboroto* still has another Sor Juanian maneuver in store. Although Mexico City had quelled its rebellion, Sigüenza tells us that Cortés's former allies, the Tlaxcalans, immediately began their own revolts, starting the cycle anew. *Alboroto* thus concludes with an ominous iteration of the Dark Empress's last appearance in the *PS* as she retreats to a new sphere, "rebelling once again."

While Sigüenza closes his text with a peremptory mention of the Count de Galve's success in subduing the Tlaxcalan insurrections, the well-informed creole author would have been all too aware that Mexico City's one-night rebellion had already played itself out more fully and drastically at other moments in his capital and in other spheres of the colonial world. Baroque Latin American literary culture, from Juan Rodríguez Freile's *El Carnero* (1638) on, had already told many stories of uproar, protest, women, sin, and plagues, stories that, as did Sigüenza's, exploited the dark sides of wonder. An endpoint on several levels for the Mexican Archive, *Alboroto* is also an inception point for my final chapter, which ranges through shocking, scandalous texts saturated with the uproar that had already taken its place as a defining characteristic of their Spectacular Cities.

However, the Mexico City that in 1692 collapsed into rebellion and, as Sigüenza would have it, phoenix-like, immediately rebounded into an orderly entity, has one final synoptic lesson to impart. We circle back to the marketplace and to Villalpando's painting of 1695, two touchstones of our preceding chapters. The Count de Galve, scheduled to depart for Spain the next year, commissioned the painting as a souvenir of his accomplishments in Mexico, just as he likely did Sigüenza's *Alboroto*.[40] Villalpando essentially complied with the viceroy's wishes, opening but a small crack in the official story. Only the partially crumbling façade of the viceregal palace reminds the painting's viewers of the riots that had devastated the Zócalo and nearly three hundred of its shop stalls. On the other hand, the Zócalo's thriving Parián market, built at the viceroy's behest in the aftermath of the riots and *not yet completed* in 1695, monopolizes the forefront of the painting. Bounded, neatly symmetrical, literally a clean, well-lighted place, the Parián commemorates both a signal achievement of the viceroy and the Ordered City that persisted as a nostalgic but imperative dream in the late seventeenth century.

In basically erasing or disappearing the 1692 disruptions specifically from the marketplace, Villalpando's tableau shares the same magical thinking and representation in which several of his forebears' texts had indulged. Cortés's *Cuarta carta-relación* magically restores the marketplace to prosperity and order far too soon after the conquest of Tenochtitlán. In the thick of the early seventeenth-century Spanish economic crisis, the colonialist fictions of Balbuena's "Grandeza" sell Mexico City to the crown as a robust emporium thoroughly devoted to engorging the royal coffers. Sigüenza's *Alboroto* verbally desecrates the marketplace, scene of the rebels' crime, as an "ill-founded village and a pigsty" (125, 260) and induces its readers to buy into the viceroy's effective rehabilitation of the city from chaos "without resort to any torture at all." Such colonialogical magical thinking will at long last evanesce in the exposés that occupy chapter 7.

Seven   BABEL
             Wild Work of the Baroque

> en que la arquitectura / a la geometría se rebela
> *[in which architecture rebels against geometry]*
> LUIS DE GÓNGORA Y ARGOTE, "SEGUNDA SOLEDAD"
> [SECOND SOLITUDE] (1613)

> No habrá remedio para este hospital de nervios.
> *[There will be no solution for this hospital of nerves.]*
> CÉSAR VALLEJO, "TRUENOS"
> [THUNDERBOLTS] (1918)

I. BAROQUE TIMES

Irving A. Leonard's watershed, prizewinning *Baroque Times in Old Mexico* (1959) purveys its subject in the spectacular terms that have excited readers, stimulated scholars, and, to no small degree, spurred the present study.[1] Taking as its epigraph the roster of Mexico's grandeurs in the eight-line "Argumento" of "La grandeza mexicana," *Baroque Times* resurrects an opulent, pleasure-sated, festive colonial Mexico that breathes the same air as Bernardo de Balbuena's poem. *Baroque Times* also steeps itself in Balbuena's dazzling literary milieu, to complex effect. For Leonard largely predicates his assessment of colonial Mexico itself on the ostentatious, recondite literary culture of the Baroque that owes its inception to Balbuena, comes to fruition in spectacular esoterica, and, according to *Baroque Times,* encounters its emblem in seventeenth-century festival poetry contests. We have heard Leonard vilify the frivolous intricacy of the festival poems, which he regards as hardly worthy of the name.

From these maligned cultural artifacts, Leonard goes on to pillory the festive, Balbuenian world of "Baroque times" that his book spiritedly brings to life. As the cultural historian would have it, the ceremonial poetry contests, which garnered creoles luxury items but no real agency or social mobility, symptomatize a colonial Baroque society that Leonard at heart views as static and repressed. A pivotal moment in his study denounces the tendency of the Baroque literary culture

> to shift from content to form, from ideas to details, to give new sanction to dogmas, to avoid issues, and to substitute subtlety of language for subtlety of thought; it served to repress rather than liberate the human spirit, and to divert by spectacles, by overstatement, and by excessive ornamentation. (28)

"Such, in essence," concludes Leonard, "was the spirit of the so-called 'Baroque Age' as manifested in the Hispanic world" (28).

By no means entirely erroneous, Leonard's influential construction of colonial Baroque times nonetheless maneuvers within an infinite loop, a limited, self-justifying sphere. The delightfully if anachronistically Romantic Leonard, who reproduces the optic and stylistics of Romantic historians such as W. H. Prescott, to an extent becomes a prisoner of his penchant for the spectacular. That is, arrested by the Romantic spectacularity of Latin American Baroque times, he remains captive to their scintillating surface. This occasions in the author a profound unease with a colonial world he deems fundamentally diseased by virtue of its complacency, inertia, and stagnation. Though in his *Books of the Brave* (1949) and his treatments of Sor Juana Inés de la Cruz and Carlos de Sigüenza y Góngora Leonard unearths challenges to Spain's stranglehold on its colonies, he persists in seeing them as small cracks in a monolithic Spanish colonial enterprise that achieved "immobility, spiritual, intellectual, cultural, political, and economic" (*Baroque Times* 223) and in appraising the challenges as anomalous, exceptional harbingers of the more liberated eighteenth century.[2]

Here, obviously, the spectacular *Baroque Times* splits from *The Spectacular City,* previous chapters of which should already have unsettled many of Leonard's preceding claims. To cement the case for spectacular *and* dynamic Baroque times, this last chapter zeroes in on some of the heftiest challenges to Leonard's circumscribed notion of Baroque times and, much more important, to the Spanish colonial enterprise itself. The contexts and texts I examine in conclusion to *The Spectacular City* should dispel any lingering illusions that the "period of stabilization" coasted serenely through the seventeenth century, generally obeisant to the viceregal order and its Ordered City. In the reality and in the discourse of the city, the energies of a conflicted and afflicted colonial society—a "hospital of nerves"—now come to the fore. They issue verbal thunderbolts that rip away at centers that have tenuously held, roiling them into a Babel that so pushes against the colonizers' would-be "geometry" of order as to utterly derange it.

For, as the agile platforms framed in chapter 1 demonstrated, other Baroque times in colonial Mexico and South America pounded beneath the tenuous stability of the seventeenth century. Destabilizing factors that spanned the seventeenth-century New World ran thick and deep. From manifold and egregious instances of colonial misrule that even the crown could not countenance, to incessant tensions between the viceregal church and state, to increasing pirate attacks on the coasts, to the decline of the ravaged Indians, to waning output from the mines, to the official audits that in the opinion of New World subjects tended to disrupt rather than fortify viceregal regimes—in all these ways the colonial New World experienced pressure from all sides. No less than its more notorious counterpart in Spain does the seventeenth century in Spanish America emerge as an era of crises and tangles. Indeed, Spain was faced to a considerably smaller degree with such matters as the multiethnicity and pluriculturalism that ineluctably marked the New World. Felipe Guaman Poma de Ayala's layered, labyrinthine representation of Cuzco intimates the ultranervous dynamism of the heterogeneous societies, which would erupt in the uprisings of colonial subjects that insistently punctuated the century throughout the Hispanic New World.

The unruly complexity of Cuzco as conveyed in Guaman Poma's resistant text opens a gateway to viceregal societies beyond Mexico that present increased strife, sharpened acrimony, and heightened defiance. Though Mexico unquestionably had a strong share of disruption and protest, the further one travels down the continent, from Colombia to Bolivia and Peru (each of which, together with the rest of Hispanic South America, still formed part of the Viceroyalty of Peru in the seventeenth century), the more exacerbated tensions and contestation appear to be. The crown's custom of first testing viceroys in Mexico and then passing seasoned rulers onto South America acknowledges the continent's thorny complexity; Leonardo Acosta observes that in Peru colonial alienation may well have reached its apogee (46). This phenomenon is as hard to ignore as it is to define. In terms of Peru, historians call attention to various determining factors. They include the confused atrocities of its conquest; delays in formulating and executing a systematic policy of urbanization (Kubler 68–69); and especially the difficulties of vying with an Indian population "far more numerous and densely concentrated than it was in Mexico" (Pagden, "Identity Formation" 66). Economic matters also bear heavily on the equation. With a vast supply of Indian labor to tap when exploiting the enormous mineral wealth of Peru, in the eyes of the colonizers the viceroyalty seemed ideally positioned to take its place as "the Spanish Crown's most profitable possession" (Brading 145). The colonizers sought to actualize that promise by instituting the brutal *mita* [forced conscription of the Indians to work in the mines] and by tethering Peru's economy to silver production, thereby forestalling the economic diversification that had bolstered Mexico's autonomy.

Modern historians may variously account for Peru's troubled situation, but at least one seventeenth-century author painfully aware of the region's travails has no problem pinpointing their source. Buenaventura de Salinas y Córdova, a creole Franciscan from Lima, in 1630 unwaveringly identifies the huge distance between the metropolis and Peru as the root of his homeland's problems. Peru, writes Salinas, is the most distant of Spain's colonies (274, 298). The infinite "mystical body" of the monarch should by all rights bridge the transatlantic gap between Spain and Peru, yet according to Salinas it has failed to do so (274). Since the long and just arm of the crown has not extended to its furthest colony, Peru has degenerated into chaos and Godlessness: "given the disposition and actions of these lands against the will and wisdom of Your Majesty, *because you are so far away,* they know neither peace nor calm, but instead immense tribulations, disruptions, affliction, anger, sadness, hatred, and rancor toward Spaniards, and loathing of God's law, which they find oppressive, bitter, and difficult to bear: they abhor God and flee from Him" (298; emphasis added). While latter-day Mexico, in the famous words of Porfirio Díaz, remains "so far from God" and "so close to the United States," for Salinas, by standing far from Spain colonial Peru also stood far from God.

The state of pandemonium and antagonism that emanated from Peru owing to its remove from the metropolis and a host of other difficulties undeniably obtained in other colonial Hispanic territories. It gained forthright expression in the spectacular, disruptive exposés that are the subjects of this chapter. Sections II and III of the chapter anatomize the features of the exposés and build bridges from Mexico to South America. Filling in some blanks of our previous investigations, the stage-setting sections disclose a radical Mexican countercanon (authored by Juan de Torquemada, Antonio de Robles, and Gregorio Martín de Guijo) that aligns the literary culture of New Spain with those of its continental neighbors. We then go south and canvass the exposés of Juan Rodríguez Freile (Bogotá), Bartolomé Arzáns de Orsúa y Vela (Potosí), Juan del Valle y Caviedes (Lima), and Buenaventura de Salinas y Córdova (Lima).

From their diverse locations, these historiographic and literary texts critical of crises further defuse Leonard's picture of stagnant Baroque times. Moreover, they militantly abrogate Balbuena's sublime, pastoral, racially monolithic Mexico City—to situate themselves in the plural, vexed, malignant spaces of Babel. Yet, city-centered, festival-involved, and authored by creoles or radicados, the Babelic texts from multiple points on the New World map still operate within the bounds of the Spectacular City.[3] By thrusting it into spaces, ideologies, and discursive modes diametrically opposed to those of "La grandeza mexicana," these Babelic texts help consolidate the currency and productivity of the Spectacular City, which template proves sufficiently elastic to accommodate the counterface of its inaugural text and literary cultures other than those of Mexico. Concomitantly, the texts under study here bring to a climax the supplementary, backfiring work of the New World Baroque. As colonial subjects strike back with animus, the Baroque that the empire bequeathed to them again steps in to act as their handmaiden. In so doing, the wild New World Baroque fulfills its potential to defy containment, trouble received ontologies, and own pluralism. Partnered with the crises of the New World, its Baroque dismantles the spurious "concierto barroco" (Sarduy 102) that colonialogical estheticizing, static erudition, hexameral nostalgia, magical thinking, syncretism and its attendant sameness, and so on had assiduously labored to maintain.

II. BABEL: ANATOMY OF THE EXPOSÉS

Antonio de Robles, a late seventeenth-century Mexican creole diarist, notes that shortly after the food riots of 1692 relayed in Sigüenza's chronicle a brazen individual hung up a poster in Mexico City that announced, "*Performing the famous comedy of it's Worse than it was*" (2:257). The urban texts in various genres that concern us here all square with the stuff of that play, if in a tragic or tragicomic mode. Having gathered steam from the 1500s to grow into a characteristic mode of the seventeenth century, the now-Baroque disruptive texts trade in and on *disturbances,* which *Webster's* principally defines as "any disquiet or disruption of the peace," "disorder," "tumult," "the state of being worried, troubled, or anxious," "agitation," and "excitement of passion." While the texts that enter the wide realm of disturbances never advocate independence from Spain, they do passionately shoulder the mission of exposing cities boiling over with sin, crime, and transgression. In an oxymoronic move that the conflictive Baroque naturalizes and that citizenship demands, the urban exposés at once loudly praise their cities and condemn them. The condemnation serves up the demon sibling of the Ordered City: convulsive, unstable New World cities whose fragile order continually threatens to succumb to chaos. Accordingly, *concierto,* verbal marker of peace and harmony, often flips into the verb *concertar,* the scheming of those who menace order.

And, as distinct from earlier creole complaint, all sectors of society now fall prey to censure. The new pantheon of evildoers in these histories of infamy includes all races and ethnicities, and officials of church and state. Insistently exhibiting the churning undersides of their cities, often viewing festivals themselves through a glass darkly, the exposés abrade the society of the spectacle and its official players. Only the crown generally escapes the texts' wrath, and that only because their authors envision the absent but necessary father that is the Spanish king as the court of final appeal, the only conceivable panacea for colonial ills. Still, according to Freile, Arzáns, and Salinas, not the king but God seems more inclined to intervene directly and remedy the wrongs of colonial society, albeit, as befits a Baroque climate of enhanced unknowability, randomly and intermittently.

Given the rare rectifications of God and the absence of the king, the dystopian New World that the exposés transmit once again encounters its signature image in Babel. Rather than the abstract Babel of Sor Juana's *Primero sueño,* the Babel grounded in history, place, and race of Sigüenza's *Alboroto* dominates these discursive landscapes. Real-time and real-space Babylons, they project St. Augustine's disordered, multiple earthly city onto the concrete scenarios of the colonial New World. The works' New World scenarios teem with the tensions and diversity that the hegemony could not tame into homogeneity, submission, or order. Guaman Poma's activist First New Chronicle here meets enterprises that, at times in solidarity with the Indians, assail the arrogance, depravity, and heterogeneity gone terribly wrong of a New World more akin to Babel than to St. Augustine's earthly city, which, after all, has some saving graces. With the Lucifer tied to Babylon (Isaiah 14:12) casting a long shadow on colonial heterotopias, the exposés can in fact depict a New World that spills over from Babel into hell. Further, concerned as they are with sin, the texts orchestrate Babel through other biblical paradigms, like the Fall, the Flood, Egypt (now more likely to represent a site of bondage than the Neoplatonists' *prisca theologia*), Judgment Day, and Redemption. The latter, predictably, eludes the New World, to the effect that "America-as-Babel displays not only the always incipient but also the unfinished" (Antelo 191).[4]

If not a definitive identity, the contingent, agitated New World herein acquires a pronounced style. Babel engenders a distinctive poetics such that while the exposés may shirk the philosophical loftiness of *Primero sueño,* they do espouse its textualization of Babel through contradiction, ambiguity, digression, and particularity. Whatever their genre, the contestatory Baroque texts erode the linear, the easily seizable, the archetypal. Freile and Arzáns dramatize the collapse of a neat architectural geometry in both politics and discourse; all of the works under study here give rein to architexture in its full tangled glory. The texturized, unidealized accounts of flawed earthly cities strongly incline toward the minute singularity of events, forsaking monumentalism and the grand narrative. Immersed in the anecdotal, they have a predilection for the body and for daily life in the New World. Daily life, together with pluralism and iconoclasm, invites into Freile's, Arzáns's, and Caviedes's projects an orality that affronts the fixed, solemn, monolithic word. The deliciously loquacious *Tratado del descubrimiento de las Indias* (1589) by the Mexican creole Juan Suárez de Peralta had already recorded the oral, vernacular speech of elite creoles, along with the gossip and rumors that spread like wildfire throughout New Spain's capital. Seventeenth-century works continue to privilege orality in histories of hearsay and in satirical compositions that turn on a scatological local vernacular.

Combating the written word and venting disturbances, the exposés batter away at the official story so potently that of the major texts I address only Torquemada's and Salinas's reached publication during the colonial period. A preponderance of the works, in fact, erect alternative archives based on documents hidden in the official archive that Salinas describes as a "confused Labyrinth" (qtd. in Cook xxxii) or from private holdings. Salinas, who for a time actually oversaw the state's documents and may have been the individual to whom Guaman Poma's manuscript was submitted,[5] as well as Torquemada, Freile, and Arzáns, articulate at length their modus operandi of combing the archives. The four authors scan the archives for suppressed records of malfeasances, records sometimes spirited into the wastebin (one meaning of Freile's title *El Carnero*). Recuperating disappeared, inflammatory material by reproducing it and, when necessary, translating it from Latin, the writers hope their revitalizing of a subterranean history will finally affect society. As Salinas writes,

> This is what the Protector [of the Indians] says in his papers, all of which he delivered to me at this Convent of my Father Saint Francisco de Lima, so that I could see the miserable state in which the unfortunate Indians, vassals of Your Majesty, find themselves. He asked me to print at the very least some portions of them so that matters of such great import to the Royal Crown, which self-interested enemies of its glory and Monarchy conceal, could be known and remedied. (297)

Principled authors like Salinas who compile the counterarchive communicate the sequestered iniquities with the umbrage and acerbity of self-appointed officers in a new, more just Inquisition. They reinvent the Inquisition, the archive, and the often-vilified *letrado,* or educated person. Arzáns asks what "penetrates, unites, moves and rules the body of man as much as learning and the learned penetrate, unite, move, and rule all members of the republic?" (3:4). Passing review and judgment on the records of the colonies, the rehabilitated letrado (in a total departure from Angel Rama's construction of him) acts as the conscience of the archive.

Since the New World abounded in individuals, especially the Mendicant clergy, intent on laying bare the immorality of conquest and colonization, the counterarchive had much on which to draw and the exposés no dearth of religiously seeded models. Beginning most conspicuously with Bartolomé de Las Casas's *Brevísima relación de la destrucción de las Indias,* the Dominicans labored in word and deed against abuses of encomienda by Spaniards and toward Indians. The Augustinians (discussed below with regard to Arzáns) joined the belligerent chorus. Yet not by chance are Torquemada and Salinas Franciscan friars, and not by chance are theirs the two texts to reach publication. The first religious order to put down roots in the New World, the ascetic, righteous, millenarian Franciscans considered it their express obligation to take the moral pulse of the environments under their charge and to broadcast their findings. Torquemada voices that obligation in his *Monarquía indiana* when he quotes a fellow Franciscan. The unnamed Franciscan provincial writes that although the king will have received information from other quarters about the creole rebellion of 1566 in Mexico City led by Martín Cortés, "the friars of this Order . . . being the first Chaplains of Your Majesty in this Land, and thus more obligated to Royal Service than others, are also obligated to declare our sentiments on matters of such import as unrest or calm in your Kingdoms" (1:633). St. Francis himself had inaugurated an activism that fed into *memoriales de agravios,* reports which enumerated offenses and proposed remedies for them. The reformist (*arbitrista*) New World Franciscan authors who follow in his footsteps throw caution to the wind and embrace the role of unflagging, unabashed truth tellers. Even when the Franciscans' writings concentrate on recuperating Indian history, they still suture historiography to the truth telling, combative memorial de agravios.

As a self-appointed moral compass of the New World, the Franciscans produced an unbroken tradition of hard-hitting denunciation that spans two centuries. The most outstanding of the first twelve Franciscans in Mexico, Toribio de Benavente (known as Motolinía), authored his watershed proindigenous report of offenses, the *Historia de los indios de la Nueva España,* in 1541. 1695 finds the Franciscan Agustín de Vetancurt promising that his text will report on the Indians in accord with the crown's concern for their "welfare, increase, calm, tranquility, and relief" (1:xix).[6] Franciscan missionary activity and writing extended to Colombia and Peru. By the time of the Inca Atahualpa's death, the Franciscans had penetrated Peru; by the start of the seventeenth century, creole Peruvian Franciscans such as Luis Jerónimo de Oré and Miguel de Agia had begun to protest the plight of the Indians, thus paving the way for Salinas's *Memorial* (1630).[7] In contrast, while the Jesuits who entered Peru in 1568 had an undeniable impact on education and on the Indians, Peruvian Jesuits eschewed the close affiliation with creoles that their Mexican counterparts had cultivated. More disparaging of the creoles as a race than the Mexican Jesuits, more fearful of the creoles gaining sway, the Lima contingent tightly controlled creoles' access to the Company of Jesus (see Lavallé, chap. 12).

The pervasiveness of the Franciscans' highly politicized religious discourse, the urgent pertinence of their activism to a New World rife with greed and corruption, and the untrammeled fire of their writings inspired secular writers as well. Hence the Franciscans, not the worldly Jesuits, prevail in this context. With the Franciscan ethos in the ascendant, Torquemada's *Monarquía indiana* looms as large in the discourse of Babel as it did in that of historiographic syncretism—and offers a paradigm for the Babelic Spectacular City. Perhaps unexpectedly, certainly efficaciously, Torquemada's inexhaustible *Monarquía* works the mainstays of the Spectacular City. The *Monarquía* marries them to Indian history and pro-Indian activism and stretches them in wayward directions that will permeate other voices, other spaces.

For one, a markedly supernatural climate of *wonder* pervades Torquemada's text, as it will the protomagical realism of Arzáns. Freely and credulously accepted, the *Monarquía*'s Franciscan wonder manifests itself in miracles, visions, apparitions, and prophecies, and in the ominous, apocalyptic portents from God that Sigüenza's *Alboroto* purloined from the Franciscan Sahagún. Supernatural events particularly inhere in the New World owing to the importance that the Franciscans, as distinct from Dominicans like Las Casas, attached to the devil's intervention in Indian religion (Brading 106). It therefore does not surprise that, when in books 3 and 4 of the *Monarquía* Torquemada relates the history of Indian *cities* and their devil-purging transformations under Spanish rule, he characterizes Tenochtitlán as a Babylon that conquest has redeemed into a New Jerusalem. Then again, accounts of precontact Indian *festivals,* like the God of the Seeds ceremony Sor Juana adapts from Torquemada, figure prominently in the *Monarquía*. Torquemada avidly tracks Indian festivals into postconquest years, where they merge with the Spanish ceremonial occasions. It very much appears that the Torquemada who termed the Indians "ceremoniáticos" (qtd. in Brading 287) himself deserves the epithet.

The *Monarquía*'s penchant for festivals flows at least in part from the symbolic weight with which its author endows them, a symbolism that goes to the very heart of his and others' Babelic works. As will Guijo and Freile, Torquemada textualizes official ceremonial events of all sorts as spectacular signs of justice or injustice, as resounding emblems the Franciscan hopes will precipitate sorely needed better rule. To underscore the need for change, Torquemada writes the history of Mexico up to 1615 as a dialectic between order and disorder, with a fierce emphasis on disorder. Incorporating legal documents from many sources into the *Monarquía* that, we recall, he construes as a legal deposition, Torquemada lays out the cases of crisis in lavish, step-by-step, forensic detail. His punctiliously annalistic text fills the slate of each year with one convoluted "alboroto"—a capacious Spanish word that can mean uproar, riot, disorder, and alarm—and one "scandal" after another. The *Monarquía*'s important account of the foundations of colonial rule, for instance, reveals a Mexico throbbing with chaos immediately after the conquest. Torquemada promotes the Franciscan-allied Cortés as a hero and then, with the hero in Honduras and presumed dead, shows a Mexico City overtaken by warring, power-hungry officials and rebellious Indians, by "great scandals, and alborotos of the masses." No one, writes Torquemada, "had the power to remedy it" (1:592). When Cortés at last returns and collaborates with the second Mexican Audiencia, a hideous spectacle of punishment ensues that parades the most seditious official through the streets in chains and in a wooden cage (1:595).

Torquemada sternly audits the rest of Mexico's viceregal officials, one by one, up to 1612. He bases his judgment of the viceroys on their treatment of the Christianized Indians, whom the Franciscan author envisages through a Las Casian lens as generally peaceful, gentle, nonmaterialistic, obedient, and humble (3: book 17, chap. 10). Unlike Las Casas, though, Torquemada falls short both of presenting all Indians in such exalted terms[8] and of harping on Hispanic abuses of the Indians. Instead Torquemada prefers to dwell on the benevolent laws regarding the Indians that Spain has set for the New World. Still immanent because generally lost in transit or in translation to the New World, the corpus of laws would presumably constitute the solution to ills that it is incumbent on a memorial de agravios to tender. Torquemada therefore devotes two chapters (3: book 17, chaps. 19–20) to transcriptions of the statutes by means of which for one hundred years Spain has tried to curb the New World's mistreatment of the Indians. As would Salinas's *Memorial*, which in imitation of Torquemada transcribes the Spanish legal corpus, the *Monarquía* allows the evanescent, righteous portions of the archive to speak anew in the midst of Babel.

III. WILD WORK OF THE BAROQUE: SPECTACULARIZING THE NEW WORLD

The relationship between the literary Baroque and projects exposing dystopian aspects of the New World is a match made in heaven—or hell. Forged in the crucible of crises, the Spanish Baroque thoroughly suits the agile platforms of Franciscan historiography and, as is self-evident, of an unhinged colonial society.[9] Dorantes de Carranza's tempestuous manifesto of Mexican creole disillusionment had early on established, to adapt the keen observation of a Cuban Neo-Baroque novel, that "*barroquismo* comes with the culture" (Cabrera Infante, *Tres tristes tigres* 399). Later in the seventeenth century, the mature Baroque delivers a full-blown vocabulary for the "barroquismo" intrinsic to labyrinthine colonial societies as well as for a greatly expanded arena of colonial complaint. The melancholic conventional repertoire of the Baroque gives form and rhetorical force to the *desengaño* [disillusionment], honor, materialism, pretense, theatricality, illness, loss, and alienation that weigh heavily on a colonial world, among other things under the grip of rampant capitalism. By the same token, as earlier chapters of *The Spectacular City* have amply borne out, extreme, abstruse Baroque stylistics fit the extreme conditions in the colonies, particularly the conditions that interdict free expression. The Baroque's ability to hold opposites in tension similarly coheres with a conflicted era and a variegated society. Excess accompanies the category crises: the excess the *Primero sueño* aptly chose as its icon of the Baroque doubly protagonizes the wild work that the Baroque repertoire enables other colonial writings to perform. Themselves inventories of "excesos" (now explicitly meaning "wrongdoings," "abuses"),[10] the disillusioned texts hammer in their moral, truthful material, which leads to excessively long tomes and to the excessive reiteration of satirical poetic themes.

Perhaps above all, the disruptive New World texts working the excess that the Baroque enfranchises depend mightily on wonder. The voracious Baroque taste for wondrously bizarre, outlandish, and shocking phenomena grants license to a verbal licentiousness (with regard to anything except religious issues) of which New World writers avail themselves to spectacularize their societies in positive and negative ways. Rare is the Babelic project that does not exploit some aspect of Baroque wonder, which can subsume both good and evil: "Those things are prodigious that go against their own nature; they inspire wonder if they are good, and if not, are considered vile," writes Arzáns (2:62). Capable of provoking extreme reactions of admiration or revilement, the wonder-laden material that the Baroque sponsors dovetails with the moralistic tendencies of the Counter-Reformation and of exposés. Arzáns proclaims that since he wishes everything in his text to benefit salvation and since "the mind is entertained and delighted by the curiosity and the strange things that history brings," he has provisioned his history with new, strange, prodigious, and shocking material (1:clxxxv). The Baroque's mighty attraction to wonder in effect permits the bizarre to override truth or verisimilitude as a didactic tool.

The explosive agency of Baroque wonder reverberates into the intensely politicized self-exoticizing that surges and ramifies in seventeenth-century New World writing. If a sense of their own strangeness or estrangement had prompted creoles like Cárdenas and Dorantes to reinvent European tropes of ex-centricity, the enhanced cachet strangeness gains in the Baroque throws down the gauntlet to seventeenth-century New World writers. Paz confirms that in "the love for the strange we find both the secret of baroque art's affinity with the criollo sensibility and the source of its fruitfulness" (58); González Echevarría observes that the "Baroque has come to be seen as an aesthetics of the strange, of the rare, representing what was new in the New World, including the people" ("Colonial Lyric" 206). Hence, the Egypt, pygmies, monsters, splendid Aztec princes of yore, museum-worthy exotica, and wonder cabinets that inhabit the texts of Balbuena, Sigüenza, Sor Juana, and Favián build an exotic Baroque imaginary for Mexico. Exoticizing infiltrates autobiography as Sor Juana tries on a panoply of spectacularizing self-images: the Mexican phoenix, the sideshow attraction, Isis, the Tenth Muse, and so on. Like Sor Juana, the Peruvian Juan de Espinosa Medrano whose major work defended the aberrant Luis de Góngora calls himself a "rare bird" (108). Moreover, Espinosa Medrano bore the nickname "El Lunarejo." Referencing the *luna,* or moon, and the *lunar,* or birthmark, that apparently marked Espinosa Medrano's face, the sobriquet exoticizes its bearer into a twofold, monstrous marvel. Perfectly appropriate, then, that Espinosa Medrano's students published a collection of his sermons in Madrid under the title *La novena maravilla* [The ninth marvel] (Millones 149).

Remarkable lines in Espinosa Medrano's defense of Góngora divulge the political motor of self-monsterizing. Confronting European prejudice head-on, the Peruvian author asks, "What can there be of value in the Indies? What can there be that pleases Europeans, who have doubts on this account? *They take us for satyrs, they presume that we are Titons, with the souls of brutes;* they cannot disabuse themselves of the belief that we merely disguise ourselves as humans" (17; emphasis added).[11] In a seemingly counterintuitive practice ratified by Baroque propensities, El Lunarejo fights fire with fire, monsters with monsters. Consistent with other authors of his times, he flings a confrontational, defiant New World identity predicated expressly on strangeness and difference at outsiders who brand Americans inhuman. Arzáns similarly spectacularizes difference through monstrous characters like the manly woman (*mujer varonil*) Floriana, "that monster of beauty and rage" (1:236), and the colossal Gasparote, a lawless, quicksilver trickster who enjoys God's protection (2:203–205). Caviedes revels in the deformities and malignancies of colonial subjects. Appropriating derogatory colonialist tropes to an extreme degree, these authors contest Balbuena's "ugly Indian" by becoming him. They replace occlusive Renaissance estheticizing of the New World into unthreatening pastoral prettiness with the anticlassical esthetic of the monstrous that Edmundo O'Gorman relates to the Aztecs in his programmatic essay from 1940, "El arte o de la monstruosidad" [On art, or monstrosity]. Against the inhuman perfection of the rational classical forms that the West idolizes (we remember Botticelli's *Venus*) and that tyrannize its Others, O'Gorman champions the irrational, disorderly, plural esthetic of the ugly and the monstrous that the Aztec serpent-woman Coatlicue—or, one could say, the exotic, grotesque entities of the New World Baroque—embodies.

O'Gorman's hallowing of a non-Western esthetic reflects national pride. So, too, in Baroque texts from the regions below the equator that Europeans persisted in associating with the monstrous antipodes do spectacularly patriotic pronouncements invariably accompany self-spectacularizing. While Vetancurt facetiously suggests that given the superiority of the New World to the Old, perhaps Europe is the antipodes (1:16), Freile, Arzáns, and Salinas content themselves with fervently extolling *patria,* or homeland, as a concept and as their beloved reality. Arzáns, who left Potosí only a couple of times, declares his local history a service "moved by love for my homeland," a love known to be "the greatest of all" positive human emotions, "justly praised as natural and intense" (1:clxxxiii). Other writers (among them, of course, Sigüenza) echo Arzáns's sentiments, emitting alongside self-exoticizing the most ardent patriotic riffs of the whole colonial period.

Wielded self-defensively by New World writers, strategic Baroque exoticizing can therefore work hand in glove with creole cultural nationalism. Sigüenza's spectacular redemption of Aztec rulers in his *Teatro de virtudes* infuses the Indian past with an exoticism that coeval texts employ to caustic effect against Spain. Torquemada, Salinas, and Arzáns appropriate the exotic golden Indian age of the past underlying Sigüenza's festival contribution and cultural nationalism. They utilize it as a platform from which to declare ancient indigenous rule superior to Spanish, at least in certain areas of major interest to the crown. Torquemada's *Monarquía* has Indians protesting that native rulers never extracted excessive tribute from their vassals (1: book 5, chap. 6). Salinas surpasses Torquemada by asserting in his first plea for the Indians that if the Spaniards "had not cruelly tyrannized all these people," the Indians who willingly paid tribute to their own just rulers would now do the same for the Spanish empire (38). Summoning the animus of Las Casas and the arguments of Guaman Poma, Salinas states that under native administration "the life, and treatment that they [the Indians] received from their masters and Kings was completely gentle, light, and agreeable; but now their servitude to the Spaniards, who bring their greed from Spain, is completely infernal, completely devoid of kindness, consolation, or relief" (38–39).[12] For his part, Arzáns terms Inca government "admirable" and notes the absence of thieves or other criminals in Inca society. Colonial rule, however, finds the Indians adopting the bad customs of "perverse" Spaniards and losing the ability to distinguish between good and evil (Arzáns 2:39). As creole cultural nationalism magnifies pre-Columbian regimes into spectacular, admonitory constructs, the indigenous past appears as a Heavenly City come to ruin in the dystopian earthly city Spain has wrought.

Finally, and most fundamentally and pervasively, New World writers rooted in earthly cities yield to the siren call of Baroque wonder's dark side. In a multitude of seventeenth-century texts, the dark wild side of the Baroque imagination that fosters the grotesque and other extreme themes gives rise to a sensationalizing tabloid sensibility. Postethnographic scandal sheets uncannily akin to the *National Enquirer,* they want to surprise and shock. Society's most titillating bizarreries—miracles, witchcraft, supernatural apparitions, aberrant matters of human interest, human monstrosities (birth defects), crimes large and small, scandals public and private, sexual wrongdoings, and public punishments—catch their prurient eye. With or without a political impetus, scandal sheets that engage with Baroque wonder exoticize and spectacularize their societies.

Though not printed until 1853, the several-volume, protojournalistic texts by each of two Mexican creoles exemplify this wild work of the Baroque. In his *Diario,* Gregorio Martín de Guijo records the events of Mexico City from 1648 to 1664. Guijo occupied such distinguished positions in the capital as secretary of the city cabildo (Sosa 79). Antonio de Robles likewise compiled a *Diario,* which covers Mexico City from 1665 to 1703. Robles served as an officer of the Inquisition and as the ecclesiastic judge of various mining towns. His diary continues Guijo's work, following his predecessor's criteria almost to the letter.[13]

Robles and Guijo also shared an involvement in two confraternities, the Congregación de San Pedro and its sister organization, the Congregación del Oratorio.[14] St. Philip Romolo Neri (Filippo de Neri) founded the Congregation of the Oratory around 1575 in a decadent Rome whose sins he would correct. St. Neri taught no specific doctrine but did frequent the streets, marketplaces, and hospitals where the lower strata of society gathered, seeking to purge them of corruption. In Mexico, the Congregación de San Pedro, which joined the Congregación del Oratorio in caring for poor clergy, differed from that group by accepting only the elite into its folds. Viceroys, knights, Audiencia councilmen, rich merchants, and so on filled the ranks of the Congregación de San Pedro (Lavrin 570–577). The two organizations powerfully imprint the two creoles' diaries. Elitist, like Suárez de Peralta's *Tratado* before them, the diaries evince basically no regard for the welfare of marginalized groups. Seeking out corruption, they immerse themselves in the lowlife conduct of all and sundry.

Guijo and Robles ply their sensational wares in diaries that dream of newspapers, diaries that fabricate a Baroque journalism in a Mexico where none existed. Had there been newspapers at the time, the writings of Guijo and Robles would probably have sold out, for the virtual Baroque journalism they conceive revolves around scandals. Indiscriminately, the two creole authors regale their potential readers with any scandal they can glean from their local environment and from the ships that communicate the latest European news. Scandals coexist in the diaries with reportage on human oddities and violent acts of nature. Guijo's and Robles's tabloids, however, eschew the sensationalizing rhetoric for which their modern avatars are infamous. In its stead, these journalists from an era without journalism manufacture a dispassionate, professional modus operandi. The exhaustive, annalistic diaries evidence no aspirations to fiction whatsoever, in either form or content. They recount real events with a zero-level, deadpan style; they treat outlandish, picaresque events in a matter-of-fact, clinical manner. Their discursive unamazement in the face of amazing occurrences keeps wonder systemic, that is, circulating in the Baroque material of the texts rather than percolating into their rhetoric. Such *nihil admirare* divests the texts of two other expectable features, namely, that they neither indulge in moralizing commentary nor outwardly subscribe to any political position, creole or otherwise. The would-be gazettes leave their readers staggered by the complexities of a Babelic Mexican society but able only to conjecture the authors' positions on them.

Of the two writers, Robles, whose diary contains fascinating material on Sor Juana and Sigüenza's era, has received more modern attention. Guijo nevertheless commands more interest as a writer, and as an exemplar of the Spectacular City. Less schematic than Robles, Guijo produces in its full, texturized dimensions a Babelic maelstrom of a society. He documents to a point of numbing satiety disruptions large and small, which he caps with spectacular, generalizing assertions like "this universally disrupted the entire kingdom" (1:10). A broad map of colonial tensions, Guijo's diary registers the turbulent relationships between church, state, and crown. An ecumenical scandal sheet, it logs the crimes, lawsuits, rebellions, and so on of all sectors of society. If Guijo's textual world accommodates the sweep of Mexicans qua criminals, it has a particular investment in the crisis of the aristocracy: the diary's material is picaresque but its protagonists generally are not. Debased elites such as petty viceroys, fractious nuns, contentious professors, and misbehaving clergy fill its pages, stirring Mexico into a frenzy. And when situations spin out of control, so does Guijo's prose. It enters the fray with a thick, particularized reporting that features labyrinthine run-on sentences, as if Guijo were overcome, or totally seduced, by the specifics.

In volume 1 of his diary (covering 1648–1651), the seemingly endless scandals Juan de Palafox detonated in the two principal cities of Mexico repeatedly send Guijo into a verbal tailspin. From 1640 to 1649, acting principally as *visitador,* or auditor, and as bishop of Puebla, Palafox attempted to reform Mexico's second city. His attacks on the entrenched privileges of the Jesuits unleashed a tug of war for power that threw Puebla into unimaginable chaos and that radiated out in expanding waves. Guijo's initial entry on Palafox, from 1648, sets the contours of subsequent bulletins:

> Under the pretext of their having become liable to censure and having disobeyed His Majesty's orders, said bishop took action in his bishopric publicly to excommunicate [the Jesuits], even depriving them of the sacraments, and they did the same with regard to him in this city [Mexico City]. And the next day, the bans that they had posted in this city against said bishop turned up covered with filth and other indecent things, and they publicly repudiated the judges' authority. (1:11)

A rallying point for colonial restiveness, the Palafox fiascos impinge on Mexico City. As the cataclysms draw Mexico City into the orbit of Puebla, Guijo's diary stakes out a new image for the second city of New Spain. From a sedate, somewhat ancillary provincial city, Puebla becomes a locus of newsworthy events that travel far and wide. Simultaneously, thanks to Palafox and Guijo, the Puebla originally intended to counteract a decadent capital emerges as the Mexican scandal city par excellence.

Event-driven as Guijo's diary is, the physical aspects of Mexico City on which it tends to alight are those that mass celebratory or punitive events entail. Enthralled by festivals of any sort, Guijo renders their stage sets and maneuvers with the wealth of detail that makes the diarist a prime source on the Mexican society of the spectacle. For Guijo, as for Torquemada, festivals can assuage the pandemonium endemic in Mexico. Stand-ins for the official story, remnants of the Ordered City, public ceremonies instill peace, law, unity, and harmony. But only fleetingly: sooner or later Guijo's Mexico City implicates any occasion, however august, in the web of scandal. The high holy day of Corpus Christi, for example, several times goes awry. In one uproarious moment during Corpus Christi in 1655, a jealous viceroy, the Duke de Albuquerque, bashes the head of an aristocrat who has showered gifts on the vicereine (2:20). More tellingly, official entries of dignitaries frequently serve as launching pads for situations that escalate into crises. Officials enter Mexico City to public acclaim in decorous, healing ceremonies. Stasis then generally, sometimes immediately, disintegrates into altercations. In Guijo's diary the officials who arrive unsullied and who seem to represent a new start for Mexico literally and symbolically fall as they enter the vortex of colonial Mexico. Infected by the Babelic New World, they die with alarming frequency shortly after setting foot in Mexico.

Under the safe haven of festivals, and only there, does the elitist Guijo suffer Mexico's classes and races to congregate all together in his text, if to perverse effect. Since his unbridled interest in crime and punishment means that the collectivity often assembles for public acts of corporeal discipline, Guijo's festivals represent pluralism at its darkest and worst.[15] With an insatiable appetite for autos-da-fé and clearly relishing the whippings, burnings, beheadings, and macabre parading of criminals and corpses that accompany them, Guijo parlays outré Baroque tastes into what borders on abject sadism. A sermon preached in 1649 that Guijo quotes articulates the author's own sadistic leanings: "Peace, peace; no, not that: rather, their heads hanging from these gallows" (1:33). Satisfying the sermon's dictum with excessive zeal, Guijo ends up depicting Mexico City in a lurid, exoticizing Baroque mode that curdles the city into a sinister police state.

IV. SIN CITIES

The noir drama of the Babelic worlds, which Guijo and Robles treat dispassionately and which the *Monarquía indiana* before them had unfolded legalistically, practically begs for literary elaboration.[16] Babel's convulsive, raw story-stuff obtains its literary due in the schools of scandal that the South American writers to whom we now turn craft by means of an expanded form of historiography and (as section V below will explore) satirical poetry. While satirical poetry customarily offends both social and verbal propriety, the accounts of their sin cities by Juan Rodríguez Freile and Bartolomé Arzáns de Orsúa y Vela finesse historiography into performing the same functions. Freile and Arzáns ambush the protocols of historiography by commingling it with fiction, a genre forbidden to the New World as of 1531. In keeping with the architecture-rupturing spirit of the Baroque, the two authors create hybrid texts that meld fiction with history as well as with moralizing, the official story, and autobiography. Freile and Arzáns remain faithful to the spirit and the literary letter of the Baroque, but their scandal sheets corrode it from within. Broadly and vividly, they leverage the Baroque into a tool for spectacularizing the "hospitals of nerves" that have arisen from the colonial hegemony. More specifically and cunningly, they enact a New World revenge on their new historiographic modus operandi by complicating the moralizing that authorizes Baroque fiction.

Freile carries out the disruptive work of the New World Baroque in *El Carnero* (The ram) (1638), an ambitious infrahistory of the first hundred years under Hispanic rule of Santafé de Bogotá, capital city of New Granada. Instead of registering the physical dimensions of Bogotá, *El Carnero* x-rays the city. It goes behind the walls of colonial life to scrutinize what happens inside the city's great cathedrals, municipal buildings, palaces, and private residences. Freile penetrates the façades and opens up a human landscape awash in passion, greed, and vice. Bogotá's citizens have materialized El Dorado into a decadent metropolis lacking higher culture and ruled by gold, sex, and lust for power. The prose in which Freile couches his city is relatively limpid for a seventeenth-century text. What makes the Bogotá of *El Carnero* a Baroque city is the excess, dynamism, and unchained ferment of its residents' lives.

Freile trawls the archive for the *petites histoires* of Bogotá's inhabitants that will become his text's most original element. In so doing, he rescues the crimes stashed away in the *carnero*, a multivalent word that literally means "ram" but that in Freile's text refers principally to the trashbin and to the common graves of paupers.[17] The calculated inversion of the text's subtitle, which places "Discovery" after "Conquest," signals that the text proposes to uncover what previous narratives have suppressed and discarded (Chang-Rodríguez 49). For example, the crimes of everyone involved in the case of Juana García except those of the woman herself remain unpunished, since "the kingdom was young, and the proceedings would taint it" (142). Official texts related to the García case ended up being thrown into the "archive of fire" (150). González Echevarría aptly designates Freile the "theoretician of the Archive" (*Myth* 99), an epithet Freile himself bears out in defining his task as a historian: "Reason tells me not to meddle in the lives of others; truth tells me to tell the truth. Both are right, but let truth prevail. And since the cases appeared in public courts and on public scaffolds, reason itself gives me license to discuss them, because it is worse for people to have committed such acts than it is for me to write about them" (172–173). Freile's ostensibly true history predicated on inflammatory cases counterweighs the heroic histories of Colombia (of Juan de Castellanos and Pedro Simón), which archivists have not, for obvious reasons, incinerated or buried.

Having opted to break into the "lives of others" that landed up in the courts or on the gallows, *El Carnero* discharges the surveillance and verbal punishment of a century of crimes in Bogotá. The text's panoptic urges carry wonder in tow, sending it into a Baroque downturn. Positive "marvel," which Freile explicitly associates with virtue (361) and indirectly with miracles, practically disappears. It cedes to the negative "novelties" he identifies with sin (357). And as Freile's panoptic exposé parades and chastises those novelties, it claims for itself the space of the plaza, which houses the gallows. Freile indirectly correlates *El Carnero* with the plaza when he rails against the criminal Juan de Mayorga: "you carried onto the public square your own people's offenses and errors, which time and oblivion had extinguished" (352). In *El Carnero*, crimes repeatedly take place, are broadcast or rumored by common folk, and are punished by the state in the plaza. Like Guijo, Freile replaces the celebratory colonial festival with the macabre spectacle of punishment, thus stigmatizing both the plaza and the spectacle. True to Baroque thematics, he frames his text as a "tablado" (331), a theater for spectacles intended to edify the reader and enhance history.

Two not-unfamiliar agendas fan the flames of *El Carnero*'s extreme Baroque righteousness, the first being creole politics. Born to one of Colombia's first settlers, Freile laces his exposé with traditional creole complaint. He addresses *El Carnero* to the king ("who gives us so much, maintaining peace and justice" [47]), bemoans the loss of encomienda, and laments Spain's rape of the New World. The hellish Colombia of *El Carnero,* Freile believes, owes to the crown's default on an immigration policy that originally allowed only old Christians accompanied by their wives, such as his parents, into the New World (135). Spain's policy and Colombia's original settlers may have died, but Freile will not let them be forgotten. Similar to Dorantes, the Colombian author memorializes the early settlers in catalogue after distended catalogue of names (chaps. 6, 7, 8, and following chap. 20), a mournful *ubi sunt* of heroic forebears.

"At the beginning of 1553," Freile also notes in an autobiographical vein, "Bishop Juan de los Barrios of the Order of Saint Francis arrived in this New Kingdom, bringing my parents with him" (134). The family debt to the Franciscans that Freile mentions here conceivably feeds the aggressively righteous textual persona the author fashions for himself. At each step glossing scandalous events with moralistic diatribes, Freile speaks as a high-minded Franciscan or other critical ecclesiastic. A more characteristically Franciscan asceticism arises as Freile shapes himself into a neostoical figure who, in a complete turnabout from Balbuena, shuns power, pleasure, and wealth. Seneca and St. Augustine, too, supply the Colombian with guideposts for a life that spurns worldly temptations, especially those of the flesh. Freile distances himself from the Babelic fleshpot of a city he has chronicled by exhorting his readers to lead a simple life working the land: "Fortunate is he who lives far from commerce, moderately, withdrawing into quiet and calm, his livelihood assured by the fruits of the land that he cultivates" (348). The pastoral laborer whom Freile here glorifies slides into line with the Franciscan Torquemada's allegorical reading of the "carnero" as a ram that herds sheep in the countryside and represents an industrious, meek, brave individual (1:619).[18]

With regard to the Indians, Freile unfortunately shares just the most jaundiced of the Franciscans' views. The founding of Bogotá leads the author to address a precontact Indian history he deems irremediably marked by the devil. Freile's censoriousness of the devil-ruled Indians engenders a scandal sheet treatment of their vices and sins not unlike Oviedo's. The Colombian chronicler portrays Indian festivals as drunken, infernal rituals; he vents his ire on the spectacular ritual of El Dorado, which kindled the avarice that still plagues Colombia (chap. 2). Freile later imports his prejudicial attitudes toward the Indians into the present and denounces their social mobility, criminality, and insurrection. Worse yet, he reproaches Indians for committing suicide to avoid conscripted work, blaming declines in the Colombian economy on them (338, 341). Freile, we see, clings to a retrograde creole mentality that construes the Amerindians primarily as a labor force for conquerors who profess to have saved them from the devil.

Astonishing, then, is the fragile hold in *El Carnero* that the law maintains on a New World supposedly rescued from the devil. Freile details the colonial regime's efforts to impose order, justice, and reason on a recalcitrant Colombia. He pays tribute to the few civil and religious leaders who have stood their moral ground and eked out some successes. Yet efforts to implant order more commonly miscarry: "In everything that I have written I find only one governor and one president who have left this Kingdom without distress and quarrels" (347). Because the "golden ages" Freile credits to upright leaders (148 *et passim*) could not coexist with the lust for real gold, advances toward order and justice fail like rejected skin grafts. In the Babelic *El Carnero*, the private scandals that explode onto the public scene, tumultuous official audits, the ineffectual system of justice, internal power struggles, unceasing insurrections in Colombia and throughout the colonies, and, of course, incorrigible greed, all overcome the flimsy scaffolding of the law. Neither a few Franciscan-style miracles nor a few acts of divine revenge can significantly mitigate the hellish climate of Colombia that Freile introduces under the aegis of Lucifer's banishment to hell and the Fall of humankind (chap. 5). If, as Freile's biblical models would have it, God has placed humankind on earth to defeat the devil, then clearly the battle has not yet been won. With redemption a long way off, the true template of *El Carnero* is not Fall and salvation but the strife between Cain and Abel.[19]

Freile's text absorbs Bogotá's raging discord into its very structure: *El Carnero* encloses an internecine struggle between official historiography and the scandalous, minute cases that threaten to overpower it. The two modes blatantly split, textually replaying the destabilizing of the Ordered City by the Spectacular City. For on the one hand the text offers a rigid chronological framework meted out into the regimes of Colombia's rulers, formal chapter headings that announce those demarcations, and schematic narration of official comings and goings. On the other,

El Carnero tenders the nonlinear cases barely hinted at in the chapter titles, downplayed in the text's subtitle as "some cases that occurred in this Kingdom, included in the history as an example, and not to be imitated to the detriment of one's conscience," and nonetheless splayed out in excessive detail. Subverting historiography, both Freile and Arzáns let their petites histoires run wild, to the point that they stand as the very embodiment of architexture. Yet the runaway, architextural cases "included in the history as an example" have a saving kinship with the particularizing exempla or anecdotes of sermons, and sermons an inalienable kinship with the two authors' flamboyantly moralistic works.

As he pushes Baroque moralizing further beyond the pale, further overdetermining it, Freile transcends the factuality of the legal archive. Under the pretext of embellishing legal cases to accentuate their exemplary qualities, the author orchestrates his outrageous tales of passion and vice with literary devices gleaned from the Baroque novella, theater, and picaresque. A staunch adversary of the bureaucratic lettered city who remarked that the reams of paperwork going to Spain occasioned more misery than the gold (269), Freile gravitates toward the relative transparency, melodramatic theatricality, and vulgar naturalism of Baroque comedias and novellas. These effects team up with the oral sources, homey exempla, colloquial dialogue, and verbal crimes (slander, accusations, cursing, gossip) that traverse *El Carnero* to liberate the New World Baroque from its elite fetters. Freile grows a vernacular, popular Baroque, a Baroque of the street, the plaza, and the marketplace. It is this Baroque, in conjunction with the era's love of sensationalism, which begets some of the New World's initial forays into fiction. Freile equates his excursions into fiction—the cases that allegedly "adorn" the history of Bogotá—with flowers ("coger las más graciosas flores," pick the most attractive flowers, 82). Like Balbuena, the Colombian writer exports a pastoral topic to the city, but to places, heights, and depths antithetical to "La grandeza mexicana."

Gendering and sexualizing the cases by linking them to flowers and deflowering, or "coger flores" (Herman 291), respectively, Freile insinuates that his text will blame women for the wholesale sinful nature of Bogotá. Indeed, the author introduces his florid cases and the story of Eve's deceptions in the same chapter (chap. 5). Women then lie at the heart of many of the cases, with Freile directing his most furious moralistic diatribes at female sinners. Nevertheless, contradictions that no reader could miss make it impossible to accept women as the root evil of the city or to accept Freile's misogyny at face value. To wit: women hardly incite *all* the scandals packed into the cases; men are often just as guilty as women; women can be innocent and wrongly accused; Freile both extols and denigrates the female sex, building catalogues of biblical female heroes (286) and villains alike (81) into his text; the seventy-year-old author notes the ridiculousness of his apparent obsession with women (285); he names the world, the devil, *and* the flesh as men's principal enemies (354).

The myriad equivocations unmask Freile's stance on women as patent scapegoating. Freile seizes upon women as a hook for his readers' Baroque prurience and as his main site for Baroque moralizing. He mines the consecrated Baroque repertoire disingenuously and expediently, converting attacks on women into a smoke screen for lambasting an earthly city riddled with colonial misrule and the undying vestiges of bedeviled Indian civilizations. What more apt, more sanctioned a vehicle could there be for the colonial order's lack of traction than a woman's honor, "subject to a thousand calamities" (353)? In line with many seventeenth-century male writers, Freile targets women as the height of disorder, holding them accountable in metaphorical or real terms for the upheaval of the times (Merrim, *Early Modern* xxx).

For a cameo of this and other features of *El Carnero* we have surveyed, let us return to the case of Juana García. Charged with a crime of diabolical magic from which other guilty parties were exculpated and the records of their misdeeds burned, Juana García stands alone on a platform in the plaza of Santo Domingo with a noose around her neck and a candle in her hands. Converted into a spectacle and a scapegoat, she cries, "All of us, every one of us, did it, and only I pay the price!" (143).

Granting that, as by now we may comfortably conclude, the nature of a text's festivals cues us into its overall project, no spectacle as focused and slender as García's shaming could adequately convey the mood of Arzáns's exorbitant *Historia de la Villa Imperial de Potosí* [History of the imperial city of Potosí] (written from 1705 to 1736; henceforth, *Potosí*). The multitude of festivals Arzáns narrates, like most everything in his more than one-million-word chronicle, are centrifugal and larger than life. A creole born in Potosí, the patriotic Arzáns recounts festivals of an overwhelming magnitude in corresponding detail. When, for example, in 1555 Potosí mounted a festival for its patron saints, Arzáns relates that the city commissioned thirty altars, twelve triumphal arches, enough rich textiles to pave the long ceremonial route, and a series of eight plays on Indian history that ended with the "tyranny and grief that the Spaniards inflicted on the Indians" (1:98).[20] If Arzáns is to be believed, hundreds of Indians from Peru's many tribes rode lions, tigers, and alligators in the opening act of a parade that commemorated the Incas (1:98). The parade culminated in a float on which sat an Indian impersonating Atahualpa, wearing a crown encrusted with pearls and huge emeralds, a chain from which hung a sun wrought of gold, and ear pendants that sported "jewels of inestimable value" (1:99). Despite its "exorbitant costs" (1:99), the festival wound on and on, generating new and varied events each day, refusing to stop after eight days and again after fifteen.

Such extravagances, real and textual, justify Lewis Hanke's appraisal of the text's festivals: "If one had to select the one symbolic institution through which the ethos of this silver city could best be seen, that institution would probably be the fiesta," and Arzáns's text "documents its history admirably" (*Bartolomé Arzáns* 40). Arzáns documents the festivals in his history of Potosí from 1545 to 1736, an annalistic, hybrid, denunciatory work, which bears uncanny resemblances to *El Carnero*. That there exists no proof of Arzáns having read Freile makes the twinning of their disruptive texts all the more representative of currents in the New World Baroque. Yet, much as the two texts from wealth-crazed regions overlap, *Potosí* deviates from *El Carnero* due precisely to Potosí's stupendous spectacularity, which respects no bounds and which attains its image in the city's wild festivals. We may therefore locate the muse of the preeminently Baroque *Potosí* in the festival.

Truth be told, the festive Potosí, "monster of wealth" (Arzáns 1:3), indulged to monstrous excess in most everything that would offend muses. Beginning in 1545, the silver mines of the mountain of Potosí attracted vast numbers of Indians, Spaniards, and other Europeans. The myth of El Dorado came to life for them, not in gold but in the silver and wealth of Potosí. By the early seventeenth century, Potosí had become the richest city in the New World and one of the richest in the world. (Though officially denominated a "villa" rather than a city, Potosí's population reached a hefty 160,000 at its peak in 1610).[21] The phrase "vale un Potosí" entered the Spanish language as an epithet for unlimited wealth. With its phenomenal prosperity and extraordinary geographical situation in climes so high and cold that for almost half a century no Hispanic babies survived birth there (1:192), Potosí developed into something of a wild west boomtown. Until the arrival of Viceroy Francisco de Toledo in 1573, it grew haphazardly, "without order, concert, or measured streets" (1:42). Potosí's inhabitants were just as unrestrained as their non-Ordered City. The nouveaux riches consumed luxury goods with a vengeance and indulged their passions and vices with equal furor. Violence, prostitution, and gambling proliferated in the city's scores of dance halls, brothels, and gaming houses.

Surrounded by these racy venues and by the festivals that flaunted Potosí's intemperance, the schoolteacher and autodidact Arzáns penned his history of a sinful, fallen city that had abandoned morality. By the time of Arzáns's writing, the city had quite concretely fallen, into demographic and economic decline. Nostalgic for its greatness, deploring its declines, Arzáns blames the city's fall on the sins that wealth has instigated. He inscribes Potosí's history in a biblical framework according to which God had visited divine vengeance on a sinful Potosí in the form of three scourges: the War of the Vicuñas of 1622–1625, a flood caused by the rupture of the Caricari dam in 1626, and the devaluation of currency around 1650. Arzáns had therefore originally planned to title his work "The Three Devastations of the Imperial City of Potosí" (Hanke, "El otro tesoro" 59). However, in the final version of the text the sins of Potosí's citizens greatly eclipse the three plagues.

It is here that similarities between *Potosí* and *El Carnero*, besides their mutual stretching of historiography into fiction, assert themselves. Year by year, in an unbroken chronological structure calibrated to the tenure of each viceroy, the Bolivian cognate of *El Carnero* dwells on the lawlessness, scandals, greed, crimes, bedlam, and so on that surfeit Potosí.[22] Because for Arzáns, "sex and sin are coterminous, if not synonymous" (Padden xxxi), private transgressions that swell into civil disorder engross the Bolivian author as much as they did Freile. The colonial regime of Potosí, too, proves incapable of stanching the chaos. Arzáns observes that some 260 homicides occurred between 1671 and 1702, only 26 of which were prosecuted (Padden xxviii). In the midst of his scandal sheet, Arzáns lauds the upstanding ecclesiastics of every religious group who have injected some order and morality into Potosí. Thus he, like the ethical clergy-writers and Freile, dedicates his history to truth (2:73). Arzáns executed the task so well that it jeopardized his life. Death threats from those whose sins the text disclosed reportedly led Arzáns into hiding, the manuscript of his exposé safely in hand (Padden xxxv).

Adopting the neostoical position common to the exposés of Freile and the Franciscans, Arzáns berates his wealth-obsessed city. He labels avarice the greatest sin (3:289). He acknowledges the all-pervasive nature of the interés Balbuena had vindicated but rues the ability of that economic mover and shaker to debauch whatever it touches. Arzáns asks, "is there anything that interés does not attempt and accomplish?" (2:40). His text's profuse, desiccated lists of the goods the city receives confirm Potosí as an emporium city and the deplorable potency of interés as what Balbuena called "sovereign of nations" ("Grandeza" 70). The moralizing practices by means of which Arzáns tongue-lashes his sin city for its materialism and other flaws would likewise offend the sybaritic Balbuena and satisfy the Franciscans and Freile. As overtly as the Colombian author, if ultimately to even more conflicted effect, Arzáns saturates his text with a formal, formulaic moralizing that follows the modus operandi of sermons. Expositions of a broad moral principle phrased in the accessible style of a sermon precede the specific cases or exempla that, as mentioned above, Arzáns unfurls in the same architextural detail as Freile.

Virtues and strains proper to Potosí, however, inevitably begin to steer Arzáns's work away from *El Carnero*. Arzáns praises the piety of Potosí's inhabitants and the charity that their great wealth promotes as his city's main virtues. He explains that Potosí lies under the planets of Jupiter, signifying magnanimity, and Mars, signifying aggression (1:5–6). Fractured into Manichean extremes of good and evil, Arzáns's Potosí is a contradictory Baroque mix, a living oxymoron. Its emblematic festivals incarnate the good (piety, charity), the bad (ostentatious materialism), and the ugly (dissension and chaos), and thus bring the oxymoronic city into sharp relief.

Because, as Arzáns writes, "this Imperial City has always been, and still is, home to sons of nearly all the nations on earth" who come to seek silver (1:255), an additional set of fractures rends the Potosí of *Potosí*. Namely, jockeying for wealth and power has bred violent ethnic rifts in the exceptionally plural city. While a census from 1610 records the presence of some forty thousand Spaniards and other Europeans in the melting pot that was Potosí (Hanke and Mendoza lxx), for Arzáns tensions have crystallized around the Basques who increasingly controlled his city's economic resources and government. Their belligerent ascent pits the Basques against other Spanish regional groups or "nations" (as the author calls them) and creoles against the Basques who disdained them. In Arzáns, of Basque origin through his paternal grandparents, a "definite creole consciousness" (Hanke and Mendoza clxix) trumps family heritage, leading the author to oppugn the Spanish upstarts.[23]

His creole pride ignited, Arzáns further devotes *Potosí* to demonstrating that although conflicts between Basques and other groups came to crisis in the War of the Vicuñas, they neither started nor ended there. Rather, ethnic rivalries permeate the history of a melting pot in which, according to Arzáns, violence never ceases. The celebration of Holy

Week in 1604, as one example among hundreds, saw a private duel between a Basque and an Extremaduran escalate into citywide war: "With these murders, the whole city rose up [*alborotóse*] and took to arms, which brought it to the brink of total destruction" (1:256). First, all ethnic and then racial groups enter the fight, and all suffer losses. Ruled by Mars, the variegated metropolis implodes time and again, to the effect that Arzáns's Potosí quintessentializes the multiple, sundered, contentious Babel. Or, given that Potosí chose St. Augustine as its patron saint (1:10 *et passim*), the most disturbed of earthly cities.

In defending the Indians whom its earthly city egregiously victimizes, *Potosí* definitively parts ways with *El Carnero*. Arzáns bridles at Spanish avarice, his compatriots' abdication of charity for the native peoples, the inhuman working conditions of Indians in the mita and mines. Because, as Arzáns argues with conceivable backing from the exposé of Salinas,[24] the lands rightfully belong to their original occupants, enslavement of the Indians contravenes human law (2:222). Because God made the Indians and made them free (3:151 *et passim*), it also contravenes natural law. Incensed by the multiply wrong enslavement of the Indians, the author at times decants his wrath into grand jeremiads that interlock with the memorial de agravios. One such tirade reminiscent of Salinas and Las Casas concludes that the Spaniards "did not conquer Peru but converted it to tyranny," a tyranny that consumed "thousands of millions of Indians" and that left Peru vastly diminished from "how it was under its own monarchs" (1:26). It follows for Arzáns that the tyrannized Indians, "exemplars of peace and brotherhood" and hence tokens of the Heavenly City in the midst of a Spanish earthly city full of "offenses against God" stemming from the colonizers' "abominable factions, passions, rancor, and deadly enmities" (1:313), must receive divine protection. And they have. In Arzáns's text, God and the Virgin Mary, via avatars like the Virgin of Copacabana, intercede and persistently work miracles for the native peoples of Potosí.

Wedding the exposé to the supernatural, *Potosí* approaches divine miracles and other wonders with an untroubled, wholehearted credulity. The supernatural salvations, cosmic portents, lore, revenants, and preternatural feats that *Potosí* endows with verisimilitude are anathema to *El Carnero* (which experimented with magic only in the Juana García case, to no good end) but entirely germane to the Franciscans and Augustinians. Despite Arzáns's ecumenical attitude toward the city's various religious groups, his defense of the Indians, neostoical perspective, and miracle-loving sensibility betray partiality for the two Mendicant orders that share each of those proclivities.²⁵ St. Augustine's role as patron saint of Potosí authorizes Arzáns's affection for the Augustinians, and the text by their first New World chronicler, the creole Antonio de la Calancha (born in La Plata), cinches it. Calancha's *Corónica moralizada del orden de S. Agustín en el Perú* [Moralizing chronicle of the order of St. Augustine in Peru] influenced Arzáns's *Potosí* more than any other printed source (Hanke and Mendoza lxi).²⁶ The Augustinian *Corónica* piles miracle on miracle. It swarms with miracles wrought upon or by afflicted clergy, Indians, women, castas, children, and so forth, many of which supernatural events Arzáns copies verbatim into his text. Arzáns outdoes even Calancha in that whereas the *Corónica* emphasizes miraculous cures, *Potosí* traffics in all kinds of miracles, including the visions and portents the Franciscans favored.

Together, though, Calancha and Arzáns seem bent on a specifically Augustinian mission. In response to skeptics who believe that miracles ceased after the death of Christ, St. Augustine asserted, "now miracles are being performed in Christ's name . . . but they do not enjoy the blaze of publicity which would spread their fame with a glory to equal that of those earlier marvels" (1034; see book 22, chap. 8). The two authors' publicizing of latter-day miracles shows divine supernatural grace to be alive and burgeoning in the New World. With pride in their own viceroyalty, they also perhaps counter Torquemada's remarks on the paucity of miracles in the conquest of Mexico (3:418).

Leaving partisan considerations aside, one realizes that the bountiful activity of the divine supernatural has written the spiritualized, pro-Indian *Potosí* into the terrain of magical realism several centuries *avant la lettre*. Yet, as magical realist fictions like Alejo Carpentier's *El reino de este mundo* [The kingdom of this world] (1949) acknowledge by aligning themselves with the Neo-Baroque, an incipient magical realist text like *Potosí* is actually capitalizing on the mechanisms of the Baroque. Although Arzáns wrote in the eighteenth century, his work does not merely display no traces of the Enlightenment (Hanke and Mendoza lxii), but in an array of ways epitomizes the New World Baroque. *Potosí* aims to shock and awe on any front. The alborotos of every sort that fill its pages seek in typical Baroque manner to control the will of readers, to "alborotar," or shake them up. Baroque locutions of wonder crowd into the text, motivated by the superlative city of Potosí itself, the "famous, always maximal, most rich and inexhaustible Cerro de Potosí; singular handiwork of God's power; nature's only miracle; perfect and permanent marvel of the world" (1:3). Festival extravagances and miracles amaze. Scandals, including violent crimes replete with obscene physical details, titillate. The predominant cast of the text is marvelous, prodigious, beyond belief—in sum, spectacular.[27] From its iconic festivals onward, the text leads one to believe that anything is possible in *Potosí*.

Arzáns has set up a Baroque discursive climate in which the fabulous and fabulation authorize each other. They suspend the criterion of verisimilitude and, the author might hope, naturalize history into the fiction he "admires and praises" (2:101). Arzáns defends fiction in Aristotelian terms that couple it with the moralizing central to his text. He says that if he praises the "fabulous creations of the imagination," "it is because although they do not yet exist they are an image of what might be, a specimen of the perils of lascivious or honest love . . . and a model of virtues to be imitated" (2:101). Nonetheless, sharply cognizant of prohibitions on fiction, the author also invokes the protection of history, of the archive. In the Counter-Reformation, miracles above all require documentation from church archives, which documentation Arzáns self-protectively flourishes. The author does not stop there. Amassing an army of buffers, Arzáns backs up his accounts with references to the some thirty-six histories of Potosí (1:clxxxiv) he has at hand. Or so he says. Unable to encounter most of the works he cites, scholars now believe that Arzáns fabricated several of his main intertexts (see Hanke and Mendoza xlix–liv, cxvi–cxvii), maybe to shield the real sources, oral and written, of his work.

Beyond protecting himself and shielding his real sources, why might Arzáns have resorted to apocryphal texts? For one, given that Arzáns took considerable liberties even with extant sources (see García Pabón, "Pensamiento andino"), the author's irrepressible creativity factors into the mix. Another answer may lie in the literary culture of Potosí, or the relative lack thereof. Although it abounded in recreational venues like gambling houses and in theatrical productions that kept the unruly public entertained (Gisbert 30–33), Potosí had comparatively little high culture. The Jesuits founded a school there in 1582, religious poets like the Sevillians Luis de Ribera and Diego Mexía de Fernangil wrote there, and artists such as Melchor Pérez Holguín painted there, yet it would be an exaggeration to call colonial Potosí a cultural center.[28] That honor in the Bolivia of the times goes to the city of La Plata (now Sucre), situated a few days' ride away, and home to the university, Audiencia, printing press, and thriving intellectual and artistic circles absent from Potosí. Since La Plata retained cultural and political primacy over

Potosí, it stands to reason that civic pride would have led Arzáns to inflate the literary culture of his home by populating it with apocryphal historians and invented poets. With specific regard to poets born and bred in Potosí, Arzáns cites several in *Potosí,* but recent historians have authenticated only one of them, Juan Sobrino (Hanke and Mendoza liv, cxvi). In any case, there can be no doubt that Potosí's principal cultural manifestations were its festivals, the most ostentatious of the entire New World (Hanke, "El otro tesoro" 70).

Reacting to a cultural arena monopolized by festivals and replicating their outsized spirit, the incorrigibly creative Arzáns proceeds to transmute the wrongdoings of his sinful city into spectacular Baroque exemplary novellas, arguably the most effervescent prose works of the Spanish American colonial period. Arzáns borrows the action-oriented plots, fondness for stories of love and revenge, stock characters of aristocratic origins, and cardboard depictions of place that characterize the Spanish novella, sometimes customizing them to the New World. The exemplary cases in which *Potosí* delights offer a veritable rogues' gallery of sinners who generally either experience Baroque desengaño and actively repent or are saved by a deus ex machina. Echoing his arguments on the Indians, Arzáns's not in the least petite histories often illustrate Miguel de Cervantes's positions on the dangers of constraining human freedom and the ways in which God's will supersedes human planning, how "man proposes but God disposes."

Though philosophically Cervantine, Arzáns's novelistic compositions nonetheless put one in mind of the hyper-Baroque Spanish novellas that sensationalized the master's *Novelas ejemplares* [Exemplary novels] (1613) not long after their publication. For *Potosí*'s densely nonlinear plots, earthy oral dialogue, and shocking tortures, rapes, cruel mothers, and dismemberments closely resemble the decadent novellas of María de Zayas y Sotomayor and Alonso de Castillo Solórzano. To placate the censors, Castillo Solórzano in particular imposed perfunctory morals on works of sheer entertainment. Arzáns, for his part, choreographs a moralizing that enables tremendous literary mobility. In *Potosí,* the interventions of God that make for an exemplary tale can occur at any juncture in a person's life, even in a last-ditch hour of repentance at the end of a thoroughly despicable trajectory. Arzáns's mobile moralizing in essence allows any story to be told and somehow transfigured into a moral tale. Aided by the divine escape clause, Arzáns can tell outrageous stories at will, in detail, and with gusto.

As Arzáns attunes his moral tales to the exemplary novel, he recognizes that even shocking stories, when too similar to one another, can jade the reader. Since, as we earlier heard Arzáns state, the reader's mind enjoys the strange things that history offers, the author strives to keep his text edgy, always surprising. Arzáns consequently activates the variety that the Baroque privileges, the same variety that assures the appeal of long Baroque festivals. Defamiliarizing his text at every turn, Arzáns has each tale shift gears from the previous one. *Potosí* successively brandishes would-be noble, cross-dressing, ghostly, picaresque, and homicidal protagonists as well as witches and Don Juans. Arzáns's unremittingly variegated text thereby assumes the cast of a literary sampler, a sin-full encyclopedia of literary figures and plots easily transplanted from the metropolis to a Babelic New World setting. The lexicon of the Baroque novella in toto appears to strike Arzáns as a ready-made language for his eclectic, electric Potosí. Thus, the Arzáns ensconced in a locale short on homegrown literature has staged a coming into culture for Potosí similar to that which Balbuena desired for his city and which Sigüenza realized in his encyclopedic *Infortunios*. Analogous to *El Carnero*, but in the more concerted and spectacular tenor that befits a boom city's ethos, *Potosí* has assimilated peninsular Baroque culture into its wild pages.

Arzáns puts a personal stamp on the Spanish Baroque novella by stocking the tales of Potosí with outlandish New World characters. The reinvigorated rogues' gallery includes upwardly mobile Indians, pretentious nouveaux riches, ambitious Orientals, adventuring manly women, monstrously large mestizos, and more. These marvelous, exotic supplements to the peninsular novella, this self-exoticizing, profoundly troubles received forms and ethical norms. Arzáns is stuck between a rock and a hard place. Should he condemn the new actors' lawlessness and prodigiousness or applaud, à la Cervantes, their freedom? Primed by the Baroque esthetic, motivated by patriotism, in the thrall of literary impulses, Arzáns cannot resist the latter path, which radically destabilizes Baroque moralizing.[29] Put simply, when Arzáns weighs the marvelous against moralizing, the marvelous wins. The stories of the new actors on the literary stage are too wonderful not to be told, and not to be told with admiration.

The battle frequently comes to a head in tales featuring New World subaltern protagonists. The wealthy, Europeanized Indian Francisco Chocata, for instance, tries to obtain the governership of the Indians by having a fellow Indian named to the post killed. In so doing, Chocata also betrays the friendship of a Spanish magistrate: "This Indian's treachery was exceedingly evil because it went against his friend, benefactor, and a respected judge whose friendship with Chocata had subjected him to criticism from the whole city" (2:120). However, the whole city, including Spaniards, begs for Chocata's life (2:120), and the general who has Chocata hanged, restoring order, may well be a criminal who deserves the same punishment! The story of the creole Floriana ("that monster of beauty and rage" [1:236]) dissolves into a more bewildering incoherence yet. While Floriana protects her honor by murdering an unwanted suitor, the young woman given over to "virtue and seclusion" and self-vigilance (1:235) soon runs off to meet a man with whom she had secretly been having an affair. However, Arzáns notes, Floriana only desired to serve God, so after her escapades she spends the rest of her life at home, in chastity and reclusion. Nun or whore? Honorable or sinful?

Not surprisingly, Arzáns's zest for spectacular storytelling deranges his overarching position on women, the Baroque's favorite scapegoats. He takes aim at the manly woman whom Spanish Golden Age literature loves to reform and punish. In one breath Arzáns indicts manly women (e.g., 2:42) and in a subsequent one, he outright vindicates them (e.g., 2:62). Other incoherencies involving the new protagonists jar *Potosí*. The pro-Indian text lets evil Indians into its pages; the work can sympathize with subalterns but almost always inveighs against blacks (Hanke and Mendoza lxxxi); quarrels between ethnic groups, to the victory of none, dissipate into sheer absurdity. For Arzáns, such monstrous, marvelous New World characters play havoc with good and evil. They disrupt Potosí itself and, equally so, *Potosí,* whose creole author refuses to lock them into conventional categories.

Decentered and unseizable, the tales of *Potosí* ultimately meet their rationale or metaphor in a specific festival, the Night of San Juan. A few tales unfold during that night of summer solstice, yet many more partake of its magical, upside-down aura. Midsummer night's dreams, they capture the fabulous genie-spirit of the city and fulfill Arzáns's palpable aspiration to forge an authentic language for his larger-than-life, oxymoronic Potosí.

V. JUDGMENT DAY

The satirical poetry of the Peruvian *radicado* Juan del Valle y Caviedes, often called the Quevedo of America, projects the carnivalesque onto a space that knows no magic or miracles, just incurable illness. In a Rabelaisian venture, Caviedes's *Diente del Parnaso* [Tooth of Parnassus] (c. 1689) passes judgment on Lima by obsessively figuring its ills through the body and by scapegoating the doctors who cannot cure the diseases of the pestilential city. Caviedes chooses laughter over inept doctors (20–21) as the only remedy for the city, whose residents' physical deformities and afflictions symptomatize its larger ills. Caviedes's wholly sick Lima suffers from the plagues that the Baroque matrix of appearance versus reality breeds: lies, hypocrisy, posturing, adulation, deceit, dishonor, and materialism. Wealth, once again the root of a New World city's evils, sets the Baroque plagues in motion.[30] Caviedes exempts only the poor and the poet from the illnesses that rage in colonial Lima. Replacing the ineffectual physician with the effectual poet and material wealth with satirical poetry, Caviedes purges the city of its ills by means of an astounding, excessive Baroque wordplay that descends into crude, vernacular obscenity. Caviedes unrelentingly spectacularizes Lima's malignities in a language as wild and diseased as the city itself.

Though Caviedes's verbal decimations of Lima rely on fiendish humor, in some of his most memorable poems the author takes philosophical stock of his city, together with his enlightened contemporaries in Mexico. Caviedes read and corresponded with Sor Juana; his boundless flow of Baroque puns as well as his empiricism compares to hers (see Merrim, "Spectacular Cityscapes" 54). Two reflective poems by Caviedes also bear the stamp of Sigüenza's famous debate with the Austrian Jesuit Eusebio Kino on the comet that appeared in 1681, in which the Mexican savant denied that the awesome phenomenon constituted a divine judgment on a sinful world. Caviedes's meditations on the comet and on the earthquakes that devastated Lima in 1687 (#213 and #263 in Reedy's edition) similarly pronounce them natural occurrences rather than divine punishments. That is, in striking contradistinction to another of his contemporaries, the completely Baroque Arzáns, Caviedes proffers the same scientific, almost Enlightenment stance on nature's eruptions as Sigüenza.

The earthquake that prompts Caviedes's scientific reflections gives rise to one of his two masterful poems on carnivalesque spectacles. "Al terremoto de Lima el día 20 de octubre de 1687" [To the earthquake in Lima of October 20, 1687] (Romance #261) depicts a natural event in spectacular terms, as a festival-like spectacle that inverts the city and its social order. Bearing horrified witness to the two tremors that rocked the city, its spectator-chronicler lists the destruction they wrought on one after another of Lima's splendid buildings. His anguished *ubi sunt* for Lima's buildings coexists with a dance of death as Caviedes describes how the earthquakes convene all of the city's inhabitants into a macabre parody of the equalizing official festival: "El plebeyo, el pobre, el noble, / sin excepción de ninguna / persona, se atropellaban / por adelantar la fuga" [The commoner, the poor, the noble, with no one exempted, trampled one another to get to the head of the escape] (465). The medieval-sounding scourge that levels the city and its inhabitants impels Caviedes to retreat somewhat from his previous scientific position on natural disasters, into biblical exegesis. He writes that the tremors may not be sent by God, but that they should cause people to meditate on their sins: "Detenga un temblor el grave / que mayor que otro se juzga, / y si no, piense que todos / tenemos igual fortuna" [May the earthquake arrest the proud man who considers himself superior to another, or if not, may it inspire him to recognize that we all share the same fate] (465). It is *as if* the earthquakes were the biblical Flood ("*como cuando en el diluvio / vengó de Dios las injurias*" [464; emphasis added]) and thus as if the tremors had visited divine judgment on the dystopian city, leaving it in ruins and purified of all but the poet-witness.

The poet's "Coloquio entre una vieja y Periquillo a una procesión celebrada en esta ciudad" [Conversation between an old woman and Periquillo about a procession held in this city] adjudicates a standard official festival. Caviedes satirizes the grand festival of Corpus Christi, viewing it as a "mojiganga burlesca" [burlesque masquerade] (210). An old woman, representing Curiosity, plies Periquillo, a truth-telling innocent, with questions about the festival he has seen in Lima. Their lively dialogue goes on to excoriate the false piety, bombastic sermons, Jesuits (with their "effeminate finery" [206]), upwardly mobile population, and prostitutes of a Lima that the poem explicitly terms Babel (212). As it turns the procession into one of Folly and Vanity, the "Coloquio" conducts a sweeping review of Peruvian society along the lines of Menippean satire.

In a second act of totalizing judgment, the satirical poem conjugates the Fiesta of Corpus with the Baroque lexicon of desengaño to raze the sinful city. The old woman inquires of Periquillo whether he perchance saw those who "primero niegan / doce artículos de fe / que uno de caballeresco" [would rather deny the twelve articles of faith than one of nobility] (209). He cynically retorts that he only espied airy devils who feed off the wind, chameleons, formless goblins, frivolous apparitions, gallant phantoms from a comedia (209). Shortly thereafter, the old woman asks the boy if all the seeming pomp of the festival taking place in this fabulous Crete, imaginary Memphis, fantastic Athens is indeed simply "perspectivas aparentes / de humo que el viento subleva / en ficticios obeliscos / a desvanecida esfera" [deceptive appearances, smoke that the wind has swirled into the false obelisks of a disappearing sphere] (212). When Periquillo replies that truly he has witnessed nothing but "cascos vanos, tripas huecas, / mucho ruido, pocas nueces" [vain shells, empty innards, much ado about nothing] (212), Caviedes adds the final touch to a poem that has wickedly decorporealized the venal, bodily Lima. Babel has shaded into Judgment Day: the pomp of the festival and its city have dissipated into end-time ruins swathed in the smoke, dust, shadows, and ultimate nothingness of Góngora's and Sor Juana's famed sonnets. Lima's final hallucinated nothingness reimagines the mystery of the Eucharist from transubstantiation into the desubstantiation of a city so fraught with Baroque disease that it vaporizes into a disillusioned phantasmagorical realm.

Babel triggers satire (Antelo 191); satire breaches social norms; satire attains some of its Baroque, New World heights or depths in the problematic Peru;[31] satire desublimates colonial tensions in an idiom worlds away from Balbuena's sublimity. These propositions, realized in Caviedes's poetry, prepare the terrain for the magnificently transgressive project of the last colonial author whom *The Spectacular City* will treat, Franciscan Buenaventura de Salinas y Córdova. Buenaventura, the name in religion that the man baptized Sancho Salinas y Córdova chose in honor of the Franciscan St. Bonaventure, well describes the New World activist and writer. Adventurously breaching all propriety and undoing his own "buenaventura," or good fortune, in the bargain, Salinas raised the bar for exposing Peru's abuses of the Indians. In the name of "lo bueno," or virtue, he subjected his Babelic Lima to a Judgment Day as vigorous and pungent as that of any satire. New World satires, however, were not published. Salinas's *Memorial de las historias del Nuevo Mundo, Pirú* [Brief on the histories of the New World, Peru] (1630), remarkably enough, was. Though printed in a limited, incomplete edition and then embargoed, the Franciscan's *Memorial* ignited other authors. It catalyzed praise and censure of Peru, creating a wake of texts, Arzáns's among them, that rivals the corpus inspired by Balbuena's "Grandeza."[32]

Salinas's adventurous, vexed life began in Lima and ended in Mexico, where he met and influenced Vetancurt.[33] The son of prominent creoles, Salinas studied with the Jesuits and then at the University of San Marcos. At the age of nine, he also entered the viceroy's retinue as a page. Everything was in place for Salinas to lead the life of a creole aristocrat at the helm of society. Then, while training for the hereditary family post as chief secretary of the Peruvian government, Salinas came in contact with the state's archives. The archives, Salinas writes, awakened him to the just Spanish laws that the viceregal regime disregarded and to the "abuses [*excesos*] and misery that the Indians have suffered" in consequence of that neglect.[34] His social consciousness aroused, in 1616 Salinas changed course and professed as a Franciscan at the Convento de Jesús de Lima. He spent more than a decade teaching and preaching in Lima and outlying regions. An inflammatory sermon on the Indians' tribulations that he preached in Cuzco in 1635 earned Salinas the animosity of the bishop there, who began to agitate against the friar. Two years later, extricating him from the predicament, the Franciscans sent Salinas to Spain and then to Rome. The friar never saw his homeland again, but he did manage to return to the New World. Between 1647 and 1653, Salinas lived in Mexico, serving as general commissioner of New Spain's Franciscans. Guijo records Salinas's death in Cuernavaca at the age of sixty-one (1:239). According to Vetancurt, Salinas died as bishop-elect of Arequipa (Cook lxix) and thus on the threshold of returning to Peru.

Salinas's first and foremost publication, the *Memorial* of 1630, encompasses the past and the present, Peru and Spain. The author apportions his text into three discourses: (1) (untitled) on the preconquest and conquest history of Peru; (2) "De los méritos y excelencias de la Ciudad de Lima," a lengthy treatise on the city; (3) "Del estado a que a llegado el Pirú" [What Peru has become], a discourse protesting abuses of the Indians and other scourges of Peru, which ends with an appendix of just Spanish laws analogous to that of Torquemada. Cut short by the embargo on its publication, the *Memorial* originally intended to support the canonization of the Franciscan Francisco Solano ends up devoting only a few final pages to hagiographic biography. Yet, as its organization attests, the text does succeed in expounding on basically all the pressing topics of its time and place. Salinas's Baroque *Memorial* subjects them to judgment brilliantly, cannily, and robustly, in a prophetic vein that predicts an end-time for a Babelic New World on the brink of imploding.

For our concerns, the *Memorial* is at once the last and the first, something of a Rosetta stone. As the text consummates the wild work of the Baroque Spectacular City with regard to both protest and praise, it revisits several central issues and texts that have driven this book. Salinas incorporates an archive that includes Columbus, Oviedo,

Acosta, Torquemada, Gregorio García, Guaman Poma, and many others (Balbuena, I will argue, being one of them). More important, the microcosmic *Memorial* pulls into its arena salient topics and timbres of seventeenth-century creole discourse. Salinas's work exemplifies the directions in which the South American continent propels that discourse, before and after his text. Finally, as one of the most disruptive, liberal texts of the seventeenth century, the *Memorial* gives voice to the colonial structures of feeling that cross into the future, whether into the wars of independence or into a politicized postcolonial consciousness. Despite its momentous accomplishments, unfortunately, the *Memorial* has not achieved the stature in the colonial canon it merits.[35] To close the body of this book I will therefore endeavor to do some small justice to Salinas's masterpiece while at the same time demonstrating its kinship with the Baroque Spectacular City.

Salinas's *Memorial* exploits the resources of the Baroque in shouts and in whispers. Monumental Baroque clusters of archival, biblical, and classical sources fortify its arguments, for the new letrado recognizes the new, activist role of erudition. Salinas writes that anyone committed to exposing the plight of the Indians should "cite all the courts, Universities, Clergymen, Friars, and any learned person [*letrado*] with experience and righteous intentions, and anyone who by any path or manner can provide light, relief, and restitution in these cases of such dire need" (290). If erudition speaks to the logical mind, Salinas's style, we see, goes to work on the emotions. His fiery writing musters cries, weeping, teaching, begging, reprehending, and castigating (290) as well as audacious, sustained metaphors like those that the early creole Dorantes had employed.[36] An expert stylist of the wild mode, Salinas also knows how to play the Baroque softly. Beneath the text's outward, consecrated, tripartite structure, Salinas subtly shapes the *Memorial* into a Baroque chiaroscuro. The first two discourses, studded with positive wonder and praise, give way to the third, a litany of negative wonder, of scandal and protest. As praise yields to protest and light to dark, Salinas covertly fits his treatise into the Baroque grid of *engaño* versus *desengaño,* deception versus disillusionment.

Salinas duly provisions the *Memorial* with Baroque, Franciscan-style miracles. Nonetheless, among the greatest marvels in the first two discourses and arguably the lightning rod for others, are Peru's creoles. Salinas maintains that the natural abundance of Peru, responsible for its famed mineral resources, produces an equal wealth of "admirable, advanced, illustrious, talented individuals" (86). A professor himself, Salinas praises creole intellectuals, saying that Peruvians need not envy the great minds of Spain because "their own are admired and envied" and that any "maravillas" its intellectuals might seek in the wide world can be found in Peru (91). The author briefly lapses into satire to lampoon those creoles too besotted with their own superiority to do a decent day's work (246). Conversely, he extols those who risk their lives to defend Peru from foreigners (276), whom Salinas demonizes with a xenophobic vehemence as overblown as his lauding of the creoles.

When the *Memorial* implores creoles to write their country's history, it precedes the Mexican Sigüenza's pleas of a similar ilk (*Teatro de virtudes* 174, 181) by almost half a century.[37] "Who has silenced so many creole tongues?" queries Salinas (83). The *Memorial* incorporates a text by a conqueror's descendant that upbraids fellow creoles who have willed the wonders of the conquest to oblivion. In shirking the historian's task, they have abdicated the patriotism that the opulent, rich Peru deserves (see Discourse 1, chap. 8). Guilt links up with seduction as Salinas cajoles creoles into writing by providing a sample of their own grand, neglected history. Contending that Peru owes much of its glory to the conquerors (272), in the first discourse the author composes a conventional creole paean to the conquest that purveys it as an epic saga. At roughly the same time that Mexican creoles were lionizing bygone days, Salinas glorifies Francisco Pizarro as an epic hero whose deeds God crowned with numerous miracles (Discourse 1, chap. 5) and the conquerors as valiant Argonauts (83). In view of Salinas's fervent patriotism and incendiary challenge to his fellow creoles, it is not hard to fathom why the *Memorial* generated a string of disciples.

Salinas's creole history of the conquest does not fail to engrave the Indians in the epic mold, as worthy adversaries who incited Spanish "maravilla" (49). However, his descriptions of the sacred Inca city, Cuzco (Discourse 1, chap. 2), had already brought Indian marvels center stage. Salinas vaunts Cuzco's stone walls as the eighth wonder of the world (26) and corrects absurdly exoticizing explanations of the Inca constructions. Quoting the Inca Garcilaso de la Vega, Salinas states that neither demons nor enchantment built the walls, just Indians and Inca ingenuity (23). In the next chapter, Salinas leads his readers on an imaginary tour of Cuzco as it stood before the conquest, wondrous and great. Salinas rhapsodizes in the same key as Bernal Díaz del Castillo when he lays out the marvels of Cuzco's palaces, which, the Peruvian says, exceeded those of any king or emperor (34). Every surface and space of the court allegedly glistened with gold: walls, tombs, statues, tableware, orchards, and fields. Salinas comments exorbitantly on the "counterfeits" in gold of nature's handiwork (34–36) with which the palaces shimmered. Far from discomfiting him as they did Cortés, the marvelous counterfeits simply confirm the grandeur of Cuzco's civilization that stems from its infinite wealth.

The praise shot through with wonder presses on undiminished from Salinas's discussion of the Inca world to that of colonial Peru, compared to which Europe "is so much less, that it seems like nothing" (96) in Discourse 2. Throughout the second discourse, he heaps accolade upon hyperbolic accolade and cites author after author. By virtue of repetition, the implausibly marvelous gradually becomes more plausible, as it did in Arzáns's *Potosí*. The archive that creates a believably fabulous climate for the *Memorial* at large does a special service for the marvelous at the beginning of the treatise on Lima. With the support of over twenty sources (including Columbus and Oviedo), a good twenty years before Antonio de León Pinelo, Salinas makes a case for Peru as the earthly paradise. He uses the words of the royal chronicler Antonio de Herrera to proclaim, "the sight of such marvelous things, which its first discoverers experienced, is not to be marveled at for there are people who declare, and hold to be true, that Paradise is hidden in some part of this Region" (102). This intensely self-exoticizing argument lays the groundwork for the theme of abundance that rules Salinas's laudatory examination of the city. As part of earthly paradise, the "City of Lima, and all its extensive valleys and mountains, exceed all of Europe, and the Ancient World in abundance" (252).

Salinas corroborates the sublime properties of Lima in a lengthy treatise on the city that wends from its rivers[38] to its physical site, urban design, mountains, and port. Intent on transmitting the grandeur of Peru's capital, "On the Merits and Excellences of the City of Lima" de facto or, I strongly suspect, deliberately mirrors "La grandeza mexicana." The first discourse of the *Memorial* had described Peru as a hub of international commerce in a paragraph laden with Balbuenian terminology: "microcosm," "ciphered," "abbreviated world," and "grandeur." Salinas's treatise on Lima then fully enters the territory of "Grandeza," at times nearly verbatim, as it salutes the emporium city, the luxury goods that stream to the city from Europe and the Orient, commerce itself, the marketplace in Lima's plaza, and so on (see Discourse 2, chap. 6). Concluding that "the whole City is a marketplace" (254), Salinas does Balbuena's textual economy and Lima's real one proud by compiling for the king what amounts to an accountant's account of Lima. The *Me-*

morial itemizes madly. It habitually breaks into exhaustive, particularized inventories, barefaced lists of goods, revenues, salaries, commercial venues, and provisions. Detail is clearly retail here, and the Salinas who wants to impress the king with Lima's economic vibrancy clearly harbors no compunctions, Balbuenian or other, about the overflow of particularity.

Abundant, a slice of earthly paradise, and a port city, Salinas's Lima resonates organically with the urban pastoral of "Grandeza." Yet, unlike Balbuena in this and other crucial regards, the Franciscan reveres nature and couches it in a gorgeous lyricism. Instead of catachrestically relocating pastoral topics into the city, Salinas celebrates the nature that, unadulterated by artifice, graces Lima; he smoothly conflates the city with the exurban countryside. There, outside the city proper, the Peruvian sites several unique festivals. Salinas diverges from Balbuena and all our other authors in spotlighting not official festivals but the unofficial, truly egalitarian festivities of the common folk. His text's festivals leave behind the society of the spectacle's equivocal, manufactured pleasures to honor the genuine, spontaneous happiness arising from a bona fide pastoral setting. The hills outside Lima, for example, receive city dwellers outfitted with guitars and refreshments who come to dance and sing. "There is not a single crag or cliff," observes Salinas, "that does not host the common folk," particularly in the weeks after the Night of San Juan (111). Salinas's counterfestivals render the pastoral countryside a refreshing, salutary supplement to the city, a far cry from Eugenio de Salazar y Alarcón's nefarious Chapultepec.

For better and for worse, the *Memorial*'s most arresting instance of joyous festivity concerns the Indians and the Spaniards. The providential, promising incident, sadly betrayed in ensuing events, occurs when Pizarro arrives at the Isla de Tumbez. As the "Indians receive him in peace, showing respect for the Spaniards and showering them with gifts" (50), the female Indian chieftain, Capullana, organizes an impromptu banquet for the conquerors on the beach. Spaniards and Indians break bread together and marvel at one another (53–54), allegedly communing as harmoniously as Puritans and Indians in the mythified Thanksgiving feast.

Salinas's "fiesta de la Capullana" is the first female-organized festival to enter our purview. This bittersweet anomaly indicates the importance Salinas attaches to racial diversity and to women. Vetancurt, another minister of plurality, likely takes his cue from the Salinas who categorically and equitably attends to each of Lima's racial groups. The concerted racial variety of Salinas's marketplace, which we glimpsed in chapter 1, suffuses the whole *Memorial*. Its new math of plurality especially hearkens to the daily, working life of society's marginalized populations. Salinas focuses on the labors of male Indians, but as the marketplace alive with females of all races implied, he is also mindful of women's work. The author obliges his readers to recognize that such things as the domestic toil of Indian women, "blackened with kitchen smoke, assigned the lowest and most vile household tasks" (285), qualify as slavery. Removing woman from vile labors and refusing to scapegoat her, the sympathetic *Memorial* assigns the feminine an exalted, positive role as the figurehead of Peru. It hails Peru as a "fertile, merciful mother," a "rich mother" (85), and a "beautiful lady" arrayed in silver (90).

Salinas's about-face in the third discourse from panegyric to exposé, and from positive to negative marvels, turns precisely on the silver that adorns the beautiful, beleaguered Peru.[39] The first chapter of "What Peru Has Become" promises to uncover the circumstances that have prostrated Peru, "the greatest misfortune being the wealth and treasures that it produces, which destroy the Indians" (271). Salinas has already sung the praises of Peru's riches hyperbolically and incessantly—too much so, one realizes, for a spartan Franciscan. The second movement of his meticulously plotted *Memorial* reveals Salinas's suspect materialism to have been a strategic ploy, an elaborate lead-in to the nucleus of the text, which disabuses readers of any illusions. As disillusionment takes over, lists of goods cede to lists of abuses wrought on those who produce them. All the positive wonders of Peru come to rest on the Indian labor responsible for the production of its wealth. The concept somewhat jibes with "Grandeza"'s epilogue, but Salinas will tell the story, the whole story, Balbuena repressed or whitewashed. Cutting to the jugular of "Grandeza" and other imperial apologetics, the *Memorial* spectacularizes the ways in which Peruvians and Spaniards, "blinded by interés and greed" (281), sabotage their greatest treasure, the Indians, to the enormous loss of a Spain widely reputed to be poor (275).

In the *Memorial*'s second discursive landscape, of negative wonders, excess tragically and illustratively reigns supreme. The excessive wealth of an outrageously lawless Peru derives from Indians exploited to an abusive excess that the warrior Salinas lays bare in wildly excessive prose. Significantly, excess here acquires the pointed, double meaning of "exceeding" or violating the law to foist excessive misery on the Indians. Salinas complains of Spaniards who, "exceeding the Instructions that they have received, always wreak great violence, ill-treatment, and excess on the Indians" (327). A loyal vassal writing to his monarch, the Peruvian assembles his catalogue of excesses to shock the Spanish king, Philip IV, into action against those who disobey royal laws protecting the Indians.[40] Salinas devises a Baroque Mirror for Princes designed to fulfill the imperative, which would shortly find full expression in Pedro Calderón de la Barca's *La vida es sueño* [Life is a dream] (1635), of rousing a dormant, uninformed king whose life is a dream (297; whether or not Salinas realizes it, the theme has a chilling pertinence to the hedonistic Philip IV, a most infelicitous addressee for the *Memorial*). One of the few official festivals that enters the *Memorial* all but satirizes the disconnect between the king and Peru as it shows officials venerating the king's only concrete presence in the New World, the royal seal, as if it were the Host (143).

To help the "Monarch of both worlds" (1) live up to his title, Salinas proposes two extreme measures. First, the *Memorial* offers its own version of the extraordinary apocryphal interview between Guaman Poma and the king from the *Nueva Corónica*. In the "Capítulo de la pregunta," or chapter of the king's questions, Guaman Poma's imagination transports him to Madrid, where the king solicits his advice on the Indians; the *Memorial* suggests that Philip IV bring Peruvian Indians to his palace and sincerely query them about their past, conversion, and treatment (282). Salinas fleshes out the imaginary encounter in the vivid, prescriptive detail that might induce the king to convert an imaginary interview into reality. Adding a daring new plotline to the Mirror for Princes, he goes so far as to recommend that the monarch learn the Indians' travails firsthand by conducting the interviews in Peru itself (313). Meanwhile and secondly, Salinas spares no effort to apprise the king, entrenched in Spain, of the Indians' torment. He presents himself as a spokesperson for the living and dying (rather than the long-deceased) Indians who surround him (272), assuming a stance quite different from Sigüenza's and Vetancurt's backward-looking creole cultural nationalism. The *Memorial* correctively abandons museums and museumizing to open onto a comprehensive, encyclopedic roster of the issues that now oppress the Indians.

In Salinas's dramatic, activist platform, certain axial paradigms of New World discourse come to crisis. Joining Guaman Poma, Salinas avows that the Spaniards have usurped lands that rightfully belong to the Indians (285), which has bred an upside-down world in which those who deserve the most receive the least (288). Indians experiencing this abysmal version of the carnivalesque also experience a new and fatal form of the Ordered City's segregation when the mita separates them from their families, making procreation impossible (294). At the same time, the similitude and commensurability that are the pillars of the Ordered City collapse in the nightmare panorama of the *Memorial*. Colonial abuses of the Indians, blares Salinas, have no match, no par (313). Even the Israelites' bondage in Egypt, the one model that might capture the ordeal of the Peruvian Indians, breaks down. Salinas expounds at length on the Israelites' suffering in a markedly nonexotic Egypt but then evacuates the comparison. The Indians' agony, he says, exceeds that of the Israelites, who at least managed to increase their numbers while indentured to the Egyptians (Discourse 3, chap. 3).[41] Only one aspect of resemblance holds fast for the New World, and counts: the Indians are human beings, not monsters. "These miserable Indians are men, not wolves, bears, tigers, or lions; nor are they camels, dromedaries, elephants, or demons" (289), declaims Salinas.

The foregoing words and other components of Salinas's platform purposefully evoke Las Casas. A post-Torquemada Franciscan reporting on a world still steeped in immorality, Salinas reverts to the extreme techniques of the Dominican's *Brevísima relación*. The Peruvian memorial de agravios shamelessly emulates the rhetorical excess, aporia, inflamed generalizations, and Manichean characterization (evil Spaniards/innocent Indians) of "the saintly Bishop of Chiapas" (318, 321) in an effort to inspire sympathy for the Indians. Salinas aims for a pathos capable of stirring the "Royal heart" (295) of the king's no-longer-mystical body. To elicit pathos, he follows Las Casas's lead and writes history on the body. Salinas adumbrates the *Memorial* with corporeal effects that range from copious mentions of his own tears to agonizing depictions of Indian bodies ravaged by the mita and the mines.

Above and beyond stylistic effects, the Peruvian version of the wild *Brevísima relación* recreates its stunning portrayal of the New World as an unmitigated hell. The Indians dying in hordes from mistreatment, fulminates Salinas, have transformed Peru into "a living image of death, and black shadow of hell" (297, quoting the Lima superintendent of the Indians, Domingo de Luna). Then again, the mismanaged diversity and bedlam that obtain in Salinas's Peru bond it with Babel as they form "a great and present pestilence: the Republic being in terribly confused and dangerous discord, to the astonishment and stupefaction of the world" (280). Salinas argues that had the productive, angelic Indians flourished, the revenue from their labors would have helped Spain reconquer the Heavenly City of Jerusalem (315). Since avaricious Spaniards have devastated the Indians, Peru can only expect the fate of Babylon, destruction. At the end of a tirade that quotes the prophet Isaiah several times, Salinas portends the annihilation of his Babelic Peru: "And soon the time will come upon us of the total destruction of the Indians, their ruin taking us unawares, and when it comes, these rich Provinces will end up barren and desolated" (277). And in the same thundering voice with which God admonished the Egyptians (310), Salinas foretells the damnation to which the Lord will subject Peru's sinners on Judgment Day (281). Nonetheless, the *Memorial* delivers hope and an apocalyptic vision of order and concert. Appropriating the words of the Spanish jurist Juan de Solórzano Pereira, the *Memorial* professes its faith that before Judgment Day a merciful God will at long last unite the Republics of the Indians and Spaniards into "a single body, single heart, and single spirit" free of scandal, sin, and injury (310), a Heavenly City on earth.

★ ★ ★

POSTSCRIPT: REDEEMING BABEL

> In the center, an occidental urban logic, all lined up, ordered, strong like the French language. On the other side, Creole's open profusion according to Texaco's logic. Mingling these two tongues, dreaming of all tongues, the Creole city speaks a new language in secret and *no longer fears Babel*. Here the well-learned, domineering, geometrical grid of an urban grammar; over there the crown of a mosaic culture to be unveiled, caught in the hieroglyphics of cement, crate wood, asbestos. The Creole city returns to the urban planner, who would like to ignore it, the roots of a new identity: multilingual, multiracial, multihistorical, open, sensible to the world's diversity. Everything has changed. (Chamoiseau, *Texaco* 220; emphasis added)

Patrick Chamoiseau's *Texaco* (1992), an exquisitely lyrical novel on Martinique's capital, also delivers hope, in the form of a postcolonial healing for the "hospitals of nerves" that reverberate from colonial foundations into the present. *Texaco* redeems Babel from a dreaded heterotopia into a utopian condition, the template for an eminently pluralistic Caribbean identity. A novelized manifesto of the Caribbean *Créolité* that the Martinican Chamoiseau and Édouard Glissant, among others, have spearheaded, *Texaco* advances the triumph of diversity, hybridity, and complexity.[42] Créolité and its *Texaco* destigmatize multiplicity and contingency, the traits of the earthly city that St. Augustine abhorred. Rejecting absolutes, they advocate an existential becoming over being and vibrant disorder over stifling order. Surely, "everything has changed" from an orthodox mentality and from a colonial ideology that would brook no disorder.

Surely, too, the path from colonial Mexico to *Texaco* or from criollismo to Créolité is a long, attenuated, and broken one. Yet Créolité reincarnates the struggling, at times combative, spirit of colonial creoles as well as their cultural nationalism. And colonial creole engagements with plurality such as Vetancurt's and Salinas's, no less than Sor Juana's premonitory juxtaposition of the blasphemous, arrogant tower with a pyramid bathed in light (*PS* ll. 412–415), shine a beacon toward a world that "no longer fears Babel." Of course, on its own the montage of eras and cultures that this postscript rehearses is hardly unmotivated, given the neocolonial status of Martinique as an overseas department of France (or Puerto Rico's in-between position), the solidarity with Latin America that Caribbean Créolité professes ("Our solidarity is first with our brothers of the neighboring islands and secondly with the nations of South America" [Bernabé et alia 904]), and the affinities between Créolité, magical realism, and the Neo-Baroque.[43] Were there world, time, and space enough, it would be satisfying to assess the fresh perspectives on all of these movements that my book and its characterization of the New World Baroque might enable, but for now and in conclusion we will simply take one last, short city tour, of Fort-de-France and Texaco.

As the creoles of *Texaco* grapple with the vestiges of colonial conquests, they launch a restorative "conquest of the city" (27), the creolization of the French bastion and capital city founded in the seventeenth century, Fort-de-France. The novel traces the battles, based on actual historical events, of Martinican creoles to infuse the French city with the jubilant, Babelic energies of Créolité. Creoles seize the grounds of the Texaco oil company on the margins of the city. There they inaugurate a supplementary society that ripples into Fort-de-France, deranging and energizing its fossilized, geometrical, urban grammar. The creole warriors have in fact vitiated the planned, colonial, Ordered City that Spain and other colonial powers mandated and that still endures in form if not always in spirit: everyone in Fort-de-France "had to choose their place, their land, their location on the checkerboard. No one was to step out of line or out of the plan. The houses rose according to the King's engineer and the Count of Blénac" (176). Pushing back at the Ordered City, the Martinican creoles supplant it with a contestatory urban logic.

A neocolonialist turned postcolonial "Urban Planner" charts the new logic. Won over to the creole city, this Urban Planner charged with razing Texaco ends up saving and theorizing it. The "Urban Planner's Notes" that track his *Bildung* themselves build an alternative poetics for the creolized city. As he comes to apprehend the city "like a Creole visionary" (388), the Urban Planner awakens to the natural, harmonious order of disorder, which embraces the contradiction and paradox dear to the Baroque: "Beauty replete with horror, order set in disorder. Beauty throbbing in horror and a secret order right in the heart of disorder" (184). The creolized Urban Planner who "no longer chooses between order and disorder, between beauty and ugliness" (184), chooses an organic art of monstrosity (we recall O'Gorman) that rises "above the insalubrious" and "whose equilibrium is violence" (148). The resulting creole city nonetheless duplicates Salinas's *Memorial* in imbuing the urban environment with the humanity of the countryside ("Texaco was what City kept of the countryside's humanity" [281]) and vaunts the peacefully pluralized city for which Salinas and others yearned as it creates a "Creole space of brand new solidarities" (320). An *"urban mangrove swamp"* (263), the Texaco that has penetrated Fort-de-France boasts a swamp's labyrinthine complexity, "entanglement" (244), and nonlinearity: "nothing which progresses or recedes, no linear progress or Darwinian elaboration. Nothing but the haphazard whirls of the living" (257). The counter "ecosystem" (263) of Texaco that culminates in the swamp, we realize, has reenfranchised not only the complexity of Babel but also the convulsive Baroque Spectacular City and aberrant ways of the colonial New World Baroque that "Babel: Wild Work of the Baroque" has strived to convey.

In the parlance of *Texaco* and Créolité, however, the swamp is a forest, Chamoiseau's take on Glissant's influential construct. Glissant distances Caribbean space and literary culture from those of Europe, "molded spatially" around "the economy of the meadow" and the "serenity of the spring" (145–146). The language of his New World literary landscape, Glissant declares, is "primarily that of the forest, which unceasingly bursts with life" (146). Opaque, dense, mobile, and overwhelming, the logic of the forest wishes to depose the reductive prisonhouse of knowability that Western culture has propagated. Glissant's forest and *Texaco* excommunicate spurious order and concert. They grant the real total license to complicate the ideal. They award the syncretism and architexture of the New World Baroque a new, magisterial primacy. With the unseating of the occlusive pastoral that Glissant and Chamoiseau advocate, the forest of Erífile that burgeoned into "La grandeza mexicana," the jungle / *silva* / *selva* of the *Primero sueño,* the marketplace of Villalpando's Zócalo, and the Spectacular City's many other Baroque projects whose architecture rebels against geometry have found a dynamic new home, a redemptive place in the present and future.

Appendix CHRONOLOGY OF
PRINCIPAL WORKS

By date of completion or publication (*), if published in the author's lifetime

- Sandro Botticelli (1455–1510): *The Birth of Venus*, c. 1484.
- Christopher Columbus (1451–1506): *Diario*, 1493.
- Hieronymus Bosch (c. 1450–1516): *Garden of Earthly Delights*, c. 1505–1510.
- Hernán Cortés (1485–1547): *Segunda carta-relación*, 1520, *1522; *Cuarta carta-relación*, 1524, *1525.
- Gonzalo Fernández de Oviedo (1478–1557): *Sumario de la natural historia de las Indias*, *1526.
- Bartolomé de Las Casas (1474–1566): *Brevísima relación de la destrucción de las Indias* *1552.
- Francisco Cervantes de Salazar (1513?–1575): Latin dialogues on Mexico City, *1554.
- Bernal Díaz del Castillo (1496–1584): *Historia verdadera de la conquista de la Nueva España*, 1551–1584.
- Spanish city-planning ordinances: "Provisión en que se declara la orden que se ha de tener en las Indias, en nuevos descubrimientos y poblaciones que en ellas se hizieron," *1573.
- Juan de la Cueva (1550?–1610): "Epístola al licenciado Sánchez de Obregón, primer corregidor de México," c. 1577.
- José de Acosta (1540–1600): *Historia natural y moral de las Indias*, *1589–1590.
- Juan de Cárdenas (1563–1609): *Primera parte de los problemas y secretos maravillosos de las Indias*, *1591.
- Eugenio de Salazar y Alarcón (1530?–1605?): "Epístola al insigne Hernando de Herrera en que se refiere al estado de la ilustre Ciudad de México"; "Bucólica: Descripción de la laguna de Méjico," c. 1597.
- Mateo Rosas de Oquendo (1559?–1612?): various poems, c. end of sixteenth century.

- Bernardo de Balbuena (1562–1627): *Siglo de oro en las selvas de Erífile*, 1601, *1608; *La grandeza mexicana*, *1604.
- Baltasar Dorantes de Carranza (1550–1604): *Sumaria relación de las cosas de la Nueva España*, 1604.
- Gregorio García (1525?–1627): *Origen de los indios del nuevo mundo, e Indias occidentales*, *1607.
- Juan de Torquemada (1557?–1624): *Monarquía indiana*, *1615.
- Felipe Guaman Poma de Ayala (fl. 1613): *El primer nueva corónica y buen gobierno*, c. 1615.
- Francisco de Bramón (dates unknown): *Los sirgueros de la Virgen sin original pecado*, *1620.
- Arias de Villalobos (1568–?): *Canto intitulado Mercurio*, 1623.
- Buenaventura de Salinas y Córdova (1592?–1653): *Memorial de las historias del Nuevo Mundo, Pirú*, *1630.
- Juan Rodríguez Freile (1566–?): *El Carnero*, 1638.
- Baltasar Gracián (1601–1558): *Agudeza y arte de ingenio*, *1642, *1648.
- Antonio de León Pinelo (1596–1660): *El Paraíso en el Nuevo Mundo*, *1650.
- Athanasius Kircher (1602–1680): *Oedipus Aegyptiacus*, *1652–1654; *Itinerarium exstaticum* *1656–1671; *Magneticum naturae regnum*, *1667; *Ars magna sciendi*, *1669.
- Alejandro Favián (1624–?): Correspondence with Athanasius Kircher, 1661–1674.
- Juan de Espinosa Medrano (1629?–1688), *Apologético en favor de don Luis de Góngora*, *1662.
- Gregorio Martín de Guijo (?–1676): *Diario*, 1648–1664.
- Carlos de Sigüenza y Góngora (1645–1700): *Glorias de Querétaro*, *1680; *Teatro de virtudes políticas que constituyen a un príncipe*, *1680; *Triunfo Parténico*, *1683; *Infortunios de Alonso Ramírez*, *1690; *Alboroto y motín de los indios de México*, 1692.
- Sor Juana Inés de la Cruz (1648?–1695): *Neptuno alegórico*, *1680; *Respuesta a Sor Filotea de la Cruz*, 1691; *El Divino Narciso* and its *Loa*, *1691, *1692; *Primero sueño*, written at an unknown date before the *Respuesta*, *1692; *Fama y obras póstumas*; *1700.
- Juan del Valle y Caviedes (1645–1697): *Diente del Parnaso*, c. 1689.
- Cristóbal de Villalpando (1645–1714): *Central Square of Mexico City*, 1695, 1695.
- Agustín de Vetancurt (1620–1700): *Teatro mexicano*, *1697–1698.
- Antonio de Robles (1648–1757): *Diario*, 1665–1703.
- Bartolomé Arzáns de Orsúa y Vela (1676–1736): *Historia de la Villa Imperial de Potosí*, 1705–1736.

NOTES

INTRODUCTION

1. Primarily chap. 2 of *La ciudad letrada* (1984). References to Angel Rama throughout this book, unless otherwise indicated, refer to *La ciudad letrada*. Translations are mine because the English version published by Duke University Press in 1994, *The Lettered City,* takes considerable license.

2. As the introduction explains later, my book focuses on writings by creoles and radicados and principally enacts the Spectacular City in Mexico. Much as chapters 1 and 7, the bookends of the study, extend the Spectacular City beyond Mexico, it lies outside the scope of this (already lengthy) book to locate the Spectacular City fully within other viceregal territories. Hence, the qualification of my claim for its ability to generate a comparative intra-Hispanic literary history.

3. The Mexican scholar José Pascual Buxó, for example, questions the tendency to enthrone "the great Amerindian works as the only and true paradigm for our present culture" (4). J. H. Elliott calls for an ecumenical perspective: "What has happened . . . is that our contemporary discovery of the presumed 'otherness' of others has embraced the non-European world to the exclusion of the conquerors, colonists, and chroniclers of the sixteenth century; the observed have been accorded a privileged status that has been denied their observers, whose individual voices, reduced to an unattractive unison, are dismissed as 'the hegemonic voices of the West.' But in reality there are many voices, among the conquerors and the conquered alike. We may not like what some of those voices are saying, but, as historians, we have an obligation to give a hearing to each and every one" ("Final Reflections" 398).

4. Mazzotti's introduction to *Agencias criollas* also provides helpful bibliography on the much-discussed overlap of creoles and mestizos. Israel, chap. 3, offers an influential treatment of mestizos, and Elizabeth Anne Kuznes a more recent one in "Ethnic and Gender Influences on 'Spanish' Creole Society in Colonial Spanish America," *Colonial Latin American Review* 4.1 (1995): 153–176.

5. I refer to scholars (to name but a few) like Solange Alberro, Rolena

Adorno, Ralph Bauer, José Joaquín Blanco, Jorge Cañizares-Esguerra, Leonardo García Pabón, Anthony Higgins, Bernard Lavallé, Yolanda Martínez-San Miguel, José Antonio Mazzotti, Mabel Moraña, Edmundo O'Gorman, Kathleen Ross, and Hernán Vidal.

6. As Blanco notes, other facets of creole life, like art, architecture, food, clothing, festivals, and language were even more mixed than their writings (*Esplendores* 17).

7. Kubler, for example, notes that in Peru "an entire generation elapsed before the campaign of systematic urbanization began under Viceroy Toledo" and that the "Christianization of the Quechua Indians was not achieved until the mid-seventeenth century." Whereas the initial colonization of Peru "lacked a dominant urban policy," in Mexico "urbanization was concomitant with initial colonization" (69).

8. Ross's more recent work discerns the same intertextuality at work in sixteenth-century creole texts. For instance, her "Sigüenza y Góngora y Suárez de Peralta: Dos lecturas de Cortés" (Mayer 2:139–149) discusses the intersection of Juan Suárez de Peralta's *Tratado* (1589) with the writings of Cortés, Sahagún, Las Casas, and Motolinía. According to Ross, what distinguishes Suárez's work from that of later creoles who take recourse to the archive of the conquest is his privileging of oral sources and orality over written works. Orality, she says, represents "the creole voice of the author" (144).

9. As I detail in chapter 6, Catalá's *Para una lectura americana del barroco mexicano* presents a notable, valuable exception to disregard of the creole Mexican Archive found in literary histories of Mexico.

10. In Peru, the Franciscan Buenaventura de Salinas y Córdova's *Memorial de las historias del Nuevo Mundo, Pirú* (1630), a text that offers hyperbolic praise of Lima and the creoles, had a similarly catalytic effect on creole writing. My last chapter discusses the neglected *Memorial* (and its possible connections to Balbuena's poem) at some length.

CHAPTER I

1. In Spanish, the lines from *Los heraldos negros* quoted in the first two paragraphs read as follows: "eje ultranervioso" ("Líneas," page 68 of the Las Américas edition); "la doncella plenitud del 1," "unidad excelsa . . . que es uno / por todos" ("Absoluta" 65); "lábrase la raza en mi palabra" ("Nostalgias imperiales" 41); "Mas ¿no puedes, Señor, . . . contra lo que acaba?" ("Absoluta" 65). The translations of the lines that appear in the text are mine but see the bilingual edition of the book, *The Black Heralds,* trans. Richard Schaaf and Kathleen Ross (Pittsburgh: LALR Press, 1990). Schaaf and Ross more precisely translate "plafones" as the architectural term "soffits." Since a soffit holds up a roof or

holds a building's columns together, I have translated the word less technically, as "platform."

2. Since Bosch's life and works remain shrouded in mystery, it is not known if or to what degree he was aware of European contact with the New World. In retrospect, however, it is practically irresistible not to view his painting of multiple worlds, exotica, travel, desire, and forbidden knowledge as emblematic of the times.

3. On the diversification of New World trade and markets that resulted in a loss of profit for the Spanish empire, see Boyer; Elliott, *Old World* chap. 3; Lynch, chap. 7; John T. TePaske and Herbert S. Klein, "The Seventeenth-Century Crisis in New Spain: Myth or Reality," *Past and Present* 90 (1981): 116–135.

4. According to Burkholder ("Bureaucrats" 90), from 1610 to 1687 creoles received 24.2 percent of initial appointments to colonial Audiencias, and from 1687 to 1750, 74.1 percent of the posts.

5. For the standard account of the alternativa, see Israel, chap. 3. I also derive my information on the clergy from Burkholder and Johnson, chap. 3.

6. Here, and throughout the book, I generally silently modernize most orthography in Spanish but not diction or punctuation.

7. Brading notes that early creole identity coalesced around "anguish, nostalgia and resentment" and that reports creoles addressed to the crown in the 1590s "both reiterate earlier grievances and introduce themes that were to haunt the creole mind until the attainment of Independence" (293). Excellent sources on the creoles and encomienda as well as on other aspects of the creole platform also include Bacigalupo, Benítez, Gallegos Rocafull, Israel, Liss, Pagden ("Identity Formation"), and Paz.

8. See Sigüenza's *Infortunios*, 31, *8–9*, and Sor Juana's Romance #37, in vol. 1 of her *Obras completas*.

9. Jean Bodin, *Methodus ad facilem historiarum cognitionem* (1566) and Juan Huarte de San Juan, *Examen de ingenios para las ciencias* (1575).

10. In Peru, *Crónica moralizada del orden de San Agustín en el Perú* (1639) by the creole Antonio de la Calancha, discussed briefly in chapter 7, contributed signally to the debate.

11. Foster's concept of "conquest culture," I believe, is central to an understanding of the colonial worlds. Foster writes, "A conquest culture is the result of processes that screen the more dynamic, expanding culture [of the donor culture, in this case, Spain], winnowing out and discarding a high percentage of all traits, complexes, and configurations found in it and determining new contexts and combinations for export. It is the result of a process in which the new face of the donor culture is precipitated out of the infinite variety of original forms and enriched by the elements produced by the contact situation itself" (12). The conquest culture of the New Worlds, in other words, rep-

resents a calculated "stripping down" or simplification of full-bodied Spanish culture (15).

12. James Lockhart and Stuart B. Schwartz present a diagram of this conventional city layout in *Early Latin America* (Cambridge: Cambridge University Press, 1983), 67.

13. See Lavallé, chap. 7. In addition to the many works of this ilk from the seventeenth century that fall under the aegis of the Spectacular City and that I will examine, one might also mention Alonso de Ovalle, *Histórica relación del reino de Chile* (1646); Juan Mogrovejo de la Cerda, *Memorias de la gran ciudad del Cuzco cabeza de los reynos del Perú* (1690); Juan Meléndez, *Tesoros verdaderos de las Indias en la gran provincia de San Juan Bautista del Perú* (1681). Of Mogrovejo, Lavallé writes that he can overwhelm with "the prolixity of his information, to the point that his text becomes an unreadable jumble" (119).

14. Foster observes that the first monumental plazas appeared in Spain at the end of the sixteenth century, starting with the plaza of Valladolid completed in 1592. The plaza of Madrid followed, in 1619 (48). According to Kubler, Mexican plazas "are unprecedented in general European practice, but for a very few exceptions" (98). On the plaza in early colonial chronicles, also see Alvaro Félix Bolaños's illuminating "A Place to Live, A Place to Think, and a Place to Die: Sixteenth-Century Frontier Cities, Plazas, and 'Relaciones' in Spanish America," in Arias and Meléndez, eds., 275–293.

15. I feel compelled to underscore the fact that despite some similarity in our titles, Debord's book elucidates only the festival machinery of my Spectacular City, not the whole of it.

16. The official entries of rulers have religious implications that align them with Corpus Christi. Strong considers the European entries to be "rooted in a view which is almost wholly biblical, in which the king as Christ or one of his scriptural prototypes, takes possession of the New Jerusalem, in which the earthly state is directly presented as a mirror of the heavenly" (10).

17. In her excellent book on Mexican festivals, as we will see in chapter 5, Curcio-Nagy also discusses how they incorporated individuals of African descent.

18. For example, Boyer notes that in 1640 the Mexico City cabildo spent thirty-five thousand pesos, "far more than its annual income," on the festival marking the arrival of Viceroy Montesclaros (472–473).

19. See Cañeque, chap. 1, and Curcio-Nagy, chap. 2, for synthetic introductions to the Mirror for Princes genre in Mexico.

20. In Peru, the account (1569) of Viceroy Toledo's entry into Lima by Tristán Sánchez or Antonio Bautista de Salazar (Ramos Sosa 33). In Mexico, Francisco Cervantes de Salazar's *Túmulo imperial* (1560), on the incredibly elaborate funerary catafalque erected in Mexico to commemorate the death of Charles V. The tomb and its verbal recreation are often identified as the first manifestations of Mannerism in Mexico (chapter 3 herein contextualizes the advent of

Mexican Mannerism), which suggests the strong influence festivals and their chronicles could exercise on the esthetics of the times.

21. In addition to the works that enter my discussion here, I refer to such works as those of Bynum, Daston and Park, Findlen (*Possessing Nature*), Impey and MacGregor, and Philip Fisher, *Wonder, the Rainbow, and the Aesthetics of Rare Experiences* (Cambridge: Harvard University Press, 1998); *The Age of the Marvelous,* ed. Joy Kenseth (Hanover: Hood Museum of Art, 1991); John Onians, "'I wonder . . .' A short history of amazement," *Sight and Insight: Essays on Art and Culture in Honour of E. H. Gombrich at 85,* ed. John Onians (London: Phaedon, 1994) 10–33; *Merchants and Marvels: Commerce, Science, and Art in Early Modern Europe,* eds. Pamela H. Smith and Paula Findlen (New York: Routledge, 2002).

22. Daston and Park offer the delicious remark allegedly pronounced by Charles V that "Columbus should have been known not as the Admiral (*Almirante*) but as the Wonderer (*Admirans*)" (147). Greenblatt states that "the production of a sense of the marvelous in the New World is at the very center of virtually all of Columbus's writings about his discoveries" (73); see his chap. 3. Also see Greene, chap. 1, for a fine discussion of how Columbus creates "a map of sensation and affect to guide those who will soon be swarming over the Americas" (74).

23. Greenblatt writes, "It is characteristic of Columbus's discourse that it yokes together actions, attitudes, or perceptions that would seem ethically incompatible" (70). He also comments that the "production of wonder then is not only an expression of the effects that the voyages had upon Columbus but a calculated rhetorical strategy, the evocation of an aesthetic response in the service of a legitimation process" (73–74).

24. Bynum has argued for the nonappropriative nature of medieval wonder, stating, "To wonder is emphatically *not* to consume and incorporate" (24).

25. See the discussion of Oviedo in my "The First Fifty Years of Hispanic New World Historiography: The Caribbean, Mexico and Central America," on the Erasmian aspects of the author's works. In *Cambridge History,* ed. González Echevarría and Pupo-Walker (78–87).

26. Oviedo's extremely important statement on variety from his chapter on the tiger reads, "It is true from what can see of the marvels of the world and the great differences among creatures, that these differences are greater in some places than in others, according to the locality or the constellations under which these animals have been bred. We see that plants which are poisonous in some areas are healthful and useful in others; and that birds in one province are of good flavor while in other places they are not prized or eaten. Some men are black, while in other lands they are very white. *Still, they are all men*" (94, 46; emphasis added).

In Pliny one finds such statements on nature's variety as, "The power and majesty of Nature in every particular action of hers seems incredible; for to say nothing of the painted peacock's feathers, of the sundry spots of tigers and panthers, of the variable colors and marks of so many creatures besides, let us come to one point only, the variety of man's speech" (trans. Philomon Holland, *Natural History* [London: Adam Islip, 1601]) 1:153. Oviedo might also be alluding to 1 Corinthians 14:10–11: "There are, it may be, so many kinds of voices in the world, and none of them is without signification. Therefore if I know not the meaning of the voice, I shall be unto him that speaketh a barbarian, and he that speaketh shall be a barbarian unto me."

27. On the exotic, I have in mind formulations like Huggan's that "the exotic is not, as is often supposed, an inherent *quality* to be found 'in' certain people, distinctive objects, or specific places; exoticism describes, rather, a particular mode of aesthetic *perception*—one which renders people, objects and places strange even as it domesticates them, and which effectively manufactures otherness even as it claims to surrender to its immanent mystery" (15). For expansions of Elliott's claims regarding the Spanish production of the exotic, see Pagden, *European Encounters* (10–11), and Bustamante's introduction to the account by the partly apocryphal Conquistador Anónimo, who echoes Oviedo's credulous, phobic list of damning Indian practices (Madrid: Polifemo, 1968). Finally, vital to any understanding of the enticements and limits of exoticizing in colonial Spanish American discourse is Rolena Adorno's "Literary Production and Suppression: Reading and Writing about Amerindians in Colonial Spanish America," *Dispositio* 11, nos. 28–29 (1986): 1–25.

28. As is well known, the most famous exponent of magical realism, Gabriel García Márquez, noted in his Nobel Prize acceptance speech of 1982, "The Solitude of America" (available on many websites) that the infinite stimuli for the imagination that Latin America provides should not blind readers to its serious problems, which also need to be seen.

29. Spadaccini and Martín-Estudillo's introduction to *Hispanic Baroques* (ix–xxxvi) synthesizes critiques of Maravall for the inadequacy of his account with regard to the ruptures of the guided culture by discrepant voices and alternative positions.

30. I allude here succinctly to a complex situation that other scholars have treated at length. On the geographic problematics of a *mundus alterius,* a standard reference is Edmundo O'Gorman, *The Invention of America* (Bloomington: Indiana University Press, 1961) 94–104. Daniel J. Boorstin's *The Discoverers* (New York: Random House, 1983), esp. part 7, offers excellent historical grounding.

31. Endorsing Ryan, in 1995 the ever-judicious Elliott qualified the views he had put forth in 1970: "I suspect that, in common with many others, I overemphasized the degree of indifference shown by early modern Europeans to the new discoveries" ("Final Reflections" 395).

32. Ryan neatly deems this a means of disguising novelty in the name of tradition (524). Historiographic syncretism has received a worthy treatment from Ryan, by the scores of literary scholars who have discussed the Inca Garcilaso

de la Vega's syncretic *Comentarios reales,* and by Catalá and Paz. From historians see Brading (whose *First America* is indispensable on the subject), Elliott, Huddleston, Keen, and Pagden *(European Encounters).* Also see Don Cameron Allen, *The Legend of Noah* (Urbana: University of Illinois Press, 1949); Giuliano Gliozzi, *Adamo e il nuovo mondo: la nascita dell'antropologia come ideologia coloniale* (Florence: La nuova Italia, 1977); Mario Góngora, *Studies in the Colonial History of Spanish America,* trans. Richer Southern (Cambridge: Cambridge University Press, 1975), chaps. 5, 6; Margaret T. Hogden, *Early Anthropology in the Sixteenth and Seventeenth Centuries* (Philadelphia: University of Pennsylvania Press, 1964), esp. chaps. 8, 10; Sabine MacCormack, "Limits of Understanding: Perceptions of Greco-Roman and Amerindian Paganism in Early Modern Europe," *America in European Consciousness: 1493-1750,* ed. Karen Kupperman, 79–129 (Chapel Hill: University of North Carolina Press, 1995).

33. The Inca Garcilaso de la Vega articulates the obligatory nature of the debate. He begins the body of his *Comentarios reales* (1609) with the following words: "In treating the New World . . . in accordance with the common custom of writers it would seem to be appropriate to treat here at the beginning whether the world is only one, or if there are many worlds" (Enrique Pupo-Walker, ed. [Madrid: Cátedra, 1996]) 143.

34. Torquemada's prologue to vol. 2, book 7 of his *Monarquía* articulates the issue precisely, if not concisely: "one of my aims in writing this long and prolix History has been to establish that the practices of these Indians, both in their religious observance and customs, were not their own inventions, born of their own whims, but that other Men of the World shared them, and that the Indians did nothing that was not a custom or feat of the ancients; and that everything, or most everything, that these other Nations of the World did can be verified and confirmed in this nation" (2:85).

35. It is important to note, along with Keen (chap. 7), the backlash against the Indians that had installed itself in Spain and Spanish discourse because of the so-called Black Legend propagated by Las Casas's *Brevísima relación de la destrucción de las Indias* (1552). The backlash was still strong in the seventeenth century.

36. See Fernando Cervantes, *The Devil in the New World: The Impact of Diabolism in New Spain* (New Haven: Yale University Press, 1994), for an examination of the modifications that the concept of the devil underwent in the New World and the Old during the colonial period.

37. With regard to the pleasurable management of the new, two familiar theoretical formulations deserve mention. First, Certeau's statement on New World travelogues: "What travel literature really fabricates is the primitive as a *body of pleasure*" (*Writing* 226). Second, Foucault's assertion that power "doesn't only weigh on us as a force that says no, but . . . it traverses and produces things, it induces pleasure, forms knowledge, produces discourse" (*The Foucault Reader,* ed. Paul Rabinow [New York: Pantheon]), 60.

38. According to Mignolo, "While the concept of *Renaissance* refers to a rebirth of classical legacies and the constitution of humanistic scholarship for human emancipation and *early modern period* emphasizes the emergence of a genealogy that announces the modern and the postmodern, the darker side of the Renaissance underlines, instead, the rebirth of the classical tradition as a justification of colonial expansion and the emergence of a genealogy (the early colonial period) that announces the modern and the postmodern" (vii).

39. Or not so insouciantly, at least in the case of *Don Quixote*. Diana de Armas Wilson, among others, views the novel as an ironic appraisal of Spain's imperial agenda. Her book adds several interesting pieces to the long-standing conversation on the presence of the New World in the *Quixote* and in other works by Cervantes.

40. In the early modern period the category of monsters included everything from the biblical pygmies and giants to figures from medieval lore, humans with birth defects and conjoined twins. As what Foucault calls a "natural form of the unnatural" (*Abnormal,* trans. Graham Burchel [New York: Picador, 2003], 56) and of category crisis, the so-called monsters that were traditionally viewed as divine portents served as apt vehicles by which to index "conditions of acute instability: foreign invasion, religious conflict, civil strife"(Daston and Park 187). Hence, they have warranted much critical attention. See, for example, *Wonders, Marvels, and Monsters in Early Modern Culture,* ed. Peter G. Platt (Newark: University of Delaware Press, 1999), and, with regard to Spain, Elena del Río Parra, *Una era de monstruos: Representaciones de lo deforme en el Siglo de Oro español* (Pamplona and Frankfurt: Universidad de Navarra and Vervuet, 2003). Along with Daston and Park (chap. 5), Río Parra (chap. 3) underscores the telling fact that Europeans, bombarded with news of the New World, paid more attention to local monsters than to exogamous ones. The great interest that Siamese or conjoined twins prompted is no less telling, suggesting, as it does, the way in which they literally conjoin self and other, the natural and the unnatural, thrills and chills.

41. Gracián's Baroque efforts are in fact omnivorous. They encompass not just seventeenth-century poetry but also classical, patristic, and Renaissance works, all of which he rates according to the degree of dissonance and mystery they present. Gracián thereby reviews and rewrites the poetic canon in keeping with his Baroque criteria.

42. As a Jesuit living in Cataluña, Gracián found himself directly embroiled in the battles between the Jesuits and the French Jansenists of the 1640s. Further, Gracián's *Criticón* (1651–1657) occasioned the famous conflicts between its author and his own order.

43. The multiple, broad, difficult works of Gracián lend themselves to a variety of approaches and have rather recently begun to receive their critical due in such works as Spadacinni and Talens's collection. See Edward H. Friedman's

"Afterword: Constructing Gracián" in that volume (355–372) for an insightful survey of new contributions to Gracián studies.

44. One recalls here Walter Benjamin's statement that the German Baroque "pile[s] up fragments ceaselessly," "in the unremitting expectation of a miracle" (178). Chapter 5 herein returns to this notion of the Baroque.

45. Apart from Leonard's *Baroque Times* (examined in chapter 7), those who view the Baroque as a wholly negative force in the New World tend to do so from a Marxist perspective. I refer to such influential scholars as Leonardo Acosta, Rama, and Vidal. John Beverley espouses the negative position in his 1987 book and in *Una modernidad obsoleta: Estudios sobre el barroco* (Los Teques, Venezuela: A.L.E.M., 1997) but shifts gears in "Nuevas vacilaciones sobre el barroco," in *Crítica y descolonización,* ed. González Stephan and Costigan (289–301).

46. Braider appropriately notes that the "baroque marks the moment when Europeans begin to digest the far-reaching implications of the accumulated social, intellectual, religious and geographical upheavals of the preceding age" (9). Other important works on the Baroque as wrought of tensions, reconciled or not, include Coutinho; Mary Gaylord, "The Making of Baroque Poetry" *The Cambridge History of Spanish Literature,* ed. David T. Gies, 222–237 (Cambridge: Cambridge University Press, 2004); Helmut Hatzfeld, *Estudios sobre el barroco* (Madrid: Gredos, 1964); Lowry Nelson Jr., *Baroque Lyric Poetry* (New York: Octagon [1961] 1979); Harold B. Segal, *The Baroque Poem* (New York: Dutton, 1974); Frank J. Warnke, *Versions of Baroque: European Literature in the Seventeenth Century* (New Haven: Yale University Press, 1972); René Wellek, *Concepts of Criticism* (New Haven: Yale University Press, 1963); Heinrich Wölfflin, *Principles of Art History,* trans. M. D. Hottinger (London: G. Bell and Sons, 1932).

47. For a synopsis of the "New World Baroque as difference" debate, see González Echevarría, "Colonial Lyric."

48. Most recent discussions consider New World writers to have utilized the Baroque in some measure strategically, defensively, and subversively. I refer the reader, for example, to the texts listed in my Works Cited by the following authors: Blanco, Bolívar Echeverría, Coutinho, González Echevarría, Martínez-San Miguel, Mazzotti, Moraña, O'Gorman, Paz, Picón-Salas, Ross, and Sabat de Rivers.

CHAPTER 2

1. I have not encountered any commentary expressly on Rama's conflation of the sixteenth- and seventeenth-century city. However, in noting that Rama's monolithic ciudad letrada overemphasizes hegemony to the detriment of resistance, Mabel Moraña suggestively states, "I think that the fundamental prob-

lem lies in the ambiguity and historical continuity on which the concept of the letrado that unites Rama's book is based. This term, which in its purest form seems best to apply to the colonial period, acquires distinct inflections in the first stage of imperial domination, and then in creole society and in the context of viceregal Baroque culture, when the emerging creole consciousness utilizes Metropolitan discourses but infuses them with a contestatory, vindictive tone." From "De *La ciudad letrada* al imaginario nacionalista: Contribuciones de Angel Rama a la invención de América," *Esplendores y miserias,* ed. Beatriz González Stephan et al., 47 (Caracas: Monte Avila, 1995).

2. My discussion of Botticelli clearly plays off Camile Paglia's in chap. 5 of *Sexual Personae: Art and Decadence from Nefertiti to Emily Dickinson* (New York: Vintage, 1991), esp. 150–151.

3. This is not, of course, to say that all enactments of the genres listed here relate to the New World.

4. In *The Order of Things* (1966), Foucault purposely detaches his definition of the episteme from concrete phenomena or circumstances: "what I am attempting to bring to light is the epistemological field, the *episteme* in which knowledge, envisaged apart from all criteria having reference to its rational value or to its objective forms, grounds its positivity" (xxii). A few years later, in *The Archaeology of Knowledge* (1969), Foucault comments on his previous position: "Lastly, in *The Order of Things,* my attention was concentrated mainly on the networks of concepts and their rules of formation. . . . The place, and the implications of the strategic choices were indicated . . . but I did little more than locate them and my analysis scarcely touched on their formation" (trans. A. M. Sheridan Smith [New York: Pantheon, 1972]), 65. Accordingly, the preponderance of Foucault's works remedy this lack.

5. Though it lies beyond the scope and purposes of my study to delve into the utopian thought that impacted the New World and that Georges Baudot has explored so well, I refer the reader to Beatriz Pastor Bodmer's *El jardín y el peregrino: Ensayos sobre el pensamiento utópico latinoamericano 1492–1695* (Amsterdam: Rodopi, 1996). Chapter 7 of Pastor's book, "Figuraciones del miedo," offers a fine treatment of the relationship between utopian thought and European anxiety vis-à-vis the New World.

6. Tlatelolco, north of Tenochtitlán and joined to it by a major causeway, was brought under Aztec rule during the reign of Axayáctl (1469–1481) and remained under Aztec control until it fell to Spanish domination in 1521. Tlatelolco housed a thriving market as well as several temples, including a Templo Mayor similar in construction to that of central Tenochtitlán and dedicated to the same gods, Huitzilopochtli and Tlaloc. On archeological excavations of Tlatelolco, see Eduardo Matos Moctezuma, *The Aztecs* (New York: Rizzoli, 1989), 203–208.

7. Cortés displays familiarity with notions of community and polis in his letter of 1519, "De la justicia y regimiento de la Rica Villa de la Veracruz a la

reina doña Juana y al emperador Carlos V, su hijo," now generally accepted as his first account from the New World. Chaps. 3–4 of Pagden (*Fall*) discuss the influence of the Aristotelian polis on Spanish debates regarding the New World.

8. Martínez-San Miguel discusses Cortés's aporia in her "Poder y narración: Representación y mediación de un deseo americano en la *Segunda carta de relación*." In *Agencias criollas,* ed. Mazzotti (99–130).

9. On Prescott's and Cortés's Moctezuma, see my "Civilización y barbarie: Prescott como lector de Cortés," *La historia en la literatura iberoamericana,* ed. Raquel Chang-Rodríguez and Gabriela de Beer, 87–96 (Hanover: Ediciones del Norte, 1989). Margo Glantz provides a fascinating discussion of the "counterfeits" in which she notes their absence from the Fourth Letter. See her "Ciudad y escritura: La Ciudad de México en las 'Cartas de relación,'" *Hispamérica* 19, 56–57 (1990): 164–174.

10. Several recent treatments of wonder deal with its negative valences, especially Campbell, introduction; Daston and Park, chap. 3; Onian.

11. In his "Carta al ama" Columbus supplies the subtext and a scholium to the *Tercera relación,* which develops his theory of the New World as terrestrial paradise.

12. When in 1528 Cortés returned to Spain, where he would die, the conqueror entered a circle of humanists. He formed in his home a kind of humanist academy that included Cervantes de Salazar. See J. H. Elliott's classic article, "The Mental World of Hernán Cortés," *Transactions of the Royal Historical Society* 17 (1967): 57. It is difficult if not impossible to determine the degree to which humanism had affected Cortés's prior thinking.

13. More's fictitious New World may nevertheless have inspired the millennial kingdom that the Franciscans strove to implant in Mexico, a utopian project that shared many of the *Utopia*'s Reformation features and ascetic aspirations.

14. Lara (102) also discerns in Philip II's urban-planning ordinances of 1573 veiled references to Ezekiel and Revelation.

15. Much as it imposed imported forms, the new Hispanic city also availed itself of the order that had characterized Tenochtitlán. Reconstructed entirely by Indian labor, colonial Mexico City utilized not only the foundations of Aztec buildings but also the broad avenues that had structured the Aztec city. Kubler concludes that "the Indian civic armature was found to be highly suitable" to Spanish needs (102).

16. Lara (103) attributes the unfortified state of colonial Mexico City either to the Spaniards' confidence that they had pacified the Indians or to biblical prophecies that the godly New Jerusalem will need no material protection. Zechariah 2:4–5, for example, reads: "Jerusalem shall be inhabited as towns without walls" for God "will be unto her a wall of fire."

17. Cervantes de Salazar makes the statement in Latin, in a letter that appears in Alonso de la Veracruz's *Dialectica resolutio cum textu Aristotelis* (1554).

I translate the Spanish version of the letter that O'Gorman's edition of Cervantes's dialogues provides (xxxvii).

18. Art historians like Kubler and James Early (*The Colonial Architecture of Mexico* [Albuquerque: University of New Mexico Press, 1994]), together with historians like O'Gorman and Benítez, have combed the text in this fashion. In his edition of the dialogues, O'Gorman even constructs a map of the walking tours. The earliest modern edition of Cervantes de Salazar's text (in Latin and Spanish), by the incomparable Joaquín García Icazbalceta—*México en 1554: Tres diálogos latinos* (Mexico: Antigua Librería de Andrade y Morales, 1875)—provides later scholars with vast amounts of information, especially on the marketplace and its wares. However, I quote from the English translation because of its easy availability to the reader as well as the quality of its introduction and annotations. The English edition also includes the Latin, photocopied from the single extant original held at the University of Texas. Since titles of the whole work vary, also for easy reference I have chosen to call it the *Dialogues*.

19. I refer to Bono, Liss, Christian. Also, Rolena Adorno, "The Warrior and the War Community: Constructions of the Civil Order in Mexican Conquest History," *Dispositio* 14, nos. 36–38 (1989): 225–246; Karl Kohut, *Pensamiento europeo y cultura colonial* (Frankfurt: Vervuet, 1997); Sergio Rivera-Ayala, "Riding High, the Horseman's View: Urban Space and Body in *México en 1554*," in Arias and Meléndez 251–274. Margarita Peña's excellent article on the Mexico City dialogues, first published in 1981, now stands as the introduction to her edition of the text: *México en 1554* (Mexico: Trillas, 1986).

20. On the possible role of Mendoza, along with the author's wealthy cousin, in luring Cervantes de Salazar to Mexico, see O'Gorman's edition, xvii. In general, I cull the biographical information on Cervantes de Salazar from Benítez, Bono, Castañeda, Icazbalceta, O'Gorman, and Peña. For a later account of Mexico City by Cervantes, which displays fuller knowledge of the city, a lesser investment in atemporal humanism, and greater involvement with creole encomienda issues, see book IV, chaps. 24–25 of his *Crónica de la Nueva España*.

21. Cervantes presents himself as an outstanding professor who persists where others have given up (31), as a member of the colonial nobility (53), as the veritable Savior of youth from "death and oblivion" for imparting knowledge to them (72), and more.

22. Among the conceivable points of convergence between Alberti's and Cervantes de Salazar's dialogues on Mexico City, I note the importance attached to planned public spaces, prescriptions for the symmetry and colonnades of the plaza and for the uniformity of other construction, and the importance of winds in determining the city's location. Kubler observes that Italianate theory was already in practice in the city's buildings. Hence, he argues that Cervantes is not describing a wholly ideal city (100). Nevertheless, one has to wonder if a

person taking a normal walk through the city in 1554 would have found it all that recognizable from Cervantes's description.

23. As Sergio Rivera-Ayala writes, the work "displays an image of the Mexican capital in which the order and harmony of its space appear as inherent characters of the colonial structure" (in Arias and Meléndez 251).

24. Indeed, in his later, more creole-involved *Crónica,* Cervantes states that the *Dialogues* had intended to notify all nations of "the grandeur and majesty" of the city (316).

25. On pages 50–51, for example, Zamora remarks that Dr. López's children now occupy their father's house and that the children "have degenerated no whit from the integrity of their father." Quoting Cicero, Alfaro retorts, "There will not, therefore, be any reason to fear that well-known saying, 'O ancient house, by what a different master you are ruled!'" Such comments, in addition to the other ways in which Cervantes praises the elite, bolster creoles' claims for the perpetuation of the privileges accorded their forebears.

26. Peña states, "The alterity of this New World is not largely conveyed by its buildings, which . . . almost always imitate those of the Metropolis, but instead by its products, exhibited in the *tianguís* [market], and language" (141); and "New Spain's *tianguís* appears in the dialogue like a gigantic panacea, all of whose herbs are 'blessed medicines'" (145).

27. Campbell's references to the "multiculturalism of seventeenth-century English consumer culture" (242) that rendered palatable "what bourgeois Europe could and would not swallow morally (culturally)" (238), together with Certeau on the "intellectual edibility" of Tupi natives in Jean de Léry's account (*Writing* 224, 231), help shape my formulation.

28. For example, Castañeda, in his introduction to the English edition of the dialogues; Liss, in her chap. 6; and Peña all take Alfaro's statement at face value and as evidence of Cervantes's laudable, sincere espousal of transculturation.

29. The engraving by Jan van der Straet/Stradanus that Certeau discusses in chap. 5 of *The Writing of History* in conjunction with visibility and knowability (even mentioning Botticelli), and that has received exorbitant critical attention, constitutes but one of many such porno-tropical depictions of America. Representations of America as a naked or seminaked woman quickly became a commonplace in the sixteenth century.

30. The autobiographical, Mexico City portion of the "Epístola" appears in Méndez Plancarte, *Poetas, Primer siglo* (20–22). In her introduction to the anthology of Spanish and some Mexican Italianate poets published in Mexico in 1577, *Flores de baria poesía* (Mexico City: Secretaría de Educación Pública, 1987) 17–19, Margarita Peña supports the possibility that Cueva compiled the work. In other words, he came, saw, and compiled an anthology! Peña conjectures that Cueva's "Epístola" does not appear in the volume owing to the poem's abundant "Mexicanisms" and lack of Italianate loftiness (37).

31. In a sonnet to his brother, "Al Inquisidor Claudio de la Cueva, mi hermano, estando en México," Cueva vents the lost pleasures, tears, annoyances, and painful memories their mutual stay in Mexico has occasioned. At the end of the poem, however, the author remarks that he and his brother must restrain their tears: "que no es gloria en esta parte / mostrar a los vencidos los despojos" [for in these parts there is no honor in revealing the wreckage to the vanquished] (in Méndez Plancarte, *Poetas, Primer siglo* 23).

32. According to Horacio Jorge Becco, *Poesía colonial hispanoamericana* (Caracas: Ayacucho, 1990), Salazar y Alarcón served in the Audiencias of Santo Domingo, Guatemala, and then Mexico. He obtained his doctorate in Mexico and went on to become minister of the Council of the Indies in 1601. He died in Spain (33).

33. In *Poetas, Primer siglo,* Méndez Plancarte presents substantial portions of the two poems by Salazar y Alarcón but prunes or omits many of their excesses to render them more fit subjects for a Mexican literary canon. To really experience these poems, for better or for worse, one needs to read them in full in Gallardo's *Ensayo de una biblioteca española de libros raros y curiosos,* from which I cite.

34. The date of the "Bucólica" has not been ascertained. However, Méndez Plancarte places Salazar's quite similar poem addressed to Herrera around 1597 (62).

35. The *Décadas* (1530) of Pedro Mártir de Anglería (Pietro Martire d'Anghiera), who never set foot in the colonies, style the New World as Hesiod's Golden Age, an Arcadia where nymphlike creatures still romp, a prelapsarian natural society.

36. Méndez Plancarte states, "The Shepherd and his Shepherdess are the viceregal couple, the Marquis and Marquise de Villamanrique: Doña Blanca Henríquez, y D. Alvaro (here Albár) Manrique de Zúñiga" (*Poetas, Primer siglo* 62). I leave it to the reader to ponder which is stranger, the reality of the twin names or the poetic treatment Salazar accords them. In any case, Gallardo includes on page 362 of his compilation a sonnet by Salazar entitled "A doña Blanca Henríquez, marquesa de Villamanrique, virreina de Nueva España" (it begins, "Blanca sobre las blancas"), which leaves no doubt that the two pastoral figures of the poem represent the viceroy and vicereine.

CHAPTER 3

1. There are several excellent shorter pieces on *La grandeza mexicana,* including those that I cite plus Oswaldo Pardo, "Giovanni Botero and Bernardo de Balbuena: Art and Economy in *La grandeza mexicana,*" *Journal of Latin American Cultural Studies* 10, no. 1 (2001): 103–117, and Daniel Torres, "De la utopía poética en *Grandeza mexicana* de Bernardo de Balbuena," *Calíope* 4, nos. 1–2

(1998): 86–93. However, there have been no modern book-length studies of Balbuena's work after Van Horne's and Rojas Garcidueñas's early monographs. Neither are there detailed, analytical, recent treatments of the trajectory of the poet's oeuvre. For bibliography on Balbuena, see Goic, González Boixo, and Sabat de Rivers *Estudios* 43–48; for biographical information, see Van Horne, *Bernardo de Balbuena*. I began to gain a sense of *Grandeza*'s signal importance when writing my "Spectacular Cityscapes" essay (Merrim 2004). The present chapter builds on and greatly extends the discussion of Balbuena in that essay.

2. Though I differ from Ryjik in arguing that *Siglo de oro* ultimately reaffirms the pastoral forest as a poetic space, my understanding of the text has profited greatly from her study of pastoral topics in Balbuena.

3. As Balbuena makes clear in the introduction to *Grandeza* (55–57), Isabel de Tobar herself was not lacking in illustrious family connections, given that she was related to the Spanish Duke de Lerma. Balbuena opts for more immediate and conceivably efficacious connections (especially since Tobar's entry into the convent seems to have provoked some kind of scandal [*Grandeza* 57]) in redirecting the addressee of *Grandeza* to the archbishop. Moreover, upon its first publication there appear to have been two versions of *Grandeza*, each dedicated to a different personage: (1) the principal edition, dedicated to Archbishop García de Mendoza y Zúñiga; (2) and a limited edition that replaces the first eight pages of *Grandeza* with a laudatory poem to the Count de Lemos, president of the Council of the Indies in Spain. Though there has been much debate on the nature of the two editions, recent scholars tend to espouse the explanation just offered, first formulated by Francisco Monterde in the prologue to his edition of *Grandeza mexicana* (Mexico City: UNAM, 1954) xli, xlv.

4. Although *Siglo de oro* contains a brief debate on the relationship between love and money (196), *El Bernardo* evinces a conventional scorn of interés (see Sabat de Rivers, *Estudios* 29–30). "Grandeza"'s favorable position on the matter in the context of the wealthy city is thus unique in Balbuena's works.

5. However, Jardine argues with regard to Europe that "by the beginning of the sixteenth century the opinion was being voiced that the merchant's was a noble profession, since it achieved prosperity for nations without war or aggression." Jardine cites the Portuguese Tomé Pires's survey of East Indies trading opportunities, the *Suma Oriental* (1515), which contains the following statement compatible with Balbuena's position: "Trading in merchandise is so necessary that without it the world would not go on. It is this that ennobles kingdoms and makes their peoples great, that ennobles cities, that brings war and peace" (327).

6. Ryjik notes the relative anonymity of the human characters that populate "Grandeza" (593).

7. I here follow the distinction between wonders as objects and wonder as a passion that Daston and Park establish on page 13 of their book and maintain throughout it.

8. On the multiple functions of the wonder cabinet see Daston and Park, chap. 2; Findlen; Mark A. Meadow, "Merchants and Marvels: Hans Jacob Fugger and the Origins of the Wunderkammer," *Merchants and Marvels*, 182–200 (reference in my chap. 1, note 21); Julian Raby, "Exotica from Islam," in Impey and MacGregor 251–258.

9. Stewart (chap. 5) and Findlen (chap. 7) discuss the role of collections in Renaissance self-fashioning. I take the term "semiophore" from Pomian, chap. 1. According to Pomian, when an object is incorporated into a collection it loses practical or use value but gains in exchange value and meaning. Clearly, the same or a magnified version of the transformation occurs in textualized objects.

10. Daston and Park, chap. 7, discuss at length the collapsing of the art–nature opposition in wonder cabinet objects. See also John Dixon Hunt, "*Curiosities* to adorn *Cabinets* and *Gardens*," in Impey and MacGregor, 193–203.

11. Dubois writes that while "periods of 'classical' production are linked to periods of unitary, often centralized, politics, to nations whose life is internally oriented," Baroque periods seem "linked to expansion, imperialism, to conquest by greater powers within the nation," and Mannerist periods "respond either to the decomposition of centralized organization or to the tyrannical reinforcement" of that organization. He also notes that Mannerism is defined by "gaps" and by "the expression of internal confliction" (182).

12. Phelan and Lafaye are important sources on the transition from the Mendicant orders to the Jesuits.

13. I owe this new information on the relationship between Rubio and Cárdenas to Domingo Ledezma. It appeared in chap. 3 of his doctoral dissertation at Brown University, "El paraíso en América: un aporte de los jesuitas en las historias naturales, 1591–1668" (2003).

14. The *Ratio atque institutio studiorum* (still the underpinnings of Jesuit pedagogy) held fast in its 1599 form until 1832. Vicencio Lanuchi, founder of the first Jesuit *colegio* in Mexico, apparently had serious doubts about the appropriateness of the audacious, liberal humanistic curriculum for New World students (Gonzalbo Aizpuru 135, 165). On Jesuit education in Mexico, also see Gerard Decorme, *La obra de los jesuítas mexicanos durante la época colonial, 1572–1767*, vol. 1 (Mexico City: Robredo, 1941).

15. Manrique's contribution to the Metropolitan Museum exhibit catalogue, *Mexico: Splendors of Thirty Centuries* (New York: Bulfinch Press, 1990), 237–242, refers tantalizingly on page 240 to treatises by Alberti, Serlio, Vignola, and Sagredo brought to Mexico by the first trained European artists and architects to infiltrate the colony. Of these treatises, as indicated in the body of the chapter, I have found Sebastian Serlio's work (translated into English by Vaughan Hart and Peter Hicks as *Sebastiano Serlio on Architecture* [New Haven: Yale University Press, 1996]), to be particularly suggestive for Mexican Mannerist literature.

16. In her *Historia de la literatura mexicana: periodo colonial* (Mexico City: Alhambra, 1989), 54, Margarita Peña posits the existence in the Mexico City of the times of one or more poetic academies, similar to those found in contemporary Seville. The anthology of Spanish and some radicado Mexican poets published in Mexico in 1577, *Flores de baria poesía,* which Peña edited (reference in my chap. 2, note 30), bears out her claim that collective literary activity and a sense of affiliation existed in the colony from at least the last quarter of the sixteenth century on.

17. Rama's dense, seminal article "Fundación del manierismo hispanoamericano por Bernardo de Balbuena" (1983) associates the birth of Latin American poetry in Balbuena with Mannerism. According to Rama, the characteristics that affiliate "Grandeza" with Mannerism—the work's epigonic relationship to European literary tradition, its hyperbole, its self-conscious artifice—all reflect a consciousness of the New World as a differential and marginal yet culminating space. Rama concludes that Balbuena's Mannerist poetry represents "a culture in the process of expanding that projected itself in space and time and generated an aberrant circuit whose energy rebounded onto itself" (21). I emphatically agree with Rama's conclusion and focus, especially his contention that Balbuena's tradition-fracturing Mannerist innovations "subvert the entire structure of the model, confuse its proportions, conjure away its centers of signification, and dissolve its rhythms and hierarchies, thus permitting an undeclared original work indirectly to emerge and to communicate a new message" (14). However, my reading of "Grandeza" strives to anchor it more specifically in the Mexican Mannerist context, which included writers other than Balbuena and which significantly impacted the poem in ways Rama does not consider.

18. I have in mind Michel Serres's construction of Hermes in *Hermes: Literature, Science, Philosophy,* ed. Josué Harari and David F. Bell (Baltimore: Johns Hopkins University Press, 1982). Rudolph Schevill's classic *Ovid and the Renascence in Spain* (Berkeley: University of California, 1913) still provides valuable background on the currency and metamorphoses of Ovid's work during the Renaissance in Europe.

19. Daston and Park 274. With regard to Ovid's influence on wonder cabinet collections, also see William B. Ashworth, "Remarkable Humans and Singular Beasts," *The Age of the Marvelous,* esp. 118, 139 (reference in my chap. 1, note 21).

20. González Echevarría aptly notes that the world of "Grandeza" is "made up, precisely, by the products of artifice. Art, industry, and craft, define each place and culture, in the same way that the poem itself is the result of art. *Grandeza mexicana* is a tribute to the artificial, to the artful, and the artful's most elaborate product is the city" ("Colonial Lyric" 210).

21. "Grandeza"'s women as flowers and convent as garden or paradise likely influenced Carlos de Sigüenza y Góngora's depiction of the Mexico City Convent of Jesús María in his *Parayso Occidental* (1684).

22. Beyond the poem mentioned here, "Oda a la vida retirada," Luis de León writes in *Los nombres de Cristo*, "pastoral life is calm and removed from the noise of the cities, and from their vices and pleasures" (1:466).

23. As Thomas Gage reports of Mexico City in 1625, church rooftops were in fact coated with gold (71). That Balbuena's hyperbolic descriptions of Mexico City, such as the claim of golden rooftops, were less exaggerated than they appear to be is the thesis of Chester C. Christian's discussion of "Grandeza."

24. See *Grandeza*, 13, 38, 114. The relative transparency of the poem's epilogue, which the poet appears to have devised after writing the body of the poem and in light of early reactions to it, may reflect an effort on Balbuena's part to pull back from the dense new esthetic of "Grandeza."

25. Several distinguished scholars, conceivably following on Pedro Henríquez Ureña's pathbreaking assertion that Balbuena represents "a new and independent form of *barroquismo*" (*La cultura y las letras coloniales en Santo Domingo* [Buenos Aires: Universidad de Buenos Aires, 1936], 55), have made this claim. See, for example, González Echevarría, "Colonial Lyric" 211; Reyes 78; Roggiano 217-21; Sabat de Rivers, *Estudios* 41. Also Emilio Carilla, *El gongorismo en América* (Buenos Aires: Instituto de Cultura Latino-Americana, 1946), 29.

26. José Moreno Villa's *Lo mexicano en las artes plásticas* (Mexico City: El Colegio de México, 1948) and George Kubler's *The Shape of Time: Remarks on the History of Things* (New Haven: Yale University Press, 1962) have been influential in this regard.

27. Rama clearly appears to have derived his conflation of the Ordered City and the Lettered City, which I discussed in chapter 2, from Mumford's dual view of the absolutist city. Certainly, the Ordered City did not disappear in colonial Latin America; it stands to this day. However, as argued previously, I believe that Rama (and Mumford?) skipped a vital historical step in not separating the sixteenth- from the seventeenth-century city.

28. I also draw my reading of Rama from Mabel Moraña's trenchant critique, "De *La ciudad letrada* al imaginario nacionalista: Contribuciones de Angel Rama a la invención de América" (reference in my chap. 2, note 1). For other critiques of Rama's focus on dominant practices, see *Angel Rama y los estudios latinoamericanos*, ed. Mabel Moraña (Pittsburgh: Instituto Internacional de Literatura Iberoamericana, 1997).

29. According to the "Compendio," the order and harmony of Pythagoreanism both originate from God: "God composed the order and course of the centuries like an exquisite poem" (132). Balbuena could hardly dispense with what he viewed as so divinely authorized an esthetic or episteme.

30. Hence, Roggiano states that "the narration immerses itself and even drowns in descriptions overloaded with enumeration" (220); Picón-Salas asserts that in Balbuena one no longer finds "great panoramic art with a central theme and narrative unity" but instead "a marked preference for pictur-

esque detail" (95); González Boixo captures the matter exactly in saying that Balbuena's happy return to the city "could even explain the most prominent literary characteristic of the poem: its accumulation of images and objects, as if Balbuena did not want to leave anything undescribed. . . . Here the Mannerist esthetic of *Siglo de Oro* becomes Baroque thanks to the 'accumulation' of elements" (24).

31. The theme of variety does occasion one lone, anomalous comment that quickly alludes to race. In chapter 1 of the poem Balbuena details the "varia traza y varios movimientos" and "varias figuras" [varying appearance, movements, and figures] of the city's inhabitants, and mentions "clérigos, frailes, hombres, y mujeres, / de diversa color y profesiones," "diferentes en lenguas y naciones" [priests, friars, men, and women of diverse colors and professions, of different languages and nations] (64–65). Balbuena, we see, mentions race but subsumes it within the issue of the many nationalities that coincide in the international city.

32. Lafaye says of "Grandeza" that the Indian, "the central figure in the writings of the first missionaries, is absent from the poem. In Mexico City, in 1602, the Indian was neither a warrior to be feared nor a soul to be saved; he was simply ignored" (54). Sadly enough, Balbuena's "disappearing" of the Indians might also derive from his father's having been indicted for abusing them (Van Horne, *Balbuena* 19–20) and from the poet's experiences as priest of the Indian town of San Pedro Lagunillas, which he yearned to leave behind.

33. I borrow somewhat from Stewart, who writes that collectors bring about "the replacement of the narrative of production by the narrative of the collection" (156).

34. As might be expected, Balbuena fails entirely to register, and presumably chooses completely to repress, the fact that (cf. Semo 55) by the end of the sixteenth century the Indians participated in all kinds of work, including the occupations "Grandeza" highlights.

35. In this regard textualized marketplaces serve the same functions as early modern paintings, such as Jan van Eyck's *The Arnolfini Marriage,* which Jardine reveals to be advertisements for the patron's possessions.

36. The aptly named philosopher Tomás de Mercado, who had taught in Mexico for many years, published in Spain his *Suma de tratos y contratos* (Salamanca, 1569; Seville, 1571). The *Suma* offers a concrete ethics for New World trade, decrying abuse of the Indies and Indians.

37. One cannot help but find a terrible irony in the fact that mercantilism would ultimately contribute to the undoing of the Spanish empire—through the devastation wrought by pirates and the Thirty Years War incited by the Netherlands as it sought to free itself from the Habsburg empire and to found a merchant republic—no less than of Balbuena himself, whose home in San Juan, Puerto Rico, pirates sacked in 1625.

CHAPTER 4

1. For an important discussion of Francisco de Terrazas in the context of the "Cortés cycle" (which I treat only insofar as it intersects with my direct concerns) and for bibliography on it, see José Amor y Vázquez, "Terrazas y su *Nuevo Mundo y Conquista* en los albores de la mexicanidad," *Nueva Revista de Filología Hispánica* 16 (1982): 395–418.

2. Another poem in the "Cartapacio" attributed to Oquendo, "Carta de las damas de Lima a las de México," mockingly claims that for praise of Mexico one should turn to "el divino Balbuena / cuyos conceptos suaves / al viejo mundo se estienden / porque en el nuevo no caben" [the divine Balbuena, whose sweet conceits spread to the Old World because the New World lacks room for them] (168). The extensive relationships between the "Cartapacio" texts and "Grandeza" merit their own study.

3. Poems that Dorantes explicitly attributes to Oquendo appear on pages 150–154 ("¡Qué buena fuera la mar!") and 233–234 ("Los que fueron al inglés") of the *Sumaria relación*. The first example derives from ll. 1521–1638 of Oquendo's *Sátira,* changing some names and adding four short stanzas to fit the Mexican context. It remains entirely unclear if the version of the *Sátira* that appears in Dorantes was recycled and circulated in Mexico by Oquendo, rewritten by Oquendo for Dorantes, and/or modified by Dorantes himself (the more standard orthography, quite distinct from Oquendo's usual style, suggests editorial intervention). Dorantes's second offering of Oquendo's work reproduces verbatim, but again with more standard orthography, ll. 635–670 of the *Sátira*.

4. Echoing Balbuena, Dorantes writes of Mexico City, "the city is so grand and as worth seeing as the greatest in Spain or any other corner of the world, and it absolutely is the greatest and best of the Indies, at least the West Indies, where things arrive from all parts, for it lacks nothing. Here one finds Spain, France, and Italy, and Rome, and Flanders" (115).

5. The "Sátira que hizo un galán a una dama criolla que le alababa mucho a México," perhaps by Oquendo, spends more than twenty stanzas acerbically debunking the native produce that its author identifies as a consecrated literary topic (Paz y Meliá 161).

6. González Echevarría refers here to colonial and modern Cuban poetry.

7. Cárdenas says of the marvels he has seen in the New World, "if Pliny were to hear about such things, they would leave him amazed and terrified" (11).

8. For example, Dorantes excoriates the Indies as a "flesh-eating wolf with an insatiable appetite for the blood of innocents, a vixen who entices and flatters everyone and then beheads them" (114).

9. On mimicry, the appropriation of colonialist practices and discourses for anticolonial purposes, see Homi Bhabha, "Signs Taken for Wonders: Questions

of Ambivalence and Authority Under a Tree Outside Delhi," *Critical Inquiry* 12, no. 1 (1985): 144–165. Relating it to mimicry, Huggan defines "staged marginality" as "a spectacularisation of sexual/ethnic difference" (xiv) and, more fully, as "the process by which marginalised individuals are moved to dramatise their 'subordinate status' for the benefit of a majority or mainstream audience. Staged marginality is not necessarily an exercise in self-abasement; it may, and often does, have a critical or even a subversive function" (87).

10. Méndez Plancarte provides excerpts of the *Mercurio* in his *Poetas novohispanos, Segundo siglo, Parte primera*, 5–13. The whole *Mercurio* appears in Genaro García, vol. 12, from which I quote.

11. Among the few who discuss Villalobos, the once-official poet, are Blanco (*La literatura*), Peña (*Historia de la literatura mexicana*, reference in my chap. 3, note 16) and Méndez Plancarte. Méndez Plancarte relates that Villalobos, author of many religious plays, was contracted (by an entity the Mexican scholar calls "the city") in 1589 and 1594 to produce works for the major festivals of Corpus Christi and San Hipólito, patron saint of the capital (xli).

12. Perhaps Villalobos expected Montesclaros, then in Spain, to convey the *Mercurio* to the Council of the Indies. This might explain in part the *Mercurio*'s double addressee and its incongruous homage to the viceroy two decades after his rule.

13. In addition to Villalobos's established involvement with festival chronicles, two pieces of information shed some light on the author's odd, anachronistic choice of subject for the second part of the *Mercurio:* Vetancurt's description of Montesclaros as an aficionado of festivals ("era el Marqués alegre y amigo de festejos" [2:214]) and Montesclaros's responsiveness to creole complaints when he was viceroy of Mexico (Israel 84).

14. As discussed in chapter 3, the sole satirical moment in "Grandeza" entailed the derision of the provinces, derision intimately related to Balbuena's personal circumstances.

15. I borrow the term "subject-in-process" from Higgins, who sees in colonial creoles "not so much a unified subject, but the unfolding of a subject-in-process, moving between different discourses, assuming diverse and contradictory positions" (5). Higgins pulls the term from Paul Smith, *Discerning the Subject* (Minneapolis: University of Minnesota Press, 1988), 35–37, 121–126. Higgins's book also demonstrates the productivity of Balbuena for the eighteenth-century creole discourse of José de Eguiara y Eguren and Rafael Landívar, a subject beyond the purview of my book.

CHAPTER 5

1. Notably, Rolena Adorno, *Guaman Poma*.
2. Especially Villancicos: 249, 258, 274, 299; and villancicos attributable to

Sor Juana: ix, xvi, xli (including the Galician language). Unless otherwise indicated, here and throughout I cite Sor Juana's works from the four-volume *Obras completas* edited by Méndez Plancarte (as OC), giving the volume number on first reference to a text and subsequently just the page number in that volume. The villancicos appear in OC:2.

3. I do not mean to imply that the ensaladas do not make serious statements under their comic guise, for they do. I have simply chosen to discuss texts by Sor Juana of a more overtly serious nature because they relate more closely to the writings of other creole authors of her milieu. On the ensaladas and related matters, see, for example: Bénassy-Berling, part 5, chaps. 1–2; Martínez-San Miguel, chaps. 4–5; Méndez Plancarte, "Estudio Liminar" to OC:2; Paz, chap. 21; Sabat de Rivers, *En busca*, part 2.

4. Relatively few scholars discuss Vetancurt: Blanco (*Esplendores*), Brading, García Icazbalceta (introduction to Mendieta), Huddleston, Keen. Also María Dolores Bravo Arriaga, "Signos religiosos y géneros literarios en el discurso de poder," *Sor Juana y su mundo,* ed. Sara Poot-Herrera, 93–139 (Mexico City: Universidad del Claustro de Sor Juana, 1995), and Jorge Cañizares Esguerra, "New World, New Stars: Patriotic Astrology and the Invention of Indian and Creole Bodies in Colonial Spanish America, 1600–1650," *American Historical Review* 104, no. 1 (1999): 33–68. To complicate matters further, scholars call Vetancurt by various names: Betancur, Betancourt, Betancurt, and Bentacurt. I adopt the most common spelling, used in the modern edition of his *Teatro mexicano,* and cull most of the biographical information on Vetancurt from the notes to that text by an unspecified editor.

5. Sigüenza, who, as we will see, takes recourse to Balbuena's "Grandeza" in his *Glorias de Querétaro,* also quotes in his *Teatro de virtudes* (203) three stanzas from Villalobos's *Mercurio* that sound exactly like "Grandeza."

6. See Vetancurt 2:193–94 for a statement on Mexico City's multiple festivals, including those of the Indians. Volume 3 of *Teatro*, on the various Franciscan missions throughout Mexico, discusses religious festivals extensively. His elaborate account of a university festival (3:117 ff.; the same festival as in Sigüenza's *Triunfo Parténico,* discussed in chapter 6), mentions that Vetancurt had written an official chronicle of the festival in Latin (3:126).

7. Vetancurt, willfully and typically, turns Balbuena's ceaseless "spring" into "summer" (2:190).

8. As chapter 7 herein discusses, Salinas's *Memorial* resulted in his exile to Spain and Italy, and then to Mexico. Vetancurt mentions Salinas several times in his *Teatro*. Unfortunately, Salinas seems to have had an insufficient effect on Vetancurt's opinion of the Indians.

9. I have in mind Williams's expansive construction of hegemony as "a whole body of practices and expectations" by means of which "the relations of domination and subordination" saturate "the whole process of living" (110).

10. My discussion of Mexico City here draws on Cope's study and Socolow's

fine introduction to *Cities and Society in Colonial Latin America,* in Hoberman and Socolow (3–18).

11. The influx of New World bullion that inflated European silver could also account in considerable measure for the Baroque crematistike esthetic of excess I mentioned in chapter 3. For a summary of the New World's impact on the Spanish economic situation see chap. 3 of *Old World* by Elliott, who asks, "How far, indeed, would Baroque art, as an art heavily dependent on gold and silver ornamentation, have been possible without the riches of the Indies?" (65).

12. In his stimulating book on the Baroque, Braider expands the Benjaminian "miracle" into "the metaphysics of immanence on which the baroque era turns" (15), a view of the Baroque well suited to the colonial context.

13. Much debate has arisen around the question of whether the capacious, transculturated Baroque can serve as a model for modernity, for Latin America at large. John Beverley's *Una modernidad obsoleta: Estudios sobre el barroco* (Los Teques, Venezuela: A.L.E.M., 1997) takes strong issue with the tendency to exalt the Baroque into such a model. On the other hand, for example, González Echevarría's *Celestina's Brood,* Bolívar Echeverría's edited collection, Irlemar Chiampi's *Barroco y modernidad* (Mexico City: FCE, 2000), and several essays in *Hispanic Baroques* (ed. Spadaccini and Martín-Estudillo) that work off Christine Buci-Glucksmann's *La Raison Baroque: de Baudelaire à Benjamin* (Paris: Galilée, 1984) argue for the Baroque's paradigmatic potential. The "Postscript" to my study offers another take on the matter. Further, the exhibition catalogue *Ultra Baroque: Aspects of Post Latin American Art,* ed. Elizabeth Armstrong and Victor Zamudio-Taylor (San Diego: Museum of Contemporary Art, 2000), claims the resistant aspects of the colonial Baroque—such as a hybridity that militates against order and classification, excess, transculturation, its mixture of the local and the global—for the postnational Latin American Ultra Baroque, an artistic movement that, as distinct from the Neo-Baroque, recuperates the early modern phenomenon "more as an attitude than a style" (4).

14. Streamlined syntheses of historiographic syncretism are lacking; works that attempt to do justice to the subject tend, rightfully, to be as complex as the primary texts themselves. Harss's introduction to his translation of the *Primero sueño* and Paz's *Sor Juana,* on the other hand, offer fine synthetic accounts of Jesuit syncretism. Yet Paz's book warrants a serious cautionary note: I believe its parts 1 and 5 quite mistakenly equate Jesuit syncretism with other forms and take Jesuit syncretism as representative of all forms of the phenomenon. I hope to have made clear that this is not the case.

15. The mestizo historian Fernando de Alva Ixtlilxochitl (1578–1650) considers not the devil but St. Thomas the Apostle in the guise of Quetzalcóatl to have guided the Toltecs. It is evident from the prologue to his *Parayso Occidental* (48) that Sigüenza, following Ixtlilxochitl and other predecessors, also

subscribes to the theory of St. Thomas as Quetzalcóatl. On Ixtlilxochitl and Sigüenza's theories, see Brading, chaps. 13 and 17, respectively.

16. Elliott notes that while sixteenth-century writers "failed to get to grips with these anomalies" of diverse origins, seventeenth-century historians searched for origins ("Final Reflections" 402–403).

17. On the Indians qua Jews, for example, Acosta writes, "Ignorant folk commonly believe that the Indians proceed from the race of Jews because they are cowardly and weak and much given to ceremony, and cunning, and lying" (87, 69).

18. I frame this divide in accord with Huddleston's thesis and exposition.

19. For example, Acosta supports the notion of a land crossing to the New World (subsequently borne out by the discovery of the Bering Strait in 1723), but with regard to who initiated the crossing he characteristically states, "Truly I have debated my point with myself and others many times and have never found an answer that satisfies me" (61, 51).

20. Modern notions of multiple migrations to the New World, the last continents to be settled by human beings, have confirmed the accuracy of the seventeenth-century eclectics.

21. Huddleston has shown that Vetancurt lifts García's "four ways of knowing" (96), which are "science, opinion, divine faith, human faith" (Vetancurt 1:208). In his introduction to Mendieta, García Icazbalceta calls attention to the accusations of plagiarism Vetancurt levied against his fellow Franciscan, Juan de Torquemada (68–74)—a most peculiar line of attack for Vetancurt given his own silent, liberal use of sources.

22. Vetancurt introduces qualifications into his discussions of the creoles and Indians that are indicative of the tangles to which issues of class and race give rise in the times. First, evidencing the creoles' Janus-faced outlook and dual agency, Vetancurt critiques the viceregal regime for its treatment of his fellow intellectuals yet praises the Spanish crown for respecting the creoles' learning, valor, and blood (1:35). Second, Vetancurt's emphasis on climate wreaks havoc with prevailing social and racial hierarchies: if climate above all else determines ability, it follows that any inhabitant born in the excellent climate of Mexico—including Indians and black slaves—would be superior to Europeans. Vetancurt recognizes the dilemma and tries to backpedal his way out of it. He reaffirms the alleged superiority of light over dark-skinned peoples but asserts that the dark-skinned peoples of Mexico are more gifted than their counterparts in Spain (1:36).

23. With regard to cultural nationalism, I have also found useful John Hutchinson, *The Dynamics of Cultural Nationalism: The Gaelic Revival and the Creation of the Irish National State* (London: Allen and Unwin, 1987), and "Nations and Culture," in *Understanding Nationalism,* ed. Montserrat Guiberneau and John Hutchinson, 74–96 (Cambridge: Polity Press, 2001).

24. On the relationship between creole patriotism and indigenous history,

see Brading, prologue and chap. 7; Keen, chap. 7; also, Leonardo García Pabón's insightful "Indios, criollos y fiesta barroca en la *Historia de Potosí* de Bartolomé Arzáns," *Revista Iberoamericana* 61, nos. 172–173 (1995): 423–439.

25. Escamilla González's article furnishes an excellent discussion of Sigüenza as a consummate cultivator of patrons and his successes in that endeavor.

26. Though it has much to offer, *Glorias de Querétaro* has inspired little modern critical interest. Hence my detailed discussion of the text. See, though, María Dolores Bravo Arriaga, "Las *Glorias de Querétaro* como 'relacion' de fiesta y su percepción del paraíso" in Mayer (1:3–34).

27. On Querétaro, see John C. Super, "The Agricultural Near North: Querétaro in the Seventeenth Century," in *Provinces of Early Mexico,* ed. Ida Altman and James Lockhart, 231–251 (Los Angeles: UCLA Latin American Center Publications, 1976). Super notes that the truly multicultural Querétaro (similar, in ways, to Cuzco) also had a black population perhaps equal to its Spanish constituency (243), and that in Querétaro "Indian languages, family solidarity, and customs maintained remarkable resiliency, especially among the Otomis, even under continual pressures from the Spanish community" (233–234). Joseph María Zelaa e Hidalgo, a proud citizen of Querétaro, offers much information on other local matters in his remarkable glossed, excised, rewritten edition of *Glorias* (1883), now available online at: http://www.archive.org/details/gloriasdequereto0ogngoog.

28. According to Bryant (Sigüenza, *Seis obras* 423), Sigüenza may have formally returned to the Jesuits before his death; he was buried in the Mexico City Jesuit Colegio de San Pedro y San Pablo. Moreover, in his *Piedad heróica de don Fernándo Cortés* (1689), Sigüenza made a more momentous contribution to Jesuit-sponsored Guadalupanism. Based on native manuscripts in his possession, Sigüenza swore in the *Piedad heróica* that the Indian Antonio Valeriano wrote, in Nahuatl, the first text on the Virgin's apparition, the *Nican mopohua*. However, no documentary proof of Sigüenza's claims has been found. See David A. Brading, *Mexican Phoenix* (Cambridge: Cambridge University Press, 2001) 117–118.

29. See Arenal for detailed verbal descriptions of both Sigüenza's and Sor Juana's arches. Pictorial recreations of Sor Juana's arch can be found in Georgina Sabat de Rivers, "El *Neptuno* de Sor Juana: Fiesta barroca y programa político," *University of Dayton Review* 16, no. 2 (1983): 63–73, and Margo Glantz, *Sor Juana Inés de la Cruz: saberes y placeres* (Mexico City: Gobierno del Estado de México, 1996) 100.

30. Sigüenza could also possibly have had in mind the festival celebrating the entry of Viceroy Marquis of Villena (1640) that Curcio-Nagy describes (41): in the same Plaza de Santo Domingo where Sigüenza's arch later stood, Villena passed under a triumphal arch the Indians had built. The arch bore native paintings and the heraldic symbol of Aztec Tenochtitlán. As part of the ceremony, the Indians explained each painting, in Nahuatl.

31. Epitomizing (Sigüenza's) Baroque erudition, *Teatro de virtudes* is a weave of others' words, all of which de facto become Sigüenza's own. To avoid making my discussion of the text equally dense, I give attributions for only the most important quotes.

32. In his *Parayso Occidental,* Sigüenza condemns the Indians' "infinite incidences of robbery, murder, sacrilege, sodomy, incest, and other even greater abominations" (48). For a compendium of Sigüenza's similar invectives against the Indians in *Alboroto* (1692), see Brading 371–372. That, as the protojournalist Robles recounts (1:291), an Indian fell off Sigüenza's arch during the festival in 1680 and almost died becomes a metaphor of its designer's low esteem for the living Indian.

33. In his edition of Sigüenza's works, Bryant states that the Mexican author published a treatise entitled, *Noticia chronológica de los reyes, emperadores, gobernadores, presidentes y vir-reyes de esta nobilíssima ciudad de México,* perhaps in the same crucial year of 1680. Of this text, only eight pages remain.

34. In his *Tratado del descubrimiento de las Indias* (written c. 1589), Suárez de Peralta briefly proposes an Egyptian or Ethiopian origin for the Mexican Indians based on the reversals of conventional gender roles the two societies share. For example, they allowed women to engage in commerce, while men stayed home weaving; in both societies women urinated in a standing position and men sitting down (a statement found in Herodotus); and a few less scandalous comparisons (Huddleston 37; Suárez de Peralta 5–6).

35. Sigüenza summarizes the resemblances between Egypt and pre-Hispanic Mexico according to Kircher thus: "they can be corroborated by commonalities in dress and sacrifices, length of the year and order of the calendar, expression of concepts through hieroglyphs and symbols, architecture of their temples, form of government, and other things that Father Athanasius Kircher attempted to enumerate in his *Oedipus Aegyptiacus*" (*Teatro de virtudes* 181).

36. As I mention later, Sigüenza writes with and against Kircher here, citing the insufficiency of Kircher's Mexican informants. In 1689, Sigüenza would again take aim at Kircher on nationalistic grounds. See Kramer's discussion of Sigüenza's quarrel with Kircher for having contended that, unlike Egyptian hieroglyphs or Chinese characters, Aztec pictographs contain no multiple or secret meanings.

37. As Sigüenza observes in his *Libra astronómica,* Kircher identifies Ham with Zoroaster, reviver of magic and idolatry; Kircher states that Ham works his magic "prompted by the Devil" (376–377).

38. Anna More, in one of the most sophisticated readings of Sigüenza's *Teatro de virtudes,* views the creole writer as a high priest of hermetic knowledge, as both its practitioner and interpreter (60). See "La patria criolla como jeroglífico secularizado en el *Teatro de Virtudes,*" in Mayer (2:47–78).

39. On how Sor Juana's personal circumstances, especially with Núñez de Miranda, impacted the *Neptuno* and "Autodefensa espiritual," see Arenal;

Brescia; Luciani (chap. 2). Also Antonio Alatorre, "La *Carta* de Sor Juana al P. Núñez (1682)," *Nueva Revista de Filología Hispánica* 35, no. 2 (1986): 591–673; Beatriz Mariscal Hay, "'Una mujer ignorante': Sor Juana, interlocutora de virreyes," *Y diversa de mí misma entre vuestras plumas ando: Homenaje internacional a Sor Juana Inés de la Cruz,* ed. Sara Poot-Herrera, 91–99 (Mexico City: El Colegio de México, 1993); Sabat de Rivers, "El *Neptuno* de Sor Juana" (reference in note 29 above): 63–73.

40. *City of God,* book XVIII, chap. 9: "Varro's explanation of the name of Athens." On page 361 of the *Neptuno,* when she discusses Harpocrates, Sor Juana cites the same book of St. Augustine's text, which also contains several portions on Isis. My readings indicate that Sor Juana tends to work with specific clusters of *City of God.* One would therefore assume her familiarity with St. Augustine's treatment of the contest between Minerva and Neptune. The syncretic, prophetic argumentation that is the *City of God*'s hallmark also pervades *El Divino Narciso* and its loa, uniting these works with both St. Augustine and the *Neptuno.*

41. Luciani's excellent discussion of Sor Juana's comedia *Amor es más laberinto* (1689) as a Mirror for Princes pairs the play with the *Neptuno.* Together, he says, the two works constitute "'bookends' to the 1680s, markers not just of the commencement of new viceregal administrations in Mexico, but also of the beginning and the end of Sor Juana's decade of maximum fame and influence" (51). See chap. 2 of Luciani's book.

42. For example, the scant three paragraphs Brading devotes to Sor Juana in *The First America* (372–373) underscore the differences between the *Teatro* and the *Neptuno;* Paz begins his chapter on the *Neptuno* (chap. 11) with the words, "Nothing could be further from the patriotic and historical interpretations of Sigüenza than the arch devised by Sor Juana" (155).

43. According to Bryant (Sigüenza, *Seis obras* 239–240), Sigüenza wrote a short piece, *Panegyrico con que la muy noble é imperial Ciudad de México, aplaudió al Excelentísimo Señor D. Thomas . . . al entrar por la triumphal Portada,* read on the day of the event in 1680. Bryant concludes that Sigüenza incorporated some of the panegyric into the lengthy poem, addressed to the viceroy at the moment he passes through the arch, which closes the *Teatro de virtudes.* The conventional poem has no Kircherian features.

44. Findlen observes that "the image that best encapsulated her vision of Isis could be found on p. 189 of the first volume of Kircher's *Oedipus*" and that "Kircher's polyvalent Isis, literally a *polymorphus Daemon,* was the origin of all female divinity, a fact he illustrated by connecting her name to many other Greco-Roman goddesses" ("Jesuit's Books" 351). Here Findlen also notes that in general Sor Juana gravitated toward illustrated encyclopedias. Yet if indeed the nun were just now gaining familiarity with Kircher, it would make sense that she especially grasp his texts through their visual images.

45. On Sor Juana and Sigüenza's collaboration in 1680, see Francisco de la

Maza, "Sor Juana y Don Carlos: Explicación de dos sonetos hasta ahora confusos," *Cuadernos americanos* 65, no. 2 (1966): 190–204. The article has led many to believe that in 1680 there existed an adversarial relationship between the two star writers. Factoring Kircher into the equation, one might conclude that rather than the animosity toward Sigüenza or mockery of his Egyptian arguments for which De la Maza argues, Sor Juana may be displaying some anxiety of influence.

46. In section 7 of his introduction, Osorio Romero posits that in Mexico City both Sigüenza and Sor Juana came into contact with a direct acquaintance, correspondent, and adept of Kircher's, Francisco Ximénez. As confessor of the Marquis and Marquise de Mancera, Ximénez would have been known to the two writers. As prefect of the Jesuit Colegio Máximo in the capital, Ximénez fielded Sigüenza's petition of 1677 to be reinstated in the Company of Jesus (Kramer 362–363). Further, according to Osorio Romero, while Sigüenza was studying with the Jesuits in Puebla, the *poblano* Alejandro Favián was writing in a Kircherian mode and mounting his Kircherian museum. In 1672 Favián sent Sigüenza a copy of the *Magneticum naturae regnum*, which Kircher had dedicated to his Puebla disciple (Trabulse, "*Itinerarium*" 31). Given the outrageous nature of Favián's Kircherian efforts that I examine in chapter 6, it stands to reason that Sigüenza never acknowledges him and that the Mexico City intellectual would want to divorce Kircher from association with the peculiar Favián and set the German Jesuit in circulation under his own more respectable scholarly aegis.

47. Certainly unbeknownst to Sigüenza and Sor Juana, Kircher had died in the Vatican just three days before the viceregal couple entered Mexico City.

48. Paz argues that Isis meets Sor Juana's needs on an intimate psychological level. Given that, in Sor Juana's genealogy, Isis is masculine and feminine, mother and widow, and goddess of signs, Paz maintains that she contains all of Sor Juana's obsessions (172). Be that as it may, Isis/Minerva gives Sor Juana grounds for some entertaining plays with gender issues that, as befits Sor Juana's needs *for the occasion,* call attention to herself. Sor Juana renders Isis doubly masculine, but the gender plays do not end there. While Sor Juana makes Neptune first and foremost the *son* of Isis, her explanations of the seventh canvas make him the *father* of Minerva/Isis; shortly after, to salvage Neptune's defeat by Minerva, Sor Juana presents the two of them as one and the same (391).

49. Works by Sor Juana that endow the Virgin Mary with characteristics of the Virgin of Guadalupe include at least poems 138, 139 (OC:1); 222, 224, 225, 226, 229, 230, 231, 232, 251, 253, 256, 257, 268, 270, 272, 273, 280, 281, 282, 306, 310 (OC:2); 409 (OC:3; I have skipped the villancicos attributable to Sor Juana). Poems #256 and #282 explicitly mention Patmos. Interestingly, the ceremonies to Mary of this nature generally took place in Mexico City. Sor Juana's festival of 1691 written for Oaxaca, conversely, contains poems associating St. Catherine of Alexandria with the rose (313, 315, 316, 320, 321, OC:2). On Sor Juana's

treatment of the Virgin of Guadalupe, often through Mary, see Bénassy-Berling (209–11); Tavard (94–98); Alberto Pérez Amador Adam, "La compuesta de flores maravilla: Francisco de Castro," *La creatividad femenina en el mundo barroco hispánico,* ed. Monike Bosse, et al., 671–685 (Kassel: Edition Reichenberger, 1999); Pamela Kirk, *Sor Juana Inés de la Cruz: Religion, Art, and Feminism,* 53–57 (New York: Continuum, 1999).

50. Cf. Méndez Plancarte's notes to ll. 446–449 of the *Neptuno* in OC:4, 606.

51. On St. Paul and Isis, also see Witt, chap. 19.

52. Martínez-San Miguel and Sabat de Rivers (*En busca*) deal extensively and effectively with Sor Juana as creole.

53. *El Divino Narciso* was first published in the third edition of vol. 1 of Sor Juana's complete works (Barcelona, 1691) and again, with her other Eucharistic plays and their loas, in the second Spanish volume of her works in Seville, 1692 (Sabat de Rivers, *En busca* 266).

54. The important loa to Sor Juana's Eucharistic play *El mártir del Sacramento, San Hermenegildo,* from which my chapter takes its epigraph, was also written for Spain. It features Columbus himself and addresses New World issues but interacts more with Columbus's providentialism than with historiographic syncretism.

CHAPTER 6

1. I derive the discussion of poetry contest pageantry from that of Leonard in *Baroque Times,* ch. 9, largely based on *Triunfo Parténico* but culled from many sources.

2. The definitions in *Webster's Unabridged* for "ether" and "ethereal" include the following: Ether: from *aither,* the upper, purer air. 1. an imaginary substance regarded by the ancients as filling all space beyond the sphere of the moon, and making up the stars and planets. 2. the upper regions of space; clear sky. Ethereal: 1. of or like the ether, or upper regions of space. 2. very light; airy; delicate. 3. heavenly; celestial; not earthly.

3. The retrospective Vetancurt also draws on the biological and climatological apologetics of Juan de Cárdenas and Diego Cisneros in ways pertinent to this chapter. Leading the way for Balbuena, Cárdenas had deemed inhabitants of the provinces coarse and dull and city dwellers lively (159). In his *Sitio, Naturaleza y Propiedades de la Ciudad de México* of 1618 (ed. José Luis Peset [Madrid: Fundación de Ciencias de la Salud, 1992]), the medical doctor Cisneros considers the temperate climate of Mexico City to have resulted in the lively minds of both creoles and Indians. Thanks to "this most beautiful machine that God created" and to the fine educational system of Mexico, the creoles are "prudent, sharp-witted, handsome, amiable, and meek" (113).

4. Of the many outstanding scholarly treatments of *Infortunios* beyond those cited in this chapter (see Irizarry's introduction for bibliography), a couple have particular pertinence to my arguments. Eleuterio Santiago-Díaz, M. A. thesis at Brown University: "*Infortunios de Alonso Ramírez*: texto enciclopédico de la Ciudad Letrada" (1982), which elucidates the presence in *Infortunios* of the genres I mention; Ester Gimbernat de González, "Mapas y texto: para una estrategia del poder," *MLN* 95 (1980): 388–99. Gimbernat de González, Sacido Romero, and Irizarry all chart the two voices in the text. Also see José F. Buscaglia-Salgado's chapter on *Infortunios* in his *Undoing Empire: Race and Nation in the Mulatto Caribbean* (Minneapolis and London: University of Minnesota Press, 2003) 128–82, which maintains that Ramírez fronts for Sigüenza's concerns about threats to the empire and to creoles.

5. In *Teatro de virtudes,* Sigüenza mentions yet another Alonso Ramírez, who helped underwrite the festival: "Alonso Ramírez de Valdés, of the order of Alcántara, sergeant major of the principality of Asturias and present magistrate of this city" (186).

6. Sor Juana contributed to *Triunfo* under the pseudonyms of Juan Sáenz del Cauri (an anagram of her name) and Felipe de Salayzes Gutiérrez. Both of her contributions won awards.

7. Blanco (*Esplendores*), Concha, and Beverley all discuss the odd course Góngora's work followed in the New World.

8. The full title of Espinosa Medrano's work reads: *Apologético en favor de don Luis de Góngora, príncipe de los poetas líricos de España, contra Manuel de Faria y Sousa, caballero portugués, que dedica al excelentísimo señor don Luis Méndez de Haro, duque conde De Olivares, &, su autor, el doctor Juan de Espinosa Medrano, Colegial Real en el insigne Seminario de San Antonio el Magno, Catedrático de artes y Sagrada Teología en él: Cura Rector de la Santa Iglesia Catedral de la Ciudad del Cuzco, cabeza de los reinos del Perú en el nuevo mundo.*

9. Blanco observes that there were "hundreds of poets" writing degraded Baroque poetry "because versification was not an art, but an etiquette, a means of distinguishing oneself in society" (*Esplendores* 72). Concha, Leonard, Rodríguez Hernández, and Vidal also relate creole proficiency in the esoteric techniques of Baroque poetry to social advancement.

10. Given the recent vogue Kircher has enjoyed, the abundance of studies on the author now available has helped me compensate for the lack of modern editions or translations of his work. See Findlen's *Athanasius Kircher* for an excellent bibliography on the German Jesuit.

11. As Findlen states, "In an age in which reports of Aztec temples, Mayan calendars, Brazilian cannibals, Chinese mandarins, and Japanese Buddhists inspired European curiosity about other cultures, Kircher helped his readers to see the commonalities within the overwhelming diversity of languages, faiths, and cultures. He underscored the universality of Christianity . . . . by find-

ing analogous evidence of Christianity in far-flung parts of the world" ("Last Man" 33).

12. In the "Segunda Crisis" of Gracián's *Criticón* (ed. Santos Alonso [Madrid: Cátedra, 1980]), "The Great Theater of the World," Andrenio contemplates the skies and raises a question that casts doubt on the received world picture: "since the supreme Artificer adorned this well-wrought dome of the earth with so many rosettes and stars, I wondered why he did not arrange them with order and concert, interweaving them into beautiful knots and forming an exquisite embroidery?" (80–81). Reaffirming that world picture and the hexameral work of the text, Critilo replies that God did endow the heavens with correspondences—correspondences that include differences and that are intended to be more complex than a simple human mind can easily grasp. Luis de Granada's hexameral work was one of the *Criticón*'s sources.

13. Remarking that certainly "Ximénez suffered attacks from men like Núñez de Miranda," Osorio Romero notes that in 1670 Rome received a report denouncing Ximénez's laxity toward students and favoritism toward those who shared his views (xxx).

14. Kircher's *Itinerarium exstaticum* was printed in several editions, each with a slightly different title: *Itinerarium exstaticum* (Rome, 1656), *Iter exstaticum secundum* (Rome, 1657), *Itinerarium extaticum coeleste* (Würzburg, 1660 and 1671). The second and subsequent editions, purged of some problematic passages, also contain a commentary on the text by Kircher's disciple, Gaspar Schott. Paz, who offers the most extensive treatment of Sor Juana and Kircher, utilizes the 1671 edition and Findlen, in "A Jesuit's Books," the 1656 edition. Findlen points out that the *Itinerarium,* with its dedication to Christina of Sweden and insistence on the New World, would have held a particular attraction for Sor Juana (353).

15. Part 6 of Octavio Paz's *Sor Juana* has much to say about the implications of the *Carta Atenagórica* for the Jesuits as well as about Kircher and the *Respuesta*. However, the Mexican critic does not discuss the impact of the Jesuit curriculum on the *Respuesta*.

16. I owe to my colleague at Brown University Kenneth Haynes the information that the original statement, "Nothing is sweeter than to know everything," appears in Greek in Cicero's letter to Atticus (4.11.2). I thank him for this and several other valuable suggestions on Kircherian and classical aspects of the chapter.

17. Though not referring to Kircher, Luciani states, "Just as her inclination is divinely instilled, the avenues by which it is explored have been prepared by the hand of God . . . . The fact that these are 'hidden,' sometimes metaphorical links, serves to emphasize her own extraordinary capacity as a seeker, whose privileged mind is able to discern the marvelous correspondences between things" (102).

18. Sigüenza, too, amassed a vast library and collected scientific instruments

and exotica. See Jorge Cañizares-Esguerra, "Spanish America: From Baroque to Modern Colonial Science" in *The Cambridge History of Science,* ed. Roy Porter, vol. 4 (Cambridge, Eng.: Cambridge UP, 2000) 819.

19. The poetry and inventories raise as many questions about Sor Juana's collection as they answer. One cannot tell if Sor Juana planned her collection or if, as Paz says, it was "an assemblage born of accident and fancy more than of a plan . . . more closely related to a magician's cave than to the museum gallery" (247); if she, like Kircher, collected specific objects, soliciting them from her correspondents; if she organized her collection in some particular way. Questions will continue to multiply, but there is little doubt about the importance Sor Juana and others attached to her collection.

20. Although, following the Christian doctrine that suits Sor Juana's purposes so well, in net terms the *PS* depicts the Soul as ungendered, the feminine grammatical gender of the word *alma* in Spanish often leads the poet to refer to the Soul in the feminine. At times, the poem also tropes the Soul explicitly as a female (e.g., "la suprema / de lo sublunar Reina soberana" [ll. 438–439], the sovereign Queen of this sublunary world, *182*), which accords with the feminine cast of the search and the nightworld as well as with female identity of the poetic speaker revealed at the end. For these reasons and for the sake of convenience throughout I refer to the Soul in the feminine.

21. Neoplatonism, Pythagoreanism, and a sublime concept of poetry abound in Balbuena's deeply Platonic "Compendio." There one also finds practically irresistible hooks for Sor Juana, including references to Hermes Trismegistus and St. Augustine that also dovetail with Kircher's poetics. Indeed, Balbuena mentions that poetry would appeal to and enlighten everyone, even the "nun in her cloister" (136)!

22. According to Ermilio Abreu Gómez (*Sor Juana Inés de la Cruz: Bibliografía y biblioteca* [Mexico City: Monografías Bibliográficas Mexicanas, 1934] 319), in 1683 Aguiar y Seijas authored a work entitled *Pastoral para la creación de una cofradía de la Doctrina Cristiana en todas las parroquias del Arzobispado de México*, a work I have not been able to consult.

23. While Paz and Méndez Plancarte discuss the Mexican sources of the loa, neither one brings out *EDN*'s relationships to Mexican pastorals. Why might this be? I believe that to establish Sor Juana as a world-class writer both scholars have concentrated massive efforts on documenting how in *EDN* and other works Sor Juana wields the lion's share of Western culture, classical and coeval. Hence, rather than primarily "Mexicanizing" Sor Juana, they pointedly Westernize her, with the odd result that the two Mexican scholars' seemingly exhaustive, definitive scholarship can impede awareness of many of her local sources.

24. *Sirgueros* is only available outside archives via the excerpted modern edition by Agustín Yáñez. Readers will find a useful introductory study of the

novel, and a comparison with Balbuena's, in Goic's "La novela hispanoamericana colonial."

25. On Bramón's tocotín and Sor Juana's loa, see page 196 of Luis Leal, "El hechizo derramado: Elementos mestizos en Sor Juana," in *Y diversa de mí misma* (reference in my Ch. 5, note 39), and Sabat de Rivers, *En busca* (288).

26. See Merrim,"Sor Juana Criolla and the Mexican Archive: Public Performances," in *Creole Subjects in the Colonial Americas: Empires, Texts, Identities,* eds. Ralph Bauer and José Antonio Mazzotti (Chapel Hill: University of North Carolina Press, 2009), especially 216–218.

27. Catalá's elucidations leave one wondering about further Guadalupan aspects of the *PS,* including the possibility that its two epistemological ventures implicate the Virgin of Guadalupe: the pyramid/mountain recalls Tepeyac, and the rose the Virgin herself.

28. On Sor Juana and María de Ágreda, see Bénassy-Berling (269-270 *et passim*). On Sor Juana and Christine de Pizan, see Electa Arenal and Amanda Powell's introduction (vii) and notes (pp. 124–129) to *The Answer/La Respuesta* (New York: The Feminist Press, 1994). Oddly, St. Augustine does not figure in Méndez Plancartes's notes to the *PS.* For his part, Paz does note that Sor Juana often cites St. Augustine. Yet, for a variety of reasons—including some questionable views on Augustinianism, Jansenism, Kircherian hermeticism, and the *PS* itself—Paz's book does not allow for the influence of St. Augustine on the *PS.*

29. At numerous points in his *First America,* Brading details the profound involvement of New World historiography with St. Augustine's *City of God.*

30. Book XVIII of *City* also contains the story of the competition between Minerva and Neptune that the *Neptuno alegórico* recounts in a skewed way.

31. The unpalatable scholastic title of Romance #2, perhaps imposed by an editor, reads, "Acusa la hidropesía de mucha ciencia, que teme inútil aun para saber y nociva para vivir" (well translated by Trueblood as: "She Condemns the Bloatedness of Much Learning, Which She Considers Useless Even as Knowledge and Harmful for Living" [*91*]). The poem was published in 1689. At its end, having established the impossibility of true knowledge, the poetic speaker decides to cast her lot with Holy Ignorance: is this a clue to or a smoke screen for the ending of the *PS?*

32. Forcione describes Alonso de Acevedo's hexameral *La creación del mundo* (early seventeenth century) in words that correlate exactly to the early parts of the *PS:* "The aim of the omnipotent but rational God is order, harmony, stasis, continuity and the elimination of chance, a universal state of being analogically represented by the familiar image of . . . the well-regulated clock" (20). Clocks appear in ll. 136 (*175*) and 205 (*176*) of the *PS.* Further, l. 165 (*175*) refers to the clocklike machinery of the world, and the section on the body portrays it in mechanical terms.

33. St. Augustine also sanctifies the human potential for learning as God-given and as a token on earth of the Heavenly City (461). His position would exonerate the Soul's indomitable quest for knowledge, the resilience after failure, and final vow to keep on trying in another sphere or on another night.

34. On the *PS* and Babel, see Jorge Checa, "Los caracteres del estrago: Babel en *Primero sueño*," in *Mujer y cultura en la colonia hispanoamericana*, ed. Mabel Moraña (Pittsburgh: Biblioteca de America, 1996) 257–271. On nominalism in Sor Juana's milieu and in the *PS*, see chs. 3–4 of Mauricio Beuchot, *The History of Philosophy in Colonial Mexico*, trans. Elizabeth Millán (Washington D. C.: Catholic University of America Press, 1998).

35. In his chapter on the *First Dream*, Paz gives a synopsis of the *Itinerarium exstaticum*, relating it to Sor Juana's text. He brings up other connections between the *PS* and Kircher, some obvious, some quite obscure. In section 8 of his introduction, on the other hand, Osorio Romero views the *PS* as "an allegation against Kircher, against his *Ars combinatorio* and against the tradition that it represents" (xlix).

36. Qtd. in Rowland, *Ecstatic Journey* (77), from the 1660 edition; emphasis added.

37. This statement caps Paz's argument that the *PS* gestures away from the Baroque to the Enlightenment and modernity. I hope to have established that the poem critiques the Baroque on and within its own grounds.

38. See ch. 7 of Cope's book, "The Riot of 1692," for the context of the riots and for a fine reading of Sigüenza's text as representing the "official story." After the riots, at the behest of Viceroy Galve, Sigüenza drew up a plan for deposing the Indians from the center of the city and redistributing them in outlying areas, a plan reproduced in "Sobre los inconvenientes de vivir los indios en el centro de la ciudad," *Boletín del Archivo General de la Nación* IX, 1 (1938): 1–34.

39. One would dearly like to know why and how Sigüenza delivered Sor Juana's funeral oration, which is now lost.

40. On Villalpando's painting vis-à-vis the Count de Galve, see Kagan (160–162), Maza, *El pintor* (159–167). On parallels between Villalpando and *Alboroto*, see Escamilla González, 198–199; e.g., "Villalpando's message, which accords with Sigüenza's, is unequivocal: authority and hierarchies have been restored; life in the kingdom of New Spain will move forward in complete order and tranquility" (100).

CHAPTER 7

1. Drawing on the colonial studies gaining force at the time in Latin America, such as Mariano Picón-Salas's *De la Conquista a la Independencia* (1944)

(which Leonard himself translated in 1962), the lively *Baroque Times* played a large role in spurring the growth of the colonial field in the United States.

2. See, for example, Leonard's landmark book of 1929 on Sigüenza, from which I derived the translations of *Alboroto*. My reading of Leonard follows the lines of Kathleen Ross's "Carlos de Sigüenza y Góngora y la cultura del Barroco hispanoamericano," *Relecturas del Barroco de Indias,* ed. Mabel Moraña, 223–243 (Hanover: Ediciones del Norte, 1994).

3. Because it cannot possibly treat all South American works that resonate with the Spectacular City, this chapter centers on exposés importantly, principally, or substantially devoted to cities. Even in that, it does not purport to be exhaustive and, to hold to a reasonable length, just treats satirical poetry briefly. For more on Caviedes's spectacularizing of Lima and for discussion of the issue in Rosas de Oquendo, see my "Spectacular Cityscapes" essay.

4. Antelo's suggestive article traces, mostly in Portuguese-language works, the history of representing the New World as Babel; see page 192 for his list of works from four centuries that mention the tower of Babel. (Oddly, the article fails to discuss St. Augustine or to cite Brading's *First America*).

5. Guaman Poma was in Lima finishing his manuscript between 1613 and 1615, and Salinas oversaw the archives from 1614 until 1615 (Cook xl). Further, Cook observes that Salinas is the only pre-twentieth-century author to impart information from Guaman Poma's text (xli).

6. In the same sentence, though, Vetancurt also promises to report on the wrongdoings of the Indians that he has witnessed in his years as an administrator.

7. Luis Jerónimo de Oré, *Symbolo Catholico Indiano* (1598), one of Arzáns's sources; Miguel de Agia, *Servidumbres personales de indios* (1604). On this and on "creole indigenism" in general, see José Antonio Mazzotti's "Indigenismos de ayer: prototipos perdurables del discurso criollo" at: http://www.fas.harvard.edu/~icop/indigenismos.html. Also see Julián Heras, *Aportes de los franciscanos a la evangelización del Perú* (Lima: Editorial Latina, 1992).

8. Always on the lookout for misdeeds and alborotos, Torquemada also finds them in non-Christianized Indians, especially those who martyred Franciscans. See vol. 3, books 18–21 of his *Monarquía.*

9. González Echevarría states, "If anything, the Baroque was a style that represented a crisis. It was through it that colonial society played out its own crisis of historical, cultural, and artistic identity" ("Colonial Lyric" 204).

10. For instance, Torquemada writes, "[The second Audiencia of Mexico] was given very specific Charges and Reports of the *excesos* believed to have been committed and of Instructions disobeyed, and asked to investigate them" (1:603).

11. The Peruvian's words parallel Sigüenza's statement, which I mentioned in chapter 5: Europeans believe that New World Indians and creoles "only walk

on two feet thanks to divine dispensation" and, even after scrutinizing them under "British microscopes," are still reluctant to grant that Americans possess "rational faculties" (*Libra* 313). On Espinosa Medrano's self-exoticizing and self-monsterizing, see González Echevarría's important reading in chap. 5 of *Celestina's Brood*. He notes that the second edition of the *Apologético* (1694) omits the abrasive lines critiquing Europeans' jaundiced views of the New World (156).

12. One need recall that Guaman Poma refers not to the Incas but to the Yarovilca Indians from whom, according to Guaman Poma, both the Incas and he himself descended (Adorno, *Guaman Poma* 5).

13. Given the similarities between Guijo and Robles, it makes sense that their diaries were both first published together, as volumes 1 (Guijo), 2, and 3 (Robles) of Manuel Orozco y Berra's *Documentos para la historia de México* in 1853. However, Robles and Guijo do differ slightly. Robles's diary includes fewer festivals, more discussion of church affairs (with a little moralizing commentary), and more news from Spain.

14. In the introduction to his edition of Guijo's diary, Romero de Terreros states that Guijo was secretary of both organizations (1:xii–xiii). Less is known about Robles, but he does devote a glowing obituary, perhaps the longest in his text, to the founder of the "most illustrious Union of San Felipe Neri," Antonio Calderón Benavides (1:58). Moreover, in the introduction to his edition of Robles's diary, Castro Leal states that the manuscript was found in the library of the Padres del Oratorio de México (xii).

15. An auto-da-fé in 1656 that Guijo recounts, for example, disciplined a Spanish woman for religious crimes, a blind beggar from Havana for bigamy, two old men who witnessed the bigamist's marriage, a male black slave and free mulatto for blasphemy, and a black creole woman for practicing witchcraft (2:67–68).

16. See Enrique Pupo-Walker's *La vocación literaria del pensamiento histórico en América* (Madrid: Gredos, 1982), still the standard reference on the subject.

17. In the prologue to his edition of Freile's text, Dario Achury Valenzuela lists some seventeen possible meanings for "carnero," ranging from those I have mentioned to such possibilities as unit of money, parchment, weapon, and worldly vices. See *El Carnero* (Caracas: Biblioteca Ayacucho, 1979) xli, l–liv.

18. In a Mirror for Princes section of the *Monarquía*, Torquemada derives a bestiary of the virtues that his royal addressee should incarnate from an emblem that King Solomon glossed. According to Torquemada, King Solomon further characterizes his pastoral "carnero" as a cautious, true leader. For a stimulating discussion of the pastoral, neostoical aspects of *El Carnero*, see chap. 1 of Ivette Hernández-Torres, *El contrabando de lo secreto: la escritura de la historia en El Carnero* (Santiago: Editorial Cuarto Propio, 2004).

19. In his last chapter Freile states, "Only man is enemy of man; for man persecutes man from envy or greed, as a legacy of those first two brothers, Cain and Abel" (353).

20. That such plays actually existed may, like other aspects of *Potosí*, strain credibility. However, Jesús Lara discovered and published a play of precisely this nature performed in Potosí. Entitled *Tragedia del fin de Atawallpa* (Cochabamba: Imprenta Universitaria, 1975), the play is a version of a sixteenth-century work originally in Spanish and Quechua. On the *Tragedia,* see Gisbert, 40–46.

21. In *The Colonial Spanish-American City* (Austin: University of Texas Press, 2005), Jay Kinsbruner classifies a *villa* as a place with two thousand to four thousand inhabitants and states that "the term *villa* could be conferred to acknowledge prodigious wealth, size, and population, as in the case of the great mining city, the Villa Imperial de Potosí" (5).

22. *Anales de la Villa Imperial de Potosí,* Arzáns's schematic first draft or blueprint of *Potosí,* as its title states, is even more annalistic. Yet it, too, contains invented material, fictional embellishments. See the modern edition of the *Anales,* ed. Alberto Crespo (La Paz: Editorial del Estado, 1970); on prior editions, see Hanke and Mendoza (xlv). As they note, Arzáns also apparently wrote parts of an exposé specifically on the deleterious effects of silver (xlvi).

23. Mendoza writes, "There is a definite creole consciousness in Arzáns. It reaches expression in his affirmation of the great natural ability, nobility, morality, and right to life and honor of the creole. . . . The strife between creoles and Spaniards is one of the fundamental themes of the *Historia*" (clxix).

24. Hanke and Mendoza confirm Salinas as one of Arzáns's sources (lxi), an assertion the many unmistakable similarities between *Potosí* and the *Memorial* corroborate.

25. Gisbert says of Arzáns, "We know that the prior of the Franciscan monastery was his friend, and it is quite likely that Arzáns consulted the monastery library" (82). That St. Francis began as an Augustinian heads off a long list of historical and theological connections between Augustinians and Franciscans.

26. The first part of Calancha's *Corónica* was published in Barcelona in 1639, and the second, incomplete part in Lima in 1653. For episodes that Arzáns derives from Calancha, see Hanke and Mendoza, cxv.

27. Even when *Potosí* "takes on the cast of a scandal sheet due to the murders, sexual crimes, battles and cruelties that it includes, it still seems to be recording unexpected and strange events worthy of so marvelous a place as Potosí," write Hanke and Mendoza (lxxviii). Diego Arzáns's brief attempts to continue his father's work perpetuate the marvelous genius loci of Potosí by rendering it in an outright teratological mode (see the last eight chapters of *Potosí*).

28. Warm thanks go to Leonardo García Pabón for helping me understand the cultural climates of Potosí and Sucre.

29. Though making the somewhat different argument that *Potosí*'s ambiguous moralizing gestures toward an outcome that only the future will realize, García Pabón anticipates my point in stating, "The difference from European thematics lies in the nature of these social and personal conflicts, for they express the process of constructing a creole social subject. This destabilizes the

moralizing structure of the tale, because the narrative voice becomes ambiguous as it tries to maintain the moral paradigm and at the same time include the process of forming a new identity" ("Introducción" xxiv).

30. In a series of philosophical-moral sonnets (poems 199, 200, 201, 206, 207, 212 in Reedy's edition), Caviedes makes a neostoical case against wealth in Peru and in general. For example, "De la vida enemiga es la riqueza / porque es centro del vicio la abundancia" [Wealth is the enemy of life because abundance is the core of vice] (386).

31. One need also consider the satirical poetry of the Brazilian Gregório de Matos (1636–1696).

32. In his chap. 6, Lavallé discusses works by Diego de Córdova Salinas (brother of Buenaventura), Antonio Gonzales de Acuña, Juan Meléndez, Alonso de Ovalle, and, of course, Calancha and Arzáns, that follow the paths set by Salinas.

33. Vetancurt was twenty-six to thirty-three years old during the period Salinas lived in Mexico; he notes that in 1618, Salinas singled him out for the honor of directing a festival (3:119). Vetancurt mentions Salinas at twelve other points in his *Teatro,* praising the Peruvian's accomplishments and referring to his writings.

34. Cook (xxxii), citing folios 26v–27 of Salinas's other major work, a defense of the creoles, Franciscans, and the crown written and published in Madrid around 1646 (lxii). I derive biographical information on Salinas from Cook's introduction.

35. Salinas's *Memorial* of 1630 is often mentioned by scholars but hard to obtain and little studied in depth. In addition to Cook, to Brading (chap. 15), and to Mazzotti's "Indigenismos de ayer"(cited in note 7 above), another exception is Jorge Barrantes Arrese's "Fray Buenaventura de Salinas y Córdova, testimonio de la dominación colonial," *1492–1992: Análisis y debate,* ed. Hernán Amat Olazábal, 283–328 (Lima: Centro de Estudios Histórico-Militares del Perú, 1992), which I have regrettably not been able to consult.

36. For example, Salinas describes the mines as a "Cold-hearted pelican, who, intent on satisfying your thirst, and the greed of man, allows your veins to be cut open, and your insides ruptured and shattered and corroded by so many Indians, maggots possessed of reason, with their steel teeth and iron hammers" (268).

37. The call for homegrown history, enshrining of precontact Indian rulers, inflamed patriotism, and other similarities between the *Memorial* and Sigüenza's *Teatro de virtudes* suggest that the Mexican read the Peruvian's text.

38. The lead position that Salinas's treatise on Lima assigns the "abundant river that runs through the middle of the city" (107) neatly relates to the author's statement that "the quantity and grandeur of the rivers, and springs of sweet water" full of gold and precious stones have led many (starting, of course, with Columbus) to identify the New World as earthly paradise (102).

39. While Salinas has not entirely refrained from protest in preceding discourses, he definitely cuts to the jugular here. To wit, the title of Discourse 3, chap. 1 reads: "Here are Revealed, Clearly and Plainly, All the Causes" of Peru's afflictions (271).

40. Salinas is not above playing a brutal, canny game. He vehemently protests the commodification of the Indians, yet, speaking to the crown's pecuniary interests, he also bills the Indians as a source of greater revenue, if Spanish laws were obeyed (312).

41. Calancha, who read Salinas (81), also compares the Indians to the Israelites in Egypt and reaches the same conclusion as his compatriot (433–434).

42. Its conflictive relationship with the *Négritude* of Aimé Césaire, architect of Martinique's departmental status in 1946, underwrites Créolité's emphatic espousing of diversity. Put simply, whereas Négritude predicates Caribbean identity on rediscovery of its links with Africa, Créolité advocates identity based on "Caribbean, European, African, Asian, and Levantine cultural elements"; as Bernabé, Chamoiseau, and Confiant write, "complexity is the very principle of our identity," and Creoleness "is in harmony with Diversity" (891–892).

43. The connections between *Texaco* and certain dimensions of the New World Baroque as *The Spectacular City* portrays it are as striking as they were inadvertent. I thank my colleague Esther Whitfield for introducing me to Chamoiseau, among many things.

WORKS CITED

Acosta, José de. *Historia natural y moral de las Indias.* Edited by Edmundo O'Gorman. Mexico City: FCE, 1940.

———. *Natural and Moral History of the Indies.* Translated by Frances M. López-Morillas. Edited by Jane E. Mangan. Durham: Duke University Press, 2002.

Acosta, Leonardo. "El barroco americano y la ideología colonialista." *Unión* (Havana) 11, no. 5 (1972): 30–63.

Adorno, Rolena. "*La ciudad letrada* y los discursos coloniales." *Hispamérica* 16, no. 48 (1988): 3–24.

———. *Guaman Poma: Writing and Resistance in Colonial Peru.* Austin: University of Texas Press, [1986] 2000.

Alba Pastor Llaneza, María. "Criollismo, religiosidad y barroco." Bolívar Echeverría 171–198.

Alberro, Solange. *Del gachupín al criollo: o de cómo los españoles de México dejaron de serlo.* Mexico City: El Colegio de México, 1992.

Alberti, Leon Battista. *On the Art of Building in Ten Books.* Translated by Joseph Rykwert, Neal Leach, and Robert Tavernor. Cambridge: MIT Press, 1988.

Anglería, Pedro Mártir de. *Décadas del Nuevo Mundo.* Translated by Joaquín Torres Asensio. Argentina: Bajel, 1944.

Antelo, Raúl. "The Baroque Gaze." Valdés and Kadir, 3:191–200.

Apuleius. *The Golden Ass, Being the Metamorphoses of Lucius Apuleius.* Translated by W. Adlington [1566], S. Gaselee. Cambridge: Harvard University Press, [1915] 1977.

Arenal, Electa. "Sor Juana's Arch: Public Spectacle, Private Battle." *Crossing Boundaries: Attending to Early Modern Women,* edited by Jane Donawerth and Adele Seef, 173–194. Newark: University of Delaware Press; London: Associated University Presses, 2000.

Arias, Santa, and Mariselle Meléndez, eds. *Mapping Colonial Spanish America: Places and Commonplaces of Identity, Culture, and Experience.* Lewisburg: Bucknell University Press, 2002.

Aristotle. *Aristotle's* Poetics. Translated by and with commentary by George

Whalley. Edited by John Baxter and Patrick Atherton. Montreal: McGill-Queen's University Press, 1997.

———. *Metaphysics*. Translated by W. D. Ross. *The Complete Works of Aristotle: Revised Oxford Translation*. Edited by Jonathan Barnes. Vol. 2. Princeton: Princeton University Press, 1984.

Arzáns de Orsúa y Vela, Bartolomé. *Historia de la Villa Imperial de Potosí*. Edited by Lewis Hanke and Gunnar Mendoza. 3 vols. Providence: Brown University Press, 1965.

Augustine, Saint. *City of God*. Translated by Henry Bettenson. Edited by G. R. Evans. London: Penguin, 1972.

Bacigalupo, Marvyn Helen. *A Changing Perspective: Attitudes Toward Creole Society in New Spain (1521–1610)*. London: Tamesis, 1981.

Balbuena, Bernardo de. *El Bernardo*. Colección Clásicos Jaliscienses. Jalisco: Gobierno del Estado de Jalisco, 1989.

———. *La Grandeza Mexicana y Compendio apologético en alabanza de la poesía*. Edited by Luis Adolfo Domínguez. Mexico City: Porrúa, 1985.

———. *Siglo de oro en las selvas de Erífile*. Colección Clásicos Jaliscienses. Jalisco: Gobierno del Estado de Jalisco, 1989.

Baudrillard, Jean. "The System of Collecting." *The Cultures of Collecting*, edited by John Elsner and Roger Cardinal, 7–24. Cambridge: Harvard University Press, 1994.

Bénassy-Berling, Marie-Cécile. *Humanisme et religion chez Sor Juana Inés de la Cruz: La femme et la culture au XVIIe siècle*. Paris: Editions Hispaniques, Publications de la Sorbonne, 1982.

Benítez, Fernando. *Los primeros mexicanos: La vida criolla en el siglo XVI*. 2d ed. Mexico City: Era, 1962.

Benjamin, Walter. *The Origin of German Tragic Drama*. Translated by John Osborne. London: NLB, 1977.

Bernabé, Jean, Patrick Chamoiseau, and Raphaël Confiant. "In Praise of Creoleness." *Callahoo* 13 (1990): 886–909.

Beverley, John. *Del* Lazarillo *al* Sandinismo: *Estudios sobre la función ideológica de la literatura española e hispanoamericana*. Minneapolis: Prisma, 1987.

Blanco, José Joaquín. *Esplendores y miserias de los criollos: La literatura en la Nueva España*. Mexico City: Cal y Arena, 1989.

———. *La literatura en la Nueva España*. Mexico City: Cal y Arena, 1989.

Bono, Dianne M. *Cultural Diffusion of Spanish Humanism in New Spain: Francisco Cervantes de Salazar's* Diálogo de la dignidad del hombre. New York: Peter Lang, 1991.

Boyer, Richard. "Mexico in the Seventeenth Century: Transition of a Colonial Society." *Hispanic American Historical Review* 57, no. 3 (1977): 455–478.

Brading, David A. *The First America: The Spanish Monarchy, Creole Patriots, and the Liberal State 1492–1867*. Cambridge: Cambridge University Press, 1991.

Braider, Christopher. *Baroque Self-Invention and Historical Truth: Hercules at the Crossroads.* Burlington: Ashgate, 2004.

Bramón, Francisco. *Los sirgueros de la Virgen.* Edited by Agustín Yáñez. Mexico City: UNAM, [1944] 1994.

Brescia, Pablo A. J. "Towards a New Interpretation of the *Carta Atenagórica.*" *Sor Juana and Vieira, trescientos años después,* edited by K. Josu Bijuesca and Pablo A. J. Brescia, 45–52. Santa Barbara: University of California, Santa Barbara, 1998.

Burkholder, Mark A. "Bureaucrats." Hoberman and Socolow 77–103.

Burkholder, Mark A., and Lyman L. Johnson. *Colonial Latin America.* New York: Oxford University Press, [1990] 1998.

Bustamante, Jesús. "La atracción de lo raro y peregrino." *Relación de la Nueva España* by El Conquistador Anónimo, edited by Jesús Bustamante, 9–69. Madrid: Polifemo, 1986.

Buxó, José Pascual. "Prefacio." Rodríguez Hernández 3–11.

Bynum, Carolyn Walker. "Presidential Address [to the American Historical Society]: Wonder." *American Historical Review* 102 (1997): 1–26.

Cabrera Infante, Guillermo. *Tres tristes tigres.* Barcelona: Seix Barral, 1965.

Calancha, Antonio de la, and Bernardo de Torres. *Crónicas agustinianas del Perú.* Vol. 1. Edited by Manuel Merino. Madrid: C.S.I.C., 1972.

Camenietzki, Carlos Ziller. "Baroque Science Between the Old and the New World: Father Kircher and His Colleague Valentin Stansel (1621–1705)." Findlen, *Kircher* 311–328.

Campbell, Mary Baine. *Wonder and Science: Imagining Worlds in Early Modern Europe.* Ithaca: Cornell University Press, 1999.

Cañeque, Alejandro. *The King's Living Image: The Culture and Politics of Viceregal Power in Colonial Mexico.* New York: Routledge, 2004.

Cárdenas, Juan de. *Primera parte de los problemas y secretos maravillosos de las Indias.* Edited by Xavier Lozoya. Mexico City: Academia Nacional de Medicina, 1980.

Carpentier, Alejo. "De lo real maravilloso americano." *Tientos y diferencias,* 102–120. Montevideo: Arca, 1967.

Carreño, Antonio. "Of 'Orders' and 'Disorders': Analogy in the Baroque Lyric (from Góngora to Sor Juana)." *Coded Encounters: Writing, Gender, and Ethnicity in Colonial Latin America,* edited by Javier Cevallos-Candau et al., 224–235. Amherst: University of Massachusetts Press, 1994.

Catalá, Rafael. *Para una lectura americana del barroco mexicano: Sor Juana Inés de la Cruz y Sigüenza y Góngora.* Minneapolis: Prisma, 1987.

Certeau, Michel de. *The Practice of Everyday Life.* Translated by Steven Rendell. Berkeley: University of California Press, 1984.

———. *The Writing of History.* Translated by Tom Conley. New York: Columbia University Press, 1988.

Cervantes de Salazar, Francisco. *Crónica de la Nueva España*. Madrid: Hispanic Society of America, 1914.

———. *Life in the Imperial and Loyal City of Mexico in New Spain and the Royal and Pontifical University of Mexico as Described in the Dialogues for the Study of the Latin Language Prepared by Francisco Cervantes de Salazar for Use in His Classes and Printed in 1554 by Juan Pablos*. Translated by Minnie Lee Barrett Shepard. Introduction by Carlos Eduardo Castañeda. Austin: University of Texas Press, 1953.

———. *México en 1554 y Túmulo imperial*. Edited by Edmundo O'Gorman. Mexico City: Porrúa, 1963.

Chamoiseau, Patrick. *Texaco*. Translated by Rose-Myriam Réjouis and Val Vinokurov. New York: Pantheon, 1997.

Chang-Rodríguez, Raquel. *Violencia y subversión en la prosa colonial hispanoamericana, siglos XVI y XVII*. Madrid: Porrúa Turanzas, 1982.

Christian, Chester C., Jr. "Poetic and Prosaic Descriptions of Colonial Mexico City." *Exploration* 9 (1981): 1–21.

Cobo, Bernabé. *Fundación de Lima*. *Obras*. Vol. 2:279–460. Biblioteca de Autores Españoles. 92. Madrid: Atlas, 1956.

Cohen, Jeffrey Jerome. "Monster Culture (Seven Theses)." *Monster Theory: Reading Culture,* edited by Jeffrey Jerome Cohn, 3–25. Minneapolis: University of Minnesota Press, 1996.

Columbus, Christopher. *Diario de a bordo*. Edited by Luis Arranz. Madrid: Historia 16, 1985.

Concha, Jaime. "La literatura colonial hispano-americana: Problemas e hipótesis." *Neohelicon* 4, no. 12 (1976): 31–50.

Cook, Warren L. "Fray Buenaventura de Salinas y Córdova: Su vida y su obra." Salinas y Córdova xxix–lxxiii.

Cope, R. Douglas. *The Limits of Racial Domination: Plebeian Society in Colonial Mexico City, 1660–1720*. Madison: University of Wisconsin Press, 1994.

Cornejo-Polar, Antonio. "Las suturas homogeneizadoras: el discurso de la armonía imposible." *Escribir en el aire: ensayo sobre la heterogeneidad socio-cultural en las literaturas andinas*, 91–158. Lima: Horizonte, 1994.

Cortés, Hernán. *Cartas de relación*. Edited by Mario Hernández. Madrid: Historia 16, 1985.

———. *Letters from Mexico*. Translated and edited by Anthony Pagden. New Haven: Yale University Press, 1986.

Coutinho, Afrânio. *Do Barroco (Ensaios)*. Rio de Janeiro: Edições Tempo Brasileiro, 1994.

Covarrubias Orozco, Sebastián de. *Tesoro de la lengua castellana o española*. Madrid: Turner, 1979.

Cueva, Juan de la. In Méndez Plancarte, *Poetas novohispanos. Primer siglo* 20–22.

Curcio-Nagy, Linda A. *The Great Festivals of Colonial Mexico City: Performing Power and Identity*. Albuquerque: University of New Mexico Press, 2004.

Darío, Rubén. *Cantos de vida y esperanza. Poesías completas.* Edited by Alfonso Méndez Plancarte. Madrid: Aguilar, 1968.

Daston, Lorraine, and Katharine Park. *Wonder and the Order of Nature 1150–1750.* New York: Zone, 1998.

Debord, Guy. *The Society of the Spectacle.* Translated by Donald Nicholson-Smith. New York: Zone, 1994.

Descartes, René. *The Philosophical Works of Descartes.* Translated by Elizabeth S. Haldane and G. R. T. Ross. Vol. 1. Cambridge: Cambridge University Press, [1911] 1978.

Díaz del Castillo, Bernal. *The Discovery and Conquest of Mexico.* Translated by A. P. Maudslay. New York: Farrar, Straus and Cudahy, 1956.

———. *Historia verdadera de la conquista de la Nueva España.* Edited by Joaquín Ramírez Cabañas. Mexico City: Porrúa, 2000.

Dorantes de Carranza, Baltasar. *Sumaria relación de las cosas de la Nueva España con noticia individual de los descendientes legítimos de los conquistadores y primeros pobladores españoles.* Edited by José María de Agreda y Sánchez. Mexico City: Jesús Medina, [1902] 1970.

Dubois, Claude-Gilbert. *Le maniérisme.* Paris: Presses Universitaires de France, 1979.

Echeverría, Bolívar, ed. *Modernidad, mestizaje cultural, ethos barroco.* Mexico City: UNAM, 1994.

Echeverría, Bolívar. "El *ethos* barroco." Bolívar Echeverría 13–36.

Elliott, J[ohn] H[uxtable]. "Final Reflections: The Old World and the New Revisited." *America in European Consciousness: 1493–1750,* edited by Karen Ordahl Kupperman, 391–408. Chapel Hill: University of North Carolina Press, 1995.

———. *The Old World and the New: 1492–1650.* Cambridge: Cambridge University Press, 1970.

Escamilla González, Iván. "El Siglo de Oro vindicado: Carlos de Sigüenza y Góngora, el conde de Galve y el tumulto de 1692." Mayer. Vol. 2:179–203.

Espinosa Medrano, Juan de. *Apologético.* Translated by Rafael Blanco Varela. Edited by Augusto Tamayo Vargas. Caracas: Ayacucho, 1982.

Faulkner, William. *Absalom, Absalom!* New York: Vintage, 1990.

Fernández de Oviedo, Gonzalo. *Natural History of the West Indies.* Translated by Sterling A. Stoudemire. Chapel Hill: University of North Carolina Press, 1959.

———. *Sumario de la natural historia de las Indias.* Edited by Manuel Ballesteros. Madrid: Historia 16, 1986.

Findlen, Paula, ed. *Athanasius Kircher: The Last Man Who Knew Everything.* New York: Routledge, 2004.

Findlen, Paula. "A Jesuit's Books in the New World: Athanasius Kircher and His American Readers." Findlen, *Kircher* 329–364.

———. "The Last Man Who Knew Everything . . . or Did He? Athanasius Kircher, S. J. (1602–1680) and His World." Findlen, *Kircher* 1–48.

———. *Possessing Nature: Museums, Collecting, and Scientific Culture in Early Modern Italy*. Berkeley: University of California Press, 1994.

Forcione, Alban K. "At the Threshold of Modernity: Gracián's *El Criticón*." Spadaccini and Talens 3–70.

Foster, George M. *Culture and Conquest: America's Spanish Heritage*. New York: Wenner-Gren Foundation for Anthropological Research, 1960.

Foucault, Michel. *The Archeology of Knowledge and the Discourse on Language*. Translated by A. M. Sheridan Smith. New York: Pantheon, 1972.

———. *The Order of Things*. New York: Vintage, 1973.

Gage, Thomas. *Thomas Gage's Travels in the New World*. Edited by J. Eric S. Thompson. Norman: University of Oklahoma Press, 1958.

Gallegos Rocafull, José M. *El pensamiento mexicano en los siglos XVI y XVII*. Mexico City: Centro de Estudios Filosóficos, 1951.

Ganster, Paul. "Churchmen." Hoberman and Socolow 137–163.

García, Genaro. *Documentos inéditos ó muy raros para la historia de México, publicados por Genaro García y Carlos Pereyra*. Vol. 12. Mexico City: Vda. de C. Bouret, 1905–1911.

García, Gregorio. *Origen de los indios del nuevo mundo, e Indias occidentales*. Mexico City: FCE, 1981.

García Berrio, Antonio. *Formación de la teoría literaria moderna*. Vol. 1. Madrid: Cupsa, 1977.

García Canclini, Néstor. *Hybrid Cultures: Strategies for Entering and Leaving Modernity*. Translated by Christopher L. Chiappari and Silvia L. López. Minneapolis: University of Minnesota Press, 1995.

García Gallo, Alfonso, ed. *Cedulario indiano, Libro cuarto*. Facs. of 1596 edition. Madrid: Ediciones Cultura Hispánica, 1946.

García Márquez, Gabriel. *Los funerales de la mamá grande*. Buenos Aires: Sudamericana, 1975.

García Pabón, Leonardo. "Introducción." *Relatos de la Villa Imperial de Potosí* by Bartolomé Arzáns de Orsúa y Vela, xiii–xxxii. La Paz: Plural, 2000.

———. "Pensamiento andino y tradición historiográfica americana en la f(ec)undación de la ciudad colonial: *La historia de Potosí* de Bartolomé Arzáns (1676–1736)." González Stephan and Costigan 493–513.

Gaylord, Mary Malcolm. "Jerónimo de Aguilar y la alteración de la lengua (la *Mexicana* de Gabriel Lobo Lasso de la Vega)." Mazzotti 73–98.

———. "El lenguaje de la Conquista y la conquista de lenguaje en las poéticas del Siglo de Oro." *Actas del IX Congreso de la Asociación Internacional de Hispanistas*. Vol. 1:469–475. Frankfurt: Vervuet, 1989.

———. "The True History of Early Modern Writing in Spanish: Some American Reflections." *Modern Language Quarterly* 57, no. 2 (1996): 213–225.

Gisbert, Teresa. *Esquema de la literatura virreinal en Bolivia.* La Paz: Universidad Mayor de San Andrés, 1968.
Glissant, Édouard. *Caribbean Discourse: Selected Essays.* Translated and edited by J. Michael Dash. Charlottesville: University Press of Virginia, [1989] 1999.
Godwin, Joscelyn. *Athanasius Kircher: A Renaissance Man and the Quest for Lost Knowledge.* London: Thames and Hudson, 1979.
Goic, Cedomil. "La novela hispanoamericana colonial." *Historia de la literatura hispanoamericana,* edited by Luis Íñigo Madrigal, 1:396–406. Madrid: Cátedra, 1982.
Gómez de Cervantes, Gonzalo. *La vida económica y social de Nueva España, al finalizar el siglo XVI.* Edited by Alberto María Carreño. Mexico City: Robredo, 1944.
Góngora y Argote, Luis de. *Obras completas.* Edited by Juan Millé y Giménez and Isabel Millé y Giménez. Madrid: Aguilar, [1943] 1967.
Gonzalbo Aizpuru, Pilar. *Historia de la educación en la época colonial: La educación de los criollos y la vida urbana.* Mexico City: El Colegio de México, 1990.
González Boixo, José Carlos. "Introducción." *La grandeza mexicana* by Bernardo de Balbuena, 1–32. Rome: Bulzoni, 1988.
González Echevarría, Roberto. *Celestina's Brood: Continuities of the Baroque in Spanish and Latin American Literature.* Durham: Duke University Press, 1993.
———. "Colonial Lyric." González Echevarría and Pupo-Walker 191–230.
———. *Myth and Archive: A Theory of Latin American Narrative.* Durham: Duke University Press, [1990] 1998.
González Echevarría, Roberto, and Enrique Pupo-Walker, eds. *The Cambridge History of Latin American Literature.* Vol. 1. Cambridge: Cambridge University Press, 1996.
González Stephan, Beatriz, and Lúcia Helena Costigan, eds. *Crítica y descolonización: El sujeto colonial en la cultura latinoamericana.* Caracas: Academia Nacional de la Historia, 1992.
Gracián, Baltasar. *Agudeza y arte de ingenio.* Edited by Evaristo Correa Calderón. 2 vols. Madrid: Castalia, 1969.
Grafton, Anthony, with April Shelford, and Nancy Siraisi. *New Worlds, Ancient Texts: The Power of Tradition and the Shock of Discovery.* Cambridge: Harvard University Press, 1992.
Greenblatt, Stephen. *Marvelous Possessions: The Wonder of the New World.* Chicago: University of Chicago Press, 1991.
Greene, Roland. *Unrequited Conquests: Love and Empire in the Colonial Americas.* Chicago: University of Chicago Press, 1999.
Guaman Poma de Ayala, Felipe. *El primer nueva corónica y buen gobierno.* http://www.kb.dk/permalink/2006/poma/info/en/frontpage.htm
Guijo, Gregorio Martín de. *Diario, 1648–1664.* Edited by Manuel Romero de Terreros. 2 vols. Mexico City: Porrúa, 1952.

Hanke, Lewis. *Bartolomé Arzáns de Orsúa y Vela's History of Potosí*. Providence: Brown University Press, 1965.

———. "El otro tesoro de las Indias: Bartolomé Arzáns de Orsúa y Vela y su *Historia de la Villa Imperial de Potosí*." *Actas del Segundo Congreso Internacional de Hispanistas*, edited by Jaime Sánchez Romeralo and Norbert Poulussen, 51–72. Nijmegen, The Netherlands: Spanish Institute of the University of Nijmegen, 1965.

Hanke, Lewis, and Gunnar Mendoza. "Bartolomé Arzáns de Orsúa y Vela: Su vida y su obra." *Historia de la Villa Imperial de Potosí* by Bartolomé Arzáns de Orsúa y Vela, edited by Lewis Hanke and Gunnar Mendoza, 1:xxvii–clxxxi. Providence: Brown University Press, 1965.

Hardoy, Jorge E., and Carmen Aranovich. "Escalas y funciones urbanas en América Hispánica hacia el año 1600—primeras conclusiones." *Actas y memorias: XXXVII Congreso Internacional de Americanistas, Buenos Aires 1966*, 171–208. Buenos Aires: 1968.

Harss, Luis. *Sor Juana's Dream*. New York: Lumen, 1986.

Hathaway, Baxter. *Marvels and Commonplaces: Renaissance Literary Criticism*. New York: Random House, 1968.

Hauser, Arnold. *Mannerism: The Crisis of the Renaissance and the Origins of Modern Art*. Translated by Eric Mosbacher. Vol. 1. New York: Knopf, 1965.

Herman, Susan. "Conquest and Discovery: Subversion of the Fall in *El Carnero*." *MLN* 108, no. 2 (1993): 283–301.

Higgins, Anthony. *Constructing the* Criollo *Archive: Subjects of Knowledge in the* Bibliotheca Mexicana *and the* Rusticatio mexicana. West Lafayette, Ind.: Purdue University Press, 2000.

Hoberman, Louisa Schell. "Hispanic American Political Theory as a Distinct Tradition." *Journal of the History of Ideas* 41 (1980): 199–218.

Hoberman, Louisa Schell, and Susan Migden Socolow, eds. *Cities and Society in Colonial Latin America*. Albuquerque: University of New Mexico Press, 1986.

Huddleston, Lee Eldridge. *Origins of the American Indians: European Concepts, 1492–1729*. Austin: University of Texas Press, 1967.

Huggan, Graham. *The Postcolonial Exotic: Marketing the Margins*. London: Routledge, 2001.

Hulme, Peter. *Colonial Encounters: Europe and the Native Caribbean, 1492–1797*. London: Methuen, 1986.

Hutchinson, John. "Cultural Nationalism and Moral Regeneration." *Nationalism*, edited by John Hutchinson and Anthony D. Smith, 122–131. Oxford: Oxford University Press, 1994.

Impey, Oliver, and Arthur MacGregor, eds. *The Origins of Museums: The Cabinet of Curiosities in Sixteenth- and Seventeenth-Century Europe*. Oxford: Clarendon, 1985.

Íñigo Madrigal, Luis. "*Grandeza mexicana* de Bernardo de Balbuena o 'El interés, señor de las naciones.'" *Versants* 22 (1992): 23–38.

Irizarry, Estelle. "Introducción." *Infortunios de Alonso Ramírez* by Carlos de Sigüenza y Góngora, edited by Estelle Irizarry, 11–75. Río Piedras: Editorial Cultural, 1990.

Israel, J. L. *Race, Class and Politics in Colonial Mexico 1610–1670*. London: Oxford University Press, 1975.

Jacobsen, Jerome V. *Educational Foundations of the Jesuits in Sixteenth-Century New Spain*. Berkeley: University of California Press, 1939.

Jardine, Lisa. *Worldly Goods: A New History of the Renaissance*. New York: Doubleday, 1996.

Juana Inés de la Cruz, Sor. *Carta de Sor Juana Inés de la Cruz a su confesor: Autodefensa espiritual*. Edited by Aureliano Tapia Méndez. Monterrey, Mexico: Impresora Monterrey, 1986.

———. *Fama y obras pósthumas del Fenix de México, Dezima Musa, Poetisa Americana, Sor Juana Inés de la Cruz*. Edited by Fredo Arias de la Canal. Mexico City: Frente de Afirmación Hispanista, 1989.

———. *Inundación castálida*. Edited by Georgina Sabat de Rivers. Madrid: Clásicos Castalia, 1982.

———. *Obras completas de Sor Juana Inés de la Cruz*. Edited by Alfonso Méndez Plancarte. 4 vols. Mexico City: FCE, 1951–1957. Vol. 1: Lírica personal; Vol. 2: Villancicos y Letras Sacras; Vol. 3: Autos y Loas; Vol. 4 (edited by Alberto G. Salceda): Comedias, Sainetes y Prosa.

Kagan, Richard L. *Urban Images of the Hispanic World, 1493–1793*. New Haven: Yale University Press, 2000.

Keen, Benjamin. *The Aztec Image in Western Thought*. New Brunswick: Rutgers University Press, 1971.

Kramer, Roswitha. "'Ex ultimo anglo orbia': Atanasio Kircher y el Nuevo Mundo." *Pensamiento europeo y cultura colonial*, edited by Karl Kohot and Sonia V. Rose, 320–377. Frankfurt: Vervuert, 1997.

Kubler, George. *Mexican Architecture of the Sixteenth Century*. New Haven: Yale University Press, 1948.

Lafaye, Jacques. *Quetzalcóatl and Guadalupe: The Formation of Mexican National Consciousness, 1531–1813*. Translated by Benjamin Keen. Foreword by Octavio Paz. Chicago: University of Chicago Press, 1976.

Lara, Jaime. *City, Temple, Stage: Eschatological Architecture and Liturgical Theatrics in New Spain*. Notre Dame: University of Notre Dame Press, 2004.

Las Casas, Bartolomé de. *Brevísima relación de la destrucción de las Indias*. Edited by André Saint-Lu. Madrid: Cátedra, 1987.

Lavallé, Bernard. *Las promesas ambiguas: Ensayos sobre el criollismo colonial en los Andes*. Lima: Pontificia Universidad Católica del Perú, Instituto Riva-Agüero, 1993.

Lavrin, Asunción. "La congregación de San Pedro: Una cofradía urbana del México colonial, 1604–1730." *Historia mexicana* 29, no. 4 (1980): 562–601.

León, Luis de. *Obras completas castellanas*. Edited by Felix García. Vol. 2. 4th ed. Madrid: Biblioteca de Autores Cristianos, 1967.

León Pinelo, Antonio de. *El Paraíso en el Nuevo Mundo*. Edited by Raúl Porras Barrenechea. Vol. 2. Lima: Imprenta Torres Aguirre, 1943.

León-Portilla, Miguel, ed. *El reverso de la conquista*. Mexico City: Joaquín Mortiz, [1964] 1996.

Leonard, Irving A. *Baroque Times in Old Mexico: Seventeenth-Century Persons, Places, and Practices*. Ann Arbor: University of Michigan Press, 1959.

Lezama Lima, José. *La expresión americana*. Santiago de Chile: Editorial Universitaria, 1969.

Liss, Peggy K. *Mexico Under Spain 1521–1526: Society and the Origins of Nationality*. Chicago: University of Chicago Press, 1975.

López de Gómara, Francisco. *La conquista de México*. Madrid: Historia 16, 1987.

López de Velasco, Juan. *Geografía y descripción universal de las Indias*. Edited by Marcos Jiménez de la Espada. Madrid: Atlas, 1971.

Luciani, Frederick. *Literary Self-Fashioning in Sor Juana Inés de la Cruz*. Lewisburg: Bucknell University Press, 2004.

Luis, de Granada. *Obras V. P. M. Fray Luis de Granada*. Edited by José Joaquín de Mora. Biblioteca de Autores Españoles. Vol. 6. Madrid: Casa Editorial Hernando, 1927.

Lynch, John. *Spain Under the Hapbsburgs*. Vol. 2. New York: New York University Press, [1969] 1981.

Malcolm, Noel. "Private and Public Knowledge: Kircher, Esotericism, and the Republic of Letters." Findlen, *Kircher* 297–309.

Manrique, Jorge Alberto. *Manierismo en México*. Mexico City: Textos Dispersos Ediciones, 1993.

———. "El manierismo en la Nueva España: Letras y artes." *Anales del Instituto de Investigaciones Estéticas* 45 (1976): 107–116.

Maravall, José Antonio. *Culture of the Baroque: Analysis of a Historical Structure*. Translated by Terry Cochran. Minneapolis: University of Minnesota Press, 1986.

Marin, Louis. *Portrait of the King*. Translated by Martha M. Houlse. Minneapolis: University of Minnesota Press, 1988.

Martínez-San Miguel, Yolanda. *Saberes americanos: Subalternidad y epistemología en los escritos de Sor Juana*. Pittsburgh: Instituto Internacional de Literatura Iberoamericana, 1999.

May, T. E. "An Interpretation of Gracián's *Agudeza y arte de ingenio*." *Hispanic Review* 16, no. 4 (1948): 275–300.

Mayer, Alicia, ed. *Carlos de Sigüenza y Góngora: Homenaje 1700–2000*. 2 vols. Mexico City: UNAM, 2002.

Maza, Francisco de la. *La ciudad de México en el siglo XVII*. Mexico City: FCE, 1968.

———. *El pintor Cristóbal de Villalpando*. Mexico City: Instituto Nacional de Antropología e Historia, 1964.

Mazzotti, José Antonio, ed. *Agencias criollas: La ambigüedad "colonial" en las letras hispanoamericanas*. Pittsburgh: Instituto Internacional de Literatura Iberoamericana, 2000.

Mazzotti, José Antonio. "Introduccion." Mazzotti 7–35.

McClintock, Anne. *Imperial Leather: Race, Gender, and Sexuality in the Colonial Conquest*. New York: Routledge, 1995.

Méndez Plancarte, Alfonso, ed. *Poetas novohispanos. Primer siglo (1521–1621)*. Mexico City: Ediciones de la Universidad Nacional Autónoma, [1942] 1991.

———. *Poetas novohispanos. Segundo siglo (1621–1721). Parte primera*. 3d ed. Mexico City: UNAM, 1995.

Mendieta, Gerónimo de. *Historia eclesiástica indiana*. Edited by Joaquín Icazbalceta. Facs. of 1870 edition. Mexico City: Porrúa, 1971.

Menéndez y Pelayo, Marcelino. *Historia de la poesía hispanoamericana*. Vol. 1. Madrid: Librería General de Victoriano Suárez, 1911.

Merrim, Stephanie. *Early Modern Women's Writing and Sor Juana Inés de la Cruz*. Nashville: Vanderbilt University Press, 1999.

———. "Spectacular Cityscapes of Baroque Spanish America." Valdés and Kadir. Vol. 3:31–57.

Mignolo, Walter D. *The Darker Side of the Renaissance: Literacy, Territoriality, and Colonization*. Ann Arbor: University of Michigan Press, 1995.

Millones, Luis. "Literary Culture During the Peruvian Viceroyalty." Valdés and Kadir. Vol. 1:133–154.

Moraña, Mabel. "The Baroque and Transculturation." Valdés and Kadir. Vol. 3:180–190.

———. *Viaje al silencio: Exploraciones del discurso barroco*. Mexico City: UNAM, 1998.

More, Thomas. *Utopia*. Translated and edited by Robert M. Adams. New York: Norton, 1975.

Morse, Richard. "The Urban Development of Colonial Spanish America." *The Cambridge History of Latin America*, edited by Leslie Bethell, 2:67–104. Cambridge: Cambridge University Press, 1984.

Mugaburu, Josephe de. *Chronicle of Colonial Lima: The Diary of Josephe and Francisco Mugaburu, 1640–1697*. Translated and edited by Robert Ryall Miller. Norman: University of Oklahoma Press, 1975.

Mujica, Barbara. "Antiutopian Elements in the Spanish Pastoral Novel." *Kentucky Romance Quarterly* 26 (1970): 263–282.

Mumford, Lewis. *The City in History: Its Origins, Its Transformations, and Its Prospects*. New York: Harcourt, Brace and World, 1961.

Muriel, Josefina. *Conventos de monjas en la Nueva España*. Mexico City: Santiago, 1946.
O'Gorman, Edmundo. *El arte o de la monstruosidad y otros escritos*. Mexico City: Planeta/Joaquín Mortiz, 2002.
———. *Meditaciones sobre el criollismo*. Mexico City: Centro de Estudios de Historia de México, 1970.
Osorio Romero, Ignacio, ed. *La luz imaginaria: Epistolario de Atanasio Kircher con los novohispanos*. Mexico City: UNAM, 1993.
Ovid. *Metamorphoses*. Translated by Horace Gregory. New York: Mentor, 1960.
Padden, R. C. "Editor's Introduction." *Tales of Potosí* by Bartolomé Arzáns de Orsúa y Vela, edited by R. C. Padden, translated by Frances M. López-Morillas, x–xxxvi. Providence: Brown University Press, 1975.
Pagden, Anthony. *European Encounters with the New World: From Renaissance to Romanticism*. New Haven: Yale University Press, 1993.
———. *The Fall of Natural Man: The American Indian and the Origins of Comparative Ethnology*. Cambridge: Cambridge University Press, 1982.
———. "Identity Formation in Spanish America." *Colonial Identity in the Atlantic World 1500–1800*, edited by Nicholas Canny and Anthony Pagden, 51–95. Princeton: Princeton University Press, 1987.
Panofsky, Erwin. *Idea: A Concept in Art Theory*. Translated by Joseph J. S. Peake. Columbia: University of South Carolina Press, 1968.
Paz, Octavio. *Las peras del olmo*. Mexico City: UNAM, 1965.
———. *Sor Juana, or, The Traps of Faith*. Translated by Margaret Sayers Peden. Cambridge: Harvard University Press, 1988.
Paz y Meliá, Antonio. "Cartapacio de diferentes versos a diversos asuntos compuestos o recogidos por Mateo Rosas de Oquendo." *Bulletin Hispanique* 9 (1907): 154–185.
Peirce, John Saunders. *The Philosophical Writings of Peirce*. Edited by Justus Buchler. New York: Dover, 1950.
Peña, Margarita. "La ciudad de México en los diálogos de Francisco Cervantes de Salazar." *Escritura* 5, no. 11 (Caracas, 1981): 125–150.
Pérez de Oliva, Hernán. *Historia de la inuención de las Yndias*. Edited by José Juan Arrom. Bogotá: Cara y Cuervo, 1965.
Phelan, John Leddy. *The Millennial Kingdom of the Franciscans in the New World*. Berkeley: University of California Press, 1970.
Picón-Salas, Mariano. *A Cultural History of Spanish America, From Conquest to Independence*. Translated by Irving A. Leonard. Berkeley: University of California Press, 1962.
Plato. *Theaetetus*. Translated by John McDowell. Oxford: Clarendon, 1973.
Plutarch. *Isis and Osiris*. penelope.uchicago.edu/Thayer/E/Roman/Texts/Plutarch/Moralia/Isis_and_Osiris*/home.html.

Pomian, Krzysztof. *Collectors and Curiosities: Paris and Venice, 1500–1800.* Translated by Elizabeth Wiles-Portier. Oxford: Polity Press, 1990.
Popkin, Richard H. "Theories of Knowledge." *The Cambridge History of Renaissance Philosophy,* edited by Quentin Skinner and Eckhard Kessler. New York: Cambridge University Press, 1988. 668–684.
Prescott, William Hickling. *The Conquest of Mexico.* New York: H. Holt, 1922.
Rabasa, José. *Inventing America: Spanish Historiography and the Formation of Eurocentrism.* Norman: University of Oklahoma Press, 1993.
Rama, Angel. *La ciudad letrada.* Hanover: Ediciones del Norte, 1984.
———. "Fundación del manierismo hispanoamericano por Bernardo de Balbuena." *University of Dayton Review* 16, no. 2 (1983): 13–22.
Ramos Sosa, Rafael. *Arte festivo en Lima virreinal (siglos XVI–XVII).* Andalucía: Junta de Andalucía, 1992.
Reyes, Alfonso. *Capítulos de literatura española.* Mexico City: Casa de España en México, 1939.
Ricard, Robert. *La conquista espiritual de México.* Translated by Ángel María Garibay K. Mexico City: Jus, 1947.
Roach, Joseph. *Cities of the Dead: Circum-Atlantic Performance.* New York: Columbia University Press, 1996.
Robles, Antonio de. *Diario de sucesos notables.* Edited by Antonio Castro Leal. 3 vols. Mexico City: Porrúa, 1946.
Rodríguez Freile, Juan. *El Carnero.* Edited by Miguel Aguilera. Medellín: Bedout, 1973.
Rodríguez Hernández, Dalmacio. *Texto y fiesta en la literatura novohispana (1650–1700).* Mexico City: UNAM, 1998.
Roggiano, Alfredo. "Bernardo de Balbuena." *Historia de la literatura hispanoamericana,* edited by Luis Íñigo Madrigal, 1:215–224. Madrid: Cátedra, 1982.
Rojas Garcidueñas, José. *Bernardo de Balbuena: La vida y la obra.* Mexico City: Instituto de Investigaciones Estéticas, 1958.
Rosas de Oquendo, Mateo. *Sátira hecha por Mateo Rosas de Oquendo a las cosas que pasan en el Pirú, año de 1598.* Edited by Pedro Lasarte. Madison: Hispanic Seminary of Medieval Studies, 1990.
Ross, Kathleen. "*Alboroto y motín de México:* Una noche triste criolla." *Hispanic Review* 55, no. 2 (1988): 181–190.
———. *The Baroque Narrative of Carlos de Sigüenza y Góngora.* Cambridge: Cambridge University Press, 1993.
———. "Historians of the Conquest and Colonization of the New World: 1550–1620." González Echevarría and Pupo-Walker 101–142.
Rowland, Ingrid D. "Athanasius Kircher, Giordano Bruno, and the *Panspermia* of the Infinite Universe." Findlen, *Kircher* 191–205.
———. *The Ecstatic Journey: Athanasius Kircher in Baroque Rome.* Chicago: University of Chicago Library, 2000.

Ryan, Michael T. "Assimilating New Worlds in the Sixteenth and Seventeenth Centuries." *Comparative Studies in Society and History* 23, no. 4 (1981): 519–538.

Ryjik, Veronika. "El mito de la nueva Arcadia: la *Grandeza mexicana* de Bernardo de Balbuena y la revaloración de los tópicos pastoriles." *Bulletin of Spanish Studies* 82, no. 5 (2005): 593–614.

Sabat de Rivers, Georgina. *En busca de Sor Juana.* Mexico City: UNAM, 1998.

———. *Estudios de literatura hispanoamericana: Sor Juana Inés de la Cruz y otros poetas barrocos de la colonia.* Barcelona: PPU, 1992.

Sacido Romero, Alberto. "La ambigüedad genérica de los *Infortunios de Alonso Ramírez* como producto de la dialéctica entre discurso oral y discurso escrito." *Bulletin Hispanique* 94 (1992): 119–139.

Salazar y Alarcón, Eugenio de. In *Ensayo de una biblioteca española de libros raros y curiosos,* edited by Bartolomé José Gallardo, 4:354–370. Madrid: Manuel Tello, 1889.

Salinas y Córdova, Buenaventura de. *Memorial de las historias del Nuevo Mundo, Pirú.* Edited by Luis E. Valcárcel. Lima: Universidad Nacional Mayor de San Marcos, 1957.

Sánchez, Francisco J. "Symbolic Wealth and Theatricality in Gracián." Spadaccini and Talens 209–229.

Sánchez, Miguel. *Imagen de la Virgen María, Madre de Dios de Guadalupe. Milagrosamente aparecida en la ciudad de México. Celebrada en su historia, con la profecía del capítulo doce del Apocalipsis.* In *Testimonios historicos guadalupanos,* edited by Ernesto de la Torre Villar and Ramón Navarro de Anda, 152–281. Mexico City: FCE, 1981.

Sarduy, Severo. *Barroco.* Buenos Aires: Sudamericana, 1974.

Schafer, Edward. *The Vermillion Bird.* Berkeley: University of California Press, 1967.

Schons, Dorothy. "The Influence of Góngora on Mexican Literature During the Seventeenth Century." *Hispanic Review* 6 (1939): 22–34.

Semo, Enrique. *Historia del capitalismo en México: Los orígenes, 1521–1763.* Mexico City: Era, [1973] 1981.

Siebert, Harald. "Kircher and His Critics: Censorial Practice and Pragmatic Disregard in the Society of Jesus." Findlen, *Kircher* 79–104.

Sigüenza y Góngora, Carlos de. *Alboroto y motín de los indios de México; Libra astronómica; Teatro de virtudes políticas que constituyen a un Príncipe.* In *Seis obras.* Edited by William G. Bryant. Caracas: Ayacucho, 1984.

———. *Glorias de Querétaro.* Querétaro: Ediciones Cimatario, 1945.

———. *Infortunios que Alonso Ramírez, natural de la ciudad de San Juan de Puerto Rico, padeció.* Edited by J. S. Cummins and Alan Soons. London: Tamesis, 1984.

———. "Letter to Admiral Pez." In *Don Carlos de Sigüenza y Góngora: A Mexi-*

can Savant of the Seventeenth Century by Irving A. Leonard. Translation of *Alboroto y motín de los indios de México*, 1692. Berkeley: University of California Press, 1929.

———. *The Misadventures of Alonso Ramírez*. Translated by Edwin H. Pleasants. Mexico City: Imprenta Mexicana, 1962.

———. *Paraíso Occidental*. Edited by Margarita Peña. Mexico City: CONACULTA, 1995.

———. *Triunfo Parténico*. Mexico City: Ediciones Xochitl, 1945.

Sosa, Francisco. *Efemérides históricas y biográficas*. Mexico City: Tip. de Gonzalo A. Esteva, 1833.

Spadaccini, Nicholas, and Luis Martín-Estudillo, eds. *Hispanic Baroques: Reading Cultures in Context*. Nashville: Vanderbilt University Press, 2005.

Spadacinni, Nicholas, and Jenaro Talens, eds. *Rhetoric and Politics: Baltasar Gracián and the New World Order*. Minneapolis: University of Minnesota Press, 1997.

Spivak, Gayatri Chakravorty. "Can the Subaltern Speak?" *Marxism and the Interpretation of Culture,* edited by Cary Nelson and Lawrence Grossberg, 271–313. Urbana: University of Illinois Press, 1988.

Stanislawski, Dan. "Earliest Town Planning in the New World." *Geographical Review* 37 (1947): 94–105.

———. "The Origin and Spread of the Grid-Pattern Town." *Geographical Review* 36 (1946): 105–120.

Stewart, Susan. *On Longing: Narratives of the Miniature, the Gigantic, the Souvenir, the Collection*. Baltimore: Johns Hopkins University Press, 1984.

Strong, Roy. *Art and Power: Renaissance Festivals: 1450–1650*. Berkeley: University of California Press, 1984.

Suárez de Peralta, Juan. *Tratado del descubrimiento de las Indias*. Edited by Federico Gómez de Orozco. Mexico City: Secretaría de Educación Pública, 1949.

Tavard, George. *Juana Inés de la Cruz and the Theology of Beauty: The First Mexican Theology*. Notre Dame: University of Notre Dame Press, 1991.

Taylor, Diana. *The Archive and the Repertoire: Performing Cultural Memory in the Americas*. Durham: Duke University Press, 2003.

Teresa de Jesús, Saint. *Libro de las fundaciones*. Edited by Víctor García de la Concha. Madrid: Espasa-Calpe, 1982.

Théry, Hervé. "The Formation of a Cultural Territory." Valdés and Kadir. Vol. 1:3–17.

Torquemada, Juan de. *Monarquía indiana*. Edited by Miguel León-Portilla. 3 vols. Mexico City: Porrúa, 1969.

Trabulse, Elías. *El círculo roto*. Mexico City: FCE, [1982] 1992.

———. "*Itinerarium Scientificum:* De Alejandro Favián a Carlos de Sigüenza y Góngora." Mayer. Vol. 2:27–36.

Trueblood, Alan S., trans. and ed. *A Sor Juana Anthology.* Cambridge: Harvard University Press, 1988.
Valdés, Mario J. "Introduction: Beyond Literary History." Valdés and Kadir. Vol. 1:xvii–xxv.
Valdés, Mario J., and Djelal Kadir, eds. *Literary Cultures of Latin America: A Comparative History.* 3 vols. New York: Oxford University Press, 2004.
Valle-Arizpe, Artemio de, ed. *Historia de la Ciudad de México según los relatos de sus cronistas.* 4th ed. Mexico City: Pedro Robredo, 1946.
Vallejo, César. *Los heraldos negros.* New York: Las Américas, n.d.
Valle y Caviedes, Juan del. *Obra completa.* Edited and prologue by Daniel Reedy. Caracas: Ayacucho, 1984.
Van Horne, John. *Bernardo de Balbuena: Biografía y crítica.* Guadalajara: Imprenta Font, 1940.
———. "Documentos del Archivo de Indias referentes a Bernardo de Balbuena." *Boletín de la Real Academia de la Historia* 96 (1930): 857–876.
Vargaslugo, Elisa. *México barroco.* Querétaro: Gráficas Monte Albán, 1993.
Vetancurt, Agustín de. *Teatro mexicano: Descripción breve de los sucessos exemplares de la Nueva-España en el Nuevo Mundo Occidental de las Indias.* 4 vols. Madrid: José Porrúa Turanzas, 1960.
Vidal, Hernán. *Socio-historia de la literatura colonial hispanoamericana: tres lecturas orgánicas.* Minneapolis: Institute for the Study of Ideologies and Literature, 1985.
Vigil, Ralph H. *Alonso de Zorita: Royal Judge and Christian Humanist, 1512–1585.* Norman: University of Oklahoma Press, 1987.
Villalobos, Arias de. *Canto intitulado Mercurio.* In *Documentos inéditos o muy raros para la historia de México, publicados por Genaro García y Carlos Pereyra,* edited by Genaro García. Vol. 12. Mexico City: Vda. de C. Bouret, 1905–1911.
Walsh, Jane MacLaren, and Yoko Sugiura. "The Demise of the Fifth Sun." *Seeds of Change: A Quincentennial Commemoration,* 17–41. Washington: Smithsonian Institution, 1991.
Webster's New Universal Unabridged Dictionary. 1983 ed.
Weismann, Elizabeth Wilder. *Art and Time in Mexico: Architecture and Sculpture in Colonial Mexico.* New York: Harper Collins, [1985] 1995.
Wheelock, Arthur K., Jr. "*Trompe-l'oeil* Painting: Visual Deceptions or Natural Truths?" *The Age of the Marvelous,* edited by Joy Kenseth, 179–191. Hanover: Hood Museum of Art, 1991.
Williams, Raymond. *Marxism and Literature.* Oxford: Oxford University Press, 1977.
Wilson, Diana de Armas. *Cervantes, the Novel, and the New World.* Oxford: Oxford University Press, 2000.
Witt, R. E. *Isis in the Graeco-Roman World.* London: Thames and Hudson, 1971.

Yates, Frances A. *Giordano Bruno and the Hermetic Tradition*. Chicago: University of Chicago Press, 1964.
Zavala, Iris. "The Three Faces of the Baroque in Mexico and the Caribbean." Valdés and Kadir. Vol. 3:174–179.
Zorita, Alonso de. *Relación de la Nueva España*. In Valle-Arizpe 259–276.

INDEX

Italicized entries indicate illustrations.

absolutism, 10, 28, 36, 45–46, 50, 154, 157
Acosta, José de, 40, 157, 162, 174, 284, 295, 320n17, 320n19; on the devil, 41–42, 160, 161, 163, 165, 191–192
admiratio, 30–31, 77, 102
Africans, 147, 148, 152, 154, 156, 181, 300n17
agile platforms, 13, 17, 27, 29, 47, 192, 257, 299n7
Aguiar y Seijas, Francisco de, 188, 189, 212, 215, 222, 238, 243, 328n22
Alberti, Leon Battista, 61–62, 63, 73, 308n22, 312n15
All, the, 10, 194, 197, 205, 206, 207, 210, 214, 216, 218, 219, 220, 227, 233
allegories, 27, 85, 112, 171, 175, 177, 178, 183, 191–192, 220–221, 226, 227, 267
Anglería, Pedro Mártir de, 84, 124, 310n35
apologetics, 7, 18, 22, 125, 131, 137, 142, 165, 198, 203, 207, 325n3. *See also* hexameral writings
aporia, 58, 66, 98, 120, 171, 236, 290, 307n8
arches, triumphal, 26; of Sigüenza, 176, 178, 321nn29–30, 322n32; of Sor Juana, 176, 183, 184, 185, 321n29, 323n42
archetypes, 11, 50, 74, 92, 120, 217, 231–232, 235, 253
architecture, 2, 26, 62, 63, 65, 72–73, 75, 105, 134, 141, 298n6, 322n35
architexture, 117, 118, 120, 126, 144, 148, 236, 253, 269, 273, 294. *See also* particularity
archives, 7, 239, 240, 253–254, 257, 266, 269, 276, 283, 286, 298n8, 331n5. *See also* Mexican Archive
Arethusa, 218, 219, 230
Aristotle/Aristotelianism, 17, 30–31, 39, 45, 57, 71, 158, 165, 206, 214, 218, 226, 230, 232, 233, 234, 235, 276, 306–307n7
Arzáns de Orsúa y Vela, Bartolomé, 19, 251, 252, 253–254, 258, 259–260, 265, 269, 270–279, 280, 282, 286, 296, 333nn22–24
Atlantis, 161, 181
Augustine, Saint, 18, 31, 64, 73, 184, 198, 221, 226–231, 234–235, 252–253, 267, 274, 275, 292, 323n40, 328n21, 329n28, 329n30, 330n33. *See also* earthly city; Heavenly City

autos-da-fé, 23, 25, 264, 332n15
Aztecs, 41, 56–57, 78, 128, 176, 177, 178, 190, 225, 242, 259, 260, 306n6. See also Indians; Moctezuma II; Tenochtitlán

Babel, 10, 145, 227, 228, 230, 232–235, 242–244, 249, 251–253, 256–258, 262–268, 274, 278, 281–283, 290–293, 330n34
Balbuena, Bernardo de, 9, 147, 155, 197, 202, 267, 278, 296; *El Bernardo*, 93, 126, 130, 311n4; ciphering by, 98, 119–120, 236, 286; "Compendio apologético," 97, 99, 100, 114, 131, 314n29, 328n21; and creole cause, 128–132, 133, 135, 143; and Dorantes, 135–140; extolling wealth, 19, 100–101, 110, 112–113, 121, 124, 126, 127, 128, 130, 142, 143, 145, 272–273; "La grandeza mexicana," 10, 40, 74, 96–102, 109–115, 117–127, 141, 246, 247, 269, 294, 311n4, 315n32, 317n14, 318n5; *La grandeza mexicana*, 95, 96–98, 99, 102, 105, 108, 122, 123, 124, 129, 139, 296, 311n3, 313n20; and Indians, 122–125, 130, 137, 156, 238, 260; liminality in, 108, 110–112; and Mannerism, 104, 108, 110, 112, 114, 144, 313n17; and metamorphosis, 108–109, 110; and Rosas de Oquendo, 133–134; and Salinas, 282, 284, 286–288, 298n10; *Siglo de oro*, 91–92, 93, 94–96, 97, 99, 100, 101, 108, 110, 111, 113, 117–118, 222–224, 311n2, 311n4, 315n30; and Sigüenza, 171–173, 181, 186, 198, 313n21, 318n5; and Sor Juana, 183, 186, 219, 220, 235–236, 328n21; and Spectacular City, 8, 92, 93, 94, 97, 127, 145; and Vetancurt, 151, 152, 164, 198, 318n7; and Villalobos, 141–145; and wonder cabinets, 102, 122, 123, 125, 203, 208, 219, 259
Baroque, 8, 43, 89, 150, 153, 157, 158, 194, 223, 257–258; esthetics of, 36, 140, 179; European, 35–36, 46, 92, 158–159; versus Mannerism, 114–115, 315n30; poetics of, 43–44, 114, 204. See also Neo-Baroque; New World Baroque
Basques, 273–274
Benavente, Toribio de. See Motolinía
Benjamin, Walter, 158–159, 232, 236, 305n44, 319n12
Bogotá, 10, 251, 265–266, 267, 269
Bosch, Hieronymus, 11, 12, 13, 34, 37, 38, 51, 52, 55, 139, 295, 299n2
Botticelli, Sandro, 11, 48, 51–52, 55, 66, 79, 88, 120, 260, 295, 306n2, 309n29. See also Venus
Bramón, Francisco de, 222–224, 296, 329n25
brevitatis formula, 98, 130, 171

cabildo, 15, 24, 68, 141, 176, 261, 300n18
Calancha, Antonio de la, 275, 299n10, 333n26, 335n41
Campbell, Mary Baine, 29, 39, 42, 56, 125, 307n10, 309n27
capitalism, 6, 19, 37, 92, 101, 103, 109, 113, 124, 143, 258. See also *interés*; materialism; mercantilism; wealth
Cárdenas, Juan de, 18, 106, 131, 136, 137–138, 139, 142, 165, 174, 259, 295, 312n13, 316n7, 325n3
carnivals/carnivalesque, 25, 26, 27, 244, 280, 289
castas, 20, 148, 154, 237, 238, 240, 244, 275. See also mestizos
catachresis, 41, 45, 112, 114, 207, 223, 287
Caviedes. See Valle y Caviedes, Juan del

Cervantes, Miguel de, 42, 222, 277, 278, 304n39
Cervantes de Salazar, Francisco, 9, 68, 73, 98, 99, 100, 125, 136, 145, 198, 204, 295, 300n20, 307n12, 308n18, 308nn20–21, 309n24; and Balbuena, 99–100, 109, 117, 119, 121, 125; *Dialogues* by, 67–80, 137, 308n22, 309n24, 309n28; and Mexico City, 66–67, 70–78, 81, 83, 86, 87, 105, 106, 120, 173, 307–308n17, 308n20, 308n22
Chamoiseau, Patrick, 291–294, 335n43
Chapultepec, 78, 86–87, 287
Charles V, 15, 34, 73, 174, 176, 300n20, 301n22
Chichimecas, 169, 173, 174, 178. See *also* Indians
cities, 2, 3, 18–19, 21, 50, 116, 256; as contact zones, 21, 147–148, 169, 175; as element of Spectacular City, 3, 4, 6–9, 13–14, 47, 154; ethnic segregation of, 20–21, 59, 63, 86, 122; of God (*see* Heavenly City); lettered (see *ciudad letrada*); of Mammon (*see* earthly city); planning of, 9, 20–21, 50, 59, 61–65, 66, 72–73, 119, 307n14 (*see also* city-planning ordinances of 1573). See *also* Bogotá; *ciudad letrada;* Cuzco; earthly city; esoteric city; Heavenly City; intellectual city; Lima; Madrid; Mexico City; Ordered City; Potosí; Puebla; Querétaro; Spectacular City; Tenochtitlán
city-planning ordinances of 1573, 20, 23, 63, 295, 307n14
ciudad letrada, 3, 100, 116–117, 197, 204, 269, 297n1, 314n27
climate, 17–18, 22, 86, 111, 137, 143, 151, 152, 153, 165, 166, 172, 320n22, 325n3
Cobo, Bernabé, 18, 20, 21

Colegio de San Pedro y San Pablo, 106, 208–209, 321n28
collections, 3, 35, 102, 103, 123, 211, 215, 216, 312n9, 313n19, 328n19
colonialogic, 39, 51, 54, 67, 84, 124, 246, 251
Columbus, Christopher, 39, 54, 58, 59, 79, 122, 136, 138–139, 243, 283, 295, 325n54; view of New World as paradise by, 37, 84, 286, 307n11; wonder in, 32–33, 35, 301nn22–23
Company of Jesus. *See* Jesuits
Corpus Christi. *See under* festivals
Cortés, Hernán, 9, 35, 49, 51, 68, 75, 77, 79, 101, 112, 125, 231, 240, 245, 257, 286, 295, 298n8, 307nn8–9; biography of, 17, 68, 307n12; *Cuarta carta-relación,* 59, 60, 152, 246, 295; description of cities by, 56–58, 60, 76; epic poems about, 17, 82, 130, 131, 316n1; *Segunda carta-relación,* 49, 56, 58, 60, 240, 295
Cortés, Martín, 75, 255
Council of the Indies, 16, 96, 126, 141, 142, 144, 310n32, 317n12
Counter-Reformation, 23, 35, 44, 105, 107, 157, 158, 161, 202, 205, 206, 207, 276
crematistike, 126, 203–204, 319n11
creoles, 4–5, 7, 16–17, 18, 21–22, 68, 107, 130, 131, 160, 163, 169, 194, 197, 251, 255, 284–285, 297n2, 298n6, 298n8, 298n10, 309n25; activism of, 16, 128–133, 135, 139, 140, 142–143, 185, 267; cultural nationalism of, 10, 132, 164, 166–167, 178, 188, 194, 204, 225, 238, 260, 261, 289, 292; discourse of, 5–8, 17, 131, 135, 140, 143, 145, 149, 163–164, 166–167, 284; education of, 105–107, 202, 325n3; identity of, 4, 5, 166, 297n4, 299n7; and Indians, 8, 137, 154, 166, 268; intellectuals among, 3, 9, 10, 26, 50,

creoles (continued)
68, 158, 165–166, 177, 182, 185, 187, 196, 197, 204, 205, 285, 320n22; nation of, 166, 167, 168, 173, 177, 182; nationalism of, 4, 5–6, 17, 133, 160, 166; patriotism of, 8, 133, 149–151, 165–167, 177, 181–182, 185, 189, 193–194, 285; roles of, 5, 15–16, 45–46, 144, 150, 154, 189, 299n4; self-exoticizing of, 37, 132, 139–140, 186, 259, 260, 278, 286, 331–332n11; social mobility of, 69, 106, 197, 204, 248; tensions of with Spaniards, 76, 223, 255, 273–274, 333n23. See also *Créolité*; *criollismo*

Créolité, 291–293, 335n42. See also creoles; *criollismo*

criollismo, 8, 17, 22, 77, 130, 142, 292. See also *Créolité*; creoles

Cueva, Juan de la, 9, 125, 295, 309n30; and Mexico City, 80–83, 86, 120, 309n30, 310n31; six C's of, 82–83, 145, 151

Cuzco, 6, *146*, 148, 154, 249, 283, 285–286, 321n27

Debord, Guy, 24, 157, 300n15
Descartes, René, 30, 205
desengaño, 258, 277, 281, 284
devil, the, 41–42, 160–161, 163, 165, 179, 181, 186, 191, 192, 221, 253, 256, 267, 268, 270, 303n36, 319n15, 322n37
Díaz del Castillo, Bernal, 56–58, 112, 285, 295
disorder, 27, 59, 79–80, 154, 232–233, 242, 244, 252, 256–257, 260, 272, 292, 293
Dorantes de Carranza, Baltasar, 10, 108, 132, 144, 145, 259, 267, 284, 296, 316n3; and Balbuena, 135–138, 139–140, 316n4; as creole apologist, 131, 135–137, 140, 142, 145, 257–258; and Jesuits, 106, 136–137; and Mexican Archive, 16–17, 135–140, 223; self-exoticizing in, 132, 138–140, 186

earthly city, 113, 120, 127, 198, 227–231, 234, 235, 252–253, 261, 274, 292. See also Augustine, Saint; Heavenly City
Egypt/Egyptians, 162, 179–180, 181, 185–187, 205, 206, 212–213, 227, 234, 253, 259, 290, 322nn34–36, 323–324n45
Eiximenis, Francesc, 64–65, 227
El Dorado, 265, 268, 271
El Lunarejo. See Espinosa Medrano, Juan de
encomiendas, 16, 17, 68, 104, 106, 129, 130, 142, 254, 267, 299n7, 308n20
entries, viceregal, 25, 28, 85, 86, 97, 102, 105, 176, 183, 184, 264, 300n16, 300n18, 300n20, 310n36, 321n30
epistemes, 3, 14, 39, 51–55, 88, 92, 115, 117, 206
epistemologies, 2, 9, 33, 37, 44, 53, 55, 58, 61, 87, 153, 157, 158, 164, 197–198, 212, 213, 225, 226, 229, 230, 236, 242, 244, 306n4, 329n27
erudition, 73, 99, 114, 137, 158, 160, 171, 181, 184, 186, 199, 214, 284, 322n31
esoteric city, 10, 196–199, 201, 202, 205, 212, 214, 215, 216, 219, 220, 224, 226, 229, 236, 237, 239, 240–241, 244
Espinosa Medrano, Juan de, 203, 259, 296, 326n8, 331–332n11
esthetics, 14, 32, 108, 126, 129, 174, 260, 300–301n20; of Baroque, 140, 196, 259, 278; of Mannerism, 103, 112, 114, 315n30; of Renaissance, 9, 93, 103, 112, 114, 260; of Spectacular City, 118
ethnographies, 39, 40, 57, 79

Eucharist, 86, 190, 191, 192, 220, 222, 244, 282, 325n53
evangelization, 18, 23, 35, 100, 105, 122, 168, 206. *See also* Indians: Christianization of
excess, 66, 114, 126, 133, 155, 235–236, 238, 241, 258, 265, 271, 288–289, 290, 310n33, 319n11, 319n13
exotica, 35, 81, 82, 86, 102, 139, 207–208, 211, 259, 299n2, 327–328n18. *See also* exoticism
exoticism, 9, 35, 37–39, 41, 45, 55, 76, 80, 82, 121–122, 124–125, 132–134, 138–139, 190, 199, 205, 259, 260, 261, 265, 285, 302n27. *See also* creoles: self-exoticizing of
exposés, 10, 246, 250–254, 258, 266–267, 272, 274, 288, 331n3, 333n22

Faulkner, William, 1, 161
Favián, Alejandro, 208–212, 216, 259, 296, 324n46
Fernández de Oviedo, Gonzalo, 39, 53, 59, 71, 76, 77, 84, 119, 136, 157, 283, 286, 295; and Indians, 34–35, 79, 267; and museumizing, 35, 38, 56, 208; and wonder, 33–35, 37, 76, 102, 138
festivals, 5, 23, 26, 27, 105, 115, 124, 133, 148, 149, 164, 196, 198, 222, 241, 252, 264, 266, 270, 272, 273, 275–276, 278, 279, 282, 287–288, 289, 300n17; chronicles of, 8–10, 28–29, 129, 141, 150, 155, 156, 168–189, 193, 197, 198, 227, 244, 247, 260, 300–301n20, 317n11, 317n13, 318n6; of Corpus Christi, 25, 27, 190, 220, 222, 224, 237–238, 244, 245, 264, 281, 300n16, 317n11; cost of, 26, 27, 300n18; as element of Spectacular City, 3, 4, 6–9, 13–14, 47, 97, 150, 151, 154, 300n15; and Indians, 23–26, 126, 152, 156, 173–176, 178, 256, 267–268, 270–271, 287, 318n6; in Potosí, 23, 270–277; reasons for, 23–26, 98, 155–157
fiction, 234, 262, 265, 269, 272, 276
fiestas. *See* festivals
fin-de-siècle, 10, 80, 145, 198, 224–225, 226, 234, 236, 237, 241
Findlen, Paula, 206, 207, 208, 234, 312nn8–9, 323n44, 326n10, 326–327n11, 327n14
Flood (Biblical), the, 40, 165, 227, 253, 281
Foucault, Michel, 7, 40, 52–54, 71, 303n37, 304n40
Franciscans, 151, 168, 254–256, 257, 272, 273, 274, 275, 283, 318n6, 333n25; and Indians, 23, 154, 267, 331n8; in Mexico City, 64–65, 104–105; millennial kingdom of, 64, 73, 105, 113, 307n13. *See also* Mendicant orders
Freile. *See* Rodríguez Freile, Juan

gachupines, 16, 81, 135, 142, 152, 173, 238
Galve, Viceroy, 128, 198–199, 238–239, 241, 243, 244–246, 330n38, 330n40
García, Gregorio, 40, 163, 164, 180, 223, 284, 296, 320n21
Garcilaso de la Vega. *See* Vega, Garcilaso de la; Vega, (El Inca) Garcilaso de la
gift economy, 126–127, 156, 216, 219
Glissant, Édouard, 291, 293–294
Góngora y Argote, Luis de, 47, 99, 109, 114, 117, 188, 201, 202–203, 204, 259, 282, 326n7
González Echevarría, Roberto, 7, 118, 120, 137, 259, 266, 305nn47–48, 313n20, 316n6, 331n9, 331–332n11
Gracián, Baltasar, 43–46, 153, 158, 207, 226, 296, 304nn41–42, 304–305n43, 327n12

Granada, Luis de, 32, 207, 327n12
"grandeza mexicana, La." *See under* Balbuena, Bernardo de
Greenblatt, Stephen, 29, 30, 33, 36, 301nn22–23
Guadalupanism. *See* Virgin of Guadalupe
Guaman Poma de Ayala, Felipe, *146*, 147–148, 149, 153, 154, 194, 249, 252, 253–254, 261, 284, 289, 296, 331n5, 332n12
guided culture, 24–25, 35, 36, 45, 150, 155, 302n29
Guijo, Gregorio Martín de, 256, 261–265, 266, 283, 296, 332nn13–15

Ham (Noah's son), 161, 163, 164, 165, 179, 181, 186, 322n37
Harpocrates, 214, 227, 234, 240
Heavenly City, 18, 73, 105, 113, 120, 127, 198, 227–230, 234, 261, 274, 290, 291, 330n33. *See also* Augustine, Saint; earthly city
Hermes (Mercury), 72, 108, 126, 141, 144, 176, 313n18
hermeticism, 158, 162, 181–182, 240, 328n21, 329n28
heterogeneity, 39, 114, 139, 150, 153, 154, 158, 161, 236, 252
heterotopia, 154, 228, 253, 291
hexameral writings, 207, 213, 229, 233, 235, 242, 251, 327n12, 329n32. *See also* apologetics
historiographic syncretism, 40, 44, 46–47, 150, 159–162, 167, 169, 206, 236, 251, 294, 319n14; and Acosta, 40, 41–42, 161; and the devil, 41–42, 160–161, 191; and Dorantes, 139; and García, 40, 163, 164; and Garcilaso de la Vega (El Inca), 302–303n32, 303n33; and Guaman Poma, 147–148; and Kircher, 162, 179–180, 186–187, 205; and Las Casas, 39, 41; and origin theories, 40–41, 161–163, 164–165, 178, 179–181, 186, 320n16, 322n34; and Sigüenza, 163, 168, 170, 175, 178–180, 186–187, 189; and Sor Juana, 163, 182, 186–191, 193–194, 221, 224, 323n40, 325n54; and Torquemada, 40, 41, 160–161, 162–163, 179, 224, 256; and Vetancurt, 160, 163–167, 179, 181
historiography, 7, 39, 135, 139, 149, 157, 159, 161, 167, 223, 224, 251, 255, 257, 265, 268, 269, 272
Huitzilopochtli, 177, 179, 181, 184, 190, 225, 306n6
humanism, 31, 39, 66, 67, 68–69, 70–71, 76, 80, 99, 106–107, 109, 119, 157, 202–203, 212, 307n12, 308n20, 312n14
hyperbole, 2, 10, 98–99, 114, 129, 131, 140, 151, 286, 288, 298n10, 313n17, 314n23

Incas, 13, 27, 261, 271, 285, 286, 322n12. *See also* Indians
Indians, 5, 57, 105, 122, 123, 148, 168–169, 249, 254, 256, 267; activism for, 10, 160, 255–256, 260–261, 274, 282–284, 288–291, 335n40; Christianization of, 23, 34–35, 57–58, 69, 75, 122, 191–192, 257, 298n7; and creoles, 5, 8, 137, 154, 166, 268; disparagement of, 8, 34–35, 79, 81–82, 122–123, 130, 165, 178, 267–268, 302n27, 315n32, 322n32; diversity of, 152–153; and festivals, 23–24, 156, 173–176, 256, 267–268, 270–271, 287; as *indio feo*, 8, 123, 126, 130, 139, 260; labor of, 65, 86, 104, 106, 123, 124, 126, 250, 268, 288, 307n15; metonymy of with nature, 77–78; in Peru, 249–250, 271, 282, 283, 285,

288–291, 298n7; riots by, 237–239, 240, 242, 243, 245, 268, 330n38; segregation of, 20, 59, 60, 63, 75–76, 78, 86, 122, 152, 154–155, 176, 290, 330n38; similitude of with Spanish, 55, 88, 190–192; syncretic origins of, 40–41, 156, 161–163, 164–165, 178, 179–181, 320n17, 322nn34–35, 331n8; texts of, 4, 5, 7, 160, 167, 179, 240; and Virgin of Guadalupe, 169, 173–174. *See also* Aztecs; Chichimecas; Incas

intellectual city, 197, 198, 201, 202, 204, 208, 219, 220, 224–225, 226, 230, 235, 239, 241

interés, 100–101, 113, 120, 124, 126, 134, 142, 272–273, 288, 311n4. *See also* capitalism; wealth

intertextuality, 7, 39, 136, 144, 221, 240, 298n8. *See also* Mexican Archive

Isis, 180, 185–186, 187–189, 227, 228, 234, 259, 323n40, 323n44, 324n48

Jesuits, 9, 105–106, 121, 149, 181, 182, 209, 210, 222, 223, 263, 281, 282, 304n42, 312n12, 324n46; and Balbuena, 9, 113, 121, 127; and creoles, 9, 18, 106–107, 136–137, 142, 169, 255; and education, 106, 107, 158, 202–203, 212, 214, 234, 255, 276, 312n14, 321n28, 327n15; and Kircher, 162, 187, 205–208, 213, 234, 327n15; Ratio Studiorum of, 106, 212, 312n14; and Sigüenza, 169, 171, 177, 180, 187, 321n28, 324n46; and Sor Juana, 182–183, 187, 193, 209, 212, 214, 218, 327n15; syncretism of, 162, 169, 189, 212, 319n14

Jews, 161–162, 163, 164, 181, 290, 320n17

journalism, 7, 17, 27, 42, 261, 262, 322n32

Juana Inés de la Cruz, Sor, 10, 17, 145, 149, 150, 163, 183, 197, 201, 204, 209, 248, 256, 259, 280, 282, 292, 296, 318n3, 323n44; and Augustine, 226–231, 235; *Carta Atenagórica*, 188, 212, 327n15; collection poems by, 215–219, 227, 328n19; *El Divino Narciso*, 160, 190, 220–224, 227, 240, 296, 323n40, 325n53, 328n23; *ensaladas*, 149, 318n3; *Fama y obras póstumas*, 193, 296; feminism of, 184, 189, 243; and Kircher, 185–187, 198, 209, 210, 212–215, 218, 221, 226, 233–235, 323n44, 323–324n45, 327n14, 328n21, 330n35; Loa to *El Divino Narciso*, 160, 190–194, 220–224, 296, 323n40, 325nn53–54, 328n23, 329n25; *Neptuno alegórico*, 85–86, 180, 182–189, 191, 193, 213, 296, 322n39, 323nn40–42, 324n48, 329n30; *Primero sueño*, 187, 198, 202, 210, 214, 215, 217–219, 220, 223, 225–227, 229–237, 240–245, 252, 253, 258, 294, 296, 328n20, 329nn27–28, 329nn31–32, 330nn34–35, 330n37; *Respuesta*, 212–215, 217, 218, 235, 296; Romances, 192, 216, 229, 299n8, 329n31; and Sigüenza, 183–186, 189, 323–324n45, 326n6; Sonetos, 186, 188, 217, 219, 238, 239; as Tenth Muse, 224, 259; transatlantic campaign of, 189–193, 222; triumphal arch of, 176, 183, 184, 185, 321n29, 323n42; and Virgin of Guadalupe, 188, 193, 324–325n49

Judgment Day, 253, 280, 282, 291

Kircher, Athanasius, 188, 205–215, 296, 324n47, 326n10; and the All, 10, 195, 197, 205, 206, 207, 210, 233; *Ars magna sciendi*, 195, 206, 207, 296; and esoteric city, 197, 205, 214; and

Kircher, Athanasius (*continued*)
  Favián, 208–212, 324n46; *Itinerarium*, 186, 210, 234, 296, 327n14, 330n35; museum of, 10, 207–208, 211, 215, 216; *Oedipus Aegyptiacus*, 162, 179–180, 186, 206, 296, 322n35, 323n44; and Sigüenza, 180, 181, 185–187, 209, 240, 322nn35–37, 324n46; and Sor Juana, 185–187, 198, 209, 210, 212–215, 218, 221, 226, 233–235, 323n44, 323–324n45, 327n14, 328n21, 330n35; and syncretism, 162, 179–180, 205, 206, 322n35

Laguna, Marquis de la, 176, 180, 190, 198–199
Las Casas, Bartolomé de, 18, 32–33, 39, 41, 55, 65, 226, 254, 256, 257, 261, 274, 290, 295, 298n8, 303n35
Leon, Luis de, 53, 111, 314n22
Leonard, Irving A., 2, 27, 201–202, 247–248, 251, 305n45, 325n1, 326n9, 330–331n1, 331n2
León Pinelo, Antonio de, 37, 44, 139, 286, 296
Lezama Lima, José, 46, 47, 159, 167
Lima, 6, 10, 19, 20, 22, 23, 26, 63, 250, 251, 280–283, 286–288, 298n10, 300n20, 331n3, 331n5, 334n38
locus amoenus, 52, 53, 54, 84, 88, 110, 111
López de Gómara, Francisco, 17, 68, 76

Madrid, 10, *12*, 20, 63, 68, 83, 133, 170, 173, 182, 190, 192, 193, 222, 224, 237, 241, 259, 300n14, 334n34
magical realism, 33, 35, 275, 292, 302n28
Mancera, Marquis de, 184, 188, 324n46
Mannerism, 103–104, 107–110, 112, 114–115, 117, 131, 139, 144, 223, 300–301n20, 312n11, 312n15, 313n17, 315n30
Maravall, Antonio, 24–25, 36, 302n29
maravillas, 32–33, 57, 60, 77, 95, 259, 285. *See also* wonder
marketplaces, 294; confluence of groups in, 21, 22, 288; as metonymy for city, 56–57, 60, 128, 286; order in, 56–57, 59, 79, 245–246; textualized, 9, 22–23, 56, 75–76, 81–82, 84, 93, 121, 124–127, 137, 142, 144–145, 152, 173, 269
materialism, 70, 100–101, 125, 127, 197, 273, 288
memoriales de agravios, 255, 257, 274, 290
Mendicant orders, 9, 105, 120, 127, 154, 254, 274–275, 333n25. *See also* Franciscans
Mendieta, Gerónimo de, 104, 105, 226
Mendoza y Zúñiga, García de, 96, 97, 100, 102, 105, 311n3
mercantilism, 101, 125–130, 142, 210. *See also* capitalism
Mercury. *See* Hermes
mestizos, 4, 5, 75, 152, 238, 278, 297n4. *See also castas*
Mexican Archive, 10, 266, 283, 298n9; and Cervantes de Salazar, 67, 70, 84; creation of, 7–8, 16; and Dorantes, 135, 136, 138, 139; and Sigüenza, 198, 237, 239–241, 243–245; and Sor Juana, 198, 220, 222–225. *See also* intertextuality
Mexico City, 6, 7, 9, 65, 87, 128, 152, 154, 176, 179, 186, 257, 264–265, 307nn15–16; compared with Europe, 71–72, 82, 95, 98, 100, 152, 185, 186, 316n4 (*see also* resemblance); as international crossroads, 6, 121, 129, 132, 149; lagoon in, 85–86, 109; literary history of, 8, 50–51, 55, 61,

80–83, 93, 120, 141, 144, 151–152, 168, 223, 261, 298n9; as Ordered City, 50, 51, 60, 64, 65, 67, 73, 80, 154–155; population of, 18, 104, 148, 238; praise of, 8, 96, 98–100, 126, 127, 134, 135–136, 140, 142, 149, 151, 165, 246, 251, 316n4; riots in, 10, 237–245, 251, 330n38; second life-project of, 93, 104, 113, 129; as Spectacular City, 6, 8, 125, 151; university in, 6, 67, 68, 69–70, 71, 74, 83, 100, 106, 150, 198, 209, 223; wealth of, 19, 142, 143, 151, 195, 200. See also Chapultepec; Tenochtitlán

Minerva, 49–50, 70, 183–184, 185, 227, 323n40, 324n48, 329n30

miracles, 30–32, 33, 35, 110, 171, 256, 261, 266, 268, 274, 275–276, 284, 285. See also wonder

Mirror for Princes, 28, 100, 177, 184, 289, 300n19, 323n41, 332n18

Mizraim, 179, 180, 185

Moctezuma II, 57, 58, 78, 85, 87, 178, 307n9

modernity, 6, 36, 109, 205, 208, 319n13, 330n37

monsters, 32, 42–43, 45, 55, 108, 110, 122–123, 139, 174–175, 259, 261, 290, 304n40

Montesclaros, Marquis de, 141, 300n18, 317nn12–13

moralizing, 31, 241, 262, 265, 267, 269, 270, 273, 275, 276, 277–278, 332n13, 333–334n29

More, Thomas, 62, 65, 70, 307n13

Motolinía, 113, 255, 298n8

Mugaburu, Joseph de, 26–27

multiplicity, 13, 147, 150, 155, 157, 159, 161, 163, 164, 187, 194, 228, 229, 235, 238, 292. See also plurality

Mumford, Lewis, 116, 117, 120, 126, 314n27

Natural Magician, 32, 34, 53, 138, 206, 213

nature, 103, 152, 208; in Balbuena, 109, 110, 112, 119, 287; in Cervantes de Salazar, 77–78; in Dorantes, 136–138; in Fernández de Oviedo, 34, 76; in Salinas, 287; in Sor Juana, 222

Neo-Baroque, 159, 258, 275, 292, 319n13. See also Baroque; New World Baroque

Neoplatonism, 31, 44, 50, 51, 53, 61–62, 84, 158, 162, 206, 213, 220, 233, 253, 328n21. See also Plato/Platonism

neostoicism, 111, 127, 267, 272, 274, 332n18, 334n30

Neptune, 85–86, 179, 180–181, 183–185, 323n40, 324n48, 329n30

New Jerusalem, 18, 64, 256, 300n16, 307n16

New World Baroque, 6, 9, 149, 202, 235, 236, 248, 258, 265, 271, 275, 292, 294, 330n37, 335n43; difference from Old World Baroque, 46–47, 158–159, 269, 305n47; genesis of, 4, 46, 114–115, 118, 159; and Spectacular City, 3–4, 8, 10, 47, 129, 251, 293; views of, 45–46, 305n45. See also Baroque

novels and novellas, 7, 31, 42, 45, 53, 222, 223, 224, 269, 277–278

Núñez de Miranda, Antonio, 182–183, 187, 209, 322n39, 327n13

O'Gorman, Edmundo, 133, 260, 293, 302n30, 307–308n17, 308n18

Oquendo. See Rosas de Oquendo, Mateo

order, 59, 63, 66, 74, 242, 245, 246, 256, 268, 272, 309n23; of Aztec cities, 56–58, 307n15; and concert, 49, 51, 54–55, 57, 61, 64, 74, 84, 101, 117,

order (*continued*)
120, 153, 158, 174, 206, 207, 228, 233, 242, 271, 291, 327n12; and Indians, 79–80, 174; and Mannerism, 103–104; and New World Baroque, 4, 119; will to, 61, 84

Ordered City, 14, 39, 61, 62, 66, 88, 148, 233, 246, 249, 252, 264, 271, 292–293; as Apollonian, 9, 55, 79, 116, 118; and Balbuena, 9, 92–93, 115, 117, 118, 119, 121, 124, 127, 236; breakdown of, 9, 80, 92–93, 104, 105, 108, 112, 118, 150, 236, 242, 268, 290; and Cervantes de Salazar, 9, 66–67, 71, 73–75, 79, 82, 87; and Cortés, 9, 49, 59, 61; and Cueva, 82–83; in New World, 49–50, 61, 63–65, 79, 154–155; and Rama, 49–50, 314n27; and Salazar y Alarcón, 9, 83, 84–86, 87–88, 110, 111

Orientalism, 42, 121–122, 132, 138

Ovid, 106, 108–109, 113, 124, 127, 223, 230, 313nn18–19

Oviedo. *See* Fernández de Oviedo, Gonzalo

Palafox, Juan de, 44, 263–264

panegyrics, urban, 21–22, 82–83, 98, 101, 115, 288

paradise, *12*, 111, 222, 313n21; city as, 110, 172, 286–287; New World as, 37, 83, 84, 136, 138, 139, 165, 307n11, 334n38; in Salazar y Alarcón, 83–86

particularity, 28, 37, 49, 73, 83, 116, 143, 148, 173, 253, 263, 269; in Balbuena, 9, 92, 93, 117, 118, 119, 120, 121, 126, 133, 151, 236; in Salinas, 22, 287; in Sor Juana, 185, 214; in Villalpando, 11, 92. *See also* architexture

pastorals, 45, 53, 78, 88, 106, 122–123, 172, 221–222, 260, 294, 332n18; and Balbuena, 91–92, 94, 110–113, 117, 123–124, 127, 137, 223, 251, 269, 287; and Salazar y Alarcón, 83–86, 88, 110, 111; and Sor Juana, 221–224, 328n23. *See also* urban pastorals

Paz, Octavio, 26, 120, 139–140, 236, 259, 303n32, 319n14, 323n42, 324n48, 327nn14–15, 328n23, 329n28, 330n35, 330n37

period of stabilization, 14–15, 249

Peru, 14–15, 16, 28, 37, 108, 135, 138, 249–250, 255, 271, 274, 282, 283, 286, 288, 289, 298n7, 298n10, 299n10, 300n20, 334n30

Pizarro, Francisco, 285, 287

Plato/Platonism, 30, 58, 61, 73, 92, 97, 117, 161, 195, 213, 218, 226, 230, 231–232, 233, 328n21. *See also* Neoplatonism

Pliny, 136, 138, 139, 316n7; and Cervantes de Salazar, 71, 73, 76, 77; and Oviedo, 34, 35, 157, 301–302n26

plurality, 44, 115, 157, 160, 163, 166–167, 176, 249, 251, 253; dark side of, 264; in New World, 148, 149–150, 151, 154, 159, 168, 175, 186, 194; and Salinas, 287–288, 292, 293; and Sigüenza, 10, 150, 163, 168, 173, 175, 186; and Sor Juana, 10, 149, 150, 163, 182, 186, 189, 193–194, 224, 235; and Vetancurt, 10, 151, 153, 163–164, 287, 292. *See also* multiplicity

poetry contests, 26, 175, 196–198, 203, 247–248, 325n1

Potosí, 10, 19, 23, 251, 260, 270–279, 333n20, 333n27

propaganda, 9, 50, 69, 77, 83

providentialism, 59, 64, 69, 138, 156, 166, 174, 176, 178, 191, 207, 325n54

Puebla, 27, 44, 73, 106, 150, 151, 154, 168–169, 175, 208, 209, 211, 212, 263–264, 324n46

Pythagoreanism, 117, 206, 213, 214, 220, 314n29, 328n21

Querétaro, 10, 168–178, 196, 321n27
Quevedo, Francisco de, 36, 140, 201, 202

radicados, 4, 7, 8, 19, 21, 37, 107, 251, 297n2
Rama, Angel, 3, 20, 49–50, 63, 116–117, 197, 204, 254, 297n1, 305–306n1, 313n17, 314nn27–28
Ramírez, Alonso, 198–201, 241, 325n4
Reformation, 2, 105, 157
relaciones de fiestas. *See* festivals: chronicles of
Renaissance, 66, 73, 92, 103, 112, 157, 162, 204, 304n38; humanism of, 31, 109, 157–158; Ordered City in, 9, 14, 49–50, 63
resemblance, 52, 53, 55, 57, 60, 71–72, 82, 88. *See also* similitude
Robles, Antonio de, 27–28, 251, 261–263, 265, 296, 332nn13–14
Rodríguez Freile, Juan, 251–254, 256, 260, 296; *El Carnero* by, 27, 118, 245, 265–273, 278, 296; on women, 269–270
Rosas de Oquendo, Mateo, 10, 108, 133–136, 142, 295, 316nn2–3, 316n5, 331n3
Ross, Kathleen, 5, 7–8, 114, 240, 298n1, 298n5, 298n8, 304n48, 331n2

Sahagún, Bernardino de, 226, 240, 256, 298n8
Salazar y Alarcón, Eugenio de, 9, 80, 83, 110, 112, 120, 125, 145, 180, 287, 295, 310nn32–33; "Bucólica" by, 84–89, 107, 109, 111, 112, 123, 295; "Epístola," 83–84, 295
Salinas y Córdova, Buenaventura de, 19, 22–23, 251, 252, 253–254, 257, 292, 293, 296, 331n5, 333n24, 334nn33–34, 334n38; and Balbuena, 286–288; effect of on creole writing, 153, 282, 298n10, 318n8, 334nn32–33; and Indians, 254, 255, 260, 274, 282–284, 288–291, 335n40; and Peru, 250, 282, 284–286, 288, 290–291, 335n39
Sánchez, Miguel, 169, 188, 222, 226
Sarduy, Severo, 194, 251
satire, 27, 36, 108, 110, 129, 133, 136, 144, 170, 253, 258, 265, 279–282, 285, 289, 334n31
scholasticism, 157–158, 206, 226, 233
Serlio, Sebastiano, 107, 108, 312n15
Sigüenza y Góngora, Carlos de, 10, 145, 150, 163, 169, 185, 194, 197, 198, 213, 248, 251, 259, 260, 280, 296, 320n28; 321n25, 321n28, 324n46, 327–328n18; *Alboroto* by, 198, 237–246, 252, 256, 296, 330n40; *Glorias* by, 155, 168–176, 318n5, 321n26; and Indians, 237–238, 289; *Infortunios* by, 198–201, 202, 241, 278, 296, 298n8, 326n4; *Libra astronómica*, 168, 209, 322n37; as organic intellectual, 168, 186, 199; *Parayso Occidental* by, 152, 178, 313n21, 319–320n15, 322n32; protest against Europeans by, 17, 167–168, 299n8; and Sor Juana, 183–186, 225, 227, 238, 239, 240–245, 323–324n45, 330n39; *Teatro de virtudes*, 151, 160, 166, 167, 168, 176–182, 184, 185–186, 189, 260, 285, 296, 318n5, 322n38, 323nn42–43, 326n5, 334n37; triumphal arch of, 176, 178, 321nn29–30, 322n32; *Triunfo Parténico*, 196, 198, 201, 203, 209, 296
similitude, 38–39, 45, 51, 52–53, 55, 71, 74, 98, 119, 147, 153, 154, 179, 233, 290; and syncretism, 39–42, 44, 139, 159, 161. *See also* resemblance
Sor Juana. *See* Juana Inés de la Cruz, Sor

spectacles, 2, 23, 79, 248, 252, 257, 264, 266, 270, 280; festivals as, 26–27, 56, 97, 126, 155, 174, 184, 287; unifying society, 24–25. *See also* wonder

Spectacular City, 6, 8, 10, 28, 112, 125, 129, 132, 144, 148, 150, 154, 160, 164, 168, 194, 197–198, 245, 263, 283, 284, 293, 294; advent of, 89, 92–93, 94, 97, 105, 115, 116, 118, 128, 145; agile platforms of, 13–14; definition of, 2–3; as Dionysian, 9, 116; elements of, 3, 4, 6–9, 13–14, 23–24, 47, 129, 141, 221; and Indians, 5, 190, 256; materialism in, 101, 125, 127; outside Mexico, 251, 297n2, 331n3; and Ordered City, 14, 50, 92, 93, 110, 268; as Spectacular Esoteric City, 10, 198, 226, 229

speculum principis. *See* Mirror for Princes

structures of feeling, 3, 4, 133, 167, 284

Suárez de Peralta, Juan, 107, 179, 253, 262, 298n8, 322n34

syncretism. *See* historiographic syncretism

Templo Mayor, 128, 152, 190

Ten Lost Tribes. *See* Jews

Tenochtitlán, 6, 23, 49, 50, 51, 55, 56, 57–58, 59–60, 62, 85–86, 141, 190, 192, 225, 231, 240, 246, 256, 306n6, 307n15, 321n30

Tepeyac, 169, 172, 222, 329n27

Terrazas, Francisco de, 17, 135, 141, 316n1

Tlatelolco, 56–57, 122, 124, 160, 239, 240, 306n6

Tobar, Isabel de, 96, 126, 311n3

Torquemada, Juan de, 179, 251, 253, 255, 256, 265, 267, 275, 283, 284, 296, 320n21, 331n10, 332n18; and festivals, 190–191, 256, 264; and Indians, 23, 41, 160–161, 162–163, 179, 190–191, 256–257, 260, 303n34, 331n8; and Sor Juana, 220, 223, 224, 225; and syncretism, 40, 41, 160–161, 162–163, 224, 256

transculturation, 46, 76–77, 149, 309n28, 319n13

urban pastorals, 84–87, 88, 110–113, 123, 137–138, 172, 269, 287. *See also* pastorals

utopia, 70, 113, 123, 172, 291, 307n13. *See also* More, Thomas; pastorals

Vallejo, César, 13, 47, 247, 298n1

Valle y Caviedes, Juan del, 251, 253, 260, 279–282, 296, 334n30

Vatican, 162, 173, 181, 187, 209, 211, 324n47

Vega, (El Inca) Garcilaso de la, 55, 147, 160, 285, 302–303n32, 303n33

Vega, Garcilaso de la, 53, 83, 86, 92

Venus, 11, *48,* 51–52, 55, 66, 79, 88, 120, 187, 219, 260. *See also* Botticelli, Sandro

Vetancurt, Agustín de, 145, 151, 158, 185, 195, 260, 296, 317n13, 318n4, 320n21, 325n3; and Balbuena, 151, 152, 164, 198, 318n7; and cultural nationalism, 10, 164, 165–166, 289; and Indians, 148, 151, 152–153, 164–167, 178, 255, 318n6, 318n8, 320n22, 331n6; and multiplicity, 148, 150–154, 163–164, 166–167, 173, 194, 214, 287, 292; and Salinas, 153, 282, 283, 287, 289, 318n8, 334n33; and Sigüenza, 151, 152, 167, 173, 178, 179, 181, 238; and Sor Juana, 194, 214, 235; and syncretism, 160, 163–167, 179, 181

Vetruvius, 62, 63, 108

Villalobos, Arias de, 10, 17, 130, 140–

145, 151, 167, 177, 223, 225, 296, 317nn11–13, 318n5
Villalpando, Cristóbal de, 11, *90*, 92, 120, 128, 148, 149, 155, 194, 196, 245–246, 294, 296, 330n40
Virgin Mary, 52, 78, 88, 188, 225, 274, 324–325n49. *See also* Virgin of Guadalupe; Woman of Patmos
Virgin of Guadalupe, 10, 164, 168–177, 188, 193, 200, 202, 222, 225, 321n28, 324–325n49, 329n27. *See also* Virgin Mary; Woman of Patmos
Vives, Luis, 67, 88, 106

wealth, 21; and creoles, 15, 16, 105–106, 129, 143; of Jesuits, 105–106, 113, 142; of New World, 2, 14, 19, 26, 100–101, 123, 142, 151, 165, 319n11; of Peru, 20, 280, 286, 288, 334n30; of Potosí, 271, 272–273; and wonder, 101–102, 288. *See also* capitalism; interés; materialism; mercantilism
Woman of Patmos, 188, 324n49. *See also* Virgin Mary; Virgin of Guadalupe
women, 22, 86, 88, 111, 152, 189, 243, 244, 245, 269–270, 275, 278, 279, 287–288, 313n21, 322n34
wonder, 20, 35–36, 55, 66, 81, 86, 97, 134, 155, 171, 173, 211, 214, 218, 229, 256, 274, 275, 285–286; in Balbuena, 101, 108, 124; in Columbus, 32–33, 35, 301nn22–23; in Cortés, 56–59; dark side of, 221, 243, 245, 261, 284, 288; in Dorantes, 137–138; as element of Spectacular City, 3, 4, 6–9, 14, 47, 101, 150, 154; history of, 30–32; invoked by texts, 29, 37, 57–58, 97, 101, 136, 153, 168, 258–259, 262; of New World, 29, 32–34, 38, 136, 138; as object, 9, 102, 198, 210, 311n7; in Oviedo, 33–35; and wealth, 101–102, 288; wounding of, 29–30, 33, 36–37. *See also maravillas;* miracles; spectacles; wonder cabinets
wonder cabinets, 76, 109, 155, 203, 259, 312n8, 312n10, 313n19; in Balbuena, 102, 122, 123, 125, 203, 208, 219, 259; of Favián, 210–211; Kircher's museum as, 207–208, 211; New World as, 37, 118, 127, 139; prototypes of in Oviedo, 35, 56, 208; of Sor Juana, 214–219, 328n19. *See also* wonder

Ximénez, Francisco, 209, 211, 324n46, 327n13

Zócalo, 60, 66, 72, 74, 81, 128, 148, 155, 195, 238, 240, 244, 245, 294
Zorita, Alonso de, 65–67, 74, 120, 152

www.ingramcontent.com/pod-product-compliance
Lightning Source LLC
Chambersburg PA
CBHW030332240426
43661CB00052B/1609